GERMAN SONG ONSTAGE

GERMAN SONG ONSTAGE

Lieder Performance in the Nineteenth and Early Twentieth Centuries

Edited by Natasha Loges and Laura Tunbridge

Indiana University Press

This book is a publication of

Indiana University Press
Office of Scholarly Publishing
Herman B Wells Library 350
1320 East 10th Street
Bloomington, Indiana 47405 USA

iupress.indiana.edu

© 2020 by Indiana University Press

All rights reserved
No part of this book may be reproduced or utilized in any form or by any means, electronic or mechanical, including photocopying and recording, or by any information storage and retrieval system, without permission in writing from the publisher. The paper used in this publication meets the minimum requirements of the American National Standard for Information Sciences—Permanence of Paper for Printed Library Materials, ANSI Z39.48-1992.

Manufactured in the United States of America

Library of Congress Cataloging-in-Publication Data

Names: Loges, Natasha, editor. | Tunbridge, Laura [date], editor.
Title: German song onstage : lieder performance in the nineteenth and early twentieth centuries / Natasha Loges and Laura Tunbridge.
Description: Bloomington : Indiana University Press, 2020. | Includes bibliographical references and index.
Identifiers: LCCN 2019053391 (print) | LCCN 2019053392 (ebook) | ISBN 9780253047007 (hardback) | ISBN 9780253047014 (paperback) | ISBN 9780253047038 (ebook)
Subjects: LCSH: Songs, German—19th century—History and criticism. | Songs, German—20th century—History and criticism. | Songs, German—Performances.
Classification: LCC ML1400 .G47 2020 (print) | LCC ML1400 (ebook) | DDC 782.4216809/43—dc23
LC record available at https://lccn.loc.gov/2019053391
LC ebook record available at https://lccn.loc.gov/2019053392

1 2 3 4 5   25 24 23 22 21 20

Contents

Acknowledgments — vii

Introduction: Restaging German Song / Laura Tunbridge — 1

1. "Eine wahre Olla Patrida [*sic*]": Anna Milder-Hauptmann, Schubert, and Programming the Orient / Susan Youens — 10

2. Song in Concert as Observed by the Schumanns: Toward the Personalization of the Public Stage / Benjamin Binder — 52

3. From Miscellanies to Musical Works: Julius Stockhausen, Clara Schumann, and *Dichterliebe* / Natasha Loges — 70

4. Natalia Macfarren and the English German Lied / Katy Hamilton — 87

5. "For Any Ordinary Performer It Would Be Absurd, Ridiculous, or Offensive": Performing Lieder Cycles on the American Stage / Heather Platt — 111

6. The Concert Hall as a Gender-Neutral Space: The Case of Amalie Joachim, née Schneeweiss / Beatrix Borchard, Translated by Jeremy Coleman — 132

7. Nikolai Medtner: Championing the German Lied and Russian Spirit / Maria Razumovskaya — 154

8. From the Benefit Concert to the Solo Song Recital in London, 1870–1914 / Simon McVeigh and William Weber — 179

9. German Song and the Working Classes in Berlin, 1890–1914 / Wiebke Rademacher — 203

10. Lilli Lehmann's Dedicated Lieder Recitals / Rosamund Cole — 223

11 "Eine Reihe bunter Zauberbilder": Thomas Mann,
Hans Pfitzner, and the Politics of Song Accompaniment /
Nicholas Attfield   244

12 Performers' Reflections / Natasha Loges and
Laura Tunbridge   262

   Timeline   281
   Index   285

Acknowledgments

This collection arose after the conference German Song Onstage 1789–1914, which took place at the Royal College of Music and Wigmore Hall in February 2016. We are grateful to the following institutions for financial and other support: the German Historical Institute, the Royal College of Music, Wigmore Hall, Music and Letters, the British Academy, the Embassy of the Federal Republic of Germany, TORCH (The Oxford Research Centre in the Humanities), and Music Talks. We are also grateful to Janice Frisch and the staff of Indiana University Press for seeing this volume to production and to the anonymous readers for their extremely helpful suggestions. Finally, thanks to all our contributors and, as always, our families.

GERMAN SONG ONSTAGE

Introduction

Restaging German Song

Laura Tunbridge

A SINGER IN EVENING dress, a grand piano. A modest-sized audience, mostly well-dressed and silver-haired, equipped with translation booklets. A program consisting entirely of songs by one or two composers. This is the way of the Lieder recital these days. There is an assumption among performers and audiences that this performance tradition is long-standing. As this book demonstrates, however, it is not. For much of the nineteenth century, the songs of Beethoven, Schubert, Schumann, and Brahms were heard in the home and salon and, no less significantly, on the concert platform alongside orchestral and choral works. The dedicated program was rare; the dedicated audience even more so. The Lied was, then, a genre with both more private and more public associations than is commonly recalled. The purpose of this volume is to unsettle some of our assumptions about what it meant and still means to present German song onstage, in the hope that greater historical awareness will open up discussion about how and why we care about, and make a case for, Lieder.

In a generation in which the notion of period performance has become firmly established as a routine mode of interpretation, it is striking that many of our concert habits have little to do with known historical practices. Audiences sit in the dark, in silence, usually not eating, drinking, or whoring, at historically informed performances of baroque opera.[1] Similarly, Beethoven's symphonies are uninterrupted by applause between movements, and his string quartets listened to, back to back, with a veneration that would have perplexed attendees at Ignaz Schuppanzigh's first play-through.[2] It is impossible and doubtless undesirable to return to the social, economic, and sanitary situation of listeners in previous centuries. Why, though, is there a belief that today's quasi-sacred consumption of classical music, which raises so many issues about elitism and access, is the *best* way of hearing it?

This question is particularly relevant to German-language art song, a genre that flourished in the first half of the nineteenth century. Perhaps of all types of classical music, the Lied is now considered the most recondite. Its text and music require explication, its performance expertise. As illustrated in my first paragraph, the Lieder recital is considered to be formal and requiring specialist knowledge in order to be fully understood. There has not been a move to historically informed performance to the same extent as in other genres.[3] Some sing with fortepiano rather than piano, and occasionally singers adopt ornamentation in the manner of nineteenth-century editions, but the kinds of portamento and rubato noted in reviews and heard across early recordings have not been adopted.[4] Neither have the programming practices of previous generations; instead, as with Beethoven's string quartets, there is a tendency toward completion and coherence. Schubert's friends' fears about the monotony of a rendition of the entirety of *Winterreise* probably would be mocked now (in public, at least).

Taking Lieder so seriously flies in the face of what we know of nineteenth-century practices, which tended to be heterogeneous and communally minded inside and outside German-speaking territories. The domestic origins of the Lied are perhaps somewhat overstated; rarely do contemporary commentators specify what kind of home or musical life is implied.[5] The means to afford having a piano or guitar in one's house or purchasing sheet music—let alone the ability to read it—is one important and often overlooked consideration. Another ambiguous situation is the salon: when the affluent host invites guests to listen to skilled and maybe even professional musicians performing in the host's home, is that a private or public space?[6]

In its early forms, the Lied served as a vehicle for engaging with poetry in the vernacular through simple strophic musical settings, and it was popular because it catered to many levels of skill. It might be correct, then, to consider Lieder under the rubric of *Bildung*, as an educational tool that could develop poetic and musical appreciation. Yet Lieder were not yet understood as the deep engagement with the poetic-musical subject, the lyric-I, in which we are so invested today. Instead, as is evident from the *Liederspiel* roots of Wilhelm Müller's and Ludwig Berger's *Die schöne Müllerin*, song performance had a great deal to do with the entertainment of role-play.[7] There might be a didactic aspect to that entertainment—as a sort of subjective entrainment (imagine how it feels to be the suicidal miller boy)—but nonetheless it was primarily a means to while away an evening.

Certainly, when Lieder were presented on public platforms, as part of concert programs, there was little sense of them being high art in the same way as they are considered now. Schubert was represented by graceful individual songs; like Schumann's, his cycles, now stalwarts of the repertoire, were not presented in their entirety until much later in the nineteenth century. They were thereby perhaps best thought of as introductions to these composers' œuvres, counterfoils to the rest of the program's symphonic movements, virtuoso piano pieces, and concert arias.

The hybridity of nineteenth-century concert programs raises some interesting questions about how various national identities could be expressed through musical choices. The Lied was undeniably a German genre, defined by its use of the vernacular language, romantic poetic themes, and the homelands of the majority of its composers. At the same time, claims made for nation building though the creation and consumption of Lieder need to be nuanced if not critiqued. Lieder traveled around the world in versions modified for national markets. An appreciation of Lieder may have signaled engagement in cultural transfer and might be considered under the umbrella of cosmopolitanism; or it may have represented the incipient hegemony of the Austro-German musical canon, or the need for émigrés to assert their Germanic origins, in the manner of Benedict Anderson's "imagined communities."[8] The modifications—translations, programming choices, new compositional and poetic contributions—however, suggest something less all-embracing and more particular, or local. Performing German song in America or Russia during the nineteenth century was different from what was happening in central Europe. Composing Lieder elsewhere did not necessarily mean that the touchstones were Schubert or Brahms, Eichendorff or Rückert. A volume such as this points out the need to recognize that although song might be staged as representative of a German tradition, Lieder could also be restaged in different languages and national styles.

Before introducing the individual chapters of this volume, it might be worth raising questions about methodology. Much of what follows is concerned with programming; as a result, many of the chapters depend on extensive archival work that allows for the quantitative assessment of the activities of various individuals and organizations. On the one hand, that enables some of the practicalities of musical life—such as financial considerations, whose influence should never be underestimated—to be considered. On the other, that data has to be married with qualitative research to enable nuanced interpretation. There is no real way of knowing what these musicians sounded like, what kind of presence they had on the concert platform, and indeed how we might respond to them and their programs were we to encounter them today. Each author negotiates that challenge differently, taking on board aspects of social or cultural context, biography, or musical exegesis as suits them. In the process, a rich and diverse account of musical life in the long nineteenth century emerges and, partly so they can talk to each other in multiple ways, the chapters are ordered in loosely chronological order rather than quarantined into themed sections. It will thus be helpful here to draw together some of their shared concerns as a guide to the volume as a whole.

Susan Youens begins our journey in Vienna, in 1825, with a concert program that would now be thought impossibly varied. She focuses on one of the most successful singers of that milieu, Anna Milder-Hauptmann, the dedicatee of Schubert's "Suleika II." The significance of singers in the history of Lieder composition is rarely given its due and in Youens's account it is clear that Milder-Hauptmann was important not just in promoting Schubert's music but in encouraging him to pursue certain poetic themes; in this case, the orientalism of the *Westöstlicher Divan*. As Youens observes, Schubert would have been unaware that the Suleika poems in that collection were written not by Goethe but by his youthful admirer, Marianne von Willemer, another indication of the important but overlooked roles played by women. Benjamin Binder in chapter 2 also focuses on female performers, considering the assessment by Robert and Clara Schumann of singers in their circle in terms of their moral standing, which was implicitly embedded in questions of gender, nationality, and generic preference. Those judgments in turn inflected the Schumanns' appreciation of the singers' interpretative abilities, Italian opera yet again serving as vilified other to true German music. The value placed on the expression of internal emotions through Lieder (conveyed by the term *Innigkeit*), it seems, was shaped by social politics and petty bigotry as much as by grand philosophical ideals.

The Schumanns' self-appointed role as cultural gatekeepers is also apparent in Natasha Loges's chapter on the programming practices of baritone Julius Stockhausen and pianist Clara Schumann. Loges queries the ideology of fidelity to the work, or *Werktreue*, within this generation of German artists. Although Stockhausen famously presented the first complete public performances of song cycles by Schubert and Clara's late husband, they were considered experiments rather than exemplars of how to present Lieder repertoire. Clara Schumann's preferred approach was to interpolate a rendition of a cycle such as *Dichterliebe* with piano works, to avoid monotony of voice and style. It was not that Stockhausen and Clara Schumann did not take these works seriously—far from it. Instead, they recognized the need to persuade (more strongly, educate) audiences of the worth of this repertoire, and it was in part their efforts that resulted in the elevated status of Lieder within the classical music sphere.

The Lied, importantly, was also mobile. Although primarily a German-language tradition, its singers and pianists traveled extensively between venues, cities, and countries. How the genre was translated—literally and more metaphorically—for different audiences is the topic of several chapters. Anglophone perspectives are offered in the chapters by Katy Hamilton, who explores the treatment of Lieder in London, and Heather Platt, who considers the United States. Hamilton investigates the consequences of Natalia Macfarren's singable translations of Lieder by Brahms on the composer's reputation and popularity in England. She likens the impetus behind translating the songs (particularly the ensemble songs) to that guiding arrangements of instrumental repertoire; in other words, they were intended to disseminate the repertoire to a larger domestic market. Macfarren's translations were also hugely influential on subsequent attempts to render Lieder in English, encouraging the use of archaisms that in later decades negatively affected the reputations of the songs themselves.

Platt's discussion of the ways in which Lieder were programmed on the East Coast, and how that reflected the European training and experience of particular singers, is to our knowledge the first such study of German art-song performance in the mid- to late-nineteenth-century United States and attests to the importance of transatlantic cultural transfer during the period. German musicians such as August Kreissmann and Americans who had studied in Europe, such as Villa Whitney White (a student of Amalie Joachim), introduced song cycles in their recitals, in turn encouraging a greater number of individual Lieder to be programmed across the country. David Bispham used his championing of Brahms's songs as a way of promoting his concerts. As well as geographical transfer, gender played a significant role in United States performance culture: women's music clubs were important venues for recitals but, at the same time, there was considerable flexibility in attitudes about which gender should sing which songs.

Gender is also significant for Beatrix Borchard's chapter, which considers the concert hall as a feminized space within the career of Amalie Joachim, a singer whose historically aware recitals signaled a new attitude to Lieder programming. The discovery of archival materials reveals that Amalie Joachim's role in devising the influential volume *Das deutsche Lied* had been suppressed; her male collaborator instead took the credit for the collection. Although the careers of female performers continued to be circumscribed by what was deemed socially acceptable, Joachim's was an era of transition, with the newly sacralized space of the concert hall enabling women such as she to play a more prominent role in musical performance. The recitals on which *Das deutsche Lied* was based encapsulated efforts to establish the genre's long German heritage and to court both professional and amateur musicians. Amalie Joachim's role was not that of an entertainer but that of an educator who, through her nontheatrical mode of performance, attempted to persuade her audiences of the superiority of Lieder over more popular parlor songs.

The determination to forge a national identity through song is also the subject of Maria Razumovskaya's chapter, which explains the role of composer and pianist Nikolai Medtner in the promotion of Lieder in early twentieth-century Moscow. Art-song salons were effective vehicles for debating representations of Russianness. The cultural capital of the aristocracy was increasingly called into question, as was the appropriateness of using folk music to convey individual expression. In response, for romances Medtner turned to German Lieder as a musical model and to the poetry of Goethe for texts. In his heyday, Medtner was praised for having managed an integration of German and Russian cultures that other artists had not; with the outbreak of World War I and then the 1917

Revolution, however, his affinity with Brahms was reinterpreted negatively, as a sign of conservatism.

William Weber and Simon McVeigh look primarily at programming, tracking the development of the solo song recital at what became the *Ver sacrum* of Lieder singing, the Bechstein (later Wigmore) Hall. Despite reports that Lieder were routinely programmed in recitals, they demonstrate that in fact British, Italian, and French repertoires were much more prominent and that new music was heard in recitals much more often than in other venues. An alternative canon of Lieder composers was evident at the start of the twentieth century in England. Brahms took precedence over Schubert and Schumann, and while figures such as Christian Sinding and Alexander von Fielitz were accorded respect, Max Reger was not. Changes in attitude were encouraged by concerts devised by musicians of German heritage—most notably George Henschel and Elena Gerhardt. Looking backward to the musical past and forward through music of the present has proved to have been fundamental in London vocal recitals until World War I.

Beyond the conventional concert sphere, Wiebke Rademacher explodes the notion that Lieder were primarily a domestic, bourgeois art form by investigating their presence on programs in working-class concerts organized in Berlin at the start of the twentieth century. It is important to consider the social aspects of Lieder performance, which often served to define distinctions of class and gender. Rademacher explores the educational purposes programming art song might have had as a means of improving the tastes of the lower classes but points out that the repertoire was also part of choral culture. Working-class choirs in Berlin, under the auspices of the Deutscher Arbeiter-Sängerbund, were heavily politicized; they deliberately distanced their activities from the bourgeoisie by programming Lieder alongside agitational and folk songs. Music making was thus both a way to attain upward social mobility and a means through which the validity of class divides could be tested.

The creative and commercial roles played by performers is apparent in the chapters by Rosamund Cole and Nicholas Attfield. Focusing on individual musicians is a fairly standard route into discussing performance practices, but Cole's chapter pursues a different angle by considering how the financial aspect of a singer's working life influenced their artistic choices. Lilli Lehmann turned to recitals when overwhelmed by her operatic schedule and, what is more, used her programs as an opportunity to promote the songs of her friend, the composer August Bungert. Lehmann was influential both because of her performance style and because she sometimes gave recitals dedicated to one composer. What is perhaps most remarkable is that her career change is shown to have been as financially lucrative as her stage work (and sometimes more so).

Lehmann's accompanist Reinhold Herman was criticized on occasion for improvising piano interludes between songs. This was, though, a fairly common practice into the early twentieth century, as discussed by Nicholas Attfield. His chapter tackles the approach taken by Hans Pfitzner who, when accompanying songs in concert, took what would now be considered outrageous liberties with their scores—improvising interludes and recomposing sections—that both enhanced the continuity of programs and emphasized their provisional nature. It seems that even into the twentieth century, notions of *Werktreue* were far from the minds of performing artists; or, rather, that the spirit of the work was conceived in a much more flexible and imaginative way.

Because of the revisionist purpose of this volume, and its emphasis on documenting performance culture in the long nineteenth century, it seemed important to investigate the attitudes of today's musicians, to gauge the extent of the historical gap between present and past. To that end, Natasha Loges and I interviewed a number of professional singers and pianists involved in the programming of Lieder recitals. Our sample was determined in large part by availability, but it represents different generations, genders, and nationalities. A selective transcript and digest of our conversations constitutes the final chapter. From the interviews it becomes apparent that there are some deep-seated beliefs in the importance of balance within recital programs, which for many means conveying a kind of coherent drama that can be understood as a whole while allowing for contrast. Often, programs were determined by poet(s) or theme if not necessarily by composer. Few condoned the practice of eclectic programs that mixed genres, associating them with celebrity or gala performances rather than the serious Liederabend. Many were surprised to be shown Clara Schumann's program from the 1870s, which interrupted *Dichterliebe* with piano pieces by her late husband as well as music by Chopin and Mendelssohn and claimed that such a disrespectful attitude to the coherence of a cycle would now be unthinkable. Some admitted that they toyed with similar ideas and that they had been intrigued by performances that had attempted them. Indeed, while several musicians professed an interest in semistaged performances, or presentations that somehow provided alternative frames for a song cycle (poetry readings, puppetry), a strong sense emerged that the straight recital dedicated to Lieder grouped by work, poet, or composer was the gold standard.

Considerations of venue and potential audiences were also important in our interviewees, with London's Wigmore Hall assuming a gravitas that would have been almost incomprehensible to its earliest patrons. If an exclusive venue such as the Wigmore is now at one end of the spectrum, there is—to our knowledge—no equivalent to the working men's clubs that promoted Lieder in late-nineteenth-century Berlin. There are, however, increasingly numerous examples of Lieder being reworked and presented in unconventional venues. Tenor Ian Bostridge has toured a staged version of Hans Werner Henze's *Winterreise* (directed by Netia Jones). Henze's score is for small ensemble rather than piano, adding percussive sound effects to convey the wintry landscape. Bostridge forsook the conventional white tie of the recitalist for trench coat and face paint: *Winterreise* became grotesque cabaret. As part of the Spitalfields Festival in East London, in December 2017, sixteen musicians were commissioned to recompose a song from Schumann's *Dichterliebe*. Each was performed in a different room, in various Huguenot houses owned by the Landmark Trust, with the audience traipsing between them, not necessarily in the order of Schumann's cycle. The musicians involved in *Schumann Street*, as it was called, were for, the most part, from outside the classical sphere, and perhaps as a result felt greater freedom to mash up Schumann's music.[9]

The boundary between *Schumann Street* and the kind of musical arrangements of preexisting works devised in the nineteenth century is not all that clear. That the liberty is extended to the manner in which the audience consumed the cycle is even more interesting—freed from the concert hall, the listeners return to the home. Even if that home is not their own (though, interestingly, the Spitalfields Huguenot Houses are not museums but occupied residences), and even if the music they hear is mostly new rather than old, there was a pull back to past practices. History lurks in the presentation of the Lied. Acknowledging that history is not unidirectional but forked and fragmented is important, for it allows us to query claims made on behalf of a genre and set of performance practices that might deter musicians and musicologists from thinking through its historical and contemporary significance rather than liberate them to do so.

Notes

1. On audience behavior, see Michael Burden, "Pots, Privies and WCs: Crapping at the Opera in London before 1830," *Cambridge Opera Journal* 23, nos. 1–2 (July 2011): 27–50.

2. See James Johnson, *Listening in Paris: A Cultural History* (Berkeley: University of California Press, 1996).

3. On nineteenth-century performance practices, see the AHRC-funded project Transforming 19th-Century Historically Informed Performance at the University of Oxford and Clive Brown's *Classical and Romantic Performing Practice, 1750–1900* (Oxford: Oxford University Press, 1999).

4. John Potter, "Beggar at the Door: The Rise and Fall of Portamento in Singing," *Music and Letters* 87, no. 4 (2006): 523–50; Daniel Leech Wilkinson, "Listening and Responding to the Evidence of Early Twentieth-Century Performance," *Journal of the Royal Musical Association* 135, supplement 1 (2010): 45–62.

5. See, for instance, Richard Taruskin, *Music in the Nineteenth Century: The Oxford History of Western Music* (New York: Oxford University Press, 2005) 3: 119–86.

6. These issues are tackled as they pertain to chamber music in Marie Sumner Lott, *The Social Worlds of Nineteenth-Century Chamber Music: Composers, Consumers, Communities* (Urbana: University of Illinois Press, 2015).

7. Jennifer Ronyak, "'Serious Play,' Performance, and the Lied: The Stägemann *Schöne Müllerin* Revisited," *19th-Century Music* 34, no. 2 (2010): 141–67.

8. See Benedict Anderson, *Imagined Communities: Reflections on the Origin and Spread of Nationalism* (New York: Verso, 1983).

9. Reviews of *Schumann Street* were published in the *Guardian*, the *Telegraph*, the *Times*, and the *Artsdesk*. See Erica Jeal, "Schumann Street Review," *Guardian*, December 10, 2017, https://www.theguardian.com/music/2017/dec/10/schumann-street-review-spitalfields-london-dichterliebe-huguenot-houses; Richard Morrison, "Concert Review: In the Light of Air/Schumann Street at Spitalfields, E1," *Times* (London), December 11, 2017, https://www.thetimes.co.uk/article/concert-review-in-the-light-of-air-schumann-street-at-spitalfields-e1-6hqzm3og7; Ivan Hewett, Rupert Christiansen, and John Allison, "The Tallis Scholars on Snuffly but Stirring Form at St John's Smith Square, plus the Rest of December's Best Classical Concerts," *Telegraph*, December 21, 2017, http://www.telegraph.co.uk/music/classical-music/mezzo-soprano-cecilia-bartoli-best-worst-barbican-plus-decembers/; Helen Wallace, "Schumann Street, Spitalfields Festival Review—Illumination on a Winter's Night," artsdesk, December 13, 2017, http://www.theartsdesk.com/classical-music/schumann-street-spitalfields-festival-review-illumination-winters-night.

Bibliography

Anderson, Benedict. *Imagined Communities: Reflections on the Origin and Spread of Nationalism*. New York: Verso, 1983.

Brown, Clive. *Classical and Romantic Performing Practice, 1750–1900*. Oxford: Oxford University Press, 1999.

Burden, Michael. "Pots, Privies and WCs: Crapping at the Opera in London before 1830." *Cambridge Opera Journal* 23, nos. 1–2 (July 2011): 27–50.

Johnson, James. *Listening in Paris: A Cultural History*. Berkeley: University of California Press, 1996.

Leech Wilkinson, Daniel. "Listening and Responding to the Evidence of Early Twentieth-Century Performance." *Journal of the Royal Musical Association* 135, supplement 1 (2010): 45–62.

Potter, John. "Beggar at the Door: The Rise and Fall of Portamento in Singing." *Music and Letters* 87, no. 4 (2006): 523–50.

Ronyak, Jennifer. "'Serious Play,' Performance, and the Lied: The Stägemann *Schöne Müllerin* Revisited." *19th-Century Music* 34, no. 2 (2010): 141–67.

Sumner Lott, Marie. *The Social Worlds of Nineteenth-Century Chamber Music: Composers, Consumers, Communities*. Urbana: University of Illinois Press, 2015.

Taruskin, Richard. *Music in the Nineteenth Century*. Oxford History of Western Music. New York: Oxford University Press, 2005.

LAURA TUNBRIDGE is Professor of Music at the University of Oxford. She is author of *Schumann's Late Style*, *The Song Cycle*, and *Singing in the Age of Anxiety: Lieder Performances in New York and London between the World Wars* and coeditor of *Rethinking Schumann*.

1 "Eine wahre Olla Patrida [sic]"

Anna Milder-Hauptmann, Schubert, and Programming the Orient

Susan Youens

ALL ONE NEED do to astonish present-day musicians is to display various early-nineteenth-century European concert programs, with their variety-over-unity approach to programming and their frequent mixture of certifiably "great" music (in the present-day canon) with lighter fare.[1] In particular, today's singers desirous of a theme for their programs or any other sort of coherent design are understandably flabbergasted by concerts such as this one given by the famous singer Anna Pauline Milder-Hauptmann on January 13, 1825 in Vienna (see table 1.1).[2]

1. The opening work was the overture to Mozart's *La clemenza di Tito*. Opera overtures were a frequent component of programs organized by singers.[3]
2. Next came "Der Troubadour" and "Concertscene für Gesang, Orchester und Guitarre," by Carl Blum, composed expressly for Anna Milder.[4] Carl Wilhelm August Blum was a guitarist as well as a singer, librettist, and comic opera composer.[5]
3. Then came a harp fantasy, performed by Xavier Desargues, a visiting French harp virtuoso.[6]
4. The first half ended with a duet by Giacomo Meyerbeer, sung by the famous bass-baritone Eduard Devrient (1801–77)[7] and Anna Milder. We discover in the review from Berlin (see note 2) that the duet was from Giacomo Meyerbeer's *Margherita d'Anjou*, first performed in 1820; whether the reference is to the "opéra en trois actes" or the two-act *opera semiseria* is not known.
5. The second half of the program also began with a Mozart opera overture, the overture to *Le nozze di Figaro*.
6. Next came "Große Scene" by Haydn—we find out in the Berlin review (see note 2) that it was *Berenice, che fai*, Hob. XXIVa: 10, from May 1795, composed during Haydn's second London visit.
7. Subsequently was "Variations for the Violin," composed by Carl Möser ("Moeser") (1774–1851), who was a friend of Prince Louis Ferdinand (Beethoven's Third Piano Concerto was dedicated to him). I wonder

Table 1.1. Program for a concert on January 13, 1825, with Anna Pauline Milder-Hauptmann.

Concert: Anzeigen
Donnerstag den 13. Januar 1825
Im Saale des Königlichen Schauspielhauses
Großes
Vocal= und Instrumental=Concert,
Gegeben
Von der Königlichen Sängerin
Anna Milder.

Erster Theil

1. Ouvertüre aus der Oper: Titus, von Mozart
2. Der Troubadour, Gedicht von C. v. Holtei, als Concertscene für Gesang, Orchester und Guitarre, eigends für die Koncertgeberin componirt von Carl Blum, und gesungen von derselben.
3. Phantasie für die Harfe, ausgeführt von dem Königl. Kammermusikus und ersten Harfenisten Hrn. Desargus.
4. Duett von J. Meyerbeer gesungen vom Königl. Sänger Herrn Devrient und Anna Milder.

Zweiter Theil

5. Ouvertüre aus der Oper: Figaro, von Mozart.
6. Große Scene von Haydn, gesungen von Anna Milder.
7. Variationen für die Violine, componirt von Carl Moeser, gespielt von dessen Schüler dem Königl. Eleven Carl Ebner.
8. Terzett von Beethoven, gesungen von der Königl. Sängerin Mad. Seidler, den Königl. Sängern Herren Stümer und Sieber.
9. Duett aus Romeo und Julietta, von Zingarelli, gesungen von Mad. Seidler und Anna Milder.
10. Die Forelle, Lied von Schubert, gesungen von Anna Milder.

Billets zu 1. Rthlr. sind in der Musikhandlung des Herrn Schlesinger, unter den Linden Nr. 34., und des Herrn Gröbenschütz, an der Schleusenbrücke; im Schauspielhause beim Kastellan Hrn. Adler, und Abends an der Kasse zu haben.
Der Anfang ist 7 Uhr das Ende 9 Uhr.
Die Kasse wird um 6 Uhr geöffnet.

Source: Franz Schubert. *Dokumente 1817–1830*, vol. 1, ed. Till Gerrit Waidelich, assisted by Renate Hilmar-Voit and Andreas Mayer, document no. 302, p. 227. Tutzing: Hans Schneider, 1993.

whether the work in question could have been Carl Möser's *Fantaisie et variations sur des motifs de l'opéra "La vestale de Spontini,"* op. 11 (Berlin: Paez, 1825), especially as Milder-Hauptmann performed the principal role of Julia, the young vestal virgin in this *tragédie lyrique* from 1805 to 1807.

8. Then came an unidentified vocal trio by Beethoven, sung by the soprano Karoline Seidler-Wranitzsky (the first Agathe in *Der Freischütz*), the tenor

Heinrich Stümmer, and the bass Ferdinand Sieber. The Berlin critic says that the unnamed trio "seems to be an early work by the genial composer"; could it have been "Tremate, empi, tremate," op. 116 of 1802 (revised, possibly in 1814)?

9. Next, we have an unspecified duet from *Giulietta e Romeo* of 1796 by Nicola Zingarelli, sung by Seidler and Milder. The work was probably "Dunque il mio bene," clearly one of the most popular numbers in this very popular opera, albeit one that seems rather dull to contemporary eyes and ears. One notes that the part for Giulietta lies largely in the middle register (Milder's forte), with only a few modest flourishes (not Milder's forte) at the very end.[8]

10. And finally, the program closed with "Die Forelle, Lied von Schubert." "Die Forelle" is the shortest work on the list, a bonbon (but a profound one) at the close of it all.

The variety, of course, is what astonishes contemporary musicians, as does the mixture of names they know well—the holy trinity of Haydn, Mozart, and Beethoven—with names to which Time has not been kind. William Weber's characterization of such programs as "variations on miscellany" is apt, but so too is his cautionary note that "miscellany" at that time was not a pejorative description.[9] The mixture of local music and music from elsewhere, as well as the desire to include something for everyone, is also on display in that long-ago evening's entertainment by some of the best musicians in Vienna.

This program was advertised as "beginning at 7 and ending at 9 o'clock," but two hours is actually slim and trim compared to other contemporaneous concerts that must have really put people's *Sitzfleisch* to the test—*if* they sat through the whole thing.[10] A Berlin actor in late 1825 organized an "Abend-Unterhaltung," an evening salon, described by a critic in *Der Freimüthige* for December 26 as "A true olla podrida, composed of all possible ingredients at hand."[11] The critic was, if anything, understating the degree of miscellany: the program included the overture to Ludwig Spohr's opera *Der Berggeist*,[12] a long poem by Friedrich Kind declaimed by a famous actress, and Schubert's "Erlkönig," sung by one Herr Bader at the piano. Marching onward, there was also an unidentified duet by Saverio Mercadante, sung by Milder and Devrient; an adagio and polonaise for cello by Antoine Bohrer;[13] a vocal quartet setting of "Glaube, Hoffnung, Liebe" by Friedrich Heinrich Himmel;[14] an unspecified scene with chorus by Bernhard Adolf Marx, composed for Madame Milder; a work by the prolific male-quartet composer Franz Eisenhofer; the overture to Mozart's *La finta giardiniera*, K. 196 (1775), followed by the first scene; a fantasy with variations by Friedrich Kalkbrenner;[15] an aria with chorus from Rossini's *La Cenerentola* ("Nacqui all'affanno, al pianto," rondò with chorus from act 2, scene 3?); Mozart's trio "Mandina amabile," K. 480, composed for Francesco Bianchi's 1783 comic opera *La villanella rapita*;[16] the male quartet version of Schubert's "Der Gondelfahrer,"

D809; Carl Blum's ballad "Der Goldschmiedgesell;"[17] and a chorus of Russians from Ernst Raupach's drama *Alangbu*, with guitar accompaniment.[18] I would have needed strong drink to survive all that. The critic's sarcasm in thus invoking *olla podrida* bespeaks an early ripple in a changing tide, a reaction already forming against the admixture of light works in popular taste with serious compositions on concert programs.

About Anna Milder

My current interest in such occasions centers on Anna Milder-Hauptmann, Beethoven's first Leonore and one of the most extraordinary singers in the early nineteenth century. In particular, I look at the nexus of art song as an element in these miscellany concerts, Anna Milder's influence on composers and concert programming, and the fashion for oriental subjects with Schubert's Suleika songs as the focus (see fig. 1.1 for depictions of her).

I will happily echo Brahms in declaring that "Suleika I" is among Schubert's loveliest works,[19] and it subsequently gained a companion piece in another Suleika song created expressly for Milder. The genesis of "Suleika II" is a familiar tale, beginning with Milder's attempt to make contact with Schubert in the autumn of 1824. He was in Hungary with the Esterházy family, and therefore, she wrote him on December 24, 1824, to say "how much I enjoy your songs, and what enthusiasm they arouse in audiences where I have performed them."[20] This was the prelude to her solicitation of both an opera and more songs from him; Schubert, whose pleasure at hearing from Leonore one can well imagine, duly sent her *Alfonso und Estrella* and several songs, including "Suleikas zweiter Gesang," dedicated to her. She loved the song, she told him in a return letter from Berlin written on March 8, 1825, declaring it "magical" and telling him that it brought her to tears, as did the first Suleika song and "Geheimnis," D491 from 1816, clearly also included in the package.[21] I would guess that Schubert's setting of "Geheimnis" was a case of the composer turning Johann Mayrhofer's heartfelt compliment to *him* into a compliment to *her*: "You sing, and the sun shines and Spring is near," the poet wrote, and what singer wouldn't want to hear *that*?[22] And yet, such rarefied beauty as was on display in "Suleika I" and "Geheimnis" were not, Milder told Schubert, meant for the public, who merely wanted their ears tickled. She turned down *Alfonso und Estrella* because it did not have a part suitable for her and requested a new opera from him, preferably in one act and on an oriental subject, with the soprano as the chief character.[23] She also requested that he set to music "Der Nachtschmetterling," which Walther Dürr has surmised was probably Johann Gottfried Ritter von Leitner's poem "Der Jüngling und der Nachtschmetterling" (The youth and the moth),[24] in a style "addressed to a wider public."[25] One can imagine her savoring the dramatic possibilities, the mothlike fluttering in both piano and vocal parts, afforded by this dialogue poem.

Fig. 1.1 a–b. Depictions of Anna Milder-Hauptmann. (a) Axis Images / Alamy Stock Photo (b) UtCon Collection / Alamy Stock Photo.

Well before the Christmas 1824 letter to Schubert, matters of taste and repertoire were part of her life story. At age sixteen, she was taken in hand and tutored by the composer Sigismund von Neukomm (1778–1858), who was one of Haydn's students, and then by Antonio Salieri.[26] In one thoroughly delicious anecdote, Neukomm brought her to Haydn, for whom she sang "a bravura aria from an old German opera much beloved by the Salzburgers" (I wish I knew what it was). After the aria, Haydn made his famous comment "My child, you have a voice like a house" ("Liebes Kind, Sie haben eine Stimme wie ein Haus"), upon which he turned to Neukomm and said, "You, however, should burn this score on the spot—she should not sing such trash."[27] In April 1803, at age seventeen, she was engaged by Emanuel Schikaneder for the Theater an der Wien, where she appeared for her debut as Juno in Franz Süßmayr's Singspiel *Der Spiegel von Arkadien* of 1794. (This was an offspring of *Die Zauberflöte* with a libretto also by Schikaneder.)[28] One of the most popular numbers in this work was the bravura aria "Juno wird dich stets umschweben," its tempo allegro, its meter 4/4, its tessitura stratospheric, with an uncomfortable emphasis on the *passagio* and quite a few melismas, as one can see from Süßmayr's exuberant treatment of the word *Seite* (see example 1.1).

But for Milder's sake and to her specifications, the composer provided an alternate aria on the same words (most of them), its music conceived in a *very* different vein: here, the tempo is andante, the meter 6/8, the tessitura largely in the middle of the voice, and passage work placed only at the end, as shown in example 1.2. This version was published in Berlin in 1838, with a prefatory homage to the recently deceased singer; it is quite moving that her friends chose this earliest specimen of her fame to herald her passing, thereby tracing an arc from beginning to end and choosing a work emblematic of the singularity of her voice.[29]

From the start, Milder impelled change: composers wanted to write for her, and they tailored their works to her unique traits. There are numerous anecdotes in which writers try to describe how she sounded, stressing difference from everyone else as they did so. The Bohemian composer Johann Wenzel Tomaschek (Václav Jan Tomášek), in his *Selbstbiographie*, writes of attending the Akademie im großen Redoutensaal in Vienna at which Beethoven's *Der glorreiche Augenblick*, op. 136, and Seventh Symphony, op. 92, were performed in 1814, with Milder-Hauptmann the soprano soloist in the cantata. Tomaschek invokes "the colossal voice of Madame Milder" resounding through the entire space, with the violin soloist helpless against such power.[30] One of the most detailed descriptions of her sound, her technique, and her artistry comes from the Berlin composer and music critic Johann Carl Friedrich Rellstab, father of the Schubert poet Ludwig Rellstab and an important figure in Berlin's musical life. He heard her in Vienna in 1811 and wrote a travel report from that city for the *Vossische Zeitung*, saying that no other performer had aroused his curiosity as much as she did and that he

Example 1.1. Franz Xaver Süßmayr, "Juno wird dich stets umschweben," from *Der Spiegel von Arkadien* (1794).

Example 1.2. Franz Xaver Süßmayr, "Juno wird dich stets umschweben," composed for Anna Milder-Hauptmann (Berlin: Moritz Westphal, 1838).

Example 1.2. (continued)

had studied her voice every day for the duration of his visit. Among the qualities that most impressed him was the particular beauty of her "middle voice" and the fact that from the top to the bottom, her voice was equally strong, full, and lovely. Trills and mordents were not her forte, he said, nor were bravura passages, but she had every nuance of soft and loud, strong and limpid—like the best Cremona violins, Rellstab rhapsodizes.[31]

In fact, her voice was often compared to instruments, especially the woodwinds. When she sang a role in Ignaz von Seyfried's opera *Cyrus* in 1803, Haydn's biographer Georg August Griesinger wrote to say that her tone was "purest metal" ("reinste Metall"), and that she was adept at sustaining notes powerfully and for a long time, without elaborate ornamentation ("Schnörkel").[32] Still another critic, writing about the July 18, 1814, performance of *Fidelio* for *Der Sammler*, wrote that Milder was not an adherent of any of the usual singing methods, that she was a "new school" unto herself, and that the "rare clarinet-like sound of her voice" was extraordinary.[33] Schubert would exploit that quality, pairing it with itself, as it were, in "Der Hirt auf dem Felsen"; he may have first encountered Wilhelm Müller's words for the first section in "Der Berghirt," op. 4 no. 1, by Milder's pianist-composer sister Jeannette Bürde (example 1.3, in which one notes Bürde's use of by-then-customary Swiss yodel motifs).[34]

The echo effects between the clarinet and the voice in Schubert's D965 would have been a nod both to Milder's fame as the first Emmeline in Joseph Weigl's *Die Schweizer Familie* of 1809—another hugely popular Singspiel in its day—and the timbral resemblance of her voice to that instrument. When Napoleon heard her sing Lilla in Martin y Soler's *Una cosa rara* in 1809, he reportedly exclaimed, "Now there's a voice—I have not heard such a voice for a long time" (Voilà une voix, depuis longtemps je n'ai pas entendu une telle voix).[35] He offered her a royal position in Paris with perquisites galore, but she was romantically involved at the time with the court jeweler Peter Hauptmann; they married in 1810, and she bore him both a daughter (in 1811) and another child whose name is not known. But the marriage broke up, and Milder left Vienna in 1815; her life thereafter is actually bound up with the history of gay Berlin, and she took a cultivated Berlin Jewish woman named Friederike Liman (1770–1844), a close friend of the famous salonnière Rahel Varnhagen von Ense, as her partner around 1817. Liman had previously been in a liaison with the singer and actress Friederike Bethmann-Unzelmann, who died in 1815 (this after Liman's youthful marriage to and separation from Carl August Liman). In a letter from Liman to Rahel on March 26, 1816, some seven months after Bethmann-Unzelmann's death, Friederike describes Milder as "good-hearted . . . not stupid, as many believe, and somewhat childlike" (Hertzens gut . . . nicht dum, wie viele glauben und etwaß kindisches).[36] The flare-up of sexual attraction—"my fever" was her designation for Milder—would burn out quickly, or so she reports (one is allowed to wonder), allowing her to become a "pure Plato or Plata," a contemporaneous designation for platonic same-sex relationships.[37] According to Karl August Varnhagen von Ense in his sketch of Liman's friendship with Rahel, Liman's attachment to Unzelmann had generated pernicious gossip, but Milder was so revered that no such unpleasantness troubled them thereafter.[38] One hopes his account was true.

Example 1.3. Jeannette Bürde, "Der Berghirt," op. 4 no. 1, measures 1–14.

Another, and quite wonderful, anecdote about Milder and her partner can serve as segue to a discussion of the two Suleika songs. In the summer of 1823, Liman and Milder were in Marienbad, where Milder visited Goethe on 15 August. After her departure, Goethe wrote to his daughter-in-law Ottilie and to Carl Friedrich Zelter, the latter on 24 August, that she sought to make small songs large and that the memory brought tears to his eyes; the songs were, we learn from Friederike, Conradin Kreutzer's "Lebe wohl, lebe wohl, mein Lieb" and "Will ruhen unter den Bäumen hier" from *Neun Wanderlieder von Ludwig Uhland* of

1818. (Schubert respected this work.)³⁹ "Goethe was completely dissolved in tears" (Gö war gans aufgelöst in trähnen), she reports. In 1828, Goethe would inscribe a "splendid edition," a *Prachtexemplar*, of his drama *Iphigenie auf Tauris* for Carl Friedrich Zelter to present to Milder on the twenty-fifth anniversary of her ascending the stage; this ageless tale, the great poet declared, achieved a higher goal when it was set to music by Gluck and sung by her.⁴⁰ It is Goethe's repeated statement to both correspondents that she made small pieces of music large that I find fascinating; the word surely has connotations of something beyond the extraordinary size of her voice, as it identifies how she could imbue "small songs" with profundity and grandeur. The Suleika songs are, of course, also "large" in their amplitude: these are not miniature *Lieder* but extended *Gesänge*, each in two different tempi with rich tonal plans.

Having received the Suleika songs from Schubert, Milder performed either just "Suleika II," with her sister accompanying, or both at a concert in Berlin on June 9, 1825, before leaving for Paris.⁴¹ Among the other works performed that evening were the overture to *Così fan tutte*, "Gruss an die Schweiz" by Carl Blum,⁴² a duet by Saverio Mercadante (perhaps the same one she had previously performed in Vienna in January), Schubert's "Erlkönig," and the overture to Rossini's *L'inganno felice*. By quickly surveying Blum's yodel-song written for Milder (example 1.4), we see the sort of strains Schubert would raise to a much higher level in "Der Hirt auf dem Felsen." A reviewer describing this concert in the *Königlich privilegirte Berlinische Zeitung*, however, went into raptures about Milder's "silvery-bright and golden-pure voice" (still more metal metaphors, but precious metals this time) as she portrayed these "noble children of Nature" (Swiss shepherds) in Blum's bundle of clichés.⁴³

According to a London review of this event in *The Harmonicon*, she sang "*two airs from Goethe's Westöstlichem Divan*, the music by Franz Schubert, and Erlkönig, also by Goethe and Schubert . . . which pleased extremely. This lady has the judgment and good taste to select such pieces for her performance as are calculated to afford her an opportunity for her powers of moving the soul, not of showing off the compass of her voice." The Janus-faced jab both at her somewhat restricted range and at bravura singing or, what Carl Maria von Weber called "Italian Larifari," is clear.⁴⁴

The Two Suleika Songs: Hafiz, Goethe, Marianne von Willemer, and Schubert

Schubert, of course, thought that Goethe wrote both of the poems he chose from the *Divan*; he knew nothing of Marianne, nor did any of the other composers drawn to these works. (Schubert's Shakespearean ventriloquism in music is astonishing: a German male poet had, so he thought, assumed the sensibility

Example 1.4. Carl Blum, "Gruss an die Schweiz," measures 1–29.

Example 1.4. (*continued*)

of a pseudo-Persian female persona expressing herself in a Western adaptation of an exotic verse form, and he, a twenty-four-year-old Austrian man, would set these words to music.) "Suleika I," D720, was, we know, composed in March 1821, in two versions that differ by one measure. The first version, the autographed manuscript of which resides in the Austrian National Library in Vienna, was published in 1822 by Cappi and Diabelli and dedicated to Franz von Schober. The autographed manuscript of the second, "Suleika II," D717, is lost, and the date of composition is therefore uncertain. Was it composed alongside the first, "Was bedeutet die Bewegung?," in 1821, as Otto Erich Deutsch thought was most likely, or did Schubert, at Milder's request for something "oriental," go back to Goethe's *Divan* and pluck a pendant poem from the anthology in late 1824?[45] If the latter is the case, one wonders whether he could have been at least slightly influenced by her words to him about the nature of the *first* song as too profound for hoi polloi. Schubert was hardly one to kowtow to diva behavior from singers, but such was his respect for Milder that choosing and fashioning a second song that would slant somewhat more to "the public taste" seems not unlikely, *if* its genesis was in 1824. Andreas Mayer has aptly suggested that "Der Hirt auf dem Felsen," composed four years later, is located somewhere in the middle ground between "popular" and "pure" taste in accord both with the singer's desires and the composer's refusal to write dross on command.[46] With "Suleika II," she could have her cake and eat it too: she could charm the public and do so with music of genuine worth, of the sort of "oriental subject" she had requested for an opera. She was born in Constantinople, we remember; she was only there for five years in infancy, but perhaps early childhood impressions as well as musical fashion influenced her attraction to orientalism in music.

If she performed both Suleika songs on that June day in 1825, the listeners could have heard what the two songs share, in Graham Johnson's typically astute observations:[47] the busy accompaniments with the imputation of continuous breeze, the incessant alternation of major and minor modes, the phrase repetitions, the importance of leaps of a sixth in the vocal lines (the *ballon*, the lilt, of this music is due in part to this element), and the doubling in thirds or unison or octaves between the voice and piano, especially the right-hand part. The contours of the vocal line at the start of "Suleika II" ("Ach, um deine feuchten Schwingen") recall "Ach, die wahre Herzenskunde" in "Suleika I," and the melody of "Eile denn zu meinem Lieben" in "Suleika II" is so closely akin to "Und so kannst du weiter ziehen" in number I as to defy mere coincidence (see example 1.5).

Schubert clearly had a mind somewhat like a computer, in which instantaneous recall of gestures from years earlier was a matter of nanoseconds. Furthermore, the two songs are complementary opposites in terms of large-scale design. Not only do both engage strophic variations, but also number I ends with an "Etwas langsamer" section and number II with an "Etwas geschwinder" section whose jog-trot rhythms bespeak messages borne more by horse-drawn coach than by wind: a *galop* (a lively dance of Hungarian or German origin that became popular in Vienna in the 1820s, just in time for Schubert to appropriate it) in 3/4 meter rather than the customary duple meter.[48] But if there is undeniably complementarity, there is also difference, possibly originating with the composer's awareness of Milder's preference for popular taste in the second song. The East Wind song, composed in Beethoven's "dark key" ("schwarze Tonart") of B minor, is remarkable for profundity without intrusion by anything "popular." The West Wind song, in contrast, is in B-flat major, as far away tonally as one can go from B minor, while the clip-clopping *galop* is recognizably a nod to Vienna's Redouten.

We owe a small troupe of bygone people thanks for the existence of these songs, beginning with one of medieval Persia's most important poets, Khwaja Shams-ud Din Muhammed Hafez-e Shirazi, best known by his pen name Hafiz, born in the garden city of Shiraz in south central Persia (Iran) circa 1315. He died there in 1389 or 1390. The 486 ghazals in his *Divan*, or anthology, were meant to be sung (Hafiz was famous for the sweetness of his singing voice), and they are exceptionally complex, even for such a sophisticated form as this—easy comprehensibility was not his stock-in-trade.[49] All ghazals are written in couplets called "beyts," or "houses," each with a fixed rhyme at the end of the second line, except for the "matla" (which means "orient" or "rising"), that is, the first couplet with the rhyme in both lines; this couplet sets the stage by stating the subject matter and establishing the atmosphere of the poem. The other couplets are reactions to the matla and feature actions that change, viewed from different angles and progressing from one point to another along a deepening trajectory until we reach the "maqta," the objective of the ghazal contained in the final couplet and usually including the poet's name. Hafiz's ghazals often tell of the movement of opposites toward unity, such as lover and beloved, friendship and solitude, life and death, ignorance and wisdom, grief and bliss, the world that

Example 1.5. Comparisons of Franz Schubert, "Suleika I," D720 and "Suleika II," D717.
a. "Suleika I," measures 109–14; "Suleika II," measures 9–12.
b. "Suleika II," measures 129–34; "Suleika I," measures 82–89.

Example 1.5. (continued)

is passing and God who never dies, separation and union, the soul yearning to be united with itself, and so on, and they had a rich afterlife.[50] These marvelous poems entered the German-speaking world through the auspices of Joseph von Hammer-Purgstall, born in Graz in 1774 and trained at Vienna's Oriental Academy, founded by Empress Maria Theresa to teach diplomats the languages and customs of the Ottoman Empire. His translation of Hafiz was the first complete rendering into German, and it electrified Goethe when the publishing firm of Cotta sent him "some novelties" along with the books he had ordered from them in early 1814.[51] "Hafiz is my sibling," he wrote, in reaction to their shared fascination with the sensuous pleasures of life, precisely because they were both so aware of the temporal, transitory dimension of existence.[52] The vital and erotic power of this poetry, its antidogmatic skepticism, and its typically Persian conversion of images from Nature into a substitute mythology drew him into another world, one that Marianne von Willemer joined after Goethe gave her a copy as a gift later that year and began writing poetry in which she is named Suleika and he becomes Hatem.[53] When Marianne invokes "Athem," or "breath" in "Suleika I," it is a West-East play of words on the name Hatem, from the Arabic "hātim" (one who ordains or decrees) and "khātim" (which means a seal, signet ring, or stamp).[54] Goethe also translated the Song of Solomon, and it was there that he discovered the Hebrew "hotem" or "seal," cognate with the Arabic: "Set me as a seal upon thine heart, as a seal upon thy arm: for love is strong as death" (Song of Sol. 8:6). The words *Siegel* and *siegeln* thereafter resound throughout the *Divan* as part and parcel of its secret-encoded passion. Ciphers, games, masks, and veils are everywhere in this collection.

When Marianne in 1814 gave Goethe her poem "Hochbeglückt in deiner Liebe," which Hugo Wolf would later set to music so beautifully, Goethe had to recognize that she loved him. Responding as he often did to erotic situations that he accepted as hopeless (in this instance, both parties were married and of disparate ages, Goethe 65, Marianne 20), Goethe fled to Heidelberg to confer with some learned orientalists—but both Willemers followed him there. On 23 September, Marianne gave Goethe a poem beginning "Was bedeutet die Bewegung?" that she had written in the coach on the way to Heidelberg, and when they parted for the last time three days later, she gave him "Ach, um deine feuchten Schwingen." Goethe would incorporate her three poems, lightly edited, into his *Buch Suleika* in the *Divan* and would, shortly before his death in 1832, send her back the letters she had written him over the years, as "witness to the loveliest of times."[55] It was not until nine years after her death in December 1860 that Herman Grimm (his father and uncle were the Brothers Grimm) revealed the true authorship of the three poems many had already identified as among the most beautiful in the volume.

Marianne's exquisite poem "Was bedeutet die Bewegung?" begins with multiple questions about meaning—precisely the sort that so often impels poetry.[56]

Was bedeutet die Bewegung?	What does this stirring portend?
Bringt der Ost mir frohe Kunde?	Does the east wind bring me joyous tidings?
Seiner Schwingen frische Regung	The refreshing motion of its wings
Kühlt des Herzens tiefe Wunde.	Cools the heart's deep wound.
Kosend spielt er mit dem Staube,	It plays sweetly with the dust,
Jagt ihn auf in leichten Wölkchen,	Chasing it about in light clouds,
Treibt zur sichern Rebenlaube	And drives the happy swarm of insects
Der Insekten frohes Völkchen.	To the shelter of the vine leaves.
Lindert sanft der Sonne Glühen,	It gently tempers the burning heat of the sun,
Kühlt auch mir die heißen Wangen,	And cools my hot cheeks;
Küßt die Reben noch im Fliehen,	Even as it flies, it kisses the vines
Die auf Feld und Hügel prangen.	That adorn the fields and hillsides.
Und mir bringt sein leises Flüstern	And its soft whispering brings me
Von dem Freunde tausend Grüße;	A thousand greetings from my beloved;
Eh' noch diese Hügel düstern,	Before these hills grow dark,
Grüßen mich wohl tausend Küsse.	I shall be greeted by a thousand kisses.
Und so kannst du weiter ziehen!	And now you may pass on,
Diene Freunden und Betrübten.	And serve friends and those who are sad.
Dort wo hohe Mauern glühen,	There, where high walls glow,
Dort find' ich bald den Vielgeliebten.	I shall soon find my dearly beloved.
Ach, die wahre Herzenskunde,	Ah, the true message from the heart,
Liebeshauch, erfrischtes Leben	The breath of love, renewed life,
Wird mir nur aus seinem Munde,	Will come to me only from his lips,
Kann mir nur sein Atem geben.[57]	Can be given to me only by his breath.

Breezes from both east and west as messengers between lovers are a recurring element of medieval Persian verse, and both Goethe and Marianne availed themselves of it. "The musky morning breeze will gently blow again, / Once more the old world will turn young and grow again," Hafiz writes at the start of one ghazal,[58] "Sweet breeze, convey the dust of our existence to that place / Where Splendor reigns" in another. "At dawn, upon the breeze, I caught the scent of my beloved's hair," he tells us in the initial couplet of yet another poem and "Last night, news of my departed friend was brought to me upon the wind" at the start of another.[59] "O morning breeze, abet me now, tonight, because to blossom as dawn lies in wait is what I long for," and "The east breeze at daybreak brings a perfume from the beloved's hair" are other lovely specimens—Marianne surely took note of the latter.[60] Dust as metonymy for both an earthly place and humanity's envelope of flesh is also a frequent motif in Persian poetry; hence its appearance in Marianne's poem ("Kosend spielt er mit dem Staube"); if I have not been able to find a happy swarm of insects in Dick Davis's or Hammer-Purgstall's translations, her invention of them is in accord with Persian poetic conversion of Nature into symbols with mythological power.[61] Throughout five stanzas, Marianne-Suleika imagines reunion with the beloved, but in the final verse, her underlying fear that "Wiedersehen" will become "Trennung" breaks through. The Persian cliché of breezes as go-betweens (winds bring ill news, breezes bring love messages) now become something deeper: the beloved's actual breath, which is also the bearer of his poetic words and of his very life. One notices the reflexive emphasis Marianne gives the words "Wird mir" and "Kann mir" at the accented beginning of the final two lines, underscoring heartfelt personal urgency. There's a wonderful ghazal, again in Davis's superb translation, that always makes me jump forward mentally several centuries to Goethe's time when I read it because of motifs shared with the Suleika poems and the *Buch Suleika*, including its invocations of memory and hence of separation, lips and life's breath, secrecy, and *lovers who edit one another's poetry*. Here are a few beyts from it:

> May I remember always when / your glance in secrecy met mine,
> And in my face your love was like / a visibly reflected sign.
>
> May I remember always when / your chiding eyes were like my death
> And your sweet lips restored my life / like Jesus's reviving breath.
>
> May I remember always when / I was a canopy unfurled
> That shaded you, and you were like / the new moon riding through the world.
>
> May I remember always when / the jewels of verse Hafez selected
> Were set out properly by you, / arranged in order, and corrected.[62]

"Ach, um deine feuchten Schwingen" also "turns," like the east wind ghazal, in the end to go deeper, to arrive at the heart of the matter. The message-bearing breeze at first purports to be sorrow-laden, invoking the tears of lovers' grief shared by all of nature (and it is Schubert's singular perception to see that melancholy underlies rapture throughout much of "Suleika I," while determined optimism underlies enunciated sorrow throughout most of "Suleika II"). It is here that we remember Goethe's home was in the east of Germany, in Weimar, while Marianne's was in the west, in Frankfurt am Main.

Ach, um deine feuchten Schwingen,	Ah, West Wind, how I envy you
West, wie sehr ich dich beneide:	Your moist wings:
Denn du kannst ihm Kunde bringen	For you can bring him word
Was ich in der Trennung leide!	Of what I suffer being parted from him!
Die Bewegung deiner Flügel	The motion of your wings
Weckt im Busen stilles Sehnen;	Awakens a quiet longing within my breast.
Blumen, Auen, Wald und Hügel	Flowers, meadows, woods, and hills
Stehn bei deinem Hauch in Tränen.	Grow tearful at your breath.
Doch dein mildes sanftes Wehen	But your soft, gentle breeze
Kühlt die wunden Augenlider;	Cools my sore eyelids:
Ach, für Leid müßt' ich vergehen,	Ah, I should die of grief
Hofft' ich nicht zu sehn ihn wieder.	If I had no hope of seeing him again.
Eile denn zu meinem Lieben,	Hasten then to my beloved,
Spreche sanft zu seinem Herzen;	Speak softly to his heart;
Doch vermeid' ihn zu betrüben,	But forebear from causing him distress
Und verbirg ihm meine Schmerzen.	And conceal my suffering from him.
Sag ihm, aber sag's bescheiden:	Tell him, but tell him humbly,
Seine Liebe sei mein Leben,	that his love is my life,
Freudiges Gefühl von beiden	and that his nearness will bring me
Wird mir seine Nähe geben.	a joyous sense of both.

By now, the message-bearing wind is heavy, sorrow-laden, and the tears of lovers' grief are shared by all of nature. But at the hinge-word *doch*, Suleika refuses to surrender to despair, despite confessing that the thought of never seeing him again would be her death. Then in the last two stanzas, she describes the pure, unselfish quality of her love for Hatem, and she ends in affirmation and in hope. The final verb is not subjunctive possibility but firm expectation of future reunion.

West-East reciprocity in words was one thing, but what of music? While the occasional German traveler had ventured into Persia and written travelogues about their experiences in the eighteenth and nineteenth centuries, ethnomusicology was not yet a recognized scholarly discipline; the Abbé Vogler had traveled to North Africa and transcribed some of the music he heard there, but such ventures were few and far between. The perceptions of music from elsewhere were inevitably filtered through Western ears, as in Engelbert Kaempfer's 1712 *Amoenitatum exoticarum*, in which he writes of "a noise rather than an ensemble" on display in Persia and of music "unencumbered by any rules of harmony but nevertheless neither confused nor disagreeable;" he knew nothing of the *dastgāh* system of Persian melody types on the basis of which a performer produced extemporized works.⁶³ Instead, Western composers resorted to stereotypes of Janissary music on the one hand and sultry arabesque melodies laden with augmented seconds on the other; we find both in popular light operas such as Michael Kelly's *Illusion, or, The trances of Nourjahad: An Oriental Romance* of 1813—a specimen of what Ralph Locke has dubbed music of "cutthroats and casbah dancers."⁶⁴ In these works, a vague and generalized East functions as sign or metaphor, as imaginary geography, against which Westerners constructed a varied sense of self. Schubert would have known all the clichés: in fact, the opera in which he invested his greatest hopes, *Fierrabras*, is about a Moorish prince who converts at the end both to Christianity and to Charlemagne's armies. A reviewer in the *Berlinische Nachrichten* for June 11, 1825, praised Schubert for the way he "marvelously captured in tones the Oriental spirit of a poem that breathes love's ardent, radiant desire;" aside from general praise for the "rhythms, modulations, melody, and accompaniment," he does not elaborate, nor does he define Schubert's way of fashioning subliminal hints of things Oriental by indubitably Western means.⁶⁵ Had "Suleika II" been truly "Oriental," he would hardly have known what to make of it.

For Cognoscenti and Hoi Polloi

Given boundaries of length and space, I will restrict my contrast between utmost radical refinement on the one hand (Suleika I) and a more popularizing tone (Suleika II) to beginnings and endings, the frames around these two songs. Schubert begins "Was bedeutet die Bewegung?" with a bit of enigmatic magic at the outset, namely five famous introductory measures that are a masterpiece of ambiguity. These winds blow from who knows where, nor can we divine their purpose immediately. We can hear this evocative rise from *pianissimo* depths up to those two rolled chords that at last define a key in several ways: on the level of onomatopoeia, as winds rolling in gently from foreign places, bearing the symbolic dust of Persian poetry with them (the figure at the beginning of example 1.6 will be used soon after for the light clouds of dust in stanza 2).

On the level of subjectivity brought to sounding life in music, we can hear some sort of sensuous/melancholy/erotic presentiment rising from the depths of the psyche, while on the level of musical logistics, we hear a nontonic beginning with an initially ungrounded German sixth chord (Schubert loved that harmony) that finally goes to the dominant seventh and thence to tonic in measure 6, when the dust settles. Not until the wind finally arrives is B minor a certainty. The chromatic dust particles swirl around the initial harmony as it arrives in

Example 1.6. Franz Schubert, "Suleika I," D717, measures 1–5.

three stages, three cumulative beginnings that rise higher and higher until they come to full awareness, if not to understanding, with Suleika forced to ask, "Was bedeutet die Bewegung?"

The winds, having arrived, begin to harp on their message in the piano before Suleika puts her query into words, and its repetitive swaying motion is one Western musical signifier of the Oriental languorous-exotic, here contained in scalewise motion within the span of a diminished fourth D C-sharp B A-sharp. So many elements at the beginning of this song add up to foreboding, from the open fifth in the bass with the ostinato repeated pitch emphasis on the fifth scale degree (very "Gretchen am Spinnrade") to the Beethovenian rhythmic tattoo in the tenor voice: Marianne's Suleika may wonder whether the east wing brings her "happy tidings," ("frohe Kunde"), but Schubert's music tells us that darker possibilities ("tiefe Wunde") haunt *his* Suleika. We also hear his Suleika's effort to persuade herself that reunion is in the offing, as manifested in the relative major and parallel major mode invocations of the words "seiner Schwingen frische Regung kühlt des Herzens tiefe Wunde": D major and B major are the "frische Regung," Suleika thus converting B minor melancholy to doubly warmer major modes, major in the plural. We hear motions of mind and exercises in willed hope on display here. Notice too that the sequence in the vocal line in measures 19–22 states a descending perfect fourth three times, thus multiply correcting the lamenting diminished fourth contour from earlier. And the wedge marks at the start of each measure in measures 6–17 and thereafter, with certain exceptions, can have a temporal dimension, indicating an ever-so-slight lengthening of the pitches and harmonies to which they are adjoined. By this means and many others at the start, Schubert brings longing, with an undercurrent of loss already manifest, to musical life.

The "Etwas langsamer" section (example 1.7) at the close is this song's culminating glory: no wonder it so captivated Brahms. Schubert changes the key signature to B major: all other instances of parallel major earlier in this work have been inscribed in a thicket of accidentals, but now his Suleika insists that parallel major mode *shall* be the tonal climate. The "heartbeat"-tolling dominant pitches, which multiply in their doubling in measures 133–40, are expectation made incarnate, with a palpable admixture of obsession and awareness of passing time and the ticking clock; by the end, they sound at virtually every level. But B minor insists on reasserting itself at measure 118 and measure 130, two slight but telling specimens of her recognition that "he" is not there and that only his physical presence is the breath of life, not the inadequate breeze amanuensis. Schubert repeats the words of the final stanza three times; this is arialike repetition, and here it functions almost like an incantation or charm, meant to bring Suleika's beloved to her by the magic powers of this music. Schubert also fashions the figures in both voice and piano to yearn upward to the emphasized second beat, this after all those downbeat emphases throughout the "etwas lebhaft" first section; much of the character of this last section derives from these ascending inflections.

When Suleika repeats the entire opening passage of the section, there is a significant change in the piano, with the right hand shifting upward by an octave, now exactly doubling Suleika's part; both this detail and the pianissimo dynamics indicate, in classic Schubertian fashion, withdrawal into an inner world. The closing arpeggiated chord in the postlude has the third chord degree on top and the hollow open fifth from the start of the vocal part sounding at the bottom: she is still waiting. What is remarkable about this music, as so many of Schubert's subtlest songs, is its portrayal of ambivalence, of mixed emotions and unresolved feelings. It is this, in sum, that distinguishes "Suleika I" from "Suleika II," for all the undeniable fact that the second song is not merely an empty vehicle for high notes and digital dexterity, as Graham Johnson has correctly observed.

"How many different ways can I incorporate subtle, swaying motion—gracefully, charmingly seductive—into these words?" Schubert must have asked himself when he created the introduction to "Suleika II." Just tallying the layers at the beginning, we find once more the combination of an ostinato on the dominant pitch (this fuels the mood of erotic anticipation) and twofold swaying motion: the rocking back-and-forth octaves in the right hand, like the

Example 1.7. Franz Schubert, "Suleika I," D717, measures 109–43.

Example 1.7. (*continued*)

tintinnabulation of little bells, and the left hand that breaks up individual harmonies into lighter components and sends them swinging and swaying as well. Even the written-out turning figure in measure 4, with the downbeat dissonance of E against F, is a small, spicy, seductive touch (example 1.8).

When the voice enters, it is with a vocal line filled with intervallic gestures that also sway back and forth, the curvature luscious to a degree. The "come hither" quality to the upward tilt of "Schwingen" that links this phrase to the one following, beginning with the words "West, wie sehr," is another wonderful detail. Furthermore, there is a palpable Janissary effect to the "thump" of the low bass notes on the downbeats, vaguely reminiscent of *mehter* music,

Example 1.8. Franz Schubert, "Suleika II," D720, measures 1–16.

or *mehterhane* bands whose shrill winds and large percussion batteries were aped in *alla turca* works by Mozart, Beethoven, and many more. (It is a curious tidbit from history that the *mehter* ensemble was banned in 1826 and replaced, by Sultan Mahmud in 1828, with a European-style band trained by Donizetti.) In the Victoria and Albert instrument collection, there is a piano from circa 1825 by Georg Haschka with five pedals: a sustaining pedal, one with a bassoon stop, an una corda pedal, a percussion pedal, and one for cymbal and bell effects in the lower octaves, all of it perfect for Orientalizing music. We notice that the right hand is silent on the downbeat to permit the percussion pedal to resound; when Suleika bids the zephyr hurry to speak to her beloved in the "Etwas geschwinder" final section (example 1.5b), the plunge down to the percussion pedal pitches happens on every beat in three-four meter. Patting your stomach while rubbing your head seems positively easy by comparison. And with the second section in measures 40–76 (example 1.9), Schubert combines a lighter version of the Janissary thump with accented offbeat ostinato tones in a rhythmic pattern to which Hugo Wolf would later be partial, here to tell of newly awakened "stilles Sehnen" (example 1.9). In the ongoing war between hope and longing, passion and anxiety that is this song, Schubert has the piano corridor in measures 36–39 seem as if about to deliver us to G minor, the B-flat major tonic key's melancholy kin, but he deflects the song to the pastoral zephyr's F major at the last minute. (This is a temporary deferral.) The mere mention of "Sehnen," longing, darkens Nature and the music alike and does so by stages.

At the end of the first section, Suleika repeats the words "Ach, für Leid müsst' ich vergehen, / hofft' ich nicht zu sehn ihn wieder," three times (measures 92–120). On the first statement, it is the final word "wieder" that trips the end of the returned music from the beginning (measures 84–99) and a move to G major—the reiterated E-flat neighbor note to D helps convey the mixture of hope and suffering in this passage. At the end of this stanza, in the piano interlude in measures 120–27, we *seem* to be returning to B-flat major, but then Schubert's Suleika stops short of resolution for one of this composer's trademark measures of silence: a held breath, a pause in which resolutions are made, in which suffering turns into new hope. This moment always makes me think of "Dove sono" and the countess's sudden resolve "di cangiar l'ingrato cor" at the end of an aria that begins with passive pain. What follows the arresting pause in "Suleika II" is the irresistibly light and lively *galop*, with the characteristic hoofbeat rhythms made almost weightless. A quite difficult piano part must sound effortless. For the dance-mad Viennese, this would have been as catnip to a cat, and its charm is only heightened by the tiny touches of B-flat minor (measures 139–42), D flat major (measures 153–55), and G minor (measures 160–63) along the way, as this Suleika too repeats Marianne's words over and over, not to bring out the different emotional layers but to revel in the dance of love (example 1.10).

In the end, Milder received from Schubert music for those who could easily appreciate such vivacity, as do we, but Schubert refuses to end with all-out display. The dreamy musing "mit halber Stimme" ("with half voice") as the scherzo dies away restores a measure of interiority to a Suleika II who is elsewhere less profound than the singer we meet in "Suleika I." How lovely that her final vocal phrase begins as a fanfare, loud and triumphant, and yet hints at the end, by the descent to quietude, at her capacity to mull over the totality of love in more inward fashion.

Whenever I hear the two Suleika songs, I recall Marianne von Willemer's poem "Was ist Gesang?" written, we are told, for a singer.

Example 1.9. Franz Schubert, "Suleika II," D720, measures 35–49.

Example 1.10. Franz Schubert, "Suleika II," D720, measures 135–58.

Example 1.10. (continued)

Was ist Gesang?

Was ist Gesang? Was, kaum gehört,
Dich faßt, dich hält, dich mit sich nimmt
Und, wie durch Liebe schön bethört,

In seinen Ton die Seele stimmt,
Dich Ernst macht, dann bald hoch dich schwingt
Zu dem was heilig, ewig groß,
Bald dich zum Mitgefühle stimmt
Mit Erdenschönheit, Menschenloos,

Was du erlebt, in dir erneut
Und rein und mild dir's nun gewährt,
So daß, was schmerzte, sich verklärt,
Was freute, inniger erfreut.

What Is Song?

What is song? It's that which no sooner
Heard, takes you, holds you, carries you along
And, as when delightfully perturbed by love,
Attunes your soul unto its harmony,
Brings you down to earth, then swings you high,
Up to what is eternal, holy, great,
Soon to attune you to sympathy
With the world's beauty, the fate of men,
Revives within you your experience
And with purity and gentleness grants it
Currency, so that which pained you is now
Transfigured, what brought you joy is more heartfelt and sincere.

Was dieß nicht wirkt, ist nicht Gesang, Ist Klang nur, höchstens hübscher Klang.[66]	That which fails to bring about all this, that is not song, Is nought but sound, a pretty sound at best.

Schubert resists "merely pretty sound" in both Suleika songs, but the allusions to Viennese *Gemütlichkeit* and pseudo-Oriental charm in "Suleika II" are nowhere in evidence in "Suleika I": pure "Gesang" in Marianne's most elevated sense.

* * *

In the fascinating diary of Lili Parthey, whose father Gustav Parthey once praised Milder for "ennobling the thoroughly frivolous content of Mozart's *Marriage of Figaro*"[!] with her performance of Susanna,[67] we encounter still more lively anecdotes of this extraordinary singer. Lili, who married the composer Bernhard Klein, was herself a singer, albeit not of professional quality, and is touchingly possessive about "Dove sono"—"*my* aria," she called it—and was a trifle jealous when someone else sang it at a salon with the young Felix Mendelssohn as the main attraction and Anna Milder performing as well.[68] The anecdote she recounted on Whitsunday, May 18, 1823, is utterly charming: Milder and Klein went to dine with friends in the Tiergarten, and then the little group sang their way through Karl Ditters von Dittersdorf's *Der Apotheker und der Doktor* of 1786. "None of us knew the notes," she confided.[69] In another entry for June 6, 1823, Lili described a piano rehearsal with Milder singing the role of Dido in Klein's opera of the same name and wrote, "I cannot describe how beautiful, how directly appealing to my heart, and how inwardly moving is this lone woman as portrayed by Milder. I could sit still forever and just listen and watch."[70] Anna Milder had that effect on a great variety of people fortunate enough to hear her. We are fortunate that Schubert was among her fans; that Lieder were an occasional component of "olla podrida" programs; and that he wrote immortal songs for her.

Notes

1. The proper term in the chapter title is not "Olla Patrida" but "olla podrida," a Spanish stew of pork, beans, and a variety of other ingredients that depend on what is at hand. See William Weber, *Great Transformation of Musical Taste: Concert Programming from Haydn to Brahms* (Cambridge: Cambridge University Press, 2008), for much more on this subject. Weber (1–2), however, rightly warns against placing too much emphasis on "miscellany programs" and observes that there were limits, that formal and informal types of music were

usually kept apart; that is, no tavern songs or the less refined specimens of male-chorus songs were to be found in programs featuring the likes of Anna Milder-Hauptmann.

2. See Till Gerrit Waidelich, Renate Hilmar-Voit, and Andreas Mayer, *Franz Schubert: Dokumente 1817–1830* (Tutzing, Ger.: Hans Schneider, 1993), 1: 227 (doc. no. 302), for a facsimile of the program. In the review of the concert in the *Königlich privilegirte Berlinische Zeitung* (later the *Vossische Zeitung*) for January 19, 1825 (229–30), we are told that "Die Forelle" was the tenth "dish" in this "Kunst-Soupés" and made a truly delicious dessert; the writer points out that Schubert, "who has also composed numerous operas," was not yet well known in Berlin.

3. For example, the program for a concert directed by the violin prodigy and conductor Franz Joseph Clement (he commissioned Beethoven's Violin Concerto in D major, op. 61)—advertised in the *Wiener-Zeitung* for January 13, 1825, 37—included Schubert's male quartets "Geist der Liebe," D747 (1822, text by Friedrich Matthisson) and "Frühlingsgesang," D740 (1822, text by Franz von Schober), began with the overture to Luigi Cherubini's *Lodoïska* (1791), and ended with Mozart's *Don Giovanni* overture (Waidelich, Hilmar-Voit, and Mayer, *Franz Schubert*, 1: 226 [doc. no. 300]).

4. Other works composed for or dedicated to Anna Milder are Conradin Kreutzer, *Lieder und Romanzen von Uhland mit Begleitung der Guitarre*, op. 70 (Leipzig: Probst, 1826), Bernhard Klein, *Vier geistliche Gesänge* (Leipzig: Breitkopf and Härtel, 1819), and Joseph Wolfram, "Lied" (Bonn: Simrock, 1820).

5. This work and its composer, Carl Wilhelm August Blum (1786–1844), who studied with Antonio Salieri in Vienna and was named composer at the Prussian royal court in 1820, are invoked in *The Harmonicon 1825*, 162. The critic writes, "The concert of the greatest attraction has been that of the celebrated Madame Milder on which occasion she sung, with great effect, the Troubadour, a new song, composed expressly for her by Carl Blum, accompanied by him on the guitar" (165). Blum's operatic and vaudeville works include *Aladin die Wunderlampe* (1828), *Gänserich und Gänschen* (1822), and *Doctor Johannes Faust, der wundertätige Magus der Nordens* (1829); he also arranged Carl Maria von Weber's *Der Freischütz* for guitar accompaniment.

6. The French court harpist Xavier Desargues wrote *Cours complet de harpe*, advertised in the *Journal général de la littérature de France* (Paris: Treuttel et Würtz, 1811), 14: 281.

7. The singer, actor, theater historian, and librettist Eduard Devrient wrote *Geschichte der deutschen Schauspielkunst* (Leipzig: J. J. Weber, 1848–74) and *Briefe aus Paris, 1839: Ueber Theaterschule*, 2nd ed. (Leipzig: J. J. Weber, 1846); the libretto for Heinrich Marschner's opera *Hans Heiling* (for which he sang the title role); and *Meine Erinnerungen an Felix Mendelssohn-Bartholdy und seine Briefe an mich* (Leipzig: J. J. Weber, 1869)—to which Wagner responded with the venomous *Eduard Devrient und sein Style: Eine Studie über dessen Erinnerungen an Felix Mendelssohn-Bartholdy*, 2nd ed. (Berlin: Stilke and Van Muyden, 1869).

8. See Nicola Zingarelli and Giuseppe Foppa, *Giulietta e Romeo: Tragedia per musica, da rappresentarsi negl' imperiali regi Teatri di Corte* (Vienna: Gio. Batta Wallishausser, 1806); my excerpted copy of "Dunque il mio bene!: Duetto in the opera of *Romeo e Giulietta*" was published in London by S. Chappell circa 1825. Other excerpted versions include "Naught e'er should sever" (= Dunque il mio bene) (London: Dicks, 1873) and "Dunque il mio bene: Duetto, sung by Made. [Giuseppina] Ronzi de Begnis and Made. [Giuditta] Pasta" (London: Goulding and D'Almaine, ca. 1825).

9. Weber, *Great Transformation*, 14.

10. For more on the topic of listening at music venues in Europe and England, see William Weber, "Did People Listen in the Eighteenth Century?," *Early Music* 25, no. 4 (November 1997): 678–91, and James H. Johnson, *Listening in Paris: A Cultural History* (Berkeley: University of California Press, 1995), among others.

11. See Waidelich, Hilmar-Voit, and Mayer, *Franz Schubert*, 1: 257–58, for the program, and 258–59, for the review in *Der Freimüthige*.

12. Clive Brown, in *Louis Spohr: A Critical Biography* (Cambridge: Cambridge University Press, 1984), 170, has unkind (but accurate) words to say about the libretto for this work.

13. I have not been able to locate this work by Anton/Antoine Bohrer (1783–1863).

14. Friedrich Heinrich Himmel, *Glaube, Hoffnung, Liebe, von C. W. Hufeland, für 4 gemischte Stimmen*, op. 29 (Leipzig: A. Kühner, by 1810).

15. Kalkbrenner was a prolific composer of fantasy and variation sets: I wonder whether the *Fantasie pour le piano-forte* published in Vienna by Diabelli in 1825 could have been the chosen work, as the preference for "new" works on such programs would suggest.

16. See Wolfgang Amadeus Mozart, *Neue Ausgabe sämtlicher Werke*, Series II/7: *Arias, Scenes, Vocal Ensembles, and Choirs with Orchestra*, vol. 3, ed. Stefan Kunze (Kassel, Ger.: Bärenreiter, 1971), 143–74.

17. Carl Blum, "Der Goldschmiedsgesell," *Gesänge der Heiterkeit und Laune* (Mainz, Ger.: Schott, 1830s?), male-quartet to a text by Goethe; Ludwig Berger, Schubert, and Zelter also set this ballad to music.

18. I have not been able to locate a musical setting of the chorus of Russians from Ernst Raupach's three-act historical drama *Alangbu* about strife between the Mongolians led by the historical Batu-Khan, grandson of Genghis Khan and founder of the Golden Horde, and various principalities of the Rus'. The drama was first performed at court on February 15, 1825, in Berlin and published in *Orphea: Taschenbuch für 1827, Vierter Jahrgang* (Leipzig: Ernst Fleischer, 1827).

19. Max Kalbeck recalls Brahms saying that "Die letzte Strophe des Schubertschen Suleika-Liedes 'Was bedeutet die Bewegung?' ist die einzige Stelle, wo ich mir sagen muß, daß Goethesche Worte durch die Musik wirklich noch gehoben worden sind. Sonst kann ich das von keinem andern Goetheschen Gedichte behaupten. Die sind alle so fertig, da kann man mit Musik nicht an" (Max Kalbeck, *Johannes Brahms*, vol. 3, *1874–1885* [Tutzing, Ger.: Hans Schneider, 1976], 87).

20. See Otto Erich Deutsch, *Schubert: Die Dokumente seines Lebens* (Kassel, Ger.: Bärenreiter, 1964), 267–68.

21. Deutsch, *Schubert*, 280–81. See also Walther Dürr, "Schubert's Songs and Their Poetry: Reflections on Poetic Aspects of Song Composition," in *Schubert Studies: Problems of Style and Chronology*, ed. Eva Badura-Skoda and Peter Branscombe (Cambridge: Cambridge University Press, 1982), 8. Dürr in the early 1980s was dispelling the myth that Schubert set to music any and every kind of mediocre or worse text set in front of him.

22. Mayrhofer published "Geheimnis: An F. Schubert" in Johann Mayrhofer, *Gedichte* (Vienna: F. Volke, 1824), 9. Schubert's setting (D491) dates from October 1816; deviations in wording between song text and published version were probably due to revision from handwritten copies earlier given to the composer. See the invaluable Graham Johnson (one of the greatest Schubertians of them all), *Franz Schubert: The Complete Songs* (New Haven, CT: Yale University Press, 2014), 2: 315.

23. Milder's roles included Namouna in Gaspare Spontini's *Nurmahal, oder das Rosenfest von Caschmir* (based on Thomas Moore's famous "Eastern Romance" *Lalla Rookh*, 1817), first performed in 1821. In the history of exoticism in opera, it is worth noting that she also played the role of Lady Anne in Antonio Salieri's 1804 "Caribbean" Singspiel *Die Neger*. Monostatos had company on the operatic stage in late-eighteenth- and early-nineteenth-century Europe.

24. Johann Gottfried Ritter von Leitner, *Gedichte* (Vienna: J. P. Sollinger, 1825), 13–15, a dialogue poem in which a moth attempts to console a disconsolate, lovelorn youth ("I am too weak with grief to bear this like a man") and the youth replies that if the moth were to know just such a love, it too would be consumed in the flames.

25. Deutsch, *Schubert*, 281.

26. See the *Österreichisches biographisches Lexikon und biographische Dokumentation* (Vienna: Verlag der Österreichischen Akademie der Wissenschaften, 2003), 294, and Carl von Ledebur, *Tonkünstler-Lexicon Berlin's von den ältesten Zeiten bis auf die Gegenwart* (Berlin: Rauh, 1861), 374–77. For more information on the singer, see also Anke Charton, "Anna Milder-Hauptmann und die 'deutsche' Opernschauspielkunst," in *Akteure und ihre Praktiken im Diskurs: Aufsätze*, ed. Corinna Kirschstein and Sebastian Hauck (Leipzig: Leipziger Universitätsverlag, 2012), 228–47; Joseph Kürschner, "Milder, Pauline Anna," *Allgemeine deutsche Biographie* 21 (Leipzig: Duncker and Humblot, 1885), 742; August Pohl, "Beethovens erste Leonore: Zum 150. Geburtstag Anna Milder-Hauptmanns," *Zeitschrift für Musik* 102 (1935), 1232–34; Till Gerrit Waidelich, "Anna Milder-Hauptmann (1785–1838); Wilhelmine Schröder-Devrient (1804–1860): 'Wenn das Orchester [...] tobt, und die Sängerin sich dazu wie eine Furie geberdet.' *Cordelia* (1823), Conradin Kreutzers Oper über 'eine wahre Begebenheit im Jahre 1814' für zwei Primadonnen," in *Vom Salon zur Barrikade: Frauen der Heinezeit*, ed. Irina Hundt (Stuttgart: Metzler, 2002), 111–28. On the 25th anniversary of her ascending the stage, she was presented with a vase with the names of her most important roles on it (Leonore in *Fidelio*, Emmeline in *Die Schweizerfamilie*, the title roles in Gluck's *Alceste* and *Armida*, Clytemnestra in Gluck's *Iphigenie in Aulis*, Elvira in *Don Giovanni*, the title roles in Cherubini's *Faniska* and *Lodoïska*, Astasia in Salieri's *Axur*, and more); see Jürgen Ponert Dietmar, "Ein Stück Musikgeschichte auf Berliner Porzellan," *Keramos* 73 (1976): 29–36.

27. Cited in Ledebur, *Tonkünstler Lexicon*, 374.

28. See Franz Xaver Süßmayr, *Der Spiegel von Arkadien* (Vienna, 1794; repr., Madison, WI: A-R, 2014), parts 1, 2, and 3. "Juno wird dich stets umschweben" appears in vol. 2, act 2, 313–23.

29. Franz Xaver Süßmayr, *Arie aus der Oper "Der Spiegel von Arcadien"* (Berlin: Moritz Westphal, [1838?]): "Zum besten des Nicolaus Bürger Hospitals und zur Erinnerung an die unvergessliche Sängerin," with a biographical note on Anna Milder.

30. This passage from Tomaschek's autobiography first published in the periodical *Libussa*, vol. 5 (Prague: Medau, 1846), 357–61, is reproduced in Klaus Kopitz and Rainer Cadenbach, eds., *Beethoven aus der Sicht seiner Zeitgenossen* (Munich: Henle, 2009), 2: 994.

31. Johann Rellstab, "Reisebericht aus Wien," *Vossische Zeitung* (Berlin), the description of Milder's voice quoted in Ledebur, *Tonkünstler Lexicon*, 376: "Bei meiner ersten Anwesenheit in Wien war sie verreist, bei meiner Rückkehr aus Italien fand ich sie aber und hörte und studirte ich ihre Stimme alle Tage. Sie hat einen Umfang von a bis 3 gestrichen c. In diesem Umfange sind sämmtliche Töne gleich schön, gleich stark, gleich voll; sollte man aber doch einige vorziehen können, so wären es die bei andern Stimmen so selten schönen

Mitteltöne, d1 bis 2 gestrichen d. Es ist der Ton einer wirklich echten Steiner Geige, die ich noch der Cremoneser vorziehe. Triller, Pralltriller und Mordenten macht sie nicht, aber den Doppelschlag, Schleifer und Anschlag sehr gut punktirt und gleich. Eigentlich grosse Bravour-Passagen macht sie eben so wenig, aber sanfte gute Volaten, voluble und deutsch, auch hat sie alle Nuancen der Stärke und Schwäche."

32. Georg August Griesinger, writing to Breitkopf and Härtel in Leipzig on December 7, 1802: "Mademoiselle Mildner [sic] macht den Cambyses [Ignaz von Seyfried's opera *Cyrus*]; ihre Stimme tönt was so selten der Fall ist wie das reinste Metall, und die giebt, da ihr Lehrer [Sigismund von] Neukomm aus der Haydenschen Schule ist lange kräftige Noten ohne Schnörkel und überladene Verzierungen" (Otto Biba, ed., *"Eben komme ich von Haydn—": Georg August Griesingers Korrespondenz mit Joseph Haydns Verleger Breitkopf und Härtel, 1799–1819* [Zurich: Atlantis Musikbuch, 1987], 213).

33. The critique of the July 18, 1814, performance of *Fidelio* appears in *Der Sammler* 6, no. 118 (July 24, 1814), 471: "Es ist ein hoher Genuß, Mad. Milder singen zu hören, den sie zieht, obgleich ihr keine der hier gebräuchlichen Methoden eigen ist, und sie gleichsam eine neue Schule constituirt, immer durch *den seltenen klarinett-gleichen Ton ihrer Stimme* [italics mine] zur Bewunderung hin."

34. Jeannette Bürde, "Der Hirt auf dem Felsen," in *Vier Lieder von Wilhelm Müller*, op. 4 (Berlin: Trautwein, 1829).

35. Ledebur, *Tonkünstler Lexicon*, 375.

36. Birgit Bosold, *Friederike Liman: Briefwechsel mit Rahel Levin Varnhagen and Karl Gustav von Brinckmann sowie Aufzeichnungen von Rahel Levin Varnhagen und Karl August Varnhagen* PhD diss., University of Hamburg, 1996 [unpaged], letter no. 38, March 26, 1816.

37. Bosold, *Friederike Liman*, from Karlsruhe to Rahel in Berlin, letter no. 44, January 30, 1818.

38. Bosold, *Friederike Liman*, "Notiz über Friederike Liman" and "Aufzeichnung 'frühesten Jugendfreundinnen Rahels' vom Dezember 1835," March 26, 1816, p. 87 and letter no. 44, January 30, 1818, p. 97. Karl August wrote, "Hatte man über die Freundschaft zur Unzelmann oft üble Nachrede geführt, so achtete und ehrte man die zur Milder nun allgemein, lobte die Treue, die Zärtlichkeit einer solchen Zuneigung, durch welche der Werth beide Frauen nur erhöht schien."

39. Emil Wachtel and Friedrich Fischl, *Aus Goethes Marienbadertagen* (Mariánské Lázně, Czech Rep.: J. J. Weber, 1932), 88. A thrilled Friederike also describes the encounter in a letter to Rahel from Marienbad on August 16, 1823 (Bosold, *Friederike Liman*, letter no. 54). In another letter, written to Rahel from Wiesbaden on August 14, 1827, she recounts a concert Milder performed in Göttingen, after which students crying "Hurrah" followed their coach from the venue to the hotel (Bosold, *Friederike Liman*, letter no. 55). When the duo traveled to Saint Petersburg in 1830 and Milder performed for Nicholas I and the czarina Alexandra Feodorovna, Milder sang, we are told, act 2, scene 1, of Spontini's *Olympie* (1819) and Carl Blum's "Gruss an die Schweiz: für eine Singstimme mit Begleitung des Pianoforte oder der Guitarre" (Munich: Joseph Aibl, [183–?]). See Bosold, *Friederike Liman*, letter no. 56.

40. Ledebur, *Tonkünstler Lexicon*, 377. The poet's encomium is as follows: "Dies unschuldsvolle, fromme Spiel, / Das edlen Beifall sich errungen, / Erreichte doch ein höh'res Ziel, / Betont von Gluck, von Dir gesungen."

41. See Waidelich, Hilmar-Voit, and Mayer, *Franz Schubert*, 1: 245–49 (doc. nos. 335–40).

42. Carl Blum, "Gruss an die Schweiz, grosse Scene und Lied, furs Orchester componirt" (Berlin: E. H. G. Christiani, [1829?]), and Blum, "Gruss an die Schweiz: für eine Singstimme."

43. Waidelich, Hilmar-Voit, and Mayer, *Franz Schubert* 1: 247 (doc. no. 338).

44. Andreas Mayer, "'Gluck'sches Gestöhn' und 'welsches Larifari': Anna Milder, Franz Schubert und der deutsch-italienische Opernkreig," *Archiv für Musikwissenschaft* 52, no. 3 (1995), 171–204. Mayer points out (p. 184) that *welsches* in Weber's context has a double meaning, encompassing both the French occupiers of Vienna, who savored Italian opera, and the creators of Italian operatic styles.

45. Otto Erich Deutsch et al., *Franz Schubert: Verzeichnis seiner Werke in chronologischer Folge* (Munich: Deutscher Taschenbuch; Kassel, Ger.: Bärenreiter, 1983), 173.

46. Mayer, "Gluck'sches Gestöhn," 194–204.

47. Graham Johnson's *Franz Schubert*, 3: 288–91, argues convincingly that "Suleika II" is "no empty vehicle for high notes and digital dexterity," that it is an effective foil to the profundities of "Suleika I" and outlines the links between the two songs.

48. See Gloria Giordano, "Il Galop, un 'frenetico tumult,'" *Chorégraphie* 1, no. 1 (1993): 89–94. The title refers to the use of *galops* as rousing finales for balls.

49. The most useful introduction to Persian poetics, the history of the ghazal, and Hafiz for those not conversant with medieval Persian is the introduction by Dick Davis to *Faces of Love: Hafez and the Poets of Shiraz* (Washington, DC: Mage, 2012), ix–lxxii.

50. For more on Hafiz, see Michael Glünz and Johann Bürgel, eds., *Intoxication, Earthly and Heavenly: Seven Studies on the Poet Hafiz of Shiraz* (Bern: Peter Lang, 1991); Leonard Lewisohn, *Hafiz and the Religion of Love in Classical Persian Poetry* (London: I. B. Tauris, 2014); Annemarie Schimmel, "Hafiz and His Contemporaries," in *The Cambridge History of Iran*, ed. Peter Jackson and Lawrence Lockhart (Cambridge: Cambridge University Press, 1986), 929–47.

51. See Joseph von Hammer-Purgstall, *Der Diwan von Mohammed Schemsed-din Hafis* (Stuttgart: J. G. Cotta, 1812–13). See also Hannes Galter and Siegfried Haas, eds., *Joseph von Hammer-Purgstall: Grenzgänger zwischen Orient und Okzident* (Graz, Austria: Leykam 2008); Baher Elgohary, *Joseph Freiherr von Hammer-Purgstall (1774–1856): ein Dichter und Vermittler orientalischer Literatur* (Stuttgart: Akademischer Verlag Heinz, 1979); Paula Fichtner, *Terror and Toleration: The Habsburg Empire Confronts Islam, 1526–1840* (London: Reaktion, 2008); Ingeborg Solbrig, *Hammer-Purgstall und Goethe: "dem Zaubermeister das Werkzeug"* (Bern: Herbert Lang, 1973).

52. Siegfried Unseld, *Goethe and his Publishers*, trans. Kenneth Northcott (Chicago: University of Chicago Press, 1996), 220. Because Goethe's *Der west-östliche Divan*, first published by Cotta in Stuttgart (1819), is such an important and beautiful work of literature, there is a massive scholarly bibliography on the subject; I will cite only a few: Katharina Mommsen, *"Orient und Okzident sind nicht mehr zu trennen": Goethe und die Weltkulturen* (Göttingen, Ger.: Wallstein, 2012), 45–242 in particular; Marina Warner, "Oriental Masquerade: Goethe's West-Eastern Divan," chap. 15 in *Stranger Magic: Charmed States and the Arabian Nights* (Cambridge, MA: Harvard University Press, 2012); Edgar Lohner, ed., *Studien zum West-östlichen Divan Goethes* (Darmstadt, Ger.: Wissenschaftliche Buchgesellschaft, 1971); and Shafiq Shamel, *Goethe and Hafiz: Poetry and History in the West-östlicher Divan* (Oxford: Peter Lang, 2013).

53. For more on Marianne von Willemer, see Carmen Kahn-Wallerstein, *Marianne von Willemer: Goethes Suleika* (Frankfurt: Insel, 1984); Dagmar von Gersdorff, *Marianne*

von Willemer und Goethe: Geschichte einer Liebe (Frankfurt: Insel, 2003); Hans-Joachim Weitz, *Marianne und Johann Jakob Willemer: Briefwechsel mit Goethe; Dokumente, Lebens-Chronik, Erläuterungen* (Frankfurt: Insel, 1965); Jürgen Behrens, Petra Maisak, and Christoph Perels, eds., *Leben und Rollenspiel Marianne von Willemer, geb. Jung 1784–1860: Ausstellung Freies Deutsches Hochstift—Frankfurter-Museum* (Frankfurt: Freies Deutsches Hochstift—Frankfurter Goethe Museum, 1984); *"Denn das Leben ist die Liebe . . .": Marianne von Willemer und Goethe im Spiegel des West-östlichen Divans* (Frankfurt: Freies Deutsches Hochstift—Frankfurter Goethe-Museum, 2014); Markus Wallenborn, *Frauen. Dichten. Goethe: Die productive Goethe-Rezeption bei Charlotte von Stein, Mariann von Willemer und Bettina von Arnim* (Tübingen, Ger.: Niemeyer, 2006); and Hans-Joachim Weitz, ed., *Sollst mir ewig Suleika heissen: Goethes Briefwechsel mit Marianne und Johann Jakob Willemer* (Frankfurt: Insel, 1995).

54. See Dorothee Metlitzki, "On the Meaning of 'Hatem' in Goethe's *West-Östlicher Divan*," *Journal of the American Oriental Society* 117, no. 1 (January–March 1997), 148–49.

55. Dated March 3, 1831, the poem enclosed with the package of Goethe's letters is very moving: "Vor die Augen meiner Lieben, / Zu den Fingern, die's geschrieben—/Einst mit heissestem Verlangen / So erwartet, wie empfangen— / Zu der Brust, der sie entquollen, / Diese Blätter wandern ["wandern"] sollen; / Immer liebevoll bereit, / *Zeugen allerschönster Zeit*" (Bettina von Brentano, *Goethe und Marianne von Willemer: Die Geschichte einer Liebe* [Kassel, Ger.: Harriet Schleber, 1945], 85).

56. One thinks irresistibly of Heine's (very different) Lorelei poem, beginning "Ich weiß nicht, was soll es bedeuten."

57. Goethe altered Marianne von Willemer's original in small but significant ways: for example, where she wrote "Ostwind" in line 2 ("Bringt der Ostwind frohe Kunde"), Goethe substitutes "Ost mir." Marianne's beginning is one of joyous anticipation of an imminent reunion, whereas Goethe's alteration tilts the balance toward something more personal, with a tinge of uncertainty. And Marianne's fourth stanza reads "Und mich soll sein leises Flüstern / Von dem Freunde lieblich grüßen; / Eh' noch diese Hügel düstern, / Sitz' ich still zu seinen Füßen" ("Before these hills grow dark, I will sit quietly at his feet"). She always stoutly maintained the superiority of her version over Goethe's, with its more conventional "thousand kisses," the number "thousand" being his preferred symbol for things that are infinite and uncountable. *Her* line was a statement of fact: she *did*, poetically speaking, "sit at his feet" and greet him lovingly.

58. Davis, *Faces of Love*, 126 and 22.

59. Davis, *Faces of Love*, 54 and 31.

60. Davis, *Faces of Love*, 14.

61. "Though longing for you scatters on the wind / All my life's work, / Still, by the dust on your dear feet, I have kept faith with you" (Davis, *Faces of Love*, 26); "My cypress-slender love, by the dust on which you tread, / Don't hesitate to visit my dust when I am dead" (108); "My body's dust is as a veil spread out to hide / My soul—happy that moment when it's drawn aside!" (124); and "Sit by my dust with wine and music: from my imprisonment / Beneath the ground, within my grave, Dancing, drawn by your scent, I will arise" (120).

62. Davis, *Faces of Love*, 76–77 (beyts 1–2, 7, and 9).

63. Engelbert Kaempfer, *Amoenitatum exoticarum politico-physico-medicarum fasciculi v* (Lemgo: H. W. Meyer, 1712), and Walther Hinz, ed., *Am Hofe des persischen Großkönigs (1684–1685)* (Thienemann: Tübingen, 1977).

64. Ralph Locke, "Cutthroats and Casbah Dancers, Muezzins and Timeless Sands: Musical Images of the Middle East," *19th-Century Music* 22, no. 1 (Summer 1998): 20–53.

65. Waidelich, Hilmar-Voit, and Mayer, *Franz Schubert*, 1: 248.

66. Theodor Creizenach, *Briefwechsel zwischen Goethe und Marianne von Willemer (Suleika); herausgeben mit Lebensnachrichten und Erläuterungen von Theodor Creizenach* (Stuttgart: J. G. Cotta, 1878), 325.

67. Gustav Parthey, *Jugenderinnerungen: Handschrift für Freunde* (Berlin: Schade, 1871), 2: 325, has a long passage devoted to Anna Milder on 83–87. See, in particular, "In Mozarts Figaro sang die Milder die Susanne, zwar nicht mit der Leichtigkeit einer französischen Soubrette, aber mit jenem bezaubernden Schmelz der Stimme, der sogar den durch und durch frivolen Inhalt des Stückes adelte. In der Erkennungsscene des zweiten Aktes [sic!—Act III] zwischen Bartolo, Marzelline und Figaro waren ihr verwunderten Ausrufe: Seine Mutter! Sein Vater! Von so hinreißender Gewalt, daß sie niemals verfehlten, einen lauten Beifall hervorzurufen. Der alte Zelter sagte in seiner derben Art: dem Weibsbilde kömmt der Ton armsdick zur Kehle heraus!"

68. Lili Parthey, *Tagebücher aus der Berliner Biedermeierzeit*, ed. Bernhard Lepsius (Berlin: Gebrüder Paetel, 1926), 269. How one would have liked to be at this soirée for some sixty people at Milder's house, with Carl Friedrich Zelter, Caroline Seidler, the Reichardts, Rahel von Varnhagen, the beautiful Friederike Robert (Heine was captivated), the Mendelssohns, and more! See also David L. Montgomery's marvelous introduction to this important source in "From Biedermeier Berlin: The Parthey Diaries; Excerpts in Translation, with Commentary and Annotation," *Musical Quarterly* 74, no. 2 (1990): 197–216.

69. Parthey, *Tagebücher*, 275. At an earlier rehearsal of Klein's *Dido*, on January 29, Lily was deeply moved by Milder's performance of the final scene. "And how she sang it! This is a unique woman and voice" (Parthey, *Tagebücher*, 265). Similar notices are a leitmotif of the diaries, as when she heard a performance of Spontini's *Olympe/Olympia* on January 14, 1822: "Milder had wonderful numbers—and how marvelously she sings!" (207) and her praise for Milder in *La Vestale* ("superb," 112).

70. Parthey, *Tagebücher*, 277.

Bibliography

Behrens, Jürgen, Petra Maisak, and Christoph Perels, eds. *Leben und Rollenspiel Marianne von Willemer, geb. Jung 1784–1860*. Ausstellung Freies Deutsches Hochstift—Frankfurter-Museum. Frankfurt: Freies Deutsches Hochstift—Frankfurter Goethe-Museum, 1984.

Biba, Otto, ed. *Eben komme ich von Haydn: Georg August Griesingers Korrespondenz mit Joseph Haydns Verleger Breitkopf und Härtel, 1799–1819*. Zurich: Atlantis Musikbuch, 1987.

Blum, Carl. "Der Goldschmiedsgesell." *Gesänge der Heiterkeit und Laune*. Mainz, Ger.: Schott, 1830s?

———. "Gruss an die Schweiz: Für eine Singstimme mit Begleitung des Pianoforte oder der Guitarre." Munich: Joseph Aibl, [183–?].

———. "Gruss an die Schweiz, grosse Scene und Lied, furs Orchester componirt." Berlin: E. H. G. Christiani, [1829?].

Bosold, Birgit. *Friederike Liman: Briefwechsel mit Rahel Levin Varnhagen and Karl Gustav von Brinckmann sowie Aufzeichnungen von Rahel Levin Varnhagen und Karl August Varnhagen.* PhD diss., University of Hamburg, 1996.

Brentano, Bettina von. *Goethe und Marianne von Willemer: Die Geschichte einer Liebe.* Kassel, Ger.: Harriet Schleber, 1945.

Brown, Clive. *Louis Spohr: A Critical Biography.* Cambridge: Cambridge University Press, 1984.

Bürde, Jeannette. "Der Hirt auf dem Felsen." In *Vier Lieder von Wilhelm Müller,* op. 4. Berlin: Trautwein, 1829.

Charton, Anke. "Anna Milder-Hauptmann und die 'deutsche' Opernschauspielkunst." In *Akteure und ihre Praktiken im Diskurs: Aufsätze,* edited by Corinna Kirschstein and Sebastian Hauck, 228–47. Leipzig: Leipziger Universitätsverlag, 2012.

Davis, Dick. *Faces of Love: Hafez and the Poets of Shiraz.* Washington, DC: Mage, 2012.

Deutsch, Otto Erich. *Schubert: Die Dokumente seines Lebens.* Kassel, Ger.: Bärenreiter, 1964.

Deutsch, Otto Erich, Werner Aderhold, Walther Dürr, and Arnold Feil, eds. *Franz Schubert: Verzeichnis seiner Werke in chronologischer Folge.* Munich: Deutscher Taschenbuch, 1983.

Dietmar, Jürgen Ponert. "Ein Stück Musikgeschichte auf Berliner Porzellan." *Keramos* 73, no. 6 (1976): 29–36.

Dürr, Walther. "Schubert's Songs and Their Poetry: Reflections on Poetic Aspects of Song Composition." In *Schubert Studies: Problems of Style and Chronology,* edited by Eva Badura-Skoda and Peter Branscombe, 1–24. Cambridge: Cambridge University Press, 1982.

Elgohary, Baher. *Joseph Freiherr von Hammer-Purgstall (1774–1856): Ein Dichter und Vermittler orientalischer Literatur.* Stuttgart: Heinz, 1979.

Fichtner, Paula. *Terror and Toleration: The Habsburg Empire Confronts Islam, 1526–1840.* London: Reaktion, 2008.

Galter, Hannes, and Siegfried Haas, eds., *Joseph von Hammer-Purgstall: Grenzgänger zwischen Orient und Okzident.* Graz, Austria: Leykam, 2008.

Gersdorff, Dagmar von. *Marianne von Willemer und Goethe: Geschichte einer Liebe.* Frankfurt: Insel, 2003.

Giordano, Gloria. "Il Galop, un 'frenetico tumult.'" *Chorégraphie* 1, no. 1 (1993): 89–94.

Glünz, Michael, and Johann Bürgel, eds., *Intoxication, Earthly and Heavenly: Seven Studies on the Poet Hafiz of Shiraz.* Bern: Peter Lang, 1991.

Hammer-Purgstall, Joseph von. *Der Diwan von Mohammed Schemsed-din Hafis.* Stuttgart: J. G. Cotta, 1812–1813.

Himmel, Friedrich Heinrich. *Glaube, Hoffnung, Liebe, von C. W. Hufeland, für 4 gemischte Stimmen,* op. 29. Leipzig: A. Kühner, by 1810.

Hinz, Walther, ed. *Am Hofe des persischen Großkönigs (1684–1685).* Erdmann: Tübingen, Ger.: 1977.

Johnson, Graham. *Franz Schubert: The Complete Songs.* 3 vols. New Haven, CT: Yale University Press, 2014.

Johnson, James H. *Listening in Paris: A Cultural History.* Berkeley: University of California Press, 1996.

Kaempfer, Engelbert. *Amoenitatum exoticarum politico-physico-medicarum fasciculi v.* Lemgo, Ger.: H. W. Meyer, 1712.

Kahn-Wallerstein, Carmen. *Marianne von Willemer: Goethes Suleika.* Frankfurt: Insel, 1984.

Kalbeck, Max. *Johannes Brahms*. Vol. 3, *1874–1885*. Tutzing, Ger.: Hans Schneider, 1976.
Kopitz, Klaus, and Rainer Cadenbach, eds. *Beethoven aus der Sicht seiner Zeitgenossen*. 2 vols. Munich: Henle, 2009.
Kürschner, Joseph. "Milder, Pauline Anna," *Allgemeine deutsche Biographie*. Vol. 21. Leipzig: Duncker und Humblot, 1885.
Ledebur, Carl von. *Tonkünstler-Lexicon Berlin's von den ältesten Zeiten bis auf die Gegenwart*. Berlin: Rauh, 1861.
Leitner, Johann Gottfried, Ritter von. *Gedichte*. Vienna: J. P. Sollinger, 1825.
Lewisohn, Leonard. *Hafiz and the Religion of Love in Classical Persian Poetry*. London: I. B. Tauris, 2014.
Locke, Ralph. "Cutthroats and Casbah Dancers, Muezzins and Timeless Sands: Musical Images of the Middle East." *19th-Century Music* 22, no. 1 (Summer 1998): 20–53.
Lohner, Edgar, ed. *Studien zum West-östlichen Divan Goethes*. Darmstadt, Ger.: Wissenschaftliche Buchgesellschaft, 1971.
Mayer, Andreas. "'Gluck'sches Gestöhn' und 'welsches Larifari': Anna Milder, Franz Schubert und der deutsch-italienische Opernkreig." *Archiv für Musikwissenschaft* 52, no. 3 (1995): 171–204.
Metlitzki, Dorothee. "On the Meaning of 'Hatem' in Goethe's *West-östlicher Divan*." *Journal of the American Oriental Society* 117, no. 1 (January–March 1997): 148–51.
Mommsen, Katharina. *"Orient und Okzident sind nicht mehr zu trennen": Goethe und die Weltkulturen*. Göttingen, Ger.: Wallstein, 2012.
Montgomery, David L. "From Biedermeier Berlin: The Parthey Diaries: Excerpts in Translation, with Commentary and Annotation." *Musical Quarterly* 74, no. 2 (1990): 197–216.
Mozart, Wolfgang Amadeus. *Neue Ausgabe sämtlicher Werke, Series II/7: Arias, Scenes, Vocal Ensembles, and Choirs with Orchestra*, vol. 3. Edited by Stefan Kunze. Kassel, Ger.: Bärenreiter, 1971.
Österreichisches biographisches Lexikon und biographische Dokumentation. Vienna: Verlag der Österreichischen Akademie der Wissenschaften, 2003–15.
Parthey, Gustav. *Jugenderinnerungen: Handschrift für Freunde*. Berlin: Schade, 1871.
Parthey, Lili. *Tagebücher aus der Berliner Biedermeierzeit*. Edited by Bernhard Lepsius. Berlin: Gebrüder Paetel, 1926.
Pohl, August. "Beethovens erste Leonore: Zum 150. Geburtstag Anna Milder-Hauptmanns." *Zeitschrift für Musik* 102 (1935): 1232–34.
Schimmel, Annemarie. "Hafiz and His Contemporaries." In *The Cambridge History of Iran*, edited by Peter Jackson and Lawrence Lockhart, 929–47. Cambridge: Cambridge University Press, 1986.
Shamel, Shafiq. *Goethe and Hafiz: Poetry and History in the "West-östlicher Divan."* Oxford, UK: Peter Lang, 2013.
Solbrig, Ingeborg. *Hammer-Purgstall und Goethe: "Dem Zaubermeister das Werkzeug."* Bern: Herbert Lang, 1973.
Süßmayr, Franz Xaver. *Arie aus der Oper "Der Spiegel von Arcadien."* Berlin: Moritz Westphal, [1838?].
———. *Der Spiegel von Arkadien*. Vienna, 1794; repr., Madison, WI: A-R, 2014.
Unseld, Siegfried. *Goethe and His Publishers*. Translated by Kenneth Northcott. Chicago: University of Chicago Press, 1996.

Wachtel, Emil, and Friedrich Fischl, eds. *Aus Goethes Marienbadertagen*. Mariánské Lázně, Czech Rep.: J. J. Weber, 1932.
Waidelich, Till Gerrit. "Anna Milder-Hauptmann (1785–1838); Wilhelmine Schröder-Devrient (1804–1860): 'Wenn das Orchester [. . .] tobt, und die Sängerin sich dazu wie eine Furie geberdet.' *Cordelia* (1823), Conradin Kreutzers Oper über 'eine wahre Begebenheit im Jahre 1814' für zwei Primadonnen." In *Vom Salon zur Barrikade: Frauen der Heinezeit*, edited by Irina Hundt, 111–28. Stuttgart: Metzler, 2002.
Waidelich, Till Gerrit, Renate Hilmar-Voit, and Andreas Mayer. *Franz Schubert: Dokumente 1817–1830*. 2 vols. Tutzing, Ger.: Hans Schneider, 1993.
Wallenborn, Markus. *Frauen. Dichten. Goethe: Die productive Goethe-Rezeption bei Charlotte von Stein, Mariann von Willemer und Bettina von Arnim*. Tübingen, Ger.: Niemeyer, 2006.
Warner, Marina. "Oriental Masquerade: Goethe's West-Eastern Divan." In *Stranger Magic: Charmed States and the Arabian Nights*, chap. 15, 309–24. Cambridge, MA: Harvard University Press, 2012.
Weber, William. "Did People Listen in the Eighteenth Century?" *Early Music* 25, no. 4 (November 1997): 678–91.
———. *The Great Transformation of Musical Taste: Concert Programming from Haydn to Brahms*. Cambridge: Cambridge University Press, 2008.
Weitz, Hans-Joachim, ed. *Marianne und Johann Jakob Willemer: Briefwechsel mit Goethe; Dokumente, Lebens-Chronik, Erläuterungen*. Frankfurt: Insel, 1965.
———, ed. *Sollst mir ewig Suleika heissen: Goethes Briefwechsel mit Marianne und Johann Jakob Willemer*. Frankfurt: Insel, 1995.
Zingarelli, Nicola, and Giuseppe Foppa. *Giulietta e Romeo: Tragedia per musica, da rappresentarsi negl' imperiali regi Teatri di Corte*. Vienna: Gio. Batta Wallishausser, 1806.

SUSAN YOUENS is J. W. Van Gorkom Professor Emerita of Music at the University of Notre Dame. She is author of *Schubert, Müller, and "Die schöne Müllerin"*; *Hugo Wolf and His Mörike Songs*; *Schubert's Late Lieder: Beyond the Song-Cycles*; and *Heinrich Heine and the Lied*.

2 Song in Concert as Observed by the Schumanns

Toward the Personalization of the Public Stage

Benjamin Binder

IN A REVIEW of some classic Lieder recitals on film screened at Lincoln Center in 2014, the *New York Times* critic Zachary Woolfe drew attention to the artifice that underlies what often seems to many concert audiences to be the revelation of a singer's authentic, real-life personality on stage:

> [Lieder recitals] appear to dispense with illusion—no sets or costumes, just a singer and a pianist—but they are not necessarily more real for it. Seemingly transparent, they are also opaque. They don't offer a singer unadorned, as many claim, but rather demand the most subtle and difficult kind of performance: the performance of self.
> How would you act if you had to act like you?[1]

It is casually assumed that Lieder singers in concert are more or less being themselves, either because they have stepped down from the operatic stage and out of theatrical costume for the evening, or because they are not generally associated with the operatic stage to begin with. Following Woolfe, however, it would be more precise to say that they are acting like themselves.

We can refine the levels of identity at play here in terms borrowed from the performance studies scholar Philip Auslander.[2] A recital performance of Schubert's "Du bist die Ruh," D776, by Renée Fleming promises to give us a glimpse of the genuine "person," Renée Fleming, who lies beneath not only the "character" or protagonist of Schubert's song (whose dramatic specificity is already highly attenuated as in so many Lieder), but also the public "persona" "Renée Fleming"—that is, Renée Fleming *qua* opera star and concert artist, with a distinctive interpretive style and manner that cuts across all her performances.[3] The aura of sincerity, intimacy, and candor that is often felt in Lieder performance derives in no small part from the apparent possibility that the singer's person is shining through the layers of persona and character, layers that seem to be more permeable than usual because of the poetic and performing conventions of the genre. It is the potential intermingling and overlap of these three layers of identity that can make a Lieder recital so compelling as a convincing presentation of self. For Woolfe, this is what makes Lieder performance pertinent to our own age of social media, "with our lives—carefully crafted visions of our lives—ever more on public display. Simultaneously honest and untrustworthy, both a performance and not, Lieder [performance] has never been so relevant and valuable."

In the past decade or so, musicologists have begun to historicize our assumptions about the honesty and trustworthiness of the relationship between person, persona, and character in classical music performance, particularly in the realm of nineteenth-century instrumental music, where, instead of a character, performers are charged with portraying a "work." Mary Hunter has shown how the performer's task in early-nineteenth-century musical aesthetics was not simply to follow the instructions of the score, but rather to reanimate the composer's work as it was originally conceived by channeling the very soul of the composer in the depths of their own soul. In this view of performance as self-transformation, the performer's "lower self" aims to identify fully with the composer's "higher" or "better" self, as Novalis might have put it. Musicality was therefore moral, in that it betrayed the performer's inner worth and substance as a person, or perhaps a troubling lack thereof.[4] Meanwhile, Karen Leistra-Jones has described how certain performers in the middle to late nineteenth century such as Joseph Joachim and Johannes Brahms took pains deliberately to perform their musicality by consciously cultivating an on-stage persona of selfless devotion to the work. By staging their authenticity as musicians (and, consequently, as human beings), these *Werktreue* performers set themselves against figures like Franz Liszt, whose flamboyant theatricality and showmanship in concert would therefore have to indicate inauthenticity—that is, a disturbing lack of transparency between person, persona, and work. Moreover, authentic musical performance was linked to a type of music—absolute music—that was itself thought to be substantial rather than theatrical. Honest, unshowy musicians chose to play honest, unshowy music, displaying good bourgeois values of earnestness and moral rectitude.[5]

When Robert and Clara Schumann contemplated the realm of vocal music on the nineteenth-century concert stage, the type of music they linked most consistently to theatrical and inauthentic performers and performance was Italian opera, while the genre of greatest substance and authenticity was, for them, the German Lied. A performance of a Lied was at the same time a performance of a singer's personal sincerity, depth of feeling, musicality, and Germanness, all closely interrelated qualities that Robert and Clara would have summed up in two words: *Wahrheit* and *Innigkeit*. In an article from 1840, for example, Robert wrote the following about a song by Norbert Burgmüller, whose poetic text he believed to have been written by the composer himself:

> [Burgmüller's] composition came into being during a painful time, [it is] deeply melancholy, but inspiring of the most heartfelt sympathy ("zur innigsten Theilnahme anregend"), and true ("wahr"). *True*—does your little heart not tremble, composers, when you hear this word? Embed yourselves ever more cozily in your pretty song-lies, yet it will bring you no higher than to be sung by some other Judas lips, seductively enough, perhaps. But if a truthful singer ("ein wahrhaftiger Sänger") steps again among you, then flee with your affected art, or learn Truth, if it's still possible.[6]

In the following study of the Schumanns' reception of some concert singers from the 1830s, 1840s, and 1850s, I want to suggest that what Robert and Clara most wanted to experience on the concert stage was an *inniger Vortrag* of a German Lied by a *wahrhaftiger Sänger* (or *Sängerin*), a sincere and truthful performance in which person, persona, and character transparently aligned in an act of heartfelt self-disclosure. For the Schumanns, the performance of German song turned the concert stage into a proving ground for a singer's moral and musical worth, a crucible of bourgeois subjectivity in performance that sometimes continues to serve as a framework for the reception of Lieder singers today.

We can begin with the Belgian soprano Elisa Meerti, who served as *erste Sängerin* for the 1839–40 season of subscription concerts at the Leipzig Gewandhaus. In his review of the season later that spring, Robert wrote,

> The public's sympathy for [Meerti] increased visibly with each evening; she doesn't quite count as one of those glittering bravura talents who know how to conquer the public on their first appearance; one recognized her virtues only gradually, as she only unfolded them little by little in all their charm.... Only in her farewell concert did she sing a German Lied by Mendelssohn ["Frühlingslied" from op. 34], which at least in us resonated longer than all the rest [i.e., Italian and French pieces], so did it seem to come from such a sincere, warm soul ("innigem Gemüth"); for she has in her voice and her delivery something exquisitely noble and demure about her.[7]

In Robert's recollection, Meerti's moving Lied performance represented the culminating high point of her season in that it finally revealed the full measure of her tender personality;[8] two days before this performance, in fact, Robert had a social call from Meerti and wrote to Clara that he found her to be "a good, genuine girl" (*ein gutes, echtes Mädchen*).[9] Moreover, the shy, incremental manner in which Meerti unveiled her virtues as a performer created a stage persona that harmonized well with the qualities of nobility and modesty that Robert so admired in Meerti's singing.

Meerti's farewell concert took place on January 16, 1840, but despite Robert's claim to the contrary, this was not the first time that she had sung Lieder during that season, as Robert himself noted in a letter to Clara from December 1, 1839: "Now I want to tell you about Meerti, who is supposed to be a splendid young lady, by the way. She recently sang German compositions for the first time [in a concert on November 29], 'Ave Maria' by Schubert and a song by Mendelssohn ['Auf Flügeln des Gesanges'], and with the most magnificent delivery and voice, such that only now have we really heard her."[10] Once again, Robert suggests that Meerti's artistic gifts could fully emerge only when they found a suitable musical vehicle, the German Lied, that also corresponded to her laudable personal qualities. To "really hear" Meerti was to hear something deeper at the level of the authentic person, through the technical, interpretive, and attitudinal attributes of her emerging stage persona. But this deeper, truer hearing only became possible when Meerti adopted song characters that resonated with the inner essence of this "splendid young lady": a virtuous maiden's prayer to the Virgin Mary on the one hand (Schubert) and an amorous yet chivalrous ode to the imaginative power of song on the other (Mendelssohn).

When Meerti returned to Leipzig in the company of her mother for the 1841–42 concert season, Clara finally got to know her and came to share Robert's judgment of her personality. As a result, however, Clara found herself puzzling over why she was nonetheless disappointed by Meerti's performance in the subscription concert on October 28, 1841, as expressed in her entry from that night in the marriage diary she shared with Robert: "We made a return visit to the Meertis. Mother and daughter please me greatly, if only she sang better—I had built up rather great expectations of her, and found myself hardly satisfied, also she sings hardly any good stuff, and precisely that not well."[11]

The "good stuff" from that evening's program must have included excerpts from Mozart's *Idomeneo* and a Lied by Mendelssohn ("Der Blumenkranz," WoO 7), but although the review of the concert in the *Allgemeine musikalische Zeitung* maintained that Meerti had been especially compelling in her performances of Lieder that season, Clara apparently did not agree.[12] About a week later, after another personal and musical encounter with Meerti, Clara settled on the reason for her dissatisfaction—Meerti was not what she seemed to be:

> On Monday evening I sang through a few of Robert's Lieder with Meerti in order to select [some] for my concert [later in the month]. But only a German heart that can feel *deeply* ("*innig*") is suitable for German Lieder.... What others have too much of, Meerti has too little of—cleverness ("Klugheit"). She is beside herself that she was criticized in Robert's journal [for certain faults

of singing technique]! this she can't believe, since after all she's in good standing with us, is supposed to sing in my concert, etc. She would have acted more prudently not to let her irritation be noticed; an arrogance lies therein which I wouldn't have looked for inside this endearing exterior.[13]

Clara's discovery of a dissonance between Meerti's "endearing exterior" persona and the "arrogant" dimension of her true personality is linked here with the idea that the Belgian Meerti is unfit to sing German Lieder. Ironically, in confessing her vexation over the bad review, Meerti also revealed herself to be insincere and not entirely good and genuine, noble and demure, as Robert had once maintained. For Clara, Robert's deeply felt Lieder ought not to be heard coming from Judas lips like these.

Clara was rather more patient with the *zweite Sängerin* in the 1840–41 Gewandhaus season: Elise List, the younger sister of Clara's dear friend Emilie List and the daughter of the railroad magnate Friedrich List. Robert and Clara despaired over Elise's preference for Italian opera and the concomitant tendencies toward superficiality and vanity in her personality that they felt could only be exacerbated by that preference.[14] In the months leading up to Elise's public debut in October, Robert and Clara recommended that she focus on Lieder instead, although privately Clara worried that Elise "lack[ed] a deeper impulse, a heartfelt understanding (*inniges Erfassen*) of the text" to truly be compelling in that repertoire.[15] Once the season began, Elise struggled mightily with stage fright; Robert wrote that "the very material of her voice was impaired"[16] and "misted over by fear" and a lack of self-assurance in public, which dampened all the natural expressivity they claimed to hear in Elise's vocal instrument at home.[17] Clara ruminated on this in the marriage diary:

> Robert thinks the only thing Elise's singing lacks is *heart, soul* ("Herz, Gemüth"). This has often occurred to me already, for her singing still has never moved me, as for example a Lied sung by [Wilhelmine Schröder-] Devrient or Pauline [Viardot-] Garcia, but it would always appear to me that she has soul in her everyday life, [so] why couldn't that express itself in her singing? I can't understand it!—I believe that once she falls in love, then she will sing with more soul as well. That love does a lot on that score is certain, I've experienced it myself. When I began to love my Robert so very profoundly ("so recht innig"), then for the first time I felt what I played, and people said that it must have been a deeper emotion that made me play so soulfully.[18]

Clara describes her own music making here as a flow of sincere expression that moves back and forth, seamlessly and harmoniously, between her authentic personal life experience and store of emotion, her public performing persona, and the work she performs—this was the mark of the successful bourgeois performing artist. In Clara's estimation, this success eluded Elise List because when Elise stepped onto the public stage to sing, she became too self-conscious to "be herself" or even to convincingly "act like herself," ultimately confirming the Schumanns' suspicion that she may not have had enough of a feeling self to draw on in the first place. Two years later, after Elise again tried and failed to launch her career, this time in Berlin, Robert offered this final assessment: "Lucky for her that she realized that she lacks the main thing for art—a warm heart that can sacrifice everything for art. Too bad about her beautiful voice; but it seems only to come from the throat."[19]

Moving to the opposite end of the spectrum in every imaginable way, we can turn to the Schumanns' reception of one of the great singers of the age, the "demonic"[20] Wilhelmine Schröder-Devrient, whose heart seemed to come directly from her throat, as the Schumanns and other critics routinely maintained.[21] A transformative artist in the history of opera whose public appearances invariably captivated Robert and Clara in both opera and song, Schröder invested her stage performances with an unprecedented degree of dramatic verisimilitude and emotional truth in a kind of method acting *avant la lettre*,[22] drawing on a range of tumultuous life experiences that expanded well beyond the boundaries of bourgeois respectability, including three marriages, four children of whom Schröder did not maintain custody, and a sexually liberated lifestyle. Robert's report in the marriage diary on Schröder's participation in the final Gewandhaus concert of the 1840–41 season reflects an awareness of this essential yet problematic relationship between Schröder's life and her art: "The performance of the Schubert Lied that Schröder sang ['Am Meer,' from *Schwanengesang*] was my favorite. My goodness, what lies within her! As though she knew all the mysteries of the heart! A bona fide actress who in this minute offers herself as a godmother [to Clara's first child—Clara was newly pregnant], and in the next [minute] could move us to tears with her painful tones! But such an artist can never be a homemaker, a wife, a mother, and she really isn't one either."[23] Here Robert is assuaging Clara's anxieties about motherhood and its effect on her own career trajectory, but he is also suggesting that in order for an artist like Schröder to give searingly heartfelt performances of any song she chooses with "demonic" flexibility, she must therefore have a kind of "demonic" flexibility in how she conducts her real life, no matter how much it might offend bourgeois sensibilities such as theirs.[24] Offstage, Robert and Clara found Schröder to be amusing, charming, and kind but with a cutting satirical edge, extravagant tastes, and a tendency toward disaster in her personal affairs.[25] These qualities may explain why Robert dedicated *Dichterliebe* to Schröder, and why "Ich grolle nicht," the most bitterly sarcastic and melodramatic song of the cycle, became a staple of her concert appearances.[26]

In a different way, the Schumanns' perception of Schröder's personality may also explain the content of the album of songs that they compiled for Schröder shortly before she collaborated with Clara in a series of soirées in the concert hall of Dresden's Hotel de Saxe in 1848–49 (see table 2.1).[27] In these soirées,

Table 2.1. Liederalbum für Wilhelmine Schröder-Devrient, circa 1848.

Robert: "Widmung," op. 25 no. 1
Robert: "Der Nussbaum," op. 25 no. 3
Robert: "Die Lotosblume," op. 25 no. 7
Robert: "Du bist wie eine Blume," op. 25 no. 24
Robert: "Intermezzo," op. 39 no. 2
Robert: "Waldesgespräch," op. 39 no. 3
Robert: "Mondnacht," op. 39 no. 5
Robert: "Schöne Fremde," op. 39 no. 6
Robert: "Frühlingsnacht," op. 39 no. 12
Robert: "Stille Liebe," op. 35 no. 8
Robert: "Erstes Grün," op. 35 no. 4
Clara: "Liebeszauber," op. 13 no. 3
Clara: "Ich hab' in deinem Auge," op. 13 no. 5

Source: Robert and Clara Schumann, *Liederalbum für Wilhelmine Schröder-Devrient*, ed. Angelika Horstmann (Kassel: Bärenreiter: 1994).

Schröder sang three of Robert's songs from the album ("Der Nussbaum," "Die Lotosblume," and "Frühlingsnacht") on repeated occasions and an unnamed song by Clara, perhaps also from the album, on February 6.[28] With the exception of "Waldesgespräch," whose ill-fated conversation between a chivalrous knight and the witch Lorelei would have had obvious dramatic and theatrical appeal in Schröder's hands, the protagonists of all the songs from the album would have inspired Schröder to call exclusively upon her "better self," suggesting again how the Schumanns believed that the character of a song (in Auslander's sense) could elevate the person of the performer under the right conditions. The album's ardent love lyrics and tender nature scenes might have been chosen for their potential salutary effect, nurturing and drawing out the more angelic parts of Schröder's demonically complex personality. In the same vein, Clara praised Schröder's performance of all eight songs of *Frauenliebe und -leben* at a soirée in 1848, exclaiming "There is but one Devrient!,"[29] and she singled out Schröder's public performance of "Du Ring an meinem Finger" two weeks later at the Hotel de Saxe, writing that she could not imagine the song sung more beautifully[30]—a fascinating claim considering that Schröder had just gone through a bitter divorce from her second husband eight months earlier.

By the same token, the Schumanns also appreciated moments when Schröder's charismatic public persona transfigured the character of the song she was performing. At the end of the final concert of the 1840–41 season at the Gewandhaus, Schröder sang Mendelssohn's "Volkslied," op. 47 no. 4, with the composer at the piano (see example 2.1). The first three stanzas of Feuchtersleben's

Example 2.1. Felix Mendelssohn, "Volkslied," op. 47 no. 4.

poem reflect on the initial idea that "in God's plan, it is certain that one will part from what one loves most," but at the end of the final stanza, the poet offers some consolation by reminding us that "when people part from one another, they say 'Auf Wiedersehen'"—that is, they look forward to seeing each other again, perhaps in the hereafter. In her performance of the song, Schröder directed the words "Auf Wiedersehen" directly to the audience and gave a little curtsey, as if to say goodbye to her public before departing for her next engagement. The reviewer for the *Allgemeine musikalische Zeitung* was horrified by this "common stage effect" and wrote that Schröder's breaking of the fourth wall "profaned" Mendelssohn's "magnificent and characteristically true" (*wahr*) composition.[31] Robert's review, on the other hand, embraced Schröder's gesture, reporting that the audience even "joined in to sing [with her] in joyous agreement,"[32] perhaps to the accompaniment of the piano interlude in measures 23–24.[33] In contrast to the negative review in the *Allgemeine musikalische Zeitung*, Robert heard "truth" in Schröder's performance because of an especially resonant harmony between person, persona, and character, in which Schröder's genuine feelings informed her stage persona and commandeered the character of the song in her performance. For Robert, any violation of *Werktreue* in Schröder's delivery was trumped by its powerful expression of *Wahrheit*.

Clara was especially close with another giant of the operatic stage who figured prominently in the Schumanns' discussion of Lieder singing: Pauline Viardot-Garcia. Ever since Clara met Viardot in 1838, she regarded the singer as an unfailingly sincere and warmhearted friend, genuine and unaffected in everything she did and said offstage, and a consummate musician to boot, with a warm and expressive voice.[34] These personal and musical qualities led Clara to suggest in March 1840 that Robert dedicate his recently composed opus 24, *Liederkreis*, to Viardot, noting that Viardot "is a being who is capable of grasping your songs in their German spirit"[35]—this despite Viardot's Spanish ancestry and Parisian operatic career. Four months later, in a letter to Emilie List, Clara reaffirmed her personal judgment of Viardot in expressing her relief at having finally received a letter from the singer after a long and unaccountable gap in their correspondence, saying that receiving the letter "so pleased me, since I believed I had been totally forgotten by her, and *almost* succumbed to the temptation to equate her with other singers with respect to character, for I thought she had been spoiled by her triumph in the end. But her letter still shows me the old friend ('die Alte') and her beautiful open character. I must write to her soon. I will put aside the Lieder for her and send them to her *as soon as* she gets to Paris."[36] In Clara's mind, Viardot's increasing renown after the triumph of her dazzling operatic debuts in London and Paris the previous year had the potential to corrupt her "beautiful open character" (or rather, her "person," in Auslander's sense) with the pretention and inflated ego of the prima donna, but this recent letter reassured Clara that Viardot's virtue and thoughtfulness were still intact, leading her to return once again to the idea that Viardot ought to sing Robert's newly published Lieder, most likely the *Liederkreis*, op. 24. By January 1841, Clara was still waiting for this performance to happen, writing in the marriage diaries that "*Pauline Garcia[-Viardot] would be the only one, I believe, who would understand Robert's Lieder completely truthfully (ganz wahrhaft)*—if only I could hear one of them from her sometime!"[37]

In the meantime, Viardot did not always live up to Clara's ideal of *Wahrheit* when she sang the Lieder of other composers. In her comments about Elise List from October 1840 quoted earlier, Clara mentions Viardot along with Schröder as the two singers whose Lieder singing could move her because they possessed sufficient heart and soul at the personal level to infuse their portrayal of a song's character with genuine emotion that was directly connected to their true selves. Yet only a month earlier, Clara had articulated her disappointment in Viardot's Lieder singing in the marriage diaries at the level of Viardot's performance persona: "I heard Pauline sing Schubert's 'Gretchen [am Spinnrade],' which she performed more as though grasping for effect instead of with the inner ardor expressed so magnificently by [Goethe's] words just as much as by Schubert's music. Pauline has delighted me every time [she performs], only she left me unsatisfied precisely in this *German* Lied, which I really cannot believe from this creature who is musical through and through, who usually understands everything in its total truth (*in seiner ganzen Wahrheit*) with the greatest rapidity!"[38]

Clara's assessment of Viardot's singing throughout the 1840s continued to reflect a tension between Viardot's unimpeachable excellence as a person and musician and her tendency to "grasp for effect" in her performances.[39] For Clara, this defect was an unfortunate consequence of Viardot's professional engagement with the operas of Bellini, Meyerbeer, Halévy, and the like; in terms of content and style, the demands of that repertoire infected Viardot's performance persona with a manipulative theatricality that made it difficult for her to connect her true personality to the song characters she portrayed. Even if Viardot the person possessed the "inner ardor" demanded by Goethe and Schubert's Gretchen, Clara felt that Viardot the performer could not channel it freely and sincerely, at least not on this occasion. In Clara's view, the theatrical approach might work for Viardot's French and Italian operatic roles, but in the Lied, it was a fatal flaw.

It was Jenny Lind, the bourgeois opera star *par excellence*, who refused to succumb to this supposed flaw and, in so doing, proved to be the most perfect realization of the Schumanns' long-cherished ideals for the singing of Lieder in concert. Lind became a sensation because her relatable public persona so thoroughly matched what many observers reported to be her real-life personality. She was gracious and modest, natural and unaffected in her conduct and dress onstage and off, a benefactor to the poor, and a sterling model of female propriety, totally circumventing the theater stereotypes of unapproachable diva or working-class profligate. Moreover, Lind would take on only operatic characters and songs that fit this persona, or else she reinterpreted them after her own image; for example, Sonia Gesse-Harm describes how, in Lind's hands, the title role of Bellini's *Norma* became "a compassionate, self-sacrificing wife and a loving mother" instead of the "merciless priestess" audiences normally encountered.[40]

It is not surprising, then, that the Schumanns came down with an intense and enduring bout of Jenny Lind fever after meeting and collaborating with her for concerts in Leipzig and Vienna in 1846–47. Clara teamed up with Lind to rehearse and perform Lieder by her husband and Felix Mendelssohn in Hamburg in March 1850, and the experience was a revelation. One quote from Clara's diary will have to stand for many similar expressions of simultaneous admiration for Lind's unassuming thoughtfulness as a person and penetrating insight as a Lied performer:

> In the afternoon Lind visited us for a little Lieder rehearsal that turned into something more, for she sang a whole lot of Robert's songs, and *how* she sang them, with what truth ("Wahrheit") with what heartfelt sincerity ("Herzinnigkeit") and simplicity, how she sang *at sight* "Marienwürmchen" and "Frühlingsglaube" from the album, having not known it before—this will remain unforgettable; what a magnificent, divinely gifted creature she is, what a pure, genuinely artistic soul, how everything she says is refreshing, how she always comes up with the right thing [and] expresses it with a few words, in short: I have probably never loved and honored a woman more than her. These Lieder will resound forever in my heart, and were it not an injustice, I would like to say that I never want to hear them sung by anyone any longer except her.[41]

Clara's intemperate "injustice" of ruling out any other singer for these songs reveals the perfect fit she perceived between Lind's reflective and considerate personality (lacking in Schröder), the intuitive and spontaneous musicianship and interpretive directness of her performance persona (corrupted in Viardot), and the sweet, gentle, childlike characters of the two cited songs, both of which most likely came from Robert's recent *Liederalbum für die Jugend*, op. 79, published just four months earlier in November 1849.[42] In the Hamburg concerts, Lind sang a variety of Robert's songs in the same vein, including "Der Nussbaum," "O Sonnenschein," "Stille Liebe," and "Der Himmel hat eine Thräne geweint."[43] In certain private circumstances, Lind could sometimes be prone to fickle, diva-like antics,[44] but the Schumanns' own encounters with Lind bear no witness to such behavior. For them, Lind was in no way "acting like" herself but always simply "being herself," *wahr* and *innig* to the core, whenever she was on stage, in rehearsal, or in the drawing room.

The Schumanns' ideology of public Lieder performances proved to have considerable staying power. It has its roots in the literary, musical, and performative discourses and practices of Goethe and his contemporaries relating to song that Jennifer Ronyak explores extensively in her recent book on the subject.[45] It lingers today in the unexamined assumptions about authenticity, sincerity, and intimate revelation in Lieder singing that Woolfe felt the need to lay bare in his 2014 review quoted earlier. Yet if for Woolfe the Lied's relative lack of character specificity (in comparison with opera) engenders a provocative mélange of transparent personal expression and carefully crafted dissimulation that can help us explore the ways we perform ourselves to each other in an image-conscious, technologically mediated world, for the Schumanns this tension was unbearable. They welcomed Lieder in concert, but because song had to share a large public stage with opera arias and extracts, they perceived a risk that the theatrical means necessary for dramatic impersonation (which they sometimes viewed as "grasping for effect") would somehow corrupt the presentation and appreciation of song, even if in actual practice many singers drew on the same techniques to bring truth to their performances in both genres, including the private performance of song. In order to conceive of the stage as a safe space for Lieder, the Schumanns had to find a way to distinguish truth (that is, their idea of truth) from fakery and avoid being duped by a disingenuous song performance, and they found their solution in the example of Jenny Lind, the supreme bourgeois performing artist. In Lind's carefully programmed Lieder performances, person, persona, and character seemed to fuse in a magical synthesis that proved to be the apotheosis of the Schumanns' vision for the personalization of the public stage through song.

Notes

1. Zachary Woolfe, "The Singer's Artifice, Flickering on Film: Lincoln Center Screens Bygone Lieder Performances," *New York Times*, February 7, 2014, http://nyti.ms/1eFWKll.

2. Philip Auslander, "Musical Personae," *Drama Review* 50, no. 1 (Spring 2006): 100–119, esp. 101–2.

3. Auslander's use of the word *persona* is therefore not the same as that of Cone in *Composer's Voice*. Cone's concept of persona, long familiar to students and scholars of the Lied, is more or less equivalent to Auslander's *character*.

4. Mary Hunter, "'To Play as if from the Soul of the Composer': The Idea of the Performer in Early Romantic Aesthetics," *Journal of the American Musicological Society* 58, no. 2 (Summer 2005): 357–98.

5. Karen Leistra-Jones, "Staging Authenticity: Joachim, Brahms, and the Politics of *Werktreue* Performance," *Journal of the American Musicological Society* 66, no. 2 (Summer 2013): 397–436.

6. Robert Schumann, "Drei gute Liederhefte," *Neue Zeitschrift für Musik* 13, no. 30 (November 29, 1836): 118. "Die Composition ist in schmerzlicher Zeit entstanden, tiefmelancholisch, aber zur innigsten Theilnahme anregend, und wahr. *Wahr*—zittert euch nicht euer kleines Herz, Componisten, wenn ihr dieses Wort hört? Bettet euch immer weicher in eure schönen Gesangslügen, ihr bringt's doch nicht höher, als von einigen andern Judaslippen gesungen zu werden, vielleicht verführerisch genug. Aber, tritt dann wieder einmal ein wahrhaftiger Sänger unter euch, so flüchtet mit eurer erheuchelten Kunst, oder lernt Wahrheit, wenn es noch möglich ist." All translations in this chapter are my own.

7. Robert Schumann, "Musikleben in Leipzig, während des Winters 1839/40 (Fortsetzung)," *Neue Zeitschrift für Musik* 12, no. 38 (May 8, 1840), 151: "Die Theilnahme des Publicums für die erstgenannte [i.e., Meerti] steigerte sich mit jedem Abende zusehends; sie gehört eben nicht zu jenen glänzenden Bravourtalenten, die sich schon bei'm ersten Auftreten ihr Publicum zu erobern wissen; ihre Vorzüge erkannte man erst allmählig, wie sie sie auch nach und nach erst in all' ihrer Liebenswürdigkeit entfaltete. . . . Erst in ihrem Abschiedsconcert sang sie ein deutsches Lied von Mendelssohn, was in uns wenigstens länger fortklingt als all' das andere, aus auch so innigem Gemüth schien es zu kommen; wie sie denn in Stimme und Vortrag etwas vorzüglich Edles und Sittsames an sich hat."

8. The review of this concert in the *Allgemeine musikalische Zeitung* echoed Robert's sentiments in strongly emphasizing the degree to which Meerti's personal qualities of "unpretentiousness and modesty" (*Anspruchlosigkeit und Bescheidenheit*) played the pivotal role in engendering the public's "heartfelt sympathy" (*innige Theilnahme*) with her and were just as relevant as Meerti's musical talent to the public's warm reception of her. See *Allgemeine musikalische Zeitung* 42, no. 4 (January 22, 1840): 76.

9. Eva Weissweiler and Susanna Ludwig, eds., *Robert and Clara Schumann, Briefwechsel: Kritische Gesamtausgabe* (Frankfurt: Stroemfeld/Roter Stern, 2001), 3: 871.

10. Weissweiler and Ludwig, *Schumann, Briefwechsel*, 2: 809. "Da will ich Dir gleich von der Meerti erzählen, die übrigens ein vortreffliches Mädchen sein soll. Sie sang neulich zum erstenmal deutsche Compositionen von Schubert das Ave Maria, und v. Mendelssohn ein Lied, und mit herrlichstem Vortrag und Stimme, daß wir sie erst jetzt recht gehört haben." "Auf Flügeln des Gesanges" is specifically cited as the Mendelssohn selection in the review of Meerti's concert in the *Allgemeine musikalische Zeitung*, 41, no. 49 (December 4, 1839): 978.

11. See Gerd Nauhaus, ed., *Robert Schumann: Tagebücher* (Leipzig: Deutscher Verlag für Musik, 1987), 2: 189–90. Quotations from the marriage diaries by Clara Schumann will be indicated as such. Clara: "Der *Meerti* machten wir einen Gegenbesuch. Mutter und Tochter gefallen mir sehr, sänge sie nur besser—ich machte mir ziemlich große Erwartungen von ihr, und fand mich wenig befriedigt, auch singt sie so wenig Gutes, und, gerade Das nicht gut."

12. See *Allgemeine musikalische Zeitung* 43, no. 44, November 3, 1841, 909.

13. Nauhaus, *Schumann Tagebücher*, 2: 191 (Clara, November 7, 1841): "Montag Abend sang ich mit der *Meerti* einige Lieder vom Robert durch, um für mein Concert auszusuchen. Doch zu deutschen Liedern gehört nur ein deutsches Herz, das *innig* fühlen kann. . . . Was Andere zu viel besitzen, hat die *Meerti* zu wenig—Klugheit. Sie ist außer sich, daß sie in Roberts Zeitung getadelt wird! das kann sie nicht begreifen, da sie doch gut mit uns steht, in meinem Concert singen soll ect: Sie thäte gescheidter sich nichts von Aerger merken zu lassen; es liegt darin eine Arroganz, die ich in diesem lieben Äußeren nicht gesucht hätte."

14. See, for example, Clara's letter to Emilie List, June 24, 1841, in Eugen Wendler, *"Das Band der ewigen Liebe": Clara Schumanns Briefwechsel mit Emilie und Elise List* (Stuttgart: J. B. Metzler, 1996), 105.

15. Nauhaus, *Schumann Tagebücher*, 2: 105 (Clara, September 24, 1840): "Von Roberts Liedern sang [Elise] Einige, doch scheint mir, zu deutschen Liedern fehlt ihr eine tiefere Regung, ein inniges Erfassen des Textes, ich kann mich darüber gar nicht so aussprechen, es ist Etwas, das ich nicht zu benennen weiß."

16. Nauhaus, *Schumann Tagebücher*, 2: 112 (Robert, October 11–18, 1840): "[Elisens] Angst war freilich groß und that selbst dem Material der Stimme Eintrag."

17. Robert Schumann, "Zweites Abonnementconcert, den 11 October." *Neue Zeitschrift für Musik* 13, no. 36 (October 31, 1840): 144. "An der Schönheit der Stimme, wie sie auch durch die Aengstlichkeit umflort schien, konnte Niemand zweifeln, der nur einige Tacte gehört, eben so wenig über die gute Schule, in der sie gebildet ist, so daß man deutlich sah, die Sängerin wollte nichts, als was sie sicher konnte. Aber freilich, was man unter vier Augen auf das trefflichste kann, kann man unter tausenden noch nicht zur Hälfte so gut, und geht dies bedeutenden Künstlern und Männern so, um wie viel mehr einer Novizin, einem achtzehnjährigen Mädchen."

18. Nauhaus, *Schumann Tagebücher*, 2: 117 (Clara, October 24, 1840): "Robert meint, das Einzige was Elisens Gesange fehlte, sey *Herz, Gemüth*. Dies ist's was mir oft schon einfiel, denn niemals noch rührte mich ihr Gesang, wie z.B. ein Lied von der *Devrient* oder *Pauline Garcia* gesungen, aber immer wollte es mir doch scheinen, als habe sie im gewöhnlichen Leben Gemüth, warum sollte sich das nicht auch im Gesang äußern können? ich begreife es nicht!—Ich glaube, wenn sie einmal lieben wird, dann wird sie auch mit mehr Seele singen. Daß die Liebe dabei viel thut, ist gewiß, das hab ich an mir erfahren. Als ich so recht innig meinen Robert zu lieben anfing, da fühlte ich erst was ich spielte, und die Leute sagten, eine tiefere Regung müsse es seyn, die mich so seelenvoll spielen mache."

19. Nauhaus, *Schumann Tagebücher*, 2: 255 (Robert, February 17, 1843): "Zu ihrem Glück, daß sie es eingesehen hatte, daß ihr zur Kunst die Hauptsache fehle,—ein warmes Herz, daß alles für die Kunst aufopfern kann. Schade um die schöne Stimme; aber sie scheint nur aus der Kehle zu kommen."

20. Robert used this adjective to describe Schröder, Paganini, Napoleon, and Adolph Henselt in a letter to Clara of January 2, 1838. See Weissweiler and Ludwig, *Schumann, Briefwechsel*, 1: 65.

21. See, for example, the reviews of Schröder's performances of Leonore in Beethoven's *Fidelio* from the 1830s cited in Stephen Meyer, "*Das wilde Herz*: Interpreting Wilhelmine Schröder-Devrient," *The Opera Quarterly* 14, no. 2 (Winter 1997/98), 26. For similar examples from the Schumanns' writings, see Robert Schumann, "Concerte: Zwanzigstes Abonnementconcert, den 18ten März," *Neue Zeitschrift für Musik* 14, no. 29 (April 9, 1841): 118, and Berthold Litzmann, *Clara Schumann: Ein Künstlerleben durch Tagebüchern und Briefen*, 3rd ed. (Leipzig: Breitkopf und Härtel, 1907), 2: 119.

22. Thomas Grey makes the connection to method acting in discussing Wagner's admiration for Schröder in the introduction to his translation of excerpts from writings by Claire von Glümer and Henry Chorley on Schröder's career. See Claire von Glümer and Henry Chorley, "Wilhelmine Schröder-Devrient and Wagner's Dresden," in *Richard Wagner and His World*, trans. and ed. Thomas Grey (Princeton, NJ: Princeton University Press, 2009), 204.

23. Nauhaus, *Schumann Tagebücher*, 2: 155 (Robert, March 14–21, 1841): "Der Vortrag des Liedes v. Schubert, das die Schr. sang, war mir das Liebste. Was ruht doch in ihr! Als wüßte sie alle Geheimniße des Herzens! Eine echte Schauspielerin die in dieser Minute sich zu Gevatter bittet, und uns in der andern zu Thränen rühren könnte mit ihren schmerzlichen

Tönen! Aber eine Hausfrau, ein Weib, eine Mutter kann eine solche Künstlerin nicht sein, und sie ist es wohl auch nicht."

24. According to Schröder's first biographer, Alfred von Wolzogen, Schröder herself was known to make the very same argument when confronted by public criticism of her offstage lifestyle choices (Alfred von Wolzogen, *Wilhelmine Schröder-Devrient: Ein Beitrag zur Geschichte des musikalischen Dramas* [Leipzig: F. A. Brockhaus, 1863], 91).

25. For examples, see Clara's remarks in Weissweiler and Ludwig, *Schumann, Briefwechsel*, 3: 1177 (from Clara to Robert, April 11, 1842); Litzmann, *Clara Schumann*, 119–20 (Clara's diary from January 24, 1849); and Kazuko Ozawa-Müller, "Clara Schumann und Wilhelmine Schröder-Devrient," in *Clara Schumann, 1819–1896: Katalog zur Ausstellung*, ed. Ingrid Bodsch and Gerd Nauhaus (Bonn: Stadtmuseum Bonn, 1996), 185 (letter to Ferdinand Hiller, April 11, 1849). See also Robert's remarks in Nauhaus, *Schumann Tagebücher*, 2: 236 (August 6–22, 1842).

26. For a contemporary observation along these lines on "Ich grolle nicht," see Claire von Glümer, *Erinnerungen an Wilhelmine Schröder-Devrient* (Leipzig: J. A. Barth, 1862), 119.

27. Robert and Clara Schumann, *Liederalbum für Wilhelmine Schröder-Devrient*, ed. Angelika Horstmann (Kassel, Ger.: Bärenreiter, 1994).

28. For information on Clara's programming for these soirées, see April Prince, "Der anmutreichen, unschuldsvollen Herrin: Clara Schumann's Public Personas," PhD diss., University of Texas at Austin, 2009, 334–37. See also Ozawa-Müller, "Clara Schumann und Wilhelmine Schröder-Devrient," 180.

29. Litzmann, *Clara Schumann*, 118 (diary entry of October 14, 1848): "Soiree zu Ehren der Schröder-Devrient, die Roberts 'Frauenliebe und Leben,' alle 8 Lieder, ganz herrlich sang! Es war für uns ein hoher Genuß, und wieder mußten wir ausrufen: 'es gibt doch nur eine Devrient!'"

30. Litzmann, *Clara Schumann*, 119 (diary entry of October 31, 1848).

31. "Nachrichten: Leipzig," *Allgemeine musikalische Zeitung* 43, no. 15 (April 14, 1841): 315–16. "Entschieden missfallen hat uns in der That unbegreifliche Verkennen der tiefen und ernsten Bedeutung des so wunderschönen Volksliedes von Feuchtersleben, zumal da F. Mendelssohns treffliche, karakteristisch wahre Komposizion desselben schon an sich für jedes musikalische Gemüth ein solches Verkennen unmöglich machen könnte. Die ersten 3 Verse trug Mad. Schröder-Devrient vortrefflich vor und man bemerkte die grosse Wirkung hiervon an allen Zuhörern; als sie aber bei der in der Dichtung und Komposizion, denn beide gehen hier recht eigentlich Hand in Hand, so schönen Schlusswendung, das hier sehr ernst und bedeutungsvoll erscheinende 'auf's Wiederseh'n!' speziell auf sich und das Publikum bezog, mit einer freundlichen Verbeugung begleitete und mithin geradezu profanirte, war auch alle edlere Wirkung hin, und was in der Seele der Zuhörer lang und tief nachgeklungen hätte, ging so als ein gewönlicher Coulisseneffekt schnell und spurlos vorüber."

32. Robert Schumann, "Concerte: Zwanzigstes Abonnementconcert," 118. "Das Publicum hörte wie gebannt, und als sie zum Schluß Mendelssohn's mit den Worten 'auf Wiedersehn' endigendes Volkslied sang, stimmten alle in freudiger Zustimmung ein."

33. A few months later, members of the Gewandhaus would restage Schröder's gesture toward Mendelssohn by singing the "Volkslied" to him on the evening of July 28, 1841, with the composer joining in for the last verse. Mendelssohn departed for Berlin the next day. See R. Larry Todd, *Mendelssohn: A Life in Music* (New York: Oxford University Press, 2003), 409.

34. For characteristic assessments of Viardot by Clara along these lines, see Wendler, "*Band der ewigen Liebe*," 73 (Clara to Emilie List, July 7, 1840); Nauhaus, *Schumann Tagebücher* 2: 197 (Clara, December 17, 1841) and 267 (Clara, August 1843).

35. Weissweiler and Ludwig, *Schumann, Briefwechsel* 3: 985 (Clara to Robert, March 14, 1840): "Welche Bedenken hast Du, lieber Robert, gegen die Dedication [of the op. 24 *Liederkreis*] an Pauline? ich rathe Dir gewiß dazu; das ist ein Wesen, das Deine Lieder aufzufassen vermag in ihrem deutschen Sinn."

36. Wendler, "*Band der ewigen Liebe*" (Clara to Emilie List, July 7, 1840, 72): "Es hat mich so sehr gefreut, da ich mich von ihr ganz und gar vergessen glaubte, und *beinah* in die Versuchung gerieth, sie anderen Sängerinnen in der Hinsicht des Charakters gleichzustellen, denn ich dachte, sie sey am Ende durch die Triumphe verdorben. Doch der Brief zeigt sie noch ganz die Alte und ihren schönen offenen Charakter. Ich muss ihr nächstens schreiben. Die Lieder hebe ich auf für sie und sende sie ihr, *sobald* sie nach Paris kommt."

37. Nauhaus, *Schumann Tagebücher* 2: 140 (Clara, January 16, 1841): "Es erreicht doch Keiner das Ideal, das ich von Roberts Liedern in mir trage! *Pauline Garcia* wäre das Einzige, glaube ich, die sie ganz wahrhaft erfassen würde—könnte ich nur einmal Eines von ihr hören!"

38. Nauhaus, *Schumann Tagebücher* 2: 105 (Clara, September 24, 1840): "Es drängte sich mir dasselbe Gefühl einmal auf, als ich von Pauline *Garcia* das Gretchen von Schubert hörte, was sie mehr nach Effect haschend vortrug, als mit dieser inneren Gluth, wie diese Worte, sowie Schuberts Musik so herrlich es aussprechen. Pauline *Garcia* hat mich jedes Mal entzückt, nur gerade bei diesen *deutschen* Lied ließ sie mich unbefriedigt, was ich eigentlich gar nicht begreife bei diesem durch und durch musikalischen Wesen, die sonst Alles in gröster [sic] Schnelligkeit in seiner ganzen Wahrheit erfaßt!"

39. For another example of Clara's reception of Viardot along these lines, see Nauhaus, *Schumann Tagebücher* 2: 268 (Clara, August 1843). See also the testy exchange of letters between Clara and Viardot in January 1848, translated into French and discussed in Beatrix Borchard, "'Ma chère petite Klara—Pauline de mon cœur': Clara Schumann et Pauline Viardot, une amitié d'artistes franco-allemande," *Cahiers Ivan Tourguéniev* 20 (1997): 135–37.

40. See Sonia Gesse-Harm, "Casta Diva: Zur Rezeption Jenny Linds in der Musikkultur um 1850," *Musikforschung* 62, no. 4 (October–December 2009): 347–63, esp. 354–55.

41. Cited in Litzmann, *Clara Schumann*, 208–9: "Vormittags besuchte uns die Lind zu einer kleinen Lieder-Probe, aus der aber noch mehr wurde, denn sie sang eine ganze Menge von Roberts Liedern, und *wie* sang sie sie, mit welcher Wahrheit, mit welcher Herzinnigkeit und Einfachheit, wie sang sie 'Marienwürmchen', 'Frühlingsglaube' aus dem Album, das sie nicht kannte, *vom Blatt*—das bleibt einem unvergeßlich; welch ein herrliches gottbegabtes Wesen ist das, welch eine reine echt künstlerische Seele, wie erfrischt einen alles, was sie sagt, wie trifft sie immer das Rechte, spricht es aus mit wenig Worten, kurz nie wohl liebte und verehrte ich ein weibliches Wesen mehr als sie. Diese Lieder werden ewig in meiner Seele klingen, und wäre es nicht ein Unrecht, so möchte ich sagen, nie will ich mehr die Lieder von andern hören als von ihr."

42. Robert's *Liederalbum für die Jugend* contains "Marienwürmchen," as well as several songs with *Frühling* in the title, but none by the name of "Frühlingsglaube" specifically. With the second song title, it is possible that Clara was instead referring to Schubert's famous "Frühlingsglaube," D686, although it is hard to imagine that Lind would "not have known" that song already, even if she was sight-reading from Clara's album.

43. For information on the programming for these concerts, see Nauhaus, *Schumann Tagebücher*, 3: 783–84.
44. For example, see Gesse-Harm, "Casta Diva," 357–58.
45. Jennifer Ronyak, *Intimacy, Performance, and the Lied in the Early Nineteenth Century* (Bloomington: Indiana University Press, 2018).

Bibliography

Auslander, Philip. "Musical Personae." *Drama Review* 50, no. 1 (Spring 2006): 100–119.

Borchard, Beatrix. "'Ma chère petite Klara—Pauline de mon cœur': Clara Schumann et Pauline Viardot, une amitié d'artistes franco-allemande." *Cahiers Ivan Tourguéniev, Pauline Viardot, Maria Malibran* 20 (1997): 127–43.

Cone, Edward. *The Composer's Voice*. Berkeley: University of California Press, 1974.

Gesse-Harm, Sonia. "Casta Diva: Zur Rezeption Jenny Linds in der Musikkulture um 1850." *Musikforschung* 62, no. 4 (October–December 2009): 347–63.

Glümer, Claire von. *Erinnerungen an Wilhelmine Schröder-Devrient*. Leipzig: J. A. Barth, 1862.

Glümer, Claire von, and Henry Chorley. "Wilhelmine Schröder-Devrient and Wagner's Dresden." In *Richard Wagner and His World*, translated and edited by Thomas Grey, 201–29. Princeton, NJ: Princeton University Press, 2009.

Hunter, Mary. "'To Play as if from the Soul of the Composer': The Idea of the Performer in Early Romantic Aesthetics." *Journal of the American Musicological Society* 58, no. 2 (Summer 2005): 357–98.

Leistra-Jones, Karen. "Staging Authenticity: Joachim, Brahms, and the Politics of *Werktreue* Performance." *Journal of the American Musicological Society* 66, no. 2 (Summer 2013): 397–436.

Litzmann, Berthold. *Clara Schumann: Ein Künstlerleben durch Tagebüchern und Briefen*, 3rd ed. 3 vols. Leipzig: Breitkopf und Härtel, 1907.

Meyer, Stephen. "*Das wilde Herz*: Interpreting Wilhelmine Schröder-Devrient." *Opera Quarterly* 14, no. 2 (Winter 1997/98): 23–40.

Nauhaus, Gerd, ed. *Robert Schumann: Tagebücher*. 2 vols. Leipzig: Deutscher Verlag für Musik, 1971–87.

Ozawa-Müller, Kazuko. "Clara Schumann und Wilhelmine Schröder-Devrient." In *Clara Schumann, 1819–1896: Katalog zur Ausstellung*, edited by Ingrid Bodsch and Gerd Nauhaus, 179–86. Bonn: Stadtmuseum Bonn, 1996.

Prince, April. "Der anmutreichen, unschuldsvollen Herrin: Clara Schumann's Public Personas." PhD diss., University of Texas at Austin, 2009.

Ronyak, Jennifer. *Intimacy, Performance, and the Lied in the Early Nineteenth Century*. Bloomington: Indiana University Press, 2018.

Schumann, Robert. "Concerte: Zwanzigstes Abonnementconcert, den 18ten März." *Neue Zeitschrift für Musik* 14, no. 29 (April 9, 1841): 117–18.

———. "Drei gute Liederhefte." *Neue Zeitschrift für Musik* 13, no. 30 (November 29, 1836).

———. "Musikleben in Leipzig, während des Winters 1839/40 (Fortsetzung)." *Neue Zeitschrift für Musik* 12, no. 38 (May 8, 1840), 151.

———. "Zweites Abonnementconcert, den 11 October." *Neue Zeitschrift für Musik* 13, no. 36 (October 31, 1840): 144.

Schumann, Robert, and Clara Schumann. *Liederalbum für Wilhelmine Schröder-Devrient*. Edited by Angelika Horstmann. Kassel, Ger.: Bärenreiter, 1994.

Todd, R. Larry. *Mendelssohn: A Life in Music*. New York: Oxford University Press, 2003.

Weissweiler, Eva, and Susanna Ludwig, eds. *Robert and Clara Schumann, Briefwechsel: Kritische Gesamtausgabe*, 3 vols. Frankfurt: Stroemfeld/Roter Stern, 2001.

Wendler, Eugen, ed. *"Das Band der ewigen Liebe": Clara Schumanns Briefwechsel mit Emilie und Elise List*. Stuttgart: Metzler, 1996.

Wolzogen, Alfred von. *Wilhelmine Schröder-Devrient: Ein Beitrag zur Geschichte des musikalischen Dramas*. Leipzig: F. A. Brockhaus, 1863.

BENJAMIN BINDER is Associate Professor of Music at Duquesne University. He is also a collaborative pianist.

3 From Miscellanies to Musical Works
Julius Stockhausen, Clara Schumann, and Dichterliebe

Natasha Loges

The song cycle eludes definition. As John Daverio has eloquently argued, the genre "discloses a paradoxical movement between the artlessness, the noble simplicity demanded by the Lied tradition, and the artfulness that a cyclic form should display.... We expect that the Lieder in question will amount to more than a mere collection, that they will exhibit elements of musicopoetic cohesiveness extending beyond the individual Lied to encompass the entire set."[1]

Several things can be inferred from this description. The first is well known, namely that the individual Lieder that collectively constitute a cycle occupy a nebulous aesthetic space that shifts between small-scale, accessible miniatures and high art, sometimes within the same song. The second—namely, the implication that a cycle is always apprehended as an unbroken whole, whether via a score, recording or performance—is worthy of pause, because, as I have shown elsewhere, this was certainly not the case for the early concert history of the song cycle, starting in the mid-nineteenth century.[2] At that time, within the standard patterned miscellany concert format, cycles were frequently broken up, presented as subgroups of songs usually interspersed with instrumental works, or in smaller selections.[3] A third, more implicit point in Daverio's use of the words "we expect" is that expectations play a role in the perception of the cyclic qualities of a group of songs, or indeed, any collection of small pieces bearing such associations. Today, audiences (both scholarly and general) are conditioned to receive song cycles as continuous wholes, so the broken-up song cycle presents intriguing challenges to this inevitability. Most commentators have dismissed this substantial performance tradition as peculiar and outdated, a blip in the song cycle's history that contravenes the composer's planned coherence in an otherwise tidy teleology of wholeness.[4] In this chapter, I will explore how the first public performers of song cycles helped shape the genre's substantial and tenacious identity as it has coalesced in both performance and scholarship and how that identity was aligned with the instrumental work concept as defined by Lydia

Goehr. I argue that such programs enabled audiences to attach the associations of serious instrumental music to song cycles.[5] Programming is an overlooked part of the "framing, staging, and placement," which Goehr has argued is a crucial way of communicating a work's status to audiences.[6] I will conclude by exploring some scholarly imperatives that have unwittingly encouraged the marginalization of this rich performance history.

My case study is seven public performances of Robert Schumann's *Dichterliebe*, op. 48, given by the baritone Julius Stockhausen (1826–1906), the Lied's "founding father," with Clara Schumann.[7] These concerts all took place in major German-speaking cities within a single decade, 1862–72. They were years of exploration and experimentation in the performance of song cycles in public; for example, Stockhausen had given the landmark first complete performance of Schubert's *Die schöne Müllerin*, D795, in 1856, and the first *Dichterliebe* in 1861.[8] He continued to perform cycles in various formats during the 1860s. In 1874, his post as director of Berlin's Stern choral society slowed his recital activities.[9] The period 1862–72 also aligns with a peak in Clara Schumann's career, before personal tragedies and declining health severely curtailed her playing.[10] Such performances laid the foundations for the subsequent "monumentalization of the canonized Lied" in the 1880s.[11]

Julius Stockhausen's and Clara Schumann's *Dichterliebe*

Stockhausen not only transformed the Lied into a concert-worthy genre, pioneered performances of complete cycles, and established the fundamental song canon, but through his considerable teaching practice, he trained the next generation to develop his legacy. As a friend and colleague of Clara Schumann, Johannes Brahms, and Joseph Joachim, he was closely associated with their musicoaesthetic ideals and, in Brahms's case, with their practical realization in performance.[12] Since his Catholic family opposed a stage career on moral grounds, and his voice lacked operatic strength anyway, the Lied (and to some extent the oratorio) was the genre through which he could realize his ambitions and also affirm his close intellectual and spiritual identification with Germany, rather than his native (French) Alsace.[13] An exceptionally capable musician, he played the piano, cello, and organ; read scores fluently; and transposed accompaniments. In keeping with the ideal of all-round cultivation, the Humboldtian *Bildungsideal*, he was intellectually curious, taking an interest, for instance, in scientific approaches to singing.[14] His diaries are peppered with quotations not only from the musical works he was performing, such as Wilhelm Müller's poetry, but also the writings of Goethe, Schiller, Jean Paul Richter, Lessing, Herman Grimm, and Schopenhauer. Naturally, he was fluent in French, but his letters suggest that he also spoke English and Italian.

Stockhausen, Clara Schumann, and Joachim were associated with a clutch of ideals about musical performance that coalesced during and particularly after their lifetimes: seriousness, humility, self-restraint, and fidelity to the composer's intentions as enshrined in the score.[15] As Karen Leistra-Jones and others have shown, such eschewing of the "flamboyant, popular, and spectacular" was in keeping with the *Werktreue* ideal.[16] These artists focused on serious, often German, music from the past in programs designed to uplift and edify. In 1849, the twenty-three-year-old Stockhausen declared, "it is the artist who educates the public, or at least one must seek to cultivate them, must attempt to force good taste and noble sensibilities upon them!"[17]

The image of Stockhausen and his colleagues as servants or priests, rather than executants or entertainers, was based on an accumulation of their statements that were recorded and repeated, on press reports that sought to locate and emphasize those qualities in their performances, and on subsequent generations' interpretation of documentary material.[18] It was also based on the repertoire they performed. Collectively, they transformed audiences' expectations of a concert from an event for entertainment and socializing to a quasi-religious worship of the (often absent) composer through their interpretation of the musical work. They were "authorized to curate the musical canon via public performance."[19] Stockhausen declared that theatrical techniques and exhibitionism had no place on the recital stage because the singer was "nothing but an interpreter of poet and composer."[20] The critical period during which these ideals worked through concert culture was not so much in their lifetimes as in the next generation, when their numerous students invoked their names to justify or legitimize their own performance decisions. Such ideals are enshrined in music conservatoires and concert halls today, although the details of these musicians' actual concert programs are not often recalled.[21]

In the performance of song cycles, however, any thought of the composer's intentions raised immediate practical problems. First, as Rufus Hallmark observes, the Lied "comes in very small packages, no match for piano sonatas, string quartets, symphonies, operas."[22] Within the mid-nineteenth-century public concert, the Lied was only a small unit within a larger whole, ideally suited to filling gaps between larger pieces or movements. With the emphasis on variety, there was no expectation that whole cycles would be performed in concerts, and Eduard Hanslick famously described Stockhausen's complete *Müllerin* as an experiment.[23] Second, song's "traditional location at the border between the popular and the serious" created a potential aesthetic gap to be bridged in the types of concerts with which Stockhausen, Clara Schumann, and Joachim were associated.[24] A song might well be contemplated as an individual item at home; it might be purchased individually, or in a volume, or in an opus branded as a *Liederkreis*. But in public performance, audiences would hear Lieder as part of larger compilations that might have little relationship with their published presentation.[25]

Furthermore, no matter what their ideals required, both Julius Stockhausen and Clara Schumann had to take heed of audiences' expectations because of their considerable financial responsibilities. By the end of 1856, Clara Schumann was widowed with seven living children; Stockhausen had five after his marriage in 1864. Therefore, neither artist could indulge in financially risky concerts that disregarded established public preferences indiscriminately. As Leistra-Jones has pointed out, "as virtuoso performers, these musicians still needed to appear before audiences and appeal to those audiences in order to succeed; they were, in other words, in the paradoxical position of being required to display an authentic self in their performances."[26] They could test and stretch audiences (and with their intellectual reputations, it is likely that audiences would have expected it of them), but they could not alienate or bore them.

It is also worth recalling that within the patterned miscellany program, constructed on a controlled alternation of genres, responsibility for each genre lay with the relevant specialist; thus, Stockhausen rarely commented on the instrumental numbers within concerts. For example, in a letter of December 15, 1859, to Friedrich Hiller, he proposed the following items for the Gürzenich Hall, Cologne's largest venue, fully restored the previous year:

Aria (aus der Oper Aetius)—Händel
Air de la Fête du Village—Boieldieu
Am Feierabend, Der Neugierige, Ungeduld—Schubert[27]

The rest of the program was up to Hiller and whoever else was booked to perform. This shared responsibility operated even when large-scale orchestral items were involved. For instance, in a concert on March 24, 1859, in Hamburg's Wörmerscher Concert Hall with Joseph Joachim, and including Brahms's Piano Concerto no. 1, Stockhausen sang a Handel aria and then offered a trio of songs connected through their subject matter: Schubert's "Frühlingsglaube," Mendelssohn's "Frühlingslied," and Schumann's "Frühlingsnacht."[28]

In all these concerts, the controlled alternation of genres was a dominating principle. For this reason, sequences were as important as individual items. Stockhausen's diaries list musical works with numbers above them to indicate the order in which they would appear in a program, as can be seen in figure 3.1. "Items" were numbered on programs, but a single item might consist of small works by several composers; equally likely, an item might consist of a single movement of a larger work, suggesting that sequences were constructed time and again. Thus, for example, on March 2, 1863, at the Gesellschaft der Musikfreunde in Vienna, one item was described as a "Liedercyklus aus Göthe's

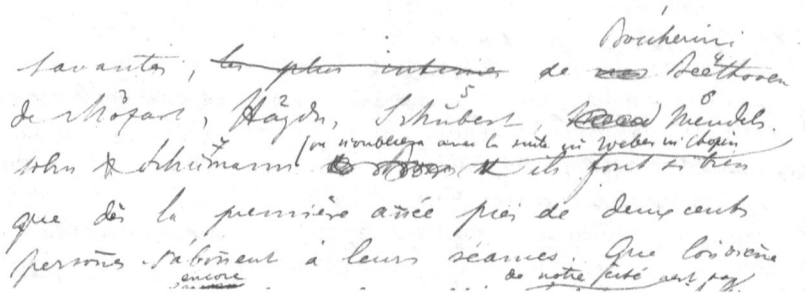

Fig. 3.1. Extract from Stockhausen's diaries, D-Fmi Frankfurt University Library, Nachlass Julius Stockhausen.

'Wilhelm Meister.'" This in turn consisted of two sub-items; the first was three Lieder (Mignon—Philine—Harfner, presumably all Schumann's settings), and the second was Schumann's *Requiem für Mignon*, op. 98b, for solo and choir.[29]

Stockhausen and Clara Schumann bonded together over the performance of her husband's songs. At their first concert together, in Ostend on August 26, 1854, when their program included songs by Schumann: "Stille," "Mondnacht," and "Frühlingsnacht."[30] When she wrote to him the following year on April 13, 1855, she reinforced that relationship with Schumann's songs when she wrote, "how happy it would make [Robert] if you would visit him with Brahms and sing for him!"[31] Their friendship and working partnership was harmonious and long-lasting.

Between 1862 and 1872, Julius Stockhausen and Clara Schumann gave seven documented evening performances of *Dichterliebe* at large venues in major cities.[32] In five cases, they were the only two concert givers (see table 3.1), and attention was shared between solo piano and piano-accompanied song. In two cases, a violinist and cellist joined them and the program was accordingly adapted (see table 3.2).

How do such performances of *Dichterliebe* relate to the ideological shift that ultimately rejected them and enshrined the Lieder cycle as an unbreakable whole? A closer look shows how the artists managed to have their cake and eat it, in other words, to conform to expected concert formats while offering their audiences a substantial, intellectual, immersive musical experience that could exceed the sum of its parts. Daverio's description quoted at the start of this chapter, in which the cycle exhibits "elements of musicopoetic cohesiveness extending beyond the individual Lied to encompass the entire set," is expanded here to embrace a multiplicity of potential experiences of the cycle. How the performers chose to present, and the audience to listen, might produce a sense of cohesiveness embracing the entire programs. If the same works are not repeated identically each time, the consistent trajectory of the evenings nevertheless suggests a contract shared

Table 3.1. Programs of Julius Stockhausen's and Clara Schumann's performances of Robert Schumann's *Dichterliebe*, op. 48.

Date	Venue	Part 1			Part 2		
		Item 1	Item 2	Item 3	Item 4	Item 5	Item 6
February 2, 1862	Kasino-Saal, Zurich	Beethoven: Piano Sonata in F minor, op. 57	Boieldieu: aria from *Jean de Paris*	D. Scarlatti: Andante and Presto; Chopin: Scherzo, op. 20	*Dichterliebe*, Part 1	Three pieces from *Kreisleriana*, op. 16	*Dichterliebe*, Part 2
November 13, 1862	Grosser Concert-Saal, Frankfurt am Main	Beethoven: Piano Sonata in F minor, op. 57	Schubert: Lied, *Der Wanderer*	Chopin: Ballade in G minor, op. 23		Three pieces from *Kreisleriana*, op. 16	
November 25, 1862	Grosser Wörmerscher Saal, Hamburg	Beethoven: Sonata quasi Fantasia in C sharp minor, op. 27 no. 2	Bononcini: romance from *Griselda*	Brahms: *Händel-Variationen*, op. 24		Three pieces from *Kreisleriana*, op. 16	
December 6, 1862	Gewandhaus, Leipzig	Beethoven: Sonata quasi Fantasia in C sharp minor, op. 27 no. 2	Grétry: aria from *La fausse magie*	Bach: Gavotte in G minor; Scarlatti: Andante and Presto in C		Schumann: Romanze in D minor, op. 32 no. 3; Andante in F sharp; Novelette in D major, op. 21 no. 2	
October 19, 1872	Saal der Liederhalle, Stuttgart	Schumann: *Fantasie*, op. 17	Schubert: Lieder *Willkommen und Abschied*; *An die Leier* (the first song accompanied by "Herr Winternitz")	Beethoven: Variations in C minor, WoO 80		Schumann: *Nachtstück* in F major, op. 23 (no. 2 or no. 4); *Scherzino* from *Faschingsschwank aus Wien*, op. 26 no. 3	Mendelssohn: Scherzo *Sommernachtstraum*, op. 21

Table 3.2. Programs of Julius Stockhausen and Clara Schumann's performances of Robert Schumann's *Dichterliebe*, op. 48, in chamber concerts.

Date	Venue	Part 1			Part 2	
		Item 1	Item 2	Item 3	Item 4	Item 5
7 p.m., November 18, 1863	Soirée musicale, unstated venue, Hamburg, with C. Rose and E. Hegar	Beethoven: Piano Trio in E-flat major, op. 70 no. 2	*Dichterliebe*, Part 1	Bach: Prelude in G major; Handel: Sarabande, Gigue, Passacaglia, HWV 432	*Dichterliebe*, Part 2	Schumann: Novelette from opus 21; Nachtstück from opus 23 and Mendelssohn: Scherzo and capriccio in F-sharp minor
7 p.m., December 6, 1864	Unstated venue, Hamburg, with C. Rose and E. Hegar	Beethoven: Piano Trio in B-flat major, op. 97	Mendelssohn: *Variations sérieuses*, op. 54	*Dichterliebe*, Part 1	Kirchner: Album Blätter, nos. 1, 2, 5, 6 and Schumann Canon from opus 56	*Dichterliebe*, Part 2

between audiences and performers in which expectations were set and met. Therefore, deliberately or not, the programs, which include much now-canonical repertoire, encouraged the audience to construct associations between the works. As Borchard has described it, "novelty was embedded into the known, a program strategy that accommodated the public's receptivity."[33] And this applies as much to the piano works as to the songs. Beethoven, a composer strongly associated with Clara Schumann (and Joseph Joachim), is prominent.[34] Clara Schumann was of course also the primary exponent of her husband's music, and it is notable that she replaced Beethoven with Schumann's *Fantasie*, op. 17, in her last performance of *Dichterliebe* with Stockhausen, thus cementing Schumann's status alongside Beethoven's.[35]

In the first part of the duo concerts (table 3.1), an aria or Lied provided textural and stylistic variety between piano works. Stockhausen's French arias were part of his signature repertoire, recalling his background in French Alsace.[36] But they were also historical and serious pieces, like the piano works that followed them. (Brahms's *Händel-Variationen*, op. 24, were, of course, contemporary but reference an extremely important historic composer; Chopin, meanwhile, had been dead for more than a decade.) The second part is particularly interesting; the sixteen songs of *Dichterliebe* were performed in two "volumes," echoing the published presentation of the cycle, with a few piano pieces in between. This effectively mirrors the first half in reverse, with the solo piano works offering textural variety while maintaining a degree of stylistic continuity.

Clara Schumann's consistent choice of piano works show that these programs were not random assemblages in service to variety but musically engaging and artistically coherent experiences. To explore just one example, at the concert on December 6, 1862, the piano interpolations were Schumann's *Romanze* in D minor, op. 32 no. 3; a piece billed as "Andante in F-Sharp;" and the *Novelette* in D major, op. 21 no. 2. If Stockhausen sang *Dichterliebe* in the original keys (it is unlikely that Clara Schumann transposed for him, since transposing was not her strength), then no. 8, "Und wüßten's die Blumen, die kleinen," would end in A minor, and no. 9, "Das ist ein Flöten und Geigen," would start in D minor; that is, a case could be made for some tonal planning. Certainly, the *Romanze* continues the tempo, tonality, and mood of the end of *Dichterliebe*, no. 8, and its lyrical middle section recalls the cycle's opening wistful mood. The central piano work is something of a mystery, since Schumann did not compose an andante in F-sharp major; but it could be the second of his *Drei Romanzen*, op. 28 no. 2, in which the right and left thumbs sing an exquisite lyrical duet. The energy is then ramped up again in the ferociously virtuosic *Novelette*, which also has a songlike central section. Judging from the approximate duration of the two outer pieces, the interpolation would have filled a good fifteen minutes with music. The review in the *Signale für die musikalische Welt* praises the artists, with their well-established reputation for quality, and also praised the "delightful program, which exemplified the cozy character of the soirée splendidly."[37]

This consistent approach to *Dichterliebe* over a decade, the prominence, size, and location of the venues in major cities, and the prime timing of the concerts (all were at 7 p.m.) indicate that this format was both popular and successful. Practically speaking, it had other advantages: each artist was showcased equally; and the breaking of *Dichterliebe* created breathing space for Stockhausen. Such programs perhaps also helped Clara Schumann overcome her misgivings about performing her husband's piano cycle *Kreisleriana*, op. 16, in public. In one letter to Brahms in the late 1850s, she declared that she found them "unsuitable for concerts," suggesting that her own primary associations with the cycle as a private work needed overcoming.[38]

In the two chamber concerts, Clara Schumann interpolated pieces by Theodor Kirchner and Mendelssohn into *Dichterliebe*; in other words, she expanded the stylistic spectrum while maintaining some consistency (she did not interpolate Scarlatti or Bach). Audiences probably enjoyed such presentations of *Dichterliebe*, at least partly because they evoked the much-loved informality of private music making through the inclusion of song and small-scale piano pieces separately from the large opening sonata and opera aria. Beatrix Borchard, in her discussion of Clara Schumann's and Joseph Joachim's concerts, has described the experience as follows: "A particular ideal of art and the artist emerges from the realm between private and public. . . . Through the hundreds of listeners, who have purchased a ticket for money, the private becomes public."[39] Edward Kravitt, however, who has done valuable work on song concert history, regards such programs as defunct. He declares that "Clara Schumann, ignoring Stockhausen's innovation [of singing complete cycles], performed her husband's *Frauenliebe und Leben* (op. 42) in two separate parts, only four songs at a time. Conservatives delayed the change until around 1870."[40] And yet she was the first recipient of the songs, performing them in private as both singer and pianist throughout 1840, the closest living link to their creator.[41] Schumann himself described her performances of his works as if "from the source."[42] What was conservative then would be regarded as a rare exception or experiment, if not an abomination, now.

While I have focused exclusively on *Dichterliebe* here, other cycles received equally thoughtful treatment. On November 13, 1872, at the Casino in Elberfeld, Stockhausen gave a shared soirée in which the interleaving of various works bespeaks a different, but equally carefully conceived, design centered on Schumann's Piano Quintet, op. 44:

Schumann Quintet, first movement
Schubert "Der Wanderer"

Schumann Quintet, second movement
Schubert "Lindenbaum" and "Die Post"
Schumann Quintet, third and fourth movements
Brahms "Sonntag" and "Wiegenlied"
Beethoven G major Violin Romanze
Schumann "Mondnacht" and "Frühlingsnacht."[43]

On some levels, such a performance is surely demanding for its listeners, particularly because of its duration. On the other hand, it is likely that each item was applauded (this is evident from the numerous reviews that mention that encores were called for straightaway), allowing audiences to relax and reset their concentration, and perhaps also allowing them to construct a different coherence for the Quintet, in which the chamber movements and songs frame and prepare one another, rather than being heard in isolation.

Despite these concerts, midway through this period the idea of *Dichterliebe* as a cycle could still regarded with suspicion. Hanslick's review of Stockhausen's pupil Helen Magnus at the Vienna Musikverein declared, "Singing the whole of Robert Schumann's 'Dichterliebe' is a tempting experiment; it was successful, as the [audience's] response showed, however, we still would not want to endorse it. Strange, fine and brilliant as it is, the music of this song-cycle ['Liederkreis'] nevertheless weaves in a twilit, fractured light, ultimately rather too dull, as a whole. But no sense of necessity, not even a strong compulsion, forces us to encounter and perform these fifteen [sic] songs as a whole."[44] For Hanslick, *Dichterliebe* is not like *Müllerin* or *Winterreise* because those works were conceived as wholes by the poet ["schon vom Dichter als ein Ganzes, eine Einheit concipirt waren"], whereas *Dichterliebe* was not. He continues that it is Schumann who put them together, criticizes the fact that the keys don't flow, and praises the double coherence of poet and composer.

Reconsidering Song Cycle Performance in Musicology

The careful design of these *Dichterliebe* performances suggests that despite their adherence to the controlled alternation of genres, they could encourage "structured understanding." They conformed to a recognizable notion of *Werktreue*, encouraging the kind of aesthetic contemplation that is associated with the instrumental work concept.[45] But as a small-scale texted genre that was variously regarded as commercialized, popular, private, and informal, separated from the high ideals that permeated discourse about purely instrumental genres such as the sonata, symphony, or even opera, the Lied has generally sat outside such discussion of musical works.[46] Lydia Goehr, for instance, does not include Lieder in her historico-philosophical survey of the shift in status of music.[47] It was only toward the end of the nineteenth century, and even then only gradually, that the notion gained currency of a fusion of poetry and music in a concert-worthy genre, with the concomitant impact on melody, form, and declamation.[48]

I have argued that Stockhausen and Clara Schumann's interleaved *Dichterliebe* performances helped audiences draw this small-scale domestic repertoire into the world of serious, instrumental music.[49] Such mixed-genre performances may have constituted artistically coherent experiences to some listeners, preparing them for the more tightly constrained programming patterns of the Lied that coalesced during the following century. The evidence is patchy at best, as the effect of programming sequences seems not to be considered in surviving private documents like diaries, letters, or published reviews. We also cannot know the other ways in which Stockhausen and Clara Schumann presented this music, as, for example, whether specific instructions in the score to alter transpositions or changes of notes to accommodate Stockhausen's range, ornamentation, preluding, or improvisation.

What does all this mean for how Lieder cycles are understood in scholarship now? Stockhausen and Clara Schumann's interleaved programmes suggest that their cycle's cohesiveness was constructed differently from today's in order to meet their own and their audiences' definitions of an enjoyable concert; or put more strongly, it is in the performer's gift to construct that cohesiveness. The decision to *publish* a set of songs as a cycle is, of course, significant and different. Borchard has drawn attention to an 1878 review of Schumann's *Frauenliebe und -leben*, op. 42, in which the critic writes that "one may compose series and sequences, but not present them in concert," suggesting the existence of an ontological gulf to be bridged.[50]

But are such performances really defunct? I programmed a *Dichterliebe* in this way at London's Wigmore Hall in February 2016 as part of a conference, and it was very well received by the public.[51] In the future, it would be worth considering how such performances might enrich scholarly approaches to cohesion in song cycles; that is, to cross the "threshold where the individual composition meets the surrounding world."[52] Recent decades have seen much debate about the cyclical nature of *Dichterliebe*, interrogating the appropriateness of the preset organicist models that inform so much analytical enquiry. David Ferris reminds us that *Dichterliebe* is, for many, the quintessential German song cycle;[53] but he argues that "Schumann plays with the conventions of musical structure and questions that aesthetic necessity for closure within small-scale forms." Beate Perrey also challenges the cyclical nature of the set, drawing on aesthetics and literary theory of the Romantic fragment; she does not mention Clara Schumann despite her being the primary exponent of Schumann's works for nearly half a century.[54] Indeed, neither Ferris nor Perrey draws on the work's performance history. There are other issues which cannot be discussed here; for instance, most commentators rely heavily on key relationships to make their argument for coherence, even though *Dichterliebe* is frequently sung by lower male voices in mixed transposition. The selection of published keys for songs was a pragmatic as well as an artistic decision; the intended purchasers were not professionals, and transposition at sight is a demanding skill even for experienced performers.[55]

From another perspective, a recent colloquy on Lied performance has sought to extricate Lied scholarship from the comfortable hermeneutic space scholars have carved for it.[56] Jennifer Ronyak points out that to confront performance is to "challenge the taking of musical works as one's object of study," and she brings recent performance scholarship into the debate with exciting results.[57] Laura Tunbridge, in encouraging us to take recordings seriously, points to a critically important way that most of us encounter music now, encouraging us to "tease out this complex relationship between text-based hermeneutics and performance history."[58] Taking such thinking one step further, it is worth exploring how both analytical and hermeneutic approaches are affected by Stockhausen's and Clara Schumann's *Dichterliebe* performances, which were encountered by a first generation of listeners even as the drive toward organicism and coherence in musicology was emerging. Rather than history *then*, and performance versus theory versus historical performance practice *now*, this exploration would aim to acknowledge the liveness of history and to remember that today's recital practices around the Lied will constitute a history in the future.

Notes

1. John Daverio, "The Song Cycle: Journeys through a Romantic Landscape," in *German Lieder in the Nineteenth Century*, ed. Rufus Hallmark, 2nd ed., with an afterword by David Ferris (New York: Routledge, 2010), 363.

2. See Natasha Loges, "The Limits of the Lied," in *Brahms in the Home and the Concert Hall: Between Private and Public Performance*, ed. Katy Hamilton and Natasha Loges, 300–23 (New York: Cambridge University Press, 2014).

3. The most useful study of nineteenth-century concert life remains William Weber, *The Great Transformation of Musical Taste: Concert Programming from Haydn to Brahms* (New York: Cambridge University Press, 2008). See also Edward Kravitt, "The Lied in 19th-Century Concert Life," *Journal of the American Musicological Society* 18, no. 2 (1965): 207–18; and Renate Hofmann, "Julius Stockhausen als Interpret der Liederzyklen Robert Schumanns," *Schumann-Forschungen* 9 (2005): 34–46, although Hofmann's study does not consider the implications of the programs.

4. See Daverio, "Song Cycle," 364, and Edward Kravitt, *The Lied: Mirror of Late Romanticism* (New Haven, CT: Yale University Press, 1996), 22. The collection edited by Walter Bernhart, Werner Wolf, and David Mosley, *Essays on the Song Cycle and on Defining the Field* (Amsterdam: Rodopi, 2001), leaves this performance history unmentioned, focusing solely on the hermeneutic and analytical inferences to be drawn from the score. Walther Dürr relies even more heavily on the composition and publication stage to define

a cycle; see his *Das deutsche Sololied im 19. Jahrhundert: Untersuchungen zu Sprache und Musik* (Wilhelmshaven, Ger.: F. Noetzel, 2002), 255–63. Beatrix Borchard has explored this concert history in numerous publications, such as "Die Sängerin Amalie Joachim und *Die schöne Müllerin* von Franz Schubert," in *Frauen- und Männerbilder in der Musik*, ed. Freia Hoffmann (Oldenburg, Ger.: Universität Oldenburg, 2000), 69–80.

5. For a summary of the Lied in publication, see David Gramit, "The Circulation of the Lied: The Double Life of an Artwork and a Commodity," in *The Cambridge Companion to the Lied*, ed. James Parsons (Cambridge: Cambridge University Press, 2004), 302.

6. Lydia Goehr, *The Imaginary Museum of Musical Works: An Essay in the Philosophy of Music* (Oxford: Oxford University Press, 2008), 173.

7. Beatrix Borchard has explored these performances from various perspectives in "Öffentliche Intimität? Konzertgesang in der zweiten Hälfte des 19. Jahrhunderts," in *Musikbezogene Genderforschung, Liedersingen, Studien zur Aufführungsgeschichte des Liedes*, ed. Katharina Hottmann (Hildesheim, Ger.: 2012), 109–26.

8. See Natasha Loges, "Julius Stockhausen's Early Performances of Franz Schubert's *Die schöne Müllerin*," *19th-Century Music* 41, no. 3 (Spring 2018): 206–24.

9. Other cities developed distinct practices, as Stockhausen wrote ruefully of London in a letter to Brahms of March 11, 1872: "Mit Schubert, Schumann & Brahms' Liedern ist leider hier nichts auszurichten.... Einheimische Unternehmer erklären kurzweg daß gute Lieder (good songs) sich nicht bezahlt machen" (Renate Hofmann, *Johannes Brahms Briefwechsel*. Vol. 18, *Johannes Brahms im Briefwechsel mit Julius Stockhausen* [Tutzing, Ger.: Hans Schneider, 1993], 79–80).

10. See Reinhard Kopiez, Andreas Lehmann, and Janina Klassen, "Clara Schumann's Collection of Playbills: A Historiometric Analysis of Life-Span Development, Mobility, and Repertoire Canonization," *Poetics* 37, no. 1 (2009): 50–73.

11. Gramit, "Circulation of the Lied," 309.

12. Stockhausen's biography also documents the growing professional animosity between him and Joachim (Julia Wirth, *Julius Stockhausen, der Sänger des deutschen Liedes: Nach Dokumenten seiner Zeit dargestellt* [Frankfurt: Englert and Schlosser, 1927]).

13. He declared to his father in a letter on October 17, 1845, from Saint Ouen: "Es kommt mir alles Deutsche so kräftig vor" (Wirth, *Julius Stockhausen*, 62). See also his effusions on Beethoven at Wirth, *Julius Stockhausen*, 70.

14. Wirth, *Julius Stockhausen*, 48–50, 59, 61.

15. Karen Leistra-Jones, "Staging Authenticity: Joachim, Brahms, and the Politics of Werktreue Performance," *Journal of the American Musicological Society* 66, no. 2 (Summer 2013): 397–436.

16. Leistra-Jones, "Staging Authenticity," 399. Leistra-Jones has also pointed out that the stances of Joachim and Brahms were not without their ambiguities.

17. "Aber sage mir nichts davon bitte, daß das Publikum den Sänger bilde im künstlerischen Sinn! Niemals hat Vater diese Ansicht vertreten, und ich glaube im Gegenteil mit ihm und meinem alten Lehrer Nagiller, daß der Künstler das Publikum bildet, oder man muß wenigstens versuchen es zu erziehen; muß versuchen ihm guten Geschmack und edles Empfinden aufzudrängen!" Letter from Paris, February 1849 [before the 23rd] in Wirth, *Julius Stockhausen*, 105.

18. The words *priest* and *priestess* were regularly used in reference to Joachim and Clara Schumann. See Nancy Reich, *Clara Schumann: The Artist and the Woman* (Ithaca, NY: Cornell University Press, 2001), 255–57, and Beatrix Borchard, "Botschafter der reinen

Kunst—vom Virtuosen zum Interpreten: Joseph Joachim und Clara Schumann," *Basler Jahrbuch für historische Musikpraxis* 20 (1996): 95–114.

19. Leistra-Jones, "Staging Authenticity," 421.

20. Quoted in Kravitt, *The Lied*, 55.

21. "Indeed, while the critical fortunes of Brahms's music have waxed and waned since his death, the approach to performance associated with him and his circle has never entirely gone out of style" (Leistra-Jones, "Staging Authenticity," 429).

22. Rufus Hallmark, ed. *German Lieder in the Nineteenth Century* (New York: Routledge, 2010), x.

23. See Eduard Hanslick, *Geschichte des Concertwesens in Wien*. Vol. 2, *Aus dem Concertsaal. Kritiken und Schilderungen aus den letzten 20 Jahren des Wiener Musiklebens* (Vienna: Braumüller, 1870), 214.

24. Gramit, "Circulation of the Lied," 312.

25. See Natasha Loges, "Detours on a Winter's Journey: Schubert's *Winterreise* in Nineteenth-Century Concerts," August 31, 2019, unpublished manuscript in possession of the author.

26. Leistra-Jones, "Staging Authenticity," 418.

27. Reinhold Sietz, *Aus Ferdinand Hillers Briefwechsel: Beiträge zu einer Biographie Ferdinand Hillers*, vol. 6 (Cologne, Ger.: Arno, 1968), 128.

28. Stockhausen performed this group more than once. Renate and Kurt Hofmann, *Johannes Brahms als Pianist und Dirigent: Chronologie seines Wirkens als Interpret*, ed. Otto Biba (Tutzing, Ger.: Hans Schneider, 2006), 50–51.

29. Archiv der Gesellschaft der Musikfreunde in Wien, Vienna, Gesellschaft der Musikfreunde, Programmsammlung, March 2, 1863.

30. Wirth, *Julius Stockhausen*, 144.

31. "Wie würde ihn das glücklich machen, wenn Sie Ihn einmal mit Brahms besuchten und vorsängen!" Wirth, *Julius Stockhausen*, 150.

32. I am extremely grateful to Dr. Thomas Synofzik of Robert-Schumann-Haus, Zwickau, for sending me transcriptions of Clara Schumann's programs.

33. "Neues wurde also in Bekanntes eingebettet, eine Programmstrategie, die der Aufnahmefähigkeit des Publikums entgegen kam" (Borchard, "Öffentliche Intimität?," 115).

34. Borchard, "Botschafter der reinen Kunst," 96, 99.

35. Borchard and others have pointed out that Clara Schumann remained her husband's representative long after his death ("Botschafter der reinen Kunst," 106–7).

36. It is not clear why this music became obsolete, but the French background could hardly have helped, especially after the Franco-Prussian war in 1870–71, when this repertoire vanished from Austro-German concert stages.

37. *Signale für die musikalische Welt*, "Ein reizendes, ganz prächtig den gemüthlichen Soirée-Character innehaltendes Programm," "Dur und Moll," unsigned review of December 6, 1862, concert in vol. 20, no. 51 (December 11, 1862): 709.

38. "Ich finde sie aber so unpassend für's Concert" (letter to Brahms, Vienna, December 20, 1858, in Berthold Litzmann, *Clara Schumann: Ein Künstlerleben; Nach Tagebüchern und Briefen*, 4th ed. [Leipzig: Breitkopf and Härtel, 1920], 3: 46).

39. "Ein bestimmtes Kunst- und Künstlerideal wird aus dem Zwischenbereich zwischen Privatheit und Öffentlichkeit. . . . Das Private wird nun vor Hunderten von Zuhörern, die gegen Geld eine Eintrittskarte erworben haben, zum Öffentlichen" (Borchard, "Botschafter der reinen Kunst," 102).

40. Kravitt, *The Lied*, 18.

41. Benjamin Binder reminds us of this in "The Lied from the Inside Out." See Jennifer Ronyak et al., "Studying the Lied: Hermeneutic Traditions and the Challenge of Performance," *Journal of the American Musicological Society* 67, no. 2 (Summer 2014): 552.

42. See letter to Joseph Fischhof from Leipzig on December 4, 1837: "Gewiß wird sie Ihnen von meinen Compositionen vorspielen; da hören Sie sie an der Quelle" (F. Gustav Jansen, *Robert Schumanns Briefe: Neue Folge*, 2nd ed. [Leipzig: Breitkopf and Härtel, 1904], 104).

43. D-Fmi, Nachlaß Julius Stockhausen, Programme 386, Universitätsbibliothek J. C. Senckenberg, University of Frankfurt.

44. "Die ganze 'Dichterliebe' von Robert Schumann durchzusingen, ist ein verlockendes Experiment; es war ein gelungenes, wie die Aufnahme zeigte, dennoch möchten wir es nicht gerade gutheißen. Eigenartig, fein und geistvoll, wie sie ist, webt die Musik dieses Liederkreises doch in einem zu dämmerigen, gebrochenen Lichte, um nicht als Ganzes schließlich etwas abzustumpfen. Keine Nothwendigkeit, nicht einmal eine starke innere Nöthigung zwingt uns aber, diese 15 Lieder als ein Ganzes aufzufassen und vorzutragen" (Feuilleton Musik, *Neue freie Presse* 1281, March 24, 1868, n.p.).

45. Goehr, *Imaginary Museum*, vi. This type of aesthetic contemplation is explained in *Imaginary Museum*, 168–70. See also Daniel Chua, *Absolute Music and the Construction of Meaning* (Cambridge: Cambridge University Press, 2006), 6. Chua reminds us that absolute music is constructed through language, the very thing it rejects, and he therefore writes against the tendency.

46. Thus, for Chua, it is opera, and not song, that "sings in an unsung world as nostalgia for an ancient age enchanted by music" (*Absolute Music*, 29).

47. Goehr, *Imaginary Museum*, 215–8.

48. See Kravitt, *The Lied*, 4–5.

49. Goehr, *Imaginary Museum*, 89.

50. The concert took place in Hamburg on January 6, 1878. See *Allgemeine musikalische Zeitung* 13, no. 2 (January 9, 1878), col. 29. The review is quoted in Beatrix Borchard, *Stimme und Geige: Amalie und Joseph Joachim; Biographie und Interpretationsgeschichte* (Vienna: Böhlau, 2007), 333.

51. The soloists were Imogen Cooper and Stephan Loges. Cooper performed "Äußerst bewegt, Sehr langsam" after the first eight songs, and "Sehr rasch" after song eleven, "Ein Jüngling liebt ein Mädchen."

52. Kevin Korsyn, "Beyond Privileged Contexts: Intertextuality, Influence, and Dialogue," in *Rethinking Music*, ed. Nicholas Cook and Mark Everist (Oxford: Oxford University Press, 2001), 55. Korsyn is particularly eloquent on the notion of a text as a network (surely the case here) of intersections and transformations.

53. David Ferris, *Schumann's Eichendorff Liederkreis and the Genre of the Romantic Cycle* (Oxford: Oxford University Press, 2000), 25–58. For a rebuttal, see Berthold Hoeckner, "Paths through *Dichterliebe*," *19th-Century Music* 30, no. 1 (2006): 65–80.

54. See Beate Perrey, *Schumann's* Dichterliebe *and Early Romantic Poets: Fragmentation of Desire* (Cambridge: Cambridge University Press, 2002).

55. Ferris comes close to approaching this thorny question in *Schumann's Eichendorff Liederkreis*, 28. He quotes Arthur Komar, who argues that *any* sixteen songs in related keys might be arranged to form a cycle. Similarly, transposition in performance or recording might create or destroy coherences that pertain only to the score in its original keys.

56. Ronyak et al., "Studying the Lied," 543–82.

57. Ronyak et al., "Studying the Lied," 545.
58. Ronyak et al., "Studying the Lied," 558.

Bibliography

Bernhart, Walter, Werner Wolf, and David Mosley, eds., *Essays on the Song Cycle and on Defining the Field*. Amsterdam: Rodopi, 2001.

Borchard, Beatrix. "Botschafter der reinen Kunst—vom Virtuosen zum Interpreten: Joseph Joachim und Clara Schumann." *Basler Jahrbuch für historische Musikpraxis* 20 (1996): 95–114.

———. "Die Sängerin Amalie Joachim und *Die schöne Müllerin* von Franz Schubert." In *Frauen- und Männerbilder in der Musik*, edited by Freia Hoffmann, 69–80. Oldenburg, Ger.: Universität Oldenburg, 2000.

———. "Öffentliche Intimität? Konzertgesang in der zweiten Hälfte des 19. Jahrhunderts." In *Musikbezogene Genderforschung, Lieder Singen, Studien zur Aufführungsgeschichte des Liedes*, edited by Katharina Hottmann, 109–26. Hildesheim, Ger.: Olms Weidmann, 2012.

———. *Stimme und Geige: Amalie und Joseph Joachim; Biographie und Interpretationsgeschichte*. Vienna: Böhlau, 2007.

Chua, Daniel. *Absolute Music and the Construction of Meaning*. Cambridge: Cambridge University Press, 2006.

Daverio, John. "The Song Cycle: Journeys through a Romantic Landscape." In *German Lieder in the Nineteenth Century*, edited by Rufus Hallmark, with an afterword by David Ferris, 363–404. 2nd ed. New York: Routledge, 2010.

Dürr, Walther. *Das deutsche Sololied im 19. Jahrhundert: Untersuchungen zu Sprache und Musik*. Wilhelmshaven, Ger.: F. Noetzel, 2002.

Ferris, David. *Schumann's Eichendorff Liederkreis and the Genre of the Romantic Cycle*. Oxford: Oxford University Press, 2000.

Goehr, Lydia. *The Imaginary Museum of Musical Works: An Essay in the Philosophy of Music*. Oxford: Oxford University Press, 2008.

Gramit, David. "The Circulation of the Lied: The Double Life of an Artwork and a Commodity." In *The Cambridge Companion to the Lied*, edited by James Parsons, 299–314. Cambridge: Cambridge University Press, 2004.

Hallmark, Rufus, ed. *German Lieder in the Nineteenth Century*. 2nd ed. Revised by David Ferris. New York: Routledge, 2010.

Hanslick, Eduard. *Geschichte des Concertwesens in Wien*. Vol. 2, *Aus dem Concertsaal: Kritiken und Schilderungen aus den letzten 20 Jahren des Wiener Musiklebens*. Vienna: Braumüller, 1870).

Hoeckner, Berthold. "Paths through *Dichterliebe*." *19th-Century Music* 30, no. 1 (2006): 65–80.

Hofmann, Renate. *Johannes Brahms Briefwechsel*. Vol. 18, *Johannes Brahms im Briefwechsel mit Julius Stockhausen*. Tutzing, Ger.: Hans Schneider, 1993.

———."Julius Stockhausen als Interpret der Liederzyklen Robert Schumanns." *Schumann-Forschungen* 9 (2005): 34–46.

Hofmann, Renate and Kurt. *Johannes Brahms als Pianist und Dirigent: Chronologie seines Wirkens als Interpret*. Tutzing, Ger.: Hans Schneider, 2006.

Jansen, F. Gustav. *Robert Schumanns Briefe: Neue Folge.* 2nd ed. Leipzig: Breitkopf and Härtel, 1904.
Kopiez, Reinhard, Andreas Lehmann, and Janina Klassen. "Clara Schumann's Collection of Playbills: A Historiometric Analysis of Life-Span Development, Mobility, and Repertoire Canonization." *Poetics* 37, no. 1 (2009): 50–73.
Korsyn, Kevin. "Beyond Privileged Contexts: Intertextuality, Influence, and Dialogue." In *Rethinking Music*, edited by Nicholas Cook and Mark Everist, 55–72. Oxford: Oxford University Press, 2001.
Kravitt, Edward. *The Lied: Mirror of Late Romanticism.* New Haven, CT: Yale University Press, 1996.
———. "The Lied in 19th-Century Concert Life." *Journal of the American Musicological Society* 18, no. 2 (1965): 207–18.
Leistra-Jones, Karen. "Staging Authenticity: Joachim, Brahms, and the Politics of *Werktreue* Performance." *Journal of the American Musicological Society* 66, no. 2 (Summer 2013): 397–436.
Litzmann, Berthold. *Clara Schumann: Ein Künstlerleben; Nach Tagebüchern und Briefen.* 4th ed. 3 vols. Leipzig: Breitkopf and Härtel, 1920.
Loges, Natasha. "Julius Stockhausen's Early Performances of Franz Schubert's *Die schöne Müllerin.*" *19th-Century Music* 41, no. 3 (Spring 2018): 206–24.
———. "The Limits of the Lied." In *Brahms in the Home and the Concert Hall: Between Private and Public Performance*, edited by Katy Hamilton and Natasha Loges, 300–23. Cambridge: Cambridge University Press, 2014.
Perrey, Beate. *Schumann's Dichterliebe and Early Romantic Poets: Fragmentation of Desire.* Cambridge: Cambridge University Press, 2002.
Reich, Nancy. *Clara Schumann: The Artist and the Woman.* Ithaca, NY: Cornell University Press, 2001.
Ronyak, Jennifer, Benjamin Binder, Laura Tunbridge, Wayne Heisler Jr., Kira Thurman, and Jonathan Dunsby. "Studying the Lied: Hermeneutic Traditions and the Challenge of Performance," *Journal of the American Musicological Society* 67, no. 2 (Summer 2014): 543–82.
Sietz, Reinhold. *Aus Ferdinand Hillers Briefwechsel: Beiträge zu einer Biographie Ferdinand Hillers.* 7 vols. Cologne, Ger.: Arno, 1968.
Signale für die musikalische Welt. "Ein reizendes, ganz prächtig den gemüthlichen Soirée-Character innehaltendes Programm." Dur und Moll. Unsigned review of December 6, 1862, concert. 20, no. 51 (December 11, 1862): 709.
Weber, William. *The Great Transformation of Musical Taste: Concert Programming from Haydn to Brahms.* Cambridge: Cambridge University Press, 2008.
Wirth, Julia. *Julius Stockhausen, der Sänger des deutschen Liedes: Nach Dokumenten seiner Zeit dargestellt.* Frankfurt: Englert and Schlosser, 1927.

NATASHA LOGES is Head of Postgraduate Programmes at the Royal College of Music. She is author of *Brahms and His Poets: A Handbook* and coeditor of *Brahms in the Home and the Concert Hall: Between Private and Public Performance*; *Brahms in Context*; and *Musical Salon Culture in the Long Nineteenth Century.*

4 Natalia Macfarren and the English German Lied

Katy Hamilton

> She sang, of course, *"M'ama!"* and not "he loves me," an unalterable and unquestioned law of the musical world required that the German text of French operas sung by Swedish artists should be translated into Italian for the clearer understanding of English-speaking audiences.
>
> —Edith Wharton, *The Age of Innocence*, 1920[1]

> English texts have nothing to do with German songs. Why don't you say that it's necessary for your catalogue and sales in England? Then I don't mind.
>
> —Johannes Brahms to Fritz Simrock, February 24, 1887[2]

ALTHOUGH THE LIED is now primarily identified by the majority of its admirers as a public concert genre (or at the very least, a recorded genre for private consumption), the nineteenth-century conception of song was inextricably bound up with the amateur, the domestic, and the joy of a medium with which music lovers could engage themselves. In an age before recording, the Lied—along with choral music and works for piano solo and duet, above all—allowed for music lovers to *participate*.[3] The wish to play and sing such a repertoire was not, however, necessarily limited to the country in which it had been composed, and as international transport and communication networks became increasingly sophisticated during the century, both musicians and their compositions traveled more and more widely. For instrumental music, the journey presented few problems, as publishers formed alliances across countries to disseminate and advertise new works that could appear largely unchanged. For vocal music, however, the challenge was more substantial: how could a non-German speaker be expected to buy and sing a Lied that they could not understand? Although opera houses often had specific rules about the accepted languages in which works could be performed, there was no similar regulation in place for song (or indeed choral repertoire).[4] A combination of practical expediency and business sense, both from the publishers of new music and those who were in the business of reissuing older works, led to the creation of a substantial industry in translating the Lieder of Schubert, Schumann, Brahms, and others for performance in languages other than German. This chapter provides an account of the career and approaches of one particularly prolific translator, a German-born singer who spent most of her life in England: Natalia Andrae (1826–1916), later Lady Macfarren. By considering the breadth of Macfarren's activities and comparing her versions of Schubert's "Erlkönig," D328, and Brahms's *Liebeslieder-Walzer*, op. 52, with other English-language renditions, it is hoped that insights might be gained into the practical and aesthetic problems of producing Lied scores in singable translation.

Born in Lübeck in December 1826, Natalia Andrae was the daughter of a German bandmaster who seems to have brought the family to England in the 1830s and become attached to a British regiment.[5] Natalia subsequently enrolled at the Royal Academy of Music in September 1841, at the age of fourteen, to study singing. That she left again in May 1842 was probably due to the scandal of her blossoming romance with Academy professor George Alexander Macfarren (1813–87), whom she married in 1844 (he was thirteen years her senior).[6] She subsequently enjoyed a brief career as a professional contralto and performed in her husband's opera *King Charles II* in 1849, the year after the birth of their daughter.[7] She then retired from the concert platform to teach, and above all, to translate. She published her *Elementary Course for Vocalising and Pronouncing the English Language* in 1868, and her first singable English translations seem to date from the following year, a volume of songs and duets by Anton Rubinstein that appeared in 1869.[8] By the late 1870s, she had become one of the most prolific translators on the British musical scene.

The majority of Macfarren's translations were carried out for Novello and Company, whose considerable catalogue consisted primarily of choral and church repertoire. They also, however, published instrumental music (particularly for piano) and vocal albums, for which Macfarren was one of the principal translators. She also is credited with selecting and even adapting some of the songs in each volume.[9] She was one of the principal translators for this series as well, along with the Reverend John Troutbeck.[10] Indeed, the occupations of her fellow translators provide an intriguing glimpse into this world: for example, Troutbeck was a precentor of Westminster Abbey; Robert Henry Benson was a merchant banker and member of council at the Royal College of Music; and Constance Bache was a composer and pianist whose performance career was curtailed after she suffered an injury to her right hand.[11] Macfarren, of course, was extremely well connected with the musical world through her husband, who had been a conductor at Covent Garden and a friend of Mendelssohn and was a distinguished teacher and scholar. In other words, these translators were all connected with the musical world, mostly indirectly, and the women who undertook translation work were themselves musically trained and yet out of the direct limelight of public performance. These were well-educated people, either with other principal sources of income or with private wealth to support them. This sort of translation work seems to have been a respectable occupation for the cultured, therefore, rather than an independent profession.

Macfarren's work for Novello included the translation of songs by Weber, Dvořák, Beethoven, Franz, Schumann, Schubert, Mendelssohn, Rubinstein, and Tchaikovsky. When Novello began their new series of operatic vocal scores in 1871, it was Macfarren who was called on to translate a string of major works, including Beethoven's *Fidelio*; Bellini's *La Sonnambula*, *I Puritani*, and *Norma*; Donizetti's *Lucia di Lamermoor*; Mozart's *Don Giovanni* and *Die Zauberflöte*; Rossini's *Il barbiere di Siviglia*; Verdi's *Il Trovatore*, *La Traviata*, and *Rigoletto*; and Weber's *Oberon* and *Der Freischütz*.[12] In a number of cases, Macfarren was identified not only as the translator but also the editor of these vocal scores—and they suggest a considerable grasp of Italian, as well as her native German. It is probable that she was concerned with working principally from these two languages. (It is not clear from the Novello records, but it seems likely that the two Auber operas she translated might have been given to her in Italian or even German, rather than French.) Certainly, her translations of songs from seemingly more exotic languages, such as Grieg's songs, were made from German-language versions, not the original Norwegian.[13] She also contributed English versions of a number of large-scale choral compositions, including works by Max Bruch and Ferdinand Hiller, and the text of *An die Freude* for Beethoven's Ninth Symphony. Her translation work extended as far as musical textbooks: namely, Eduard Devrient's *Meine Erinnerungen an Felix Mendelssohn-Bartholdy und seine Briefe an mich* and Adolf Bernhard Marx's *Die Musik des neunzehnten Jahrhunderts und ihre Pflege*.[14]

A sizable proportion of Macfarren's translation work, therefore, was concerned with rendering the texts of songs by composers who were no longer living. Hence there could be no interference from the work's creator, and editions were produced by publishing houses with the intention of reaching a new audience who could not understand the source text (with the English words sometimes appearing alone, or above the original). Schubert's "Erlkönig" provides a useful example of the tactics and solutions Macfarren employed in her task, and the particular challenges of rendering German poetry singable in another language.

Schubert's "Erlkönig": Scott to Macfarren

Although it was the later nineteenth century that saw a major boom in the production of English-language Lieder publications, certain songs had already appeared in translation in the earlier 1800s. Franz Schubert's opus 1, "Erlkönig," D328, was issued by Wessel and Company in 1832, having been "sung with

Fig. 4.1. Opening vocal line of Schubert's Erlkönig with Walter Scott translation in underlay. Published by Wessel & Company, 1832.

great applause" in London, so the title page tells us, by Wilhelmine Schröder-Devrient.[15] Both German and English texts are given in this edition, carefully produced for the purpose—but the overall effect is tremendously confusing for the simple reason that the English version was not in fact written to be sung. Instead, Sir Walter Scott's translation of Goethe's poem, produced without any thought to musical rendition, had been shoehorned into the score and necessitated a complete rewrite of the vocal rhythm in order to accommodate it.

One of the principal difficulties of producing singable translations from German (and indeed French) is the lack of equivalent words in English that have the same rhythmic construction—above all, two-syllable verb forms with a weak second syllable.[16] For this reason, almost every English-language rendition of "Erlkönig" involves some alteration to the sung rhythm of Schubert's original. The Scott translation, however, demonstrates an exceptional level of alteration, and it is perhaps an indication of a practice in its infancy (as well as a fascinating insight into the lack of a notion of *Werktreue* as we would now apply it) that it was thought appropriate to issue such a wildly different vocal line in 1832. Scott's translation was still in print up to midcentury, albeit with minor alterations;[17] but after 1850, several new English versions appeared on the market that adhered more closely to Schubert's score. This suggests a growing appetite for Lieder in

English that reflected the original rhyme schemes as closely as possible—a skill for which Macfarren is repeatedly praised in the musical press and that surely contributed to her professional dominance in this area of activity.

In 1884, Macfarren translated "Erlkönig" for Novello as part of an album of Schubert Lieder for soprano or tenor voice. The song was singled out as among her finest texts of the volume, and it is given here in full (table 4.1), alongside Goethe's German and Scott's literary rendition.[18]

Macfarren's translation is remarkably close to Goethe's original in its details, and it is particularly impressive that she is able to match the descriptions the father gives of mists, rustling leaves, and willow trees; other writers often altered them to solve metrical difficulties. Even Scott, unencumbered by the need to match a musical rhythm, embroiders the original in a rather gothic manner with "'Twas but the wild blast as it howls through the trees" in the fourth verse. She also succeeds in placing the necessary emphasis on the final syllable of the second line of the seventh verse—"I'll take thee by *force*"—to match the sudden leap from *pp* to *fff* in Schubert's score, one of the most crucial dramatic moments of the musical setting.[19] The remainder of the text is largely idiomatic, for all that it relies on contractions of several words to save syllables ("o'er," "thou'rt," "shudd'ring"). There is one line, however, that seems to betray Macfarren's German origins: the structural reversal at the beginning of verse five, "Thou gentle boy, wilt thou with me go?" It seems an odd decision to send the verb to the end here, even to provide a rhyme with *know*, and subsequent translators have negotiated this corner without having to resort to such tactics. Still, the presence of this line could be taken as proof positive that Macfarren really was working carefully and directly from Goethe's text—the work resonates with the workings of Lois Phillips's far more recent *Lieder Line by Line* approach here—rather than aiming for a poetic approximation based on either a limited understanding of the original, or indeed a limited concern to match it in specific details.[20] Although recent German-language critiques of Lieder in translation are predominantly concerned with accuracy and adherence to the original, the very nature of a musical setting can preclude any chance of being truly accurate to the exact textual content of the German.[21] In some cases, the problem is that a phrase is too long, too short, or too awkward to transfer smoothly across languages. Macfarren's sometimes curious manipulation of language can rescue a situation by allowing a closer match to German patterns of emphasis, and it is no doubt for this reason that her texts earned the reputation of reading "so well as scarcely to give the impression that the words are not those to which the music was originally wedded."[22]

Despite the attention that Macfarren evidently paid to her task, the printing of her careful work was not so well managed. The English texts were edited

Table 4.1. Translations of "Erlkönig" by Macfarren, alongside Goethe's original German and Scott's literary rendition.

Goethe poem as set by Schubert	Walter Scott translation (Wessel)	Natalia Macfarren translation (Novello)
Wer reitet so spät durch Nacht und Wind?	O, who rides by night through the woodlands so wild?	Who rides thro' the night o'er woodland wild?
Es ist der Vater mit seinem Kind;	It is the fond father embracing his child,	It is the father with his young child.
Er hat den Knaben wohl in dem Arm,	And close the boy nestles within his lov'd arm,	The boy lies folded close in his arm,
Er fasst ihn sicher, er hält ihn warm.	From the blast of the tempest to keep himself warm.	He holds him steady and safe from harm.
"Mein Sohn, was birgst du so bang dein Gesicht?"—	"O father, see yonder, see yonder," he says	"My son, thou hidest" thy face as in fear?
"Siehst, Vater, du den Erlkönig nicht? Den Erlenkönig mit Kron und Schweif?"	"My boy upon what dost thou fearfully gaze?" "O 'tis the Erl-King with his staff and his shroud"	"The Erlking, father, see he is near, With crown and sceptre, and snow-white shroud."
"Mein Sohn, es ist ein Nebelstreif."—	"No my love 'tis but a dark wreath of the cloud."	"My son, 'tis but a passing cloud."
"Du liebes Kind, komm, geh mit mir! Gar schöne Spiele spiel ich mit dir; Manch bunte Blumen sind an dem Strand, Meine Mutter hat manch gülden Gewand."—	"O will thou go with me thou loveliest child? By many gay sports shall thy hours be beguil'd, My mother keeps for thee full many a fair toy, And many fine flow'rs shall she pluck for my boy."	"My gentle boy, oh come with me, I'll sport and play the day long with thee, And wondrous flowers shalt thou behold, And a garment shalt thou wear all of gold."
"Mein Vater, mein Vater, und hörest du nicht, Was Erlenkönig mir leise verspricht?"— "Sei ruhig, bleibe ruhig, mein Kind; In dürren Blättern säuselt der Wind."—	"O father, my father, and did you not hear, The Erl-King whispers so close in my ear?" "Be still my lov'd child, be at ease, 'Twas but the wild blast as it howls through the trees.'	"My father, my father, oh dost thou not hear What Erlking whispers so soft in mine ear?" "Nay fear not, it is nothing, my child, The leaves but rustle sharp o'er the wild."

(continued)

Table 4.1. *(continued)*

Goethe poem as set by Schubert	Walter Scott translation (Wessel)	Natalia Macfarren translation (Novello)
"Willst, feiner Knabe, du mit mir gehn? Meine Töchter sollen dich warten schön; Meine Töchter führen den nächtlichen Reihn Und wiegen und tanzen und singen dich ein."	"O wilt thou go with me, thou loveliest boy, My daughter shall tend thee with care and with joy; She shall bear thee so lightly thro' wet and thro' wild, And hug thee, and kiss thee, and sing to my child."	"Thou gentle boy, wilt thou with me go? My daughters all pretty pastimes know, My daughters nightly their gay revels keep, They'll dance and they'll sing and they'll rock thee to sleep."
"Mein Vater, mein Vater, und siehst du nicht dort Erlkönigs Töchter am düstern Ort?"	"O father, my father and saw you not plain, Th'Erl King's pale daughter glide fast through the rain?"	"My father, my father, I feel sore afraid, See Erlking's daughters in yon dark shade!"
"Mein Sohn, mein Sohn, ich seh es genau: Es scheinen die alten Weiden so grau."	"O no, my hearts treasure, I knew it full soon, It was the grey willow that danc'd to the moon."	"My son, my son, I see it full well, The grey knotted willows bend to the gale."
"Ich liebe dich, mich reizt deine schöne Gestalt; Und bist du nicht willig, so brauch ich Gewalt."— "Mein Vater, mein Vater, jetzt fasst er mich an! Erlkönig hat mir ein Leids getan!"—	"Come with me, no longer delay, Or else silly child I will drag thee away." "Oh, father! Oh, father! Now, now keep your hold, The Erl-King has seiz'd me, his grasp is so cold."	"I love thee, child, in vain wouldst thou now be perverse, For if thou'rt not willing I'll take thee by force." "My father, my father, his cold hand I feel! Erlking has hurt me, with grasp strong as steel."
Dem Vater grauset's, er reitet geschwind, Er hält in Armen das ächzende Kind, Erreicht den Hof mit Müh' und Not: In seinen Armen das Kind war tot.	Sore trembled the father, he spurr'd through the wild, Clasping close to his bosom his shuddering child. He reaches his dwelling in doubt and in dread, But clasp'd to his bosom the infant was dead.	The father shudd'ring gives spur to his steed, Holds fast his darling, and groans in his need. He reach'd his home in doubt and dread, Within his fond arms the child lay dead.

for consistency and punctuation: but a striking number of them seem to have been rushed into print without proper proofreading, and errors and omissions abound. Errors are particularly noticeable in "Erlkönig" for the simple reason that it contains so many spoken lines, and quotation marks often appear almost arbitrarily in the English texts. Even the eponymous villain's name is rendered in several ways ("Erl-King," "Erl-king," "Erlking") within the same printing. It might be argued that, with no living composer to supervise good presentation, publishing houses might well see no reason to be very particular, but translations of songs by living composers could also suffer in this way. Almost all such translations were at publishers' initiative, undertaken primarily for financial gain and reputation building abroad, with a clear goal of maximizing profits and minimizing costs. This was as true for the songs of Johannes Brahms (just seven years Macfarren's junior) as it was for the posthumous editions of Schubert's Lieder; and in the case of Brahms's Lieder, translations were often simply added into the German first edition. The resulting publications are often rather cramped in their presentation of bilingual texts, the English squeezed into what had initially been a spacious German-only score. Title pages were mostly designed only to allow space for German text in various striking fonts, and it was not always possible to even credit the translator on the front of the piece as a result. This entirely utilitarian approach—pragmatic at best, and penny-pinching at worst—stands at odds with the effort expended by Macfarren and her contemporaries to find the most effective way of rendering such Lieder into singable English.

Brahms's *Liebeslieder*, op. 52: Macfarren's Translation as Model

All four of Brahms's principal publishers (Breitkopf and Härtel, Peters, Rieter-Biedermann, and Simrock) formed associations with publishing houses in Britain to distribute scores, and each had its own preferred translators.[23] The size of the amateur market, and its commercial value to publishers and composers, made adaptability the key to success. To this end, translations were not unlike arrangements in their potential to reach a considerable number of people beyond the confines of a piece in its original form.[24] Brahms himself had suggested performative adaptability in the *Liebeslieder* by marking the vocal parts "ad libitum"; he later created a piano-only version, and various other arrangers were then commissioned by Simrock to provide scores for a range of instruments and voices.[25] In the same way, translations could carry Lieder beyond the confines of the German-speaking world—but in Brahms's case, at least, the enterprise was very much at the behest of the publisher, rather than the composer.

Brahms's remarks on printed translations are not numerous, but they indicate an impatience with the commercial necessity of producing something that he apparently considered to be artistically worthless. In a brief argument with Fritz Simrock in 1887, he first stated categorically that "English texts have nothing to do with German songs"[26] before expanding on the subject in a subsequent letter:

> Even if you had nothing else to think about, I don't understand why you would even speak one word *in favor* of the English text. Except that it's there now, and can't easily be taken away. But if it were possible, due to other extensive changes, to remove it, I would ask you to think the thing over once more. The German song that I compose has absolutely nothing to do with the English translation; that is only stuck on afterwards by the publisher—there is nothing further to say about it.... I beg you to remember that I, personally, cannot get excited about it! ... Apologies for the endless grumbling, but it is truly meant in a good and friendly way.[27]

Although Brahms responded to a request from Macfarren, via Elisabeth von Herzogenberg, for an album leaf (the mirror canon *Mir lächelt kein Frühling*, WoO25), he does not appear to have been directly in contact with any of his translators.[28] Thus, all the negotiations for translated versions of his works—such as the *Liebeslieder*, op. 52—were handled entirely through the publishing house.

Simrock, responsible for issuing the majority of Brahms's compositions, commissioned Macfarren to make translations for the second printings of many of his vocal works. She produced the first English versions of the *Schicksalslied*, op. 54; *Gesang der Parzen*, op. 89; *Zwei Motetten*, op. 74; *Sieben Lieder für Chor*, op. 62; four of his duet collections, *Gesänge für Frauenchor*, op. 17; both books of *Liebeslieder*, opp. 52 and 65; and fifteen opera of solo Lieder—more than 130 items in all.[29] Thanks to the production of these English-language versions, Brahms's growing popularity in England in the 1860s and 1870s as an instrumental composer (initially through performance of his chamber works, and later, above all, thanks to the *St-Antoni Variations*, op. 56a) could be supplemented by the increasing availability of his Lieder, now accessible to non-German-speakers for performance at home.[30] It is particularly striking that, after the significant success of Brahms's *Liebeslieder*, op. 52, in both Austro-Germany and England, the *Neue Liebeslieder*, op. 65, are the only composition of Brahms's to be published bilingually in the very first printing that Simrock issued, in 1875.[31] Indeed, the model of the *Liebeslieder* was to be profoundly influential on the next generation of British composers, with Charles Stanford, Walford Davies, Ernest Walker, and Liza Lehmann all writing collections for four singers and piano *à la* Brahms.[32]

The first song of the cycle, "Rede, Mädchen," is largely presented as a dialogue between the tenor and bass, who begin the song, and the soprano and alto—the voice of the "Mädchen" whom they are entreating. Since all eighteen of the *Liebeslieder* are written in waltz meter, the translation needs to match the lilting rhythm of the German to prevent incorrect accentuation and hinder the sense of the dance. This Macfarren achieves very gracefully, but at the expense of matching the rhyme scheme of Daumer's German (see table 4.2). Instead, she implements her own entirely idiosyncratic rhyming pattern that neatly aligns with aspects of the musical setting. Brahms himself seems relatively unconcerned with drawing out Daumer's rhymes, particularly in the second and third verses: in the second, the soprano and alto entry overlay the men's "komme" (to rhyme with "Überfromme"), and in the third, the women's "grüßen" (to rhyme with "büßen") is obscured by the men's repeat of "komme" at the bottom of the vocal texture. Macfarren's translation seems geared toward a happier resolution in the last line of the song, since by setting the second verse to the rhyme scheme ABCC, the men's repeated "wilt thou meet me?" now aligns directly with the women's "I'll meet thee" at the end of the third verse, and all four singers agree on their final vowel.[33]

Furthermore, since Brahms repeats part of the song's eighth line ("Oder willst du, *willst du*, daß ich komme?"), Macfarren can establish a repeat of "wilt thou" at this stage of the piece, which can then be revisited in the men's repetition of this line at the end of the text—a sleight of hand that avoids the problem of finding an exact equivalent for the repeated German words, "daß ich komme." This kind of reshuffling across parts, with shortened or repeated phrases in different voices, is one of the chief difficulties in creating a smooth and functional translation of the *Liebeslieder* (see example 4.1).

The sixth of the *Liebeslieder*, "Ein kleiner, hübscher Vogel" (example 4.2), poses slightly different problems. The tenor has a prominent role in delivering the narrative in this song, but the light, bouncing nature of Brahms's setting plays with the poem by frequently dividing two-syllable words using rests and melodic leaps.

As is evident from both "Erlkönig" and "Rede, Mädchen," translators are often able to derive a certain amount of latitude from matching the strong and weak emphases of an original text, but without using words of equivalent numbers of syllables (particularly since two-syllable verbs are considerably more common in German than in English). Such a divide here, however, would risk disturbing the musical effect that Brahms has set in motion. And there is also the more fundamental problem of finding a suitable English equivalent to *Vogel*. Macfarren's solutions for "kleine, hübscher Vogel" and "Rede, Mädchen" are shown in tables 4.2 and 4.3.

Macfarren succeeds in maintaining the hopping two-syllable pattern of the German, by losing a few direct equivalences ("kleiner" to "once a," "Garten" to

Example 4.1. Johannes Brahms, *Liebeslieder-Walzer*, op. 52 no. 1, "Rede Mädchen," measures 31–56 vocal parts, with German and English underlay.

Table 4.2. "Rede, Mädchen" (Georg Friedrich Daumer) with Macfarren translation.

1. Rede, Mädchen (Daumer)	Macfarren translation
Rede, Mädchen, allzu liebes,	Oh give answer, maiden fairest,
Das mir in die Brust, die kühle,	Thou whose smile my heart entrances,
Hat geschleudert mit dem Blicke	Who hast slain me with thy glances,
Diese wilden Glutgefühle!	Tell me, hath thy heart relented?
Willst du nicht dein Herz erweichen,	Or like cloister'd nun, contented,
Willst du, eine Überfromme,	Wilt thou dwell by love forsaken?
Rasten ohne traute Wonne,	Say, how long must I entreat thee,
Oder willst du, [willst du], daß ich komme?	Say, oh fairest, [wilt thou], wilt thou meet me?
Rasten ohne traute Wonne,	Nay, to dwell by love forsaken,
Nicht so bitter will ich büßen.	Were a doom for which I care not.
Komme nur, du schwarzes Auge,	Wistful eyes, take heart, despair not,
Komme, wenn die Sterne grüßen.	When the stars are bright I'll meet thee.
[Willst du daß ich komme?]	[Say, oh wilt thou meet me, wilt thou meet me?]

Source: Macfarren: J. Brahms, *Liebeslieder. Songs of Love* Op. 52 (Berlin: N. Simrock & London: Stanley Lucas, Weber & Co., 1874). Translated into English by Mrs. Natalia Macfarren.

Table 4.3. "Ein kleiner, hübscher Vogel" (Georg Friedrich Daumer) with Macfarren translation.

Ein kleiner, hübscher Vogel (Daumer)	Macfarren translation
Ein kleiner, hübscher Vogel nahm den Flug	Was once a pretty tiny birdie flew
Zum Garten hin, da gab es Obste genug.	Where fruit in garden fair hung bright to view.
Wenn ich ein hübscher, kleiner Vogel wär,	If that a pretty tiny bird I were,
Ich säumte nicht, ich täte so wie der.	I'd fly away and seek yon garden fair.
Leimruten-Arglist lauert an dem Ort;	Limetwigs and trech'ry all its branches bore,
Der arm Vogel konnte nicht mehr fort.	Ah hapless birdie, thou wilt fly no more!
Wenn ich ein hübscher, kleiner Vogel wär,	If that a pretty tiny bird I were,
Ich säumte doch, ich täte nicht wie der.	I think of yonder garden I'd beware.
Der Vogel kam in eine schöne Hand,	That birdie came in hand of ladye bright,
Da tat es ihm, dem Glücklichen, nicht and.	And there he had full store of fond delight.
Wenn ich ein hübscher, kleiner Vogel wär,	If that a pretty tiny bird were I,
Ich säumte nicht, ich täte doch wie der.	Like him to yonder garden straight I'd fly.

Source: Macfarren: J. Brahms, *Liebeslieder. Songs of Love* Op. 52 (Berlin: N. Simrock & London: Stanley Lucas, Weber & Co., 1874). Translated into English by Mrs. Natalia Macfarren.

Example 4.2. Johannes Brahms, *Liebeslieder-Walzer*, op. 52 no. 6, "Ein kleiner, hübscher Vogel," measures 3–13, tenor part only, with German underlay.

Example 4.3. Johannes Brahms, *Liebeslieder-Walzer*, op. 52 no. 6, "Ein kleiner, hübscher Vogel," measures 3–13, tenor part only, with English underlay.

"fruit in," "genug" to "to view") and by adding some extras ("birdie," "garden"). The overall effect is to retain the sense of split words that Brahms has set up (see example 4.3).

The translation of "Vogel" as "birdie" appears to have been a standard rendering at this date and seems not to have carried the somewhat childish associations that it now has. The rhyme scheme of the English matches that of the German, and the "Leimruten-Arglist" of the second verse, sometimes known as birdlime (a sticky substance used to trap birds as they land on treated branches), is rendered as obliquely in English as it is in the German. Brahms's setting includes multiple repetitions of the phrase "nicht fort," halfway through this verse, echoing between voices and piano, as the bird is held fast in the branches of the tree. The harmonies beneath the singers, in a gentle musical pun on the text, are gradually shifted and realigned to allow the music to continue. Macfarren's "no more" is not quite the ideal analogue to the German—but it is difficult to see which two English syllables might work better. (A Novello translation by W. G. Rothery has "You're caught!" but this also doesn't line up with Brahms's little musical joke.)[34] Macfarren is more successful at the very end of the song, when the repeated "wie der" is rendered as "I'd fly."

The later translations appended to "Rede, Mädchen," by Lockwood and Barker, owe much to Macfarren's work (table 4.4). Certain words and ideas are carried across directly—indeed, Lockwood's translation is so heavily indebted to Macfarren that the two texts in the table are virtually identical. Barker's 1955 translation actually adds more archaic language, rather than removing what might seem to be the old-fashioned components of Macfarren's earlier efforts (e.g., the rhyming pair "ensnarest" and "impairest" in the first verse). The image of the cloistered nun remains from 1875, even though it is not present in the original German. Barker is more ambitious, however, in "Ein kleiner, hübscher Vogel" (table 4.5), where he takes the opportunity to add text to the repetition of "Da tat es ihm, dem Glücklichen, nicht." He further varies the repetitions of "wie der" at the end, with the singers repeatedly declaring "Ah me!" until their final tutti, "Not me!" In this regard, then, Barker takes far greater liberties with Brahms's setting of Daumer's words—the chasm between the Lied and the translation is, as Brahms had grumbled to Simrock decades earlier, sufficient that there are places where the two are simply not directly connected.

Macfarren continued to produce singable English-language versions of vocal repertoire until at least the late 1880s, and many of her opera translations were subsequently reissued by Schirmer in the early 1900s.[35] The following generation of music translators, however, sought to take a different approach to the "problem" of translation. Writers such as Edward Dent and Arthur Fox-Strangways sought to adjust not only the words, as Macfarren had done, but also the cultural concepts of German poetry for British sensibilities, even aiming to "improve" on what they considered to be the simplistic approach of poets such as Wilhelm Müller.[36] Furthermore, the outbreak of World War I was to have a tremendous effect on the reception of German musical and poetic culture in Britain.[37] And even after the war, commentators seemed unable to conceive of how sung translations might benefit an audience, tying themselves in knots as they increasingly privileged both the sound and poetic depth of an original text, even to the point of absurdity, rather than focusing on the practical advantages of understanding what was being said. As Herbert Peyser observed in 1922, discussing the difficulty of singing such simple lines in Italian operas as "Apri la finestra" (Open the window) without it sounding trite and unpoetic, "to sing a sentiment is to idealize it; but to

Table 4.4. "Rede, Mädchen" translations by Natalia Macfarren, Elizabeth M. Lockwood, and George Barker.

Rede, Mädchen (Macfarren translation)	Rede, Mädchen (Elisabeth M. Lockwood translation)	Rede, Mädchen (George Barker translation)
Oh give answer, maiden fairest, Thou whose smile my heart entrances, Who hast slain me with thy glances, Tell me, hath thy heart relented?	Oh give answer, maiden fairest, Thou whose smile my heart entrances, Who hast slain me with thy glances, Tell me, hath thy heart relented?	Tell me maiden, oh my fairest, Thou whose smile my soul ensnarest, Who hast slain me with thy glances, Who thyself my joy impairest.
Or like cloister'd nun, contented, Wilt thou dwell by love forsaken? Say, how long must I entreat thee, Say, oh fairest, wilt thou meet me?	Or like cloister'd nun, contented, Wilt thou dwell by love forsaken? Say, how long must I entreat thee, Say, oh fairest, wilt thou meet me?	Will thy heart be ever hidden Like a cloistered nun unheeding? Must I sing these songs unbidden? Ever, ever silent to my pleading?
Nay, to dwell by love forsaken, Were a doom for which I care not. Wistful eyes, take heart, despair not, When the stars are bright I'll meet thee. [Say, oh wilt thou meet me?]	Nay, to dwell by love forsaken, Give a doom for which I care not. Wistful eyes, take heart, despair not, When the stars are bright I'll meet thee. [Say, oh wilt thou meet me?]	In retreat thou shouldst not languish; Canst thou never, never meet me? Let thine eyes behold my anguish; Come, oh come where the stars can greet thee. [Wilt thou ever greet me.]

Sources: Macfarren: J. Brahms, *Liebeslieder. Songs of Love Op. 52* (Berlin: N. Simrock & London: Stanley Lucas, Weber & Co., 1874). Translated into English by Mrs. Natalia Macfarren. Lockwood: J. Brahms, *Love Song Waltzes Op. 52 for piano duet (with solo and mixed voices ad libitum). Vocal Score* (London: Alfred Lengnick & Co., n.d.). English version by Elisabeth M. Lockwood. N.B. Since this edition uses the old Simrock plates, there is no separate plate number for the edition, which makes it very difficult to date. It seems likely to date from ca. 1910. Barker: J. Brahms, *Love Song Waltzes Op. 52 for piano duet (with solo and mixed voices ad libitum). Vocal Score. English version by George Barker* (Surrey: Alfred Lengnick & Co, Ltd., 1955).

Table 4.5. "Ein kleiner, hübscher Vogel" translations by Natalia Macfarren, Elizabeth M. Lockwood, and George Barker.

Macfarren translation (1875)	Lockwood translation	Baker translation (1955)
Was once a pretty tiny birdie flew Where fruit in garden fair hung bright to view. If that a pretty tiny bird I were, I'd fly away and seek yon garden fair.	Was once a pretty tiny birdie flew Where fruit in garden fair hung bright to view. If that a pretty tiny bird I were I'd fly away and seek yon garden fair.	A pretty bird so small, who winged his way, Upon an orchard pounced to steal one day. If I a pretty bird so bold could be, Why hesitate to do the same as he?
Limetwigs and trech'ry all its branches bore, Ah, hapless birdie, thou wilt fly no more! If that a pretty tiny bird I were, I think of yonder garden I'd beware.	Limetwigs and trech'ry all its branches bore, Ah, hapless birdie, thou wilt fly no more! If that a pretty tiny bird I were, I think of yonder garden I'd beware.	Limetwigs ensnared him, bitterly he fought: Unhappy bird, surely you are caught-. [He's caught!] If so if I a pretty bird could be, [S/A: And so if I...] I'd hesitate to do the same as he. [Just as he]
That birdie came in hand of ladye bright, And there he had full store of fond delight. If that a pretty tiny bird were I, Like him to yonder garden straight I'd fly. [I'd fly]	That birdie came in hand of ladye bright, And there he had full store of fond delight. If that a pretty tiny bird were I, Like him to yonder garden straight I'd fly. [I'd fly]	How sad to see that bird a captive bound! When suddenly outstretched my lady's [hand*]. Ah happy bird to touch that gentle light. And so if I a pretty bird could be, Why hesitate to do the same as he? [Ah me! Not me!]

Sources: Macfarren: J. Brahms, *Liebeslieder. Songs of Love Op. 52* (Berlin: N. Simrock & London: Stanley Lucas, Weber & Co., 1874). Translated into English by Mrs. Natalia Macfarren. Lockwood: J. Brahms, *Love Song Waltzes Op. 52 for piano duet (with solo and mixed voices ad libitum)*. *Vocal Score* (London: Alfred Lengnick & Co., n.d.). English version by Elisabeth M. Lockwood. N.B. Since this edition uses the old Simrock plates, there is no separate plate number for the edition, which makes it very difficult to date. It seems likely to date from ca. 1910. Barker: J. Brahms, *Love Song Waltzes Op. 52 for piano duet (with solo and mixed voices ad libitum)*. *Vocal Score. English version by George Barker* (Surrey: Alfred Lengnick & Co, Ltd., 1955).

*This word is missing from the printed score—I have simply inferred it from the surrounding text.

idealize the commonplace is to achieve only the sublimation of the ridiculous." He remarks that "if instead of 'open the window' the English audience heard 'Throw wide the casement,' all incentive to mirth would disappear."[38] In other words, an archaic poetic turn of phrase could be a means of retaining a serious sentiment, when the unadorned vernacular could prompt an unwanted comic effect. This change of posture perhaps explains the somewhat inconsistent attitude toward Macfarren's work during this time. Although her archaic turns of phrase may seem faintly risible to modern audiences, and despite her disinclination to improve on the words of her poets, her solutions are skillfully and elegantly rendered, and in some cases the very use of archaic language (where it could be considered poetical rather than simply dated) seems to have appealed to her successors as a means of providing translations with suitable gravitas. Thus, many later writers owe a significant debt to her texts, on which they clearly modeled their own.

Of course, the archaic nature of the *German* is never discussed in concert reviews for the simple reason that, aside from a very few skilled linguists and widely read individuals, a British concert audience still consists, in the main, of people who simply cannot listen to German Lieder with the same acuteness and depth of understanding as a native German speaker. As Leo Black has written, "even if [an Anglophone Lied aficionado] thinks he understands it all, he is most unlikely to be experiencing the words with all the deep emotional resonances that attach to a language and its nuances when one has spoken it since childhood. Too much brainwork is involved, and too little heartwork, so that one should speak of following rather than understanding."[39] Several recent projects to produce new sung English translations of major Lied cycles (such as Jeremy Sams's versions of Schubert's *Die schöne Müllerin*, D795; *Winterreise*, D911; and *Schwanengesang*, D957) suggest that there is still an appetite to hear song in the native language of the audience.[40] Although this is now a practice that will aid listeners far more than singers or pianists (a tiny minority in relation to their nineteenth-century counterparts), the directness—and often, simplicity—of such an approach might offer a way in for new admirers and advocates of this increasingly rarefied genre.

Notes

1. Edith Wharton, *The Age of Innocence* (New York: D. Appleton, 1920), 2–3.
2. Max Kalbeck, ed., *Johannes Brahms Briefwechsel* (Berlin: Deutsch Brahms-Gesellschaft, 1919, repr. Tützing, Ger.: Hans Schneider, 1974), 11: 143.
3. For one composer-specific example of the importance of domestic music making, see Katy Hamilton and Natasha Loges, eds., *Brahms in the Home and the Concert Hall: Between Private and Public Performance* (Cambridge: Cambridge University Press, 2014).

4. This is not to suggest, however, that the regulations around opera houses were straightforward; see, for instance, Lucile Desblache, "Tales of the Unexpected: Opera as a New Art of Globalization" in *Music, Text and Translation*, ed. Helen Minors (London: Bloomsbury Academic, 2013), 9–19.

5. See 1911 census of England, class RG14, piece 585, www.ancestry.co.uk. She was therefore not born, as is usually stated, in 1827. Natalia's father Heinrich Andrae is listed on her wedding certificate of 1844 as a professor of music living at St. Clement Danes. See also Pierre Degott, "Natalia Macfarren (1827–1916): A Nineteenth-Century Translator/Mediator for the Operatic Cause," in *Translators, Interpreters, Mediators. Women Writers 1700–1900*, ed. Gillian Dow (Oxford, UK: Peter Lang, 2007), 225–236.

6. Minutes of the Royal Academy of Music, May 20, 1842. My thanks to Kathy Adamson and Adam Taylor of the Royal Academy of Music for their help in tracing this information.

7. Quite how successful she would have been without the intervention of her husband is difficult to say; she was politely received by the *Times* critics, who mention her participation in a number of concerts at the Hanover Square Rooms, one of Sterndale Bennett's concerts in 1849, and a morning concert at the Royal Italian Opera (that is, Covent Garden) in 1849. *King Charles II* was reviewed by *The Times* on October 29, 1849, 8, where she is singled out for gracious, rather than enthusiastic, praise. The Macfarrens traveled to the United States in 1848, where George conducted a concert of the New York Philharmonic on February 5, 1848. Clarina Thalia, their daughter, was born there on March 23. The New York Philharmonic program can be viewed at the Leon Levy Digital Archives: https://archives.nyphil.org/, 1848 Feb 05 / Special / Macfarren (ID: 10581), accessed September 23, 2018.

8. Natalia Macfarren, *Elementary Course for Vocalising and Pronouncing the English Language* (London: Lamborn Cock, Addison, 1868), is reviewed in the *Musical Times and Singing Class Circular* 13, no. 301 (March 1, 1868): 323. The volume of *Seven Songs* by Anton Rubinstein, published by Novello, Ewer, is also reviewed in the *Musical Times and Singing Class Circular* 14, no. 314 (April 1, 1869): 55. Macfarren is identified as the translator in the details of the volume, but the reviewer makes no comment about her texts.

9. See, for example, *Twenty Songs for a Contralto Voice*, a volume of Schubert Lieder "selected, edited, and translated by Natalia Macfarren" (London: Novello, Ewer, 1882) and *Fourteen Songs* set to poems by Robert Burns, by Robert Franz, which were "edited and adapted by Natalia Macfarren" (London: Novello, Ewer, 1876).

10. This list has been compiled through a search of British Library holdings and review articles featured in *The Times* and the *Musical Times and Singing Class Circular*. Although I have also consulted the Novello Business Archives (also held by the British Library, London: GB-Lbl Add. MSS 69516–69792 and MS.Mus.817–850), none of the commission books includes details of translators' names, except in very rare circumstances—usually when a new translation is being commissioned, to distinguish it from preexisting stock. The list is therefore likely to be incomplete.

11. The Reverend John Troutbeck (1832–99) provided English versions of Bach's *St. Matthew Passion*, *St. John Passion*, and *Christmas Oratorio*, as well as of vocal works by Beethoven, Brahms, Dvořák, and Liszt. Constance Bache (1846–1903) most famously translated Humperdinck's *Hänsel und Gretel* and La Mara's *Letters of Franz Liszt*; her two brothers, Walter and Francis Edward, were also musicians. In addition to these

writers and Robert Henry Benson (1850–1929) is the more mysterious E. M. Traquair, who undertook the first translation of Brahms's *Ein deutsches Requiem*, op. 45. See Bernarr Rainbow and Rosemary Williamson, "Troutbeck, John" in *Grove Music Online: Oxford Music Online* (Oxford: Oxford University Press), accessed January 1, 2017, https://doi.org /10.1093/gmo/9781561592630.article.28475; Nicholas Temperley, "Bache: (3) Constance Bache" in *Grove Music Online: Oxford Music Online* (Oxford: Oxford University Press), accessed January 1, 2017, https://doi.org/10.1093/gmo/9781561592630.article.01697; "Obituary: Miss Constance Bache," *Musical Times and Singing Class Circular* 44, no. 276 (August 1, 1903): 539; *Who Was Who*, online edition, s.v. "Benson, Robert Henry" (Oxford: Oxford University Press, 2014), https://doi.org/10.1093/ww/9780199540884.013.U205982; and Herbert Schneider, "Brahms' Lieder in französischen, englischen und italienischen Übersetzungen: Eine vergleichende Studie," in *Das österreichische Lied und seine Ausstrahlung in Europa*, ed. Pierre Béhar and Herbert Schneider (Hildesheim, Ger.: Georg Olms, 2007), 332–33.

12. The first volumes of this vocal score series (eleven in all) are listed in the Novello commission books on October 27, 1871, for publication over the rest of the year. Other operas for which translations were undertaken by Macfarren were Daniel Auber's *Massaniello* and *Fra Diavolo*, Gaetano Donizetti's *Lucrezia Borgia*, Friedrich von Flotow's *Martha*, and Richard Wagner's *Lohengrin* and *Tannhäuser*. See Novello commission book for April 1867–July 1880, GB-Lbl MS.Mus.819.

13. In this regard, she was certainly not alone among professional translators: in 1934, Edward Dent freely admitted that "when I translated Tchaikovsky's *Eugene Onegin* I collated the German and Italian versions; when they agreed I assumed that they were correct, and when they disagreed I looked up words in a Russian dictionary until I got the sense of the passage, and found out what word came on the important note" (Edward Dent, "The Translation of Operas," *Proceedings of the Musical Association* 61 [1934–35]: 97). See also Beryl Foster, *The Songs of Edvard Grieg* (Aldershot, UK: Scolar Press, 1990), 209 and 214.

14. Eduard Devrient, *My Recollections of Felix Mendelssohn-Bartholdy, and His Letters to Me* (London: Richard Bentley, 1869), and Adolf Bernhard Marx, *The Music of the Nineteenth Century and Its Culture: System of Musical Instruction* (London: R. Cocks, 1854), the translation of which was shared with August Heinrich Wehrhan. These translations are still consulted by English-speaking scholars, particularly the Devrient recollections. See, for example, Francesca Brittan, "On Microscopic Hearing: Fairy Magic, Natural Science, and the *Scherzo Fantastique*," *Journal of the American Musicological Society* 64, no. 3 (Fall 2011): 527.

15. Schröder-Devrient made her first visit to England in 1832, where she performed the title role of *Fidelio* at the King's Theatre. See John Reed, "Schubert's Reception History in Nineteenth-Century England," in *The Cambridge Companion to Schubert*, ed. Christopher Gibbs (Cambridge: Cambridge University Press, 1997), 254.

16. This particular difficulty, along with other basic considerations of translation for singing, is discussed at length in Edward Dent, "Translation," and Arthur H. Fox-Strangways, "Translation of Songs," *Proceedings of the Musical Association* 49 (1922–23): 79–99.

17. The song was reprinted, with alterations to Scott's translation, as part of the *Musical Bouquet* in 1847 (nos. 119–20 of the series).

18. The volume is reviewed in the *Musical Times and Singing Class Circular* 25, no. 501 (November 1, 1884): 649. It is interesting that the reviewer seems to think that the version of "Erlkönig" featuring repeated quavers (rather than triplets) in the right hand of the piano is the authentic original, "the triplets being an afterthought." The English text is taken from Graham Johnson, ed., *Franz Schubert: The Complete Songs* (New Haven, CT: Yale University Press, 2014), 1: 518, which includes details of Schubert's change to Goethe's original ("Mühe" to "Müh" in the penultimate line).

19. Less successful renderings of this line, which lose the all-important quick change from cajoling to violence, include "Come quickly, or else I will tear thee away" (anonymous translation issued by Curwen; see n. 36); "And if you resist me I'll drag you from hence" ("Der Erlkönig," SS2072, trans. Robert Elkin [London, Novello & Co., 1966]); and the even more high-handed "You shall be mine, I'll seize you and should you resist / My strength shall not spare you, my will shall insist" of Arthur H. Fox-Strangways and Steuart Wilson (Oxford: Oxford University Press, 1932).

20. Most singers studying and working today will be familiar with Lois Phillips's *Lieder Line by Line and Word for Word* (London: Duckworth, 1979), which provides translations for performers that lay out direct linguistic equivalents between German and English, as well as idiomatic translations, in order to help non-German speakers understand the proper meaning and emphasis of the original poetry.

21. See, for example, Jan Kunold's schematic assessment of song translation in "Die Problematik der Musikübersetzung am Beispiel der englischen Version von Schuberts *Die schöne Müllerin*" in *Das österreichische Lied und seine Ausstrahlung in Europa*, 229–52. For a contrasting approach to this field of study, see Helen Minors, ed., *Music, Text and Translation* (London: Bloomsbury Academic, 2013).

22. *Musical Times and Singing Class Circular*, unsigned review of *Twenty Songs for a Soprano or Tenor Voice; with Pianoforte Accompaniment*, by Franz Schubert. English version by Natalia Macfarren, vol. 25, no. 501 (November 1, 1884): 649.

23. See Schneider, "Brahms' Lieder." Macfarren's work for Simrock largely ceased in the early 1880s, when a new link with the United States seems to have led Simrock to use a US translator instead.

24. For a comprehensive consideration of the impact of piano duet arrangements on the reception of repertoire from this period, see Thomas Christensen, "Four-Hand Piano Transcription and Geographies of Nineteenth-Century Musical Reception," *Journal of the American Musicological Society* 52, no. 2 (Summer 1999): 255–98.

25. Katy Hamilton, "Music inside the Home and outside the Box: Brahms's Vocal Quartets in Context," in Hamilton and Loges, *Brahms in the Home*, 283–93, explores arrangements and issues of performative flexibility within Brahms's *Liebeslieder*.

26. Kalbeck, *Brahms Briefwechsel*, 11: 143.

27. Letter of February 27, 1887 (Kalbeck, *Brahms Briefwechsel*, 11: 144).

28. See David Brodbeck, "On Some Enigmas Surrounding a Riddle Canon by Brahms," *Journal of Musicology* 20, no. 1 (Winter 2003): 73–103.

29. Macfarren translated the duets opp. 20, 61, 66, and 75 and Lieder opp. 19, 46, 47, 48, 49, 63, 69, 70, 71, 72, 84, 85, and 86. Several of these are listed in Schneider, "Brahms' Lieder" as being anonymous—Schneider's information, largely drawn from secondary sources, has been supplemented by viewing scores firsthand.

30. See Michael Musgrave, "Brahms and England," in *Brahms: Biographical, Documentary and Analytical Studies 2*, ed. Michael Musgrave (Cambridge: Cambridge University Press, 1987), 1–20. Earlier songs were issued in translation only from the 1870s, once interest in Brahms's music in England was already proven—thus, some translations appear only years after the first editions; but they were nevertheless the first English language texts available.

31. See Margit McCorkle, *Johannes Brahms: Thematisch-bibliographisches Werkverzeichnis* (Munich: G. Henle, 1984), 279. Macfarren's translations were also used in the program of at least one early concert performance of the *Neue Liebeslieder* in London. See "Monday Popular Concerts," *Musical Times and Singing Class Circular* 18, no. 418 (December 1, 1877), 592.

32. Charles Stanford, *A Cycle of Songs*, op. 68 (1897; the texts taken from Tennyson's *The Princess*); Walford Davies, *Nursery Rhymes*, op. 19 (ca. 1906); Ernest Walker, *5 Songs from England's Helicon*, op. 10 (1900); Liza Lehmann, *In a Persian Garden* (1896) and *The Daisy-Chain* (1900), among others.

33. The overall rhyme scheme of Macfarren's setting is ABBC / CDEE / FGGE. Daumer's is, more simply, ABCB / DEFE / FGHG.

34. Rothery's translation seems to be Novello's first, the spacing of the score clearly intended for a dual-language edition, unlike Simrock's. See Johannes Brahms, *Songs of Love (Liebeslieder) Waltzes for Pianoforte Duet (with Chorus ad lib.)*, trans. W. G. Rothery. Novello no. 650. (London: Novello & Co., 1915).

35. Her translation of *Lohengrin* was used for performances at the Metropolitan Opera in New York in 1886, and her *Rigoletto* at Covent Garden in 1909. See Alfred Loewenberg, *Annals of Opera 1597–1940* (London: John Calder, 1978), cols. 885 and 890, for first performances of these translations. Macfarren's translation of *Rigoletto* was even used for a stage production at Covent Garden as late as 1954; see "Covent Garden Opera," *The Times* (London), May 7, 1954, 10.

36. See Arthur Fox-Strangways, "Translation of Songs," for a lengthy discourse on the problems he finds in Müller.

37. Macfarren died in 1916; one can only imagine what she must have thought during her final few years, having made her home in England and given so much time to rendering the music of the country in which she was born intelligible to the inhabitants of her new home.

38. Herbert F. Peyser, "Some Observations on Translation," *Musical Quarterly* 8, no. 3 (July 1922): 355.

39. Leo Black, "Wort Oder Ton?," *Musical Times* 138, no. 1849 (March 1997): 21.

40. Sams's translations were performed at the Ryedale Festival and the Wigmore Hall in 2015–17 by Toby Spence, Roderick Williams, John Tomlinson, and Christopher Glynn. It is a relief to see that perhaps things are starting to change, after Laura Tunbridge's remarks just four years ago at the time of writing: "If a community were being imagined through Lieder performance in London between the wars it was one that, despite all efforts to the contrary, was less about nationalism than about cosmopolitanism; less about collective expression on a broad scale than of the coterie. It is a community that continues to dominate classical concerts at venues such as the Wigmore Hall, where today audience members cough or turn program pages at their peril, and no one would dare sing Schubert in English" (Laura Tunbridge, "Singing Translations: The Politics of Listening between the Wars," *Representations* 123, no. 1 [Summer 2013]: 76).

Bibliography

Brahms, Johannes. *Songs of Love (Liebeslieder) Waltzes for Pianoforte Duet (with Chorus ad lib.).* Novello no. 650. Translated by W. G. Rothery. 1915.

Brittan, Francesca. "On Microscopic Hearing: Fairy Magic, Natural Science, and the *Scherzo Fantastique*." *Journal of the American Musicological Society* 64, no. 3 (Fall 2011): 527–600.

Brodbeck, David. "On Some Enigmas Surrounding a Riddle Canon by Brahms." *Journal of Musicology* 20, no. 1 (Winter 2003): 73–103.

Christensen, Thomas. "Four-Hand Piano Transcription and Geographies of Nineteenth-Century Musical Reception." *Journal of the American Musicological Society* 52, no. 2 (Summer 1999): 255–98.

Degott, Pierre. "Natalia Macfarren (1827–1916): A Nineteenth-Century Translator/Mediator for the Operatic Cause." In *Translators, Interpreters, Mediators: Women Writers 1700–1900*, edited by Gillian Dow, 225–36. Oxford, UK: Peter Lang, 2007.

Dent, Edward. "The Translation of Operas." *Proceedings of the Musical Association* 61 (1934–35): 81–104.

Desblache, Lucile. "Tales of the Unexpected: Opera as a New Art of Globalization." In *Music, Text and Translation*, edited by Helen Minors, 9–19. London: Bloomsbury Academic, 2013.

Devrient, Eduard. *My Recollections of Felix Mendelssohn-Bartholdy, and His Letters to Me.* Translated by Natalia Macfarren and August Heinrich Wehrhan. London: Richard Bentley, 1869.

Foster, Beryl. *The Songs of Edvard Grieg.* Aldershot, UK: Scolar, 1990.

Fox-Strangways, Arthur H. "Translation of Songs." *Proceedings of the Musical Association* 49 (1922–23): 79–99.

Franz, Robert. *Fourteen Songs.* Edited and adapted by Natalia Macfarren. London: Novello, Ewer, 1876.

Goethe, Johann Wolfgang von. "Der Erlkönig." Translated by Arthur H. Fox-Strangways and Steuart Wilson. Oxford: Oxford University Press, 1932.

———. "Der Erlkönig." SS2072. Translated by Robert Elkin. London: Novello & Co., 1966.

Hamilton, Katy. "Music inside the Home and outside the Box: Brahms's Vocal Quartets in Context." In *Brahms in the Home and the Concert Hall: Between Private and Public Performance*, edited by Katy Hamilton and Natasha Loges, 279–99. Cambridge: Cambridge University Press, 2014.

Hamilton, Katy, and Natasha Loges, eds. *Brahms in the Home and the Concert Hall: Between Private and Public Performance.* Cambridge: Cambridge University Press, 2014.

Johnson, Graham, ed. *Franz Schubert: The Complete Songs.* New Haven, CT: Yale University Press, 2014.

Kalbeck, Max. *Johannes Brahms Briefwechsel.* Vol. 11, *Johannes Brahms: Briefe an Fritz Simrock.* Berlin: Deutsch Brahms-Gesellschaft, 1919; repr. Tützing, Ger.: Hans Schneider, 1974.

Kunold, Jan. "Die Problematik der Musikübersetzung am Beispiel der englischen Version von Schuberts *Die schöne Müllerin*." In *Das österreichische Lied und seine Ausstrahlung*

in Europa, edited by Pierre Béhar and Herbert Schneider, 229–52. Hildesheim, Ger.: Georg Olms, 2007.
Loewenberg, Alfred. *Annals of Opera 1597–1940*. London: John Calder, 1978.
Macfarren, Natalia. *Elementary Course for Vocalising and Pronouncing the English Language*. London: Lamborn Cock, Addison, 1868.
———, ed. and trans. *Twenty Songs for a Contralto Voice*. London: Novello, Ewer, 1882.
Marx, Adolf Bernhard. *The Music of the Nineteenth Century and Its Culture: System of Musical Instruction*. Translated by Natalia Macfarren. London: R. Cocks, 1854.
McCorkle, Margit. *Johannes Brahms: Thematisch-bibliographisches Werkverzeichnis*. Munich: G. Henle, 1984.
Minors, Helen, ed. *Music, Text and Translation*. London: Bloomsbury Academic, 2013.
"Miss Constance Bache (obituary)." *Musical Times and Singing Class Circular* 44, no. 276 (August 1, 1903): 539.
"Monday Popular Concerts." *Musical Times and Singing Class Circular* 18, no. 418 (December 1, 1877): 592.
Musgrave, Michael. "Brahms and England." In *Brahms: Biographical, Documentary and Analytical Studies 2*, edited by Michael Musgrave, 1–20. Cambridge: Cambridge University Press, 1987.
Musical Times and Singing Class Circular. Unsigned review of *Elementary Course for Vocalising and Pronouncing the English Language*, by Natalia Macfarren. Vol. 13, no. 301 (March 1, 1868): 323.
———. Unsigned review of *Seven Songs*, by Anton Rubinstein. Vol. 14, no. 314 (April 1, 1869): 55.
———. Unsigned review of *Twenty Songs for a Soprano or Tenor Voice*, by Franz Schubert. English version by Natalia Macfarren. Vol. 25, no. 501 (November 1, 1884): 649.
Peyser, Herbert F. "Some Observations on Translation." *Musical Quarterly* 8, no. 3 (July 1922): 353–71.
Phillips, Lois. *Lieder Line by Line and Word for Word*. London: Duckworth, 1979.
Rainbow, Bernarr, and Rosemary Williamson. "Troutbeck, John." In *Grove Music Online: Oxford Music Online*. Oxford: Oxford University Press. Accessed January 1, 2017. https://doi.org/10.1093/gmo/9781561592630.article.28475.
Reed, John. "Schubert's Reception History in Nineteenth-Century England." In *The Cambridge Companion to Schubert*, edited by Christopher Gibbs, 254–62. Cambridge: Cambridge University Press, 1997.
Rubinstein, Anton. *Seven Songs*. London: Novello, Ewer, 1869.
Schneider, Herbert. "Brahms' Lieder in französischen, englischen und italienischen Übersetzungen: Eine vergleichende Studie." In *Das österreichische Lied und seine Ausstrahlung in Europa*, edited by Pierre Béhar and Herbert Schneider, 295–366. Hildesheim, Ger.: Georg Olms, 2007.
Temperley, Nicholas. "Bache: (3) Constance Bache" in *Grove Music Online: Oxford Music Online*. Oxford: Oxford University Press. Accessed January 1, 2017. https://doi.org/10.1093/gmo/9781561592630.article.01697.
Tunbridge, Laura. "Singing Translations: The Politics of Listening between the Wars." *Representations* 123, no. 1 (Summer 2013): 53–86.
Wharton, Edith. *The Age of Innocence*. New York: D. Appleton, 1920,
Who Was Who. S.v. "Benson, Robert Henry." Online edition. Oxford: Oxford University Press. 2014. https://doi.org/10.1093/ww/9780199540884.013.U205982.

KATY HAMILTON is a freelance writer and broadcaster and coeditor of *Brahms in Context* (2019) and *Brahms in the Home and the Concert Hall* (2014). She has also published on music and concert life in nineteenth and twentieth-century Britain and Germany. She regularly provides concert notes for the Wigmore Hall, Southbank Centre, and Salzburg Festival, and is a frequent contributor to BBC Radio 3. Further information is available at http://www.katyhamilton.co.uk.

5 "For Any Ordinary Performer It Would Be Absurd, Ridiculous, or Offensive"

Performing Lieder Cycles on the American Stage

Heather Platt

IN 1879, WHEN George L. Osgood (1844–1922) performed Schumann's *Frauenliebe und -leben*, one Boston critic opined, "For many excellent artists it would be most hazardous to undertake the delivery of these songs; for any ordinary performer it would be absurd, ridiculous or offensive."[1] This was the second time Osgood performed the cycle; when he performed it in 1876, *Dwight's Journal of Music* claimed it was the first time the work had been presented in its entirety in the United States.[2] Indeed, the only Lieder cycle that was repeatedly reported as being performed in full prior to this time was Beethoven's *An die ferne Geliebte*.

Although scholars have studied nineteenth-century US performances of German symphonies and operas, to date there has not been an examination of performances of Lieder.[3] This gap has come about in part because of the difficulty in locating documentary evidence. Unlike operas or symphonies, no organizations were dedicated to the Lied, and therefore there was no institutional motivation to preserve programs. Even popular and successful women's clubs that sponsored numerous song recitals and *Männerchöre* (including New York's Liederkranz) did not archive their programs. Moreover, the small number of documents that have survived, such as handbills and program booklets, are extraordinarily difficult to locate because libraries usually do not catalog individual pieces of ephemera. A history of US performances, therefore, relies greatly on reports in journals and newspapers. From 1852 to 1881, *Dwight's Journal of Music* played a significant role in introducing readers to a variety of Lieder through its reviews of performances and short articles on composers. But the most detailed reviews concerned only Boston, and issues of the journal end right at the time when song recitals were growing in popularity and performances of cycles had begun to increase. Briefer reports in the *Musical*

Courier, which began in 1880, track the subsequent growth in popularity of recitals, but, although it covered many of the major singers and reprinted representative programs from across the country, by its very nature as a trade journal it has significant gaps in coverage and, in particular, offered little commentary on cycles. Recently, however, digitized copies of a large number of newspapers have enabled scholars to locate numerous performances of Lieder across the United States, facilitating research into the previously uncharted field of public performances of the genre.

Nevertheless these sources raise almost as many questions as they answer. Leaving aside that not all performances were reported in media outlets (especially so in the case of performances at private clubs, including *Männerchore*, as well as informal, domestic performances) and that many nineteenth-century publications are yet to be digitized, the reports do not always accurately and completely provide entire programs. Moreover, in both English- and German-language newspapers, reports of Lieder performances (and especially those prior to the emergence of high-quality music criticism in the 1890s) are often quite succinct, at best stating the names of the singer (often without naming the pianist) and titles of some of the songs. Reports do not always accurately state whether an entire cycle was performed, and titles of cycles are often incorrectly spelled or are abbreviated. Longer reports might consider the singer's performance but provide very little assessment of the actual music. These limitations notwithstanding, for the first time, enough reports have been uncovered to be able to construct the beginnings of the tradition of performing complete cycles on US stages.

This chapter begins with an overview of performances of Lieder during chamber and orchestral concerts from the 1850s to 1880, with an emphasis on the early performances of complete cycles. Song recitals, which created the infrastructure essential for the performance of lengthy cycles, began to gain currency during the late 1870s, and they became a standard element of concert life in major cities by the 1890s. At the end of the century, when an increasing number of musicians were presenting cycles, Villa Whitney White (1858–1933) and David Bispham (1857–1921) stood out for their numerous performances of cycles by a variety of composers. The last section of this chapter will briefly locate the place of cycles in these two singers' contrasting careers.

Miscellany Concerts Prior to 1880

A memorial to the tenor August Kreissmann (1823–79), despite its hyperbole, accurately reflects the state of US concert life in the middle of the century, when the general public rarely heard Lieder in concerts:

> From him the Boston public first heard the incomparable beauty of Schubert, Franz, and Schumann . . . and the immortal strains of the *Adelaide* of Beethoven. . . . People who had starved upon the inanities of modern psalmody,

who were tired of the forced brilliancy of Italian opera, and were disgusted with the commonplaces of British composers, found in the overflowing fountain of German song the sources of the keenest and most lasting pleasure.[4]

Born in Germany, Kreissmann studied at the Leipzig Conservatory in 1844 and then for two years in Milan. The tribute to him was presented at a memorial service organized by the Orpheus Club of Boston, a German men's chorus that Kreissmann had founded and conducted. Although it was presented to an organization composed of German immigrants, its sentiments mirrored earlier reviews in Anglophone presses that had extolled him as the most important Lieder performer in the United States during the 1850s and 1860s. During chamber concerts in his home base of Boston, and in guest appearances in New York and Philadelphia, he programmed songs by Schubert, Schumann, and Robert Franz, but the only cycle he performed in its entirety was Beethoven's *An die ferne Geliebte*, op. 98. Kreissmann and his German-born pianists, Otto Dresel (1826–1890), Ernst Perabo (1845–1920) and Hugo Leonhard, were part of that network of musicians, including fellow immigrants such as Theodore Thomas (1835–1905) and Leopold Damrosch (1832–85), who tirelessly advocated the programing of German repertoire in US concert and opera halls. And like them, his performances and his repertoire were championed in *Dwight's Journal of Music*.[5]

Reports of Kreissmann's activities, as well as recollections of other musicians, indicate that Lieder were performed at informal gatherings in private homes and at rehearsals and social functions of German choral organizations. But as late as the 1860s, outside Kreissmann's Boston, many of the performances in concerts were of the few Lieder that were already circulating in English-language editions, such as Schubert's "Ständchen," D957 (which was usually referred to as "Serenade"), and such songs were usually performed in English. Moreover, when Lieder were included in concerts of instrumental music, they usually accounted for only one or two numbers. These statements are true even of concerts given by German organizations, which tended to emphasize the same few popular Lieder that were sung in other venues.[6]

Chamber concerts in Boston during the 1850s and 1860s, however, sometimes included as many as ten Lieder. Such concerts enabled Kreissmann to present groups of songs from Schumann's *Dichterliebe*, op. 48. Critics repeatedly acknowledged him for introducing this cycle to Boston audiences, though apparently he performed only eight numbers from the first half of the collection. Similarly, his performance of these first eight songs during a Mason-Thomas chamber concert in New York took place at a time when Schumann's songs (in general) were rarely programmed in that city.[7] One of the earliest performances of the complete cycle took place in Chicago in 1875, when a popular local performer, Mrs. Clara D. Stacey, gave it, in English, during one of Carl Wolfsohn's piano recitals devoted to Schumann. Wolfsohn (1834–1907), a German immigrant who had worked with Theodore Thomas in New York and Philadelphia, frequently programmed Lieder. Florence French reported that his series of ten Schumann recitals included forty-four of the composer's songs, "and of these many were first productions" in Chicago.[8]

Theodore Thomas, who from the 1850s occasionally programmed Lieder during his orchestral concerts, hired George L. Osgood to perform Lieder during his orchestra's 1872–73 East Coast and Midwest tour. A Bostonian of Puritan lineage, Osgood had studied voice and concertized in Europe during 1867–71. The critical response to his performances with Thomas was quite uneven, at times revealing how little these types of songs were appreciated, even in cities with significant German populations. One reviewer, for instance, observed that although Osgood gave a "beautiful rendering" of five of the Lenau settings from Schumann's op. 90, the New York audience "had little relish for such solid musical food." Demonstrating that the Lied was still relatively new to the US stage, a few reviewers questioned the wisdom of Osgood's choice to dedicate himself to the genre, which one Boston critic referred to as a "peculiar class of songs." Still others doubted the validity of performing Lieder in large concert halls. Nevertheless, Osgood, who sometimes gave small excerpts from *Dichterliebe* and *Die schöne Müllerin*, was repeatedly praised for introducing audiences to songs of a "higher order" than the arias and ballads to which they were accustomed.[9]

Ultimately, Osgood settled in Boston and established a fine reputation as a choral director and teacher. He occasionally sang Lieder during chamber concerts, but the only cycle that he seems to have performed in full was Schumann's *Frauenliebe und -leben*. These performances, in 1876 and 1879, were during unusually long concerts that included choral and instrumental works, as well as other solo Lieder (see table 5.1). After the 1879 concert, his performance was applauded for its tenderness and sincerity, but the *Dwight's* critic remarked that *Frauenliebe* "should by good rights" be performed by a woman.[10] (To be sure, Osgood was not the first man to present the cycle; Stockhausen had performed it in Cologne in 1862.)

Prior to Osgood's performances, the most frequently presented song from this cycle was "Du Ring an meinem Finger." In 1851, US publishers released English-language editions of this song, advertising it as one of the works performed by Jenny Lind during her tour. Subsequently, in 1871, the popular US series of scores *Gems of German Songs* released the entire cycle in English, increasing the likelihood that the set was receiving domestic performances. Grace Hiltz (b. 1855–1930), a young soprano who was earning the praise of local critics, gave one of the first public English-language performances of the cycle in Chicago, in 1880.[11] Unlike Osgood, she gave the work within a song recital rather than a miscellany program.

Table 5.1. Program of Osgood's Concert on May 1, 1879, at Mechanics Hall in Boston.

1. Choruses
   a. "Benedictus" (1590) — Giovanni Gabrieli
      For three chorus, in twelve real parts
   b. "Ave Verum" — Mozart
      With accompaniment of the piano-forte and string quartet.
2. Quartet in B-flat major, op. 41 — Saint-Saëns
   For piano, violin, viola, and 'cello
3. Song series, "Frauen-Liebe und Leben" [sic] — Schumann
   The words by Von Chamisso
4. Chorus, "May Dew," op. 95 no. 1 — Rheinberger
5. Piano-forte solo—"Benediction de Dieu dans la solitude" — Liszt
   From the "Harmonies Poétiques et Réligieuses"
6. Suite of spring songs — Franz
   a. "'Tis the Dark Green Leaves," op. 20 no. 5
   b. "The Moon's to Rest Declining," op. 17 no. 2
   c. "When the Earth from Slumber," op. 22 no. 3
   d. "'Mid Blossomy Sheen," op. 14 no. 2
   e. "Thro' the Wheat and the Corn," op. 33 no. 3
   f. "The Hills Are Green," op. 11 no. 3
7. Three characteristic numbers — Rubinstein
   a. Songs
      (1.) "There Was a Monarch Golden"
      (2.) "As Sings the Lark"
   b. Chorus, "The Pine Tree," op. 39 no. 3
   c. First movement of the Trio in B-flat major, op. 52
      For piano, violin, and 'cello
8. Chorus, "Laughing and Crying" — Schubert

Song Recitals of the 1880s and 1890s

By the late 1870s, singers such as Hiltz and George Werrenrath (1838–98) had begun presenting events that were called song recitals.[12] Those that featured Lieder resembled some of Gustav Walter's Viennese *Liederabende* in that they included a few instrumental numbers, but some of Hiltz's and Werrenrath's recitals embraced almost twenty Lieder, which was more than the number Walter usually presented. Werrenrath, a Danish immigrant who had trained in Hamburg and collaborated with Gounod in recitals in Belgium, gave a series of four song recitals in Chicago in 1879. The series was sponsored by the Beethoven Society, and Wolfsohn, the society's leader, accompanied the singer. From 1881 to 1889, Werrenrath gave five similar series in Brooklyn, New York. Aside from *An die ferne Geliebte*, he did not present a complete cycle in a single performance, though he did perform individual numbers from Schubert's and Schumann's cycles. In particular, in 1881, he distributed the songs of *Die schöne Müllerin* across a series of three recitals. Similarly, Stockhausen had also spread the cycle across a series of concerts in London. This type of programming suggests that the adoption of cycles was gradual partly because of singers' concerns that audiences could not accept a recital consisting of (or dominated by) one work, rather than a reluctance to learn all the songs.

By 1880, Schubert's two cycles had been introduced to US music lovers through articles in music journals, in addition to which some of the individual songs from the cycles had been included in concerts for decades. Furthermore, the scores of the complete cycles were part of Litolff's Library of Classical Music, which was published and advertised in music journals during the 1860s. Nevertheless, it is impossible to know exactly when the cycles were first performed in their entirety. Even throughout Europe, such performances were slow to gain traction: Stockhausen's performances, including, for instance, *Die schöne Müllerin*, D795, in Vienna in 1856 and *Winterreise*, D911, in Hamburg in 1864, were considered unusual, and Karl Wallenreiter, who performed these cycles and six songs from *Schwanengesang*, D957, and Schumann's *Dichterliebe* and op. 39 *Liederkreis* during 1866–68, was one of the few to follow Stockhausen's lead.[13] In 1879 and 1880, one of Osgood's students, Julius (Jules) Jordan (1850–1927) presented *Die schöne Müllerin*, *Winterreise*, and *Schwanengesang* during two series of three recitals in Providence and Newport, Rhode Island. During the second *Schwanengesang* recital, Jordan also performed other songs by Schubert, Schumann, Rubinstein, Jensen, Liszt, and Franz "with the view of illustrating the development of German song."[14] The second series of recitals was advertised in New York papers and noted in *Dwight's*; but, in general, these performances did not attract a great deal of attention. Jordan was just at the start of his career, and the venues were not especially prominent. That other low-profile performances of cycles, including ones at schools, might have been given elsewhere is similarly suggested by the English-language performances of Schubert's cycles in 1887 by the pupils of the Cleveland School of Music.[15] In view of the pedagogical nature of these recitals, the songs of each cycle were presented by a number of students. In contrast, later professional singers, including Wilhelm Heinrich and David Bispham, sometimes chose to perform cycles in collaboration with other singers, either to add timbral variety or to rest their voices. To the same end, in Europe, Stockhausen often interspersed cycles with instrumental pieces, and one of Bispham's 1898 US performances of *Die schöne Müllerin* included four piano pieces by his accompanist Arthur Whiting. Bispham's recital notwithstanding, this interspersing of instrumental works was not the standard practice in US performances of cycles.

Despite the availability of scores and reports of complete performances, during the 1880s most professional singers continued to present only excerpts from cycles. Such is the case with George Henschel. A colleague of Brahms, Joseph

Joachim and Stockhausen, Henschel and his US-born wife, Lillian (née Bailey), toured the United States giving what they billed as vocal recitals from 1880 to 1901.[16] Their recitals had a standard outline of songs and duets, in a variety of languages, dating from the mid-seventeenth century to the nineteenth. Such diversity greatly pleased audiences and critics. Although they performed numerous Lieder, the format of the recitals did not accommodate long cycles. The only cycles George seemed to have sung in full were Beethoven's *An die ferne Geliebte*, which was not among the numbers he frequently performed, and his own *Serbisches Liederspiel* (1878), a cycle composed of ten songs for one to four voices. Henschel, however, taught a number of US singers who did perform cycles, and he inspired two of the other prominent Lieder recitalists, Max Heinrich and David Bispham.

After studying at the Dresden Conservatory, Max Heinrich (1853–1916) left Germany at the age of twenty to escape military service. After his notable 1883 performance of *Elijah* under Leopold Damrosch, he established a career performing in oratorios and song recitals in the United States and Canada; he also served as professor of singing at the Royal Academy of Music in London from 1889 to 1892.[17] Heinrich's earliest performances in the United States were for the German community of Philadelphia, but his later career focused on attracting a wider Anglophone audience. After his first "Classical Song Recitals" in Chicago and Milwaukee in 1884, he undertook multiple tours of the country, finally announcing his retirement in 1903. At various times, he lived and worked in Philadelphia, Boston, Chicago, La Jolla (California), Los Angeles, and New York. Many of his recitals comprised close to thirty songs and, unlike recitalists in Europe, he usually did not include instrumental numbers—a model that other US recitalists often followed. In order to add variety, a female singer usually contributed some numbers, though they accounted for less than half the program. Before he worked in England, most of Heinrich's song recitals consisted entirely of Lieder—something that was quite unusual in the 1880s even in Europe—but from 1892 (when he returned to the United States) he frequently juxtaposed Lieder with songs by English composers, such as Alexander Campbell MacKenzie's *Seven Spring Songs*, op. 44 (1890), or ones by US composers, including George Chadwick (1854–1931). This combination satisfied audiences and critics who felt uncomfortable with German texts and sought more variety than they perceived in a Lieder recital.

Throughout the 1880s and 1890s, when German orchestral music was dominating US concert halls and Wagner's operas were attracting an increasing number of followers, some of Heinrich's recitals included small excerpts from Schubert's cycles, resembling some of Henschel's recitals, as well as numbers from Schumann's cycles. During the 1880s, and, less frequently, the 1890s some of Heinrich's recitals also included a performance of *Frauenliebe und -leben* by one of his collaborators—Medora Henson (a pupil of Henschel; ca. 1862–1928), Mrs. Margaretha Kirpal (b. ca. 1859), or Lena Little (a US student of Stockhausen and a collaborator also of Henschel; 1853–1920). Heinrich himself, however, sang few cycles in their entirety. In 1897, he gave Dvořák's seven *Zigeunerlieder*, op. 55, with a "fire and an abandon" that pleased a critic and the audience,[18] and the first of many performances of Brahms's *Vier ernste Gesänge*, op. 121. This first performance, which was in English, took place during the Boston Symphony Orchestra's memorial for Brahms, and the orchestra's conductor, Emil Paur, provided the accompaniment. During many later performances, Heinrich accompanied himself and performed from memory, as was his usual practice. Already critics in 1897 observed that Heinrich was almost declaiming the vocal lines, rather than singing lyrically, and this tendency increased with age. Doubtlessly it characterized his last performance of this cycle in December 1915, during a memorial service that the Bohemians (a New York musicians' club) organized for their founder, the pianist Rafael Joseffy (1852–1915).[19]

Critics such as Philip Hale frequently alluded to Heinrich's poor vocal techniques but (as in the case of Ludwig Wüllner) they almost always conceded that these were compensated for by Heinrich's unusually insightful, dramatic interpretations.[20] This type of interpretation is evident in the numerous performance annotations that distinguish Heinrich's English-language editions of Lieder, which included *Dichterliebe,* and his pedagogical volume that contained numerous annotated excerpts from *Die schöne Müllerin.* These publications date from the end of Heinrich's career when he was receiving more attention from the press as a teacher than as a singer. When one of his Boston acolytes, Stephen S. Townsend (1865–1941), performed *Dichterliebe* using Heinrich's edition and an English version of the *Müllerin* cycle, Heinrich provided the piano accompaniments and informative introductions to each cycle.[21]

Heinrich and Townsend were two of the many singers who contributed to the Boston song recitals and chamber concerts organized by the blind tenor Wilhelm Heinrich (d. 1911)—no relation to Max. Born in Illinois of German parents, Wilhelm studied with Stockhausen during 1891. He marked his return from Germany to the United States with performances of *Die schöne Müllerin* in his hometown of Rockford, Illinois (where he sang his own English translation), Boston, and New York. In 1892 and 1897, he presented Schubert's *Winterreise* with Louise Rollwagen (1854–1923), a contralto from Cincinnati who, like Henschel, had studied at Joachim's Königliche Hochschule in Berlin. Heinrich and Rollwagen sang in alternation, sometimes giving one song each, at other times two or three; in all, each gave twelve songs.

Winterreise had rarely been given complete performances, and, as with reviewers in Europe, a Boston critic of Heinrich's 1892 recital cautioned that a complete performance runs the risk of becoming monotonous.[22] Hale, a leading provocative anti-Brahmsian, lobbed a similar charge at performances of Brahms's *Magelone* Romances, op. 33, a fifteen-song cycle dedicated to Stockhausen. In December 1891, Heinrich Meyn (1863–1933), a native of Hamburg who had studied with Stockhausen, presented most of the *Magelone* Romances in Boston and New York. Reviews of the Boston recital were not charitable, noting the "Magelone Lieder were simply murdered if not quite beyond recognition."[23] One might be tempted to find various personal biases of the critics as grounds for dismissing these negative assessments, but the reviews point to the significant challenges, in terms of both audience attention and performers' techniques, that long cycles still posed at the end of the century.

Turn-of-the-Century Advocates of Song Cycles

During the late 1890s, Villa Whitney White and David Bispham presented far more performances of complete song cycles than either their predecessors or their contemporaries. Unlike the other performers discussed in this chapter, White (whose family's presence in Massachusetts dated to the seventeenth century) was primarily a voice teacher. During the 1880s, she sang in church choirs and at chamber concerts in New England and taught at the Boston Conservatory. In 1891 she began studying with Amalie Joachim, a former student of Stockhausen, as well as a close friend of Brahms and a colleague of Henschel.

White assisted Joachim during her 1892 US tour. At Oberlin College, Joachim sang *An die ferne Geliebte* and ten songs from *Winterreise*, a cycle that she had sung in full in Europe. In comparison, Max Heinrich and Henschel selected significantly fewer songs for their excerpts from this cycle. Joachim's performances of *Die schöne Müllerin* in New York and Boston received mixed reviews, with one critic complaining that printed translations of the texts should have been supplied to the audience.[24] During performances of the same work at Smith and Mount Holyoke Colleges, White assisted Joachim, who was battling ill health, by performing six of the twenty songs.[25] From 1892 until 1897, White continued to study with Joachim, spending up to six months of each year in Germany. During the remaining months, she concertized in the United States, gaining national attention for her entertaining and educational lecture recitals, some of which featured performances of cycles.

In 1895 White's popularity skyrocketed when she presented a series of four lecture recitals to one of the most established music clubs in the country, the Amateur Musical Club of Chicago. Organized by women, this club hosted recitals by numerous other prominent Lieder exponents, including the Henschels, Max Heinrich, and Bispham.[26] White's success led to numerous new engagements, and in 1897–98 she traversed the country for thirteen months, performing in multiple cities in sixteen states, often giving as many as three or four recitals in each city. She performed cycles in a variety of venues, such as women's clubs (including ones devoted to music as well as ones concerned with the wider culture), universities, colleges, churches, and private homes. But only one performance of a cycle was sponsored by a German organization: in 1897 she presented Brahms's *Magelone* Romances for the Saint Paul Musikverein.[27]

By 1897 White had devised at least fifteen programs. She formulated most of them with the assistance of Heinrich Reimann (1850–1906), an organist and historian at Berlin's Klindworth-Scharwenka Conservatory who had also helped Joachim create her programs on the history of German song.[28] In her lectures, White placed each song in its historical context and explained its meaning before singing it in German. Her programs encompassed sacred and secular German songs from as far back as the Middle Ages as well as Lieder. Following Joachim's precedent, she included *An die ferne Geliebte* in a program called "The Song in the Form of the Aria from the Seventeenth Century to Beethoven." In contrast, she had separate programs for *Die schöne Müllerin* and Brahms's *Magelone* Romances.

Beginning in 1893, White regularly performed Cornelius's *Six Christmas Songs*. She included them in her program of sacred songs, or combined them with folk songs from the British Isles or Alexander von Fielitz's song cycle *Eliland— Songs of Chiemsee*.[29] White might have met von Fielitz (1860–1930), a professor at the Stern Conservatory, while in Berlin during 1896 or 1897. His 1896 song cycle set ten love songs by Kaspar Stieler (1632–1707) that tell of a monk's love for a young nun. This cycle was the most contemporary work in White's repertoire, and unlike most of her song selections, it was not performed by Joachim. Although the cycle is no longer well known, numerous other singers in the United States around the end of the nineteenth century performed it, including Mme. Nordica and Meyn.[30]

By establishing a successful career, choosing to remain unmarried, and performing at events aiding working women, White moved beyond traditional societal expectations for women. Her values might have affected her choice of repertoire and in particular her decision not to perform *Frauenliebe und -leben*. Given that by the 1890s this cycle was performed by other singers in the United States and in that it was part of Joachim's repertoire, White's choice is noteworthy, and one is left to ponder whether the fact that Chamisso's texts did not mesh with her own life experiences contributed to her choice. To be sure, it is also possible that her avoidance of the cycle related to Schumann's musical style. Although she occasionally presented a lecture recital dedicated to Schumann's songs, she performed his works less frequently than Schubert's, and, unlike Joachim, she did not perform *Dichterliebe*. She did, however, perform other popular songs by Schumann, including "Widmung," op. 25 no. 1, and "Der Nussbaum," op. 25 no. 3, as well as numbers from the *Liederalbum für die Jugend*, op. 79. (Although songs from this collection are not frequently performed on stage today, they were performed by other major Lieder recitalists of the time, including Joachim, Max Heinrich, and Bispham.)

The cycles by Beethoven, Schubert, and Brahms were the most technically challenging pieces in White's repertoire. During 1895 alone, she presented *An die ferne Geliebte* at least five times, and, between 1895 and 1898, she gave *Die schöne Müllerin* at least thirteen times. According to press reviews, it was White who premiered this cycle in Minneapolis, Saint Paul, and Portland (Oregon). She likewise premiered Brahms's *Magelone* Romances in these cities and likely also at Mount Holyoke College, and perhaps also in Chicago.

Joachim had given the complete *Magelone* cycle in Germany in 1896, and White studied these pieces with her during the summer following Brahms's death in 1897. During her subsequent US tour, White presented this cycle at least six times, with the most prominent performance being in Boston's Steinert Hall. In general, critics praised her rich voice as being well suited to these songs, but many viewed the songs themselves as dreary.[31] Although most press notices imply she gave the entire cycle, some indicate she did not perform two of the songs, no. 7, "War es dir, den diese Lippen bebten," and no. 12, "Muss es eine Trennung geben."[32] A devout Christian Scientist, White might have omitted these pieces because the passionate texts describe the yearnings of Peter, the main protagonist.

After 1898, White no longer maintained such a demanding touring and performing schedule but rather focused on teaching in the Boston area and at the Hartford School of Music in Connecticut. A 1901 reprise of the *Magelone* Romances in Hartford is one of the few locally publicized recitals from this period. In contrast, during 1906–13, she exhibited a renewed interest in giving recitals, but most of these appearances were relatively small in scale, and they were mostly confined to Boston and her last hometown of Portland, Oregon. Some of them featured Cornelius's *Six Christmas Songs*, and a 1910 Beethoven program in Portland included *An die ferne Geliebte*, but the lack of sources make it impossible to know the precise number of cycles she performed.

While White's presence on the national stage was quite brief, and despite her performances being in the context of lecture recitals, she gave far more performances of Lieder cycles than other contemporary female recitalists. Moreover, although Maria Brema, Marguerite Hall, and Ernestine Schumann-Heink established more prominent careers, the only cycle they performed was *Frauenliebe und -leben*.

As White's career reached its peak during 1897–98, David Bispham was establishing a reputation for his performances in opera, oratorio, and song recitals. Born in Philadelphia to a Quaker family that traced its history in the United States to the seventeenth century, Bispham was expected to enter the family wool business. Nevertheless, at the age of thirty, after devoting all his spare time to singing in church choirs, amateur theatricals, oratorios, and German choruses, he finally turned to a career in music. He studied with the singing teachers William Shakespeare in England and Luigi Vannuccini and Giovanni Lamperti in Italy; Henschel and Max Heinrich were among his role models.[33]

In England, Bispham established a noteworthy career, performing in theatrical genres and miscellany concerts. He made his Covent Garden debut in 1892, singing the part of Beckmesser in Wagner's *Die Meistersinger von Nürnberg*. In November 1896, he marked his return to the United States with a performance of the same role at New York's Metropolitan Opera, and he remained with that company until 1903. During the late 1890s and early 1900s he presented numerous song recitals, beginning with an 1896 appearance at a concert organized by Philadelphia's Orpheus Club, a German men's chorus he had sung with in his youth.

During January and February 1897, Bispham presented a series of four recitals with fellow singers. In the first, he gave the US premiere of Brahms's *Vier ernste Gesänge*, a cycle he had introduced to London audiences the preceding November.[34] The second concert featured a sampling of Schubert songs, and the third included English, German, and Italian songs, as well as *An die ferne Geliebte*.[35] The fourth concert, which was hastily arranged in response to the success of the preceding three, featured Brahms's *Magelone* Romances. Since Meyn had omitted some of the songs when he gave this cycle, Bispham was able to claim his was the first performance of this cycle in the United States, though for some this distinction was inconsequential.[36]

While Bispham sang the songs of the character Peter and provided the narrative, Marguerite Hall sang Magelone's songs, Lloyd d'Aubigné the minstrel's song, and Marie Engle that of the sultan's daughter. Hall and Bispham gave the final song of the cycle, "Treue Liebe," in unison. Bispham's performance received better press than Meyn's, but at least one critic doubted the contributions of multiple singers enhanced the performance, and some cautioned that the "profoundly intellectual" love songs would not be widely accepted.[37] Both Meyn's and Bispham's performances are historically significant because they took place while Brahms was still alive. The *Magelone* Romances were rarely performed in their entirety in Europe during Brahms's lifetime, and the composer himself did not advocate that type of performance.[38] Although critics in New York's English-language papers had mixed assessments of Bispham's recitals, they acknowledged the novelty of performing Brahms's cycles. In contrast, the *New Yorker Staats-Zeitung* only briefly noted these works, placing greater emphasis on Bispham's interpretations of Schubert's and Beethoven's Lieder.

In December 1898, Bispham paired Brahms's *Vier ernste Gesänge* with *Die schöne Müllerin* in recitals in Boston and New York. The *New York Times* review of the Boston recital advised the arrogant Bispham not to waste "his precious sotto voce on the death hymns of Brahms and the wailings of the miller whose love doted on green."[39] In his review of the New York recital, Leonard Liebling likewise described the Brahms songs as "very heavy fare" that "sung by a lesser artist than Bispham, . . . might have been indigestible." Bispham had gained quite a cult following, to which Liebling alluded when he reported that "the large audience of ladies . . . followed every number with bated breath."[40] But, in contrast to this positive reception, other critics in both English-language and German publications were not impressed with either the sound of Bispham's voice or his interpretation of the songs.[41]

Brahms's 1896 *Vier ernste Gesänge* received multiple performances in 1897–98, including those by Bispham, Max Heinrich, Stephen Biden (a young baritone in Chicago), and William O. Goodrich (1862–1956), a former student of Henschel who performed in Milwaukee.[42] Some of the performances were associated with commemorations of Brahms's death in April 1897; nonetheless this set was one of the few complete cycles to receive repeated US performances within two years of its creation.[43] Certainly, a cycle of only four songs is easier to program than one of twenty. Yet the technical and expressive difficulties of the work are substantial. In the following years, Bispham combined this cycle with a variety of songs, including lighter fare such as his signature piece "Danny Deever" (1897) by Walter Damrosch, as well as folk songs such as "Annie Laurie."[44] Bispham, who advocated English-language performances of opera and Lieder, did not perform cycles in English, but he made an exception for this Brahms cycle because its words were taken from the Bible, which was not originally in German. Nevertheless, he recalled that on at least one occasion he was criticized for his choice.[45]

During 1904–5, Bispham toured the country giving song recitals. The centerpiece of his tour was a series of four recitals titled "Cycle of Song Cycles." In the first program, he sang *An die Ferne Geliebte* and *Dichterliebe* while Marguerite Hall presented *Frauenliebe*. The second and third recitals consisted of *Die schöne Müllerin* and *Winterreise*, respectively; and the fourth encompassed Brahms's *Vier ernste Gesänge* and the *Magelone* Romances, with Hall performing Magelone's songs. Although numerous publications lauded this ambitious series, a number, including (perhaps surprisingly) the *New Yorker Staats-Zeitung*, cautioned that a program devoted to one composer and one composition would not attract audiences, and that even those attending would find difficulty mustering the required attention to appreciate each song. The *New York Times* was one of the few papers to show appreciation of the *Magelone* cycle, but, like critics of the other recitals, its reviewer questioned the accuracy of Bispham's introductory remarks. Reviews of Bispham's singing were mixed, and while some critics in Boston and Chicago attested to his interpretative skills, those in New York were more critical, in particular implying that Bispham was less successful with the more delicate or intimate songs.⁴⁶ To some extent, this series was a publicity stunt, designed to draw attention to Bispham's recitals in the wake of his departure from the Metropolitan Opera. Moreover, most of his recitals during this tour did not include cycles; rather, many responded to the rising tide of US nationalism by including songs by US composers.

Throughout his career, Bispham confined his performances of cycles to larger cities in the East and in Chicago. In contrast, White performed cycles throughout the country. In California, for instance, she gave *Die schöne Müllerin* in San Francisco, Los Angeles, and Redlands, whereas Bispham presented only the more popular *Dichterliebe* in San Francisco (in 1905 and 1911). But other artists, including Ludwig Wüllner, also had reservations about West Coast audiences. Wüllner, who had sung for Brahms and whose father was a colleague of Brahms, performed *Die schöne Müllerin*, *Winterreise*, *Schwanengesang*, and *Dichterliebe* in a series of New York recitals during his 1910 tour, but he does not seem to have performed these works on the West Coast. He did, however, give *Vier ernste Gesänge* in the West, as well as in Louisville, Kentucky, and Detroit, Michigan.

Advertisements as late as 1911 claim Bispham was the first to sing the *Magelone* cycle in the United States, but, ironically, the 1904–5 performances seem to be the last he gave of this cycle; furthermore, this series of recitals was also likely the last time he gave the Schubert cycles. In contrast to his limited success with German cycles, Bispham's frequent performances of Liza Lehmann's *In a Persian Garden* (1896), a cycle for four voices, was said to have created a fad that encouraged US composers to create similar cycles.⁴⁷ Aside from cycles, Bispham had an extensive repertoire of songs by Schubert, Schumann, and Brahms and, in the early years of the twentieth century, he regularly programmed Richard Strauss's Lieder (which Max Heinrich was also performing) and introduced US audiences to Lieder by Hugo Wolf.

By the end of the nineteenth century, *Dichterliebe* was presented by a greater number of singers than any other cycle, being performed by visitors from Europe such as Harry Plunket Greene (1865–1936) and US pupils of Henschel such as Charles W. Clark (1865–1925). According to a 1902 Chicago review of a performance by Stockhausen's pupil Anton Van Rooy (1870–1932), "the cycle has suffered much at the hands of incompetence."⁴⁸ This comment stands in stark contrast to the situation in the 1860s, when some critics longed for performances of the cycle.⁴⁹ Nevertheless, in many parts of the United States, performances of complete cycles were still infrequent during the closing years of the century.

In this chapter, the cycle has functioned as a barometer of the gradual incorporation of Lieder into US concert life, a previously unexplored aspect of the transatlantic transfer of European culture to the United States. Besides locating performances of cycles, it has identified the major nineteenth-century exponents of the Lied in the United States, most of whom have been ignored by modern scholars even though they were much admired by their contemporaries. This study has also dated the establishment of song recitals, which became the main vehicle for Lieder performances, to the late 1870s and has alluded to the gradual establishment of Lieder as a concert genre from Boston to the West Coast and even to Hawaii. The greater acceptance of the genre is also suggested by the shift from the performance of small excerpts of cycles to Bispham's use of cycles as a marketing tool and the establishment of the practice of performers giving multiple cycles during a single concert season.

German immigrants, in particular Kreissmann and Max Heinrich, led the efforts to bring Lieder to US stages. But there were also significant contributions from singers whose families had resided in the United States for generations, including Osgood, White, and Bispham. Many of these performers were colleagues of Thomas, Wolfsohn, and the Damrosch family, who were key figures in the establishment of the German-dominated canon in US concerts halls and opera houses. Indeed, the inclusion of Lieder in US chamber and orchestral concerts is the clearest demonstration of the link between the US dissemination of Lieder and the promotion of other larger, German genres. The significance of this connection notwithstanding, these vocalists were not merely following on the coattails of the conductors and instrumentalists; rather, they were paving their own ways and in so doing pioneering practices that would become common in Europe only decades later, as was the case when Heinrich created recitals composed entirely of Lieder. Still, a full evaluation of the significance of the achievements outlined here, including the US premieres of complete performances of the *Magelone* Romances and *Dichterliebe* predating those in England, cannot be accomplished until European performances have been more fully investigated.

Notes

1. "Music and the Drama: Mr. Osgood's Concert," *Boston Daily Advertiser*, May 8, 1879.
2. "George L. Osgood's Concert," *Dwight's Journal of Music* 36, no. 4 (May 27, 1876): 239.
3. Though concentrating on the symphony, Jessica C. E. Gienow-Hecht provides one of the most sensitive examinations of the complex nature of the US adoption of German music: *Sound Diplomacy: Music and Emotions in Transatlantic Relations, 1850–1920* (Chicago: University of Chicago Press, 2009). In general, in contrast to the treatment of opera and symphonies, Lieder are often accorded only passing reference in previous studies of US concert life. Vera Brodsky Lawrence, for instance, cites just a few performances of individual

songs, mostly by Schubert, in *Strong on Music: The New York Music Scene in the Days of George Templeton Strong*, vols. 1–3 (Chicago: University of Chicago Press, 1988–95).

4. Address by F. H. Underwood, "In Memoriam: August Kreissmann," *Dwight's Journal of Music* 39 (August 2, 1879): 123.

5. For an overview of the milieu, see Katherine K. Preston, "Art Music from 1800 to 1860," in *The Cambridge History of American Music*, ed. David Nicholls (Cambridge: Cambridge University Press, 1998), 186–213.

6. Indeed, throughout the century, the only cycle that a number of *Männerchöre* programmed was *An die ferne Geliebte*, and most of those performances were given by the popular star of German opera, Anton Schott (1846–1913). See, for instance, the report of Schott's performances at an 1887 Germania *Männerchor* concert in Chicago: "Two Enjoyable Concerts," *Chicago Tribune*, May 6, 1887, 2. For a program of a typical concert by a German organization that included one Lied (in this case, "Die Post," which was circulating in English editions), see the advertisement for the 1869 *Großes Sacred-Concerts* of the Nashville Turnverein in *Tennessee Staats-Zeitung* (Nashville), January 30, 1869, 1. In their studies of German choruses, Suzanne Snyder and Heike Bungert discuss the diverse repertoire performed by these organizations: Snyder, "The *Männerchor* Tradition in the United States: A Historical Analysis of Its Contribution to American Musical Culture" (PhD diss., University of Iowa, 1991); Bungert, "The Singing Festival of German Americans, 1849–1914," *American Music* 34, no. 2 (2016): 141–79. In general, the performance of complete cycles, which could not provide the same type of community-building experience as choral singing, was not a primary mission of these immigrant organizations.

7. Nancy Reich, "Robert Schumann's Music in New York City, 1848–1898," in *European Music and Musicians in New York City, 1840–1900*, ed. John Graziano (Rochester, NY: University of Rochester Press, 2006), 16, 22–23.

8. Florence French (comp.), *Music and Musicians in Chicago: The City's Leading Artists, Organizations and Art Buildings* (Chicago: printed by the author, 1899), 23. In contrast, Laura Tunbridge states the first performance of *Dichterliebe* in England did not take place until 1895, when it was given by Harry Plunket Greene (*Singing in the Age of Anxiety* [Chicago: University of Chicago Press, 2018], 44).

9. A. A. C., "Music in New York: Thomas and His Orchestra at Steinway Hall," *Dwight's Journal of Music* 32, no. 17 (November 30, 1872): 341; "Theodore Thomas's Concerts [Boston]," *Dwight's Journal of Music* 32, no. 18 (December 14, 1872): 351; "Our Musical Season," *Chicago Tribune*, October 13, 1872, 3.

10. "Concerts," *Dwight's Journal of Music* 39, no. 994 (May 24, 1879): 85. "Music in Boston," *Musical Record* no. 32 (May 17, 1879): 101. The program in table 5.1 was transcribed from the article in Dwight's. In general, during the nineteenth century, women often performed songs with male poetic personae, as will be evidenced in the following discussion of Amalie Joachim and White, and vice versa. For a discussion of gender and the performance of cycles, see Laura Tunbridge, *The Song Cycle* (Cambridge: Cambridge University Press, 2010), 54–55.

11. Robert Schumann, *"Woman's Love and Life": New Series of Gems of German Songs* (New York: Schirmer, 1871). A program for Hiltz's recital is held in the Frederick Grant Gleason Collection of Chicago's Newberry Library. Hershey School of Musical Art, Chicago, Programs, Box 52, folder 508.

12. Song recitals were distinct from the vocal music concerts that took place during the early decades of the century in that they mainly comprised art songs rather than a

miscellany of arias, ballads, and folk songs. These earlier concerts, which rarely included a Lied, were, however, significant in that similar concerts did not emerge in Europe until the 1850s (William Weber, "Orchestral Programs in Boston, 1841–55, in European Perspective," *American Orchestras in the Nineteenth Century*, ed. John Spitzer [Chicago: University of Chicago Press, 2012], 384).

13. For Stockhausen's performances, see, for example, *Fremden-Blatt*, April 29, 1856, [8], and *Allgemeine musikalische Zeitung*, April 6, 1864, 247. For Wallenreiter: "Dur und Moll," *Signale für die musikalische Welt* 24, no. 22 (April 1866): 400, and 26, no. 3 (January 1868): 41; "Kurze Nachrichten," *Leipziger Allgemeine Musikalische Zeitung*, January 1868, 15; "Musikfeste, Aufführungen," *Neue Zeitschrift für Musik* no. 49 (November 29, 1867): 435.

14. A. G. L. "New Port R.I.," *Dwight's Journal of Music* 40, no. 1029 (September 25, 1880): 159.

15. "Schubert Song Recitals," *Plain Dealer* (Cleveland), March 8, 1887, 5. The school's director, the tenor Alfred F. Arthur, provided an introduction for the cycles. Because Arthur trained at the Boston Conservatory and Kreissmann collaborated with faculty of that institution, it is highly likely that Arthur experienced some of the many performances of Lieder in Boston.

16. Henschel conducted the Boston Symphony Orchestra from 1881 to 1884. The songs from the Schubert cycles that he sang in Boston concerts during 1884 and 1887 are listed in *The Musical Yearbook of the United States*, vols. 1–5, ed. Calvin B. Cady and G. H. Wilson (Boston: n.p., 1883–1888), vol. 1, 40 and vol. 4, [159].

17. "Heinrich, Max," in *The American History and Encyclopedia of Music* ..., vol. 1, ed. William Lines Hubbard. Musical biographies compiled by Janet M. Green (Toledo: Irving Squire, 1908), 367.

18. "Musical Matters: Max Heinrich's Second Song Recital in Steinert Hall," *Boston Daily Advertiser*, December 8, 1897, 5.

19. This performance was given in an establishment that Brahms might well have enjoyed—Lüchow's Restaurant in Manhattan. The club, whose membership was restricted to men (many of whom were of German heritage), often held recitals there. Heinrich was described as one of the few artists "with the ability to present such songs as these in their true spirit" ("Max Heinrich Sings Brahms's 'Serious Songs' for 'the Bohemians,'" *Musical America* 23, no. 9 [January 1, 1916]: 49).

20. Philip Hale, "Mr. Max Heinrich," *Boston Journal*, December 8, 1897, 7.

21. Max Heinrich, *Correct Principles of Classical Singing* (Boston: Lothrop, Lee and Shepard, 1910). Alice Mattullath provided the English translations that Heinrich used for his published editions of Lieder and for Townsend's performances. Townsend had studied with Henschel in London and was coached by Heinrich. The performances were reviewed in "Interesting Song Recital by Stephen Townsend," *Boston Journal*, March 15, 1911, 12, and "Townsend Wins High Approval," *Boston Herald*, January 29, 1913, 4.

22. "Music and Drama: Mr. William Heinrich's Third Song Recital," *Boston Journal*, February 10, 1892, 5.

23. C. L. Capen, "Musical Matters: Brahms' Magelone Lieder," *Boston Daily Advertiser*, December 12, 1891, 2. Capen cast aspersions on the number of lessons Meyn had with Stockhausen.

24. "Mme. Joachim's First Recital," *Evening Post* [New York], April 19, 1892, 7.

25. US music journals covered some of Joachim's performances of cycles in Europe as well as her recitals in the United States. See Heather Platt, "Amalie Joachim's 1892 U.S. Tour,"

American Brahms Society Newsletter 35, no. 1 (Spring 2017): 1–8. I presented further details about White's career in "Amalie Joachim's American Protégée: Villa Whitney White," paper presented at Joseph Joachim at 185: An International Conference, Boston, June 18, 2016.

26. These performers also appeared in recitals hosted by many other women's clubs. Some of the events were scheduled during the day and mainly attended by women, while others were open to the public and were attended by men as well. Linda Whitesitt has described the important role women's clubs played in organizing classical music concerts, but no one has explored their programming of Lieder (Linda Whitesitt, "Women as 'Keepers of Culture': Music Clubs, Community Concert Series and Symphony Orchestras," in *Cultivating Music in America: Women Patrons and Activists since 1860*, ed. Ralph P. Locke and Cyrilla Barr [Berkeley: University of California Press, 1997], 65–86).

27. "Under Musikverein Auspices," *Saint Paul Globe*, October 24, 1897, 8.

28. The appendixes of Beatrix Borchard's *Stimme und Geige: Amalie Joachim und Joseph Joachim*, 2nd ed. (Wien: Böhlau, 2007), provide copies of Joachim's programs, along with lists of her repertoire. See also the edition that Reimann published: *Das deutsche Lied: Eine Auswahl deutscher Gesänge aus dem 14. bis 19. Jahrhundert aus den Programmen der historischen Lieder-Abende der Frau Amalie Joachim*, 3 vols. (Berlin: Simrock, 1891–93).

29. In programming folk songs, White was following Joachim, but numerous other Lieder recitalists, including Werrenrath, also juxtaposed Lieder and folk songs.

30. From 1905 to 1908, von Fielitz worked as a teacher and conductor in Chicago, but he later returned to the Stern Conservatory.

31. "Miss White's Recital," *Boston Herald*, March 24, 1898, 6.

32. "Handel Hall," *Inter Ocean*, November 20, 1897, 6. "Music and Drama," *Boston Evening Transcript*, March 19, 1898, 21.

33. David Bispham, *A Quaker Singer's Recollections* (New York: Macmillan 1920), 49.

34. "Music," *Athenaeum* no. 3602 (November 7, 1896): 644; "Song Recital by Mr. David Bispham," *The Sun* [New York], January 13, 1897, 7.

35. Although offering some words of praise, critics had reservations about Bispham's voice and his interpretations of Beethoven's songs. [Attributed to William James Henderson], "Mr. Bispham's Recitals: Third of His Series at the Carnegie Lyceum," *New York Times*, February 10, 1897, 7. "Gesangs-Recital," *New Yorker Staats-Zeitung*, February 10, 1897, 14.

36. Press notices for Meyn's 1891 Boston recital imply that he was to give the entire cycle, but a reviewer of Bispham's performance indicates that in New York Meyn omitted three of the songs ("Mr. Bispham's Song Recital," *New York Tribune*, February 20, 1897, 6).

37. [Attributed to William James Henderson], "Mr. Bispham's Recitals: The Whole of Brahms's "Die Schoene Magelone" Excellently Given at the Opera House," *New York Times*, February 20, 1897, 6.

38. Stockhausen seems to have given the complete work only once, though he often gave excerpts from the cycle, and his students collaborated in a complete performance. Natasha Loges, "The Limits of the Lied: Brahms's *Magelone-Romanzen* op. 33," in *Brahms in the Home and the Concert Hall: Between Private and Public Performance*, ed. Katy Hamilton and Natasha Loges (Cambridge: Cambridge University Press, 2014), 314–18. Goethe Universität, Frankfurt am Main, Universitätbibliothek, Nachlaß Julius Stockhausen, Konzertprogramme, nos. 500–501.

39. [Attributed to William James Henderson], "Mr. Bispham's Song Recital: An Unusually Serious Musical Afternoon at Mendelssohn Hall," *New York Times*, December 16, 1898, 6.

40. Leonard Liebling, "The Bispham Recital," *Musical America* 1, no. 12 (December 24, 1898): 7.

41. For excerpts from reviews of both performances, see "Bispham Recital," *Musical Courier* 37, no. 25 (December 21, 1898): 16. The *New Yorker Staats-Zeitung* discussed only the performance of the Schubert cycle ("Mendelssohn Hall," *New Yorker Staats-Zeitung*, December 16, 1898, 8). This paper also noted the number of women in the audience, even though the number was typical for matinees, including those given by many other Lieder recitalists, such as Werrenrath and the Henschels. That *Frauenliebe und -leben* became one of the cycles most frequently performed in its entirety (surpassed only by *Dichterliebe*) is perhaps in large part due to the female-dominated audiences. Adrienne Fried Block discussed the significance of matinees in "Matinee Mania: The Regendering of Nineteenth-Century Audiences in New York City," *19th-Century Music* 31, no. 3 (Spring 2008): 193–216.

42. "Music and the Drama," *Milwaukee Sentinel*, May 11, 1897, 2.

43. A small number of reviews document performances of other cycles that celebrated similar milestones; for instance, David Melamet, who was best known as a composer and conductor, gave *Die schöne Müllerin* in a recital marking the hundredth anniversary of Schubert's birth. The conductor of the *Germania Männerchor* of Baltimore, Melamet was a German immigrant who had studied at Joachim's Berlin Königliche Hochschule. The existence of reports like this suggest it is quite possible that other organizations, and not just German ones, likewise used cycles for such celebrations. There is, however, an important caveat that the vocal lines and piano parts in many cycles would likely have been too difficult for the untrained amateurs who populated groups such as *Männerchore*. See "Conzert und Theater," *Deutsche Correspondent*, February 23, 1897, 4.

44. This might have been one of the last times Bispham performed this cycle ("Bispham Will Include Old Time Favorites in Song Recital Tomorrow Afternoon," *Honolulu Star Bulletin*, May 10, 1913, 5).

45. Bispham, *Quaker Singer's Recollections*, 235–36.

46. In general, New York reviews expressed a concern that Bispham was singing too much. In New York, his Brahms recital took place the day before he performed solo roles in Brahms's *Ein Deutsches Requiem* and Bach's Cantata 140; three days later, he read Byron's "Manfred" during a concert of Schumann's incidental music; and, the day after that, he sang during Elsa Breidt's piano recital ("Bispham's zweites Recital," *New Yorker Staats-Zeitung*, November 10, 1904, 14; "Last Bispham Recital," *New York Times*, December 1, 1904, 9).

47. Fanny Morris Smith, "Woman's Work in Music: Song Cycles," *Etude* 19, no. 4 (1901): 151.

48. "Van Rooy Song Recital," *Chicago Tribune*, November 28, 1902, 13. Van Rooy was primarily a Wagnerian opera singer who performed in Europe and at the Metropolitan Opera in New York.

49. "Music in New York: Mason Thomas' Last Soiree," *Musical Review and Musical World* 14, no. 9 (April 25, 1863): 98–99.

Bibliography

Bispham, David. *A Quaker Singer's Recollections*. New York: Macmillan 1920.

Block, Adrienne Fried. "Matinee Mania: The Regendering of Nineteenth-Century Audiences in New York City." *19th-Century Music* 31, no. 3 (Spring 2008): 193–216.

Borchard, Beatrix. *Stimme und Geige: Amalie und Joseph Joachim; Biographie und Interpretationsgeschichte*. 2nd ed. Vienna: Böhlau, 2007.

Bungert, Heike. "The Singing Festival of German Americans, 1849–1914." *American Music* 34, no. 2 (2016): 141–79.

Cady, Calvin B., and G. H. Wilson. *The Musical Yearbook of the United States*, vols. 1–5. Boston: n.p., 1883–1888.

French, Florence, comp. *Music and Musicians in Chicago: The City's Leading Artists, Organizations and Art Buildings*. Chicago: printed by the author, 1899.

Gienow-Hecht, Jessica C. E. *Sound Diplomacy: Music and Emotions in Transatlantic Relations, 1850–1920*. Chicago: University of Chicago Press, 2009.

Heinrich, Max. *Correct Principles of Classical Singing*. Boston: Lothrop, Lee and Shepard, 1910.

Lawrence, Vera Brodsky. *Strong on Music: The New York Music Scene in the Days of George Templeton Strong*. 3 vols. Chicago: University of Chicago Press, 1988–95.

Loges, Natasha. "The Limits of the Lied: Brahms's *Magelone-Romanzen* op. 33." In *Brahms in the Home and the Concert Hall: Between Private and Public Performance*, edited by Katy Hamilton and Natasha Loges, 300–23. Cambridge: Cambridge University Press, 2014.

Platt, Heather. "Amalie Joachim's American Protégée: Villa Whitney White." Paper presented at Joseph Joachim at 185: An International Conference, Boston, June 18, 2016.

———. "Amalie Joachim's 1892 U.S. Tour," *America Brahms Society Newsletter* 35, no. 1 (Spring 2017): 1–8.

Preston, Katherine K. "Art Music from 1800 to 1860." In *The Cambridge History of American Music*, edited by David Nicholls, 186–213. Cambridge: Cambridge University Press, 1998.

Reich, Nancy. "Robert Schumann's Music in New York City, 1848–1898." In *European Music and Musicians in New York City, 1840–1900*, edited by John Graziano, 10–28. Rochester, NY: University of Rochester Press, 2006.

Reimann, Heinrich. *Das deutsche Lied: Eine Auswahl deutscher Gesänge aus dem 14. bis 19. Jahrhundert aus den Programmen der historischen Lieder-Abende der Frau Amalie Joachim*. 3 vols. Berlin: Simrock, 1891–93.

Snyder, Suzanne. "The *Männerchor* Tradition in the United States: A Historical Analysis of Its Contribution to American Musical Culture." PhD diss., University of Iowa, 1991.

Tunbridge, Laura. *Singing in the Age of Anxiety: Lieder Performances in New York and London between the Wars*. Chicago: University of Chicago Press, 2018.

———. *The Song Cycle*. Cambridge: Cambridge University Press, 2010.

Weber, William. "Orchestral Programs in Boston, 1841–55, in European Perspective." In *American Orchestras in the Nineteenth Century*, edited by John Spitzer, 373–94. Chicago: University of Chicago Press, 2012.

Whitesitt, Linda. "Women as 'Keepers of Culture': Music Clubs, Community Concert Series, and Symphony Orchestras." In *Cultivating Music in America: Women Patrons and Activists since 1860*, edited by Ralph P. Locke and Cyrilla Barr, 65–86. Berkeley: University of California Press, 1997.

HEATHER PLATT is Professor of Music History at Ball State University. She is author of *Johannes Brahms: A Research and Information Guide* and coeditor, with Peter H. Smith, of *Expressive Intersections in Brahms: Essays in Analysis and Meaning.*

6 The Concert Hall as a Gender-Neutral Space

The Case of Amalie Joachim, née Schneeweiss

Beatrix Borchard, Translated by Jeremy Coleman

EVERY MUSICIAN RECOGNIZES the importance of spaces for performing and listening to music, as well as for the conception of individual works. Spaces are not, however, an objective given. As the sociologist Martina Löw has stressed, they are created through actions "in which intentionality, emotionality, perception, and unconscious motifs or ideas become intermixed."[1] What always arises from this, according to Löw, is a gender-specific construction of space. The following observations, based on Löw's concept of dynamic space, explore the role that concert singing in the nineteenth century and its associated modes of performance and repertoires played in female singers' career possibilities and the arguments with which the stage and concert hall were distinguished from one another. My point of departure is the career and the cultural negotiations of the alto Amalie Joachim (1839–99), because she offers an instructive example of the close relationship between gender, the social history of performers (both male and female), the history of public concert life, the economic interests of publishers, political factors, and the gender-specific construction of spaces.

A Discovery in Tunbridge Wells

A house in Tunbridge Wells. Under a bed, a suitcase filled with a musician's letters to his brother, a wool trader in London. The sender was the violinist and composer Joseph Joachim (1831–1907), best known for his friendship and professional relationship with Johannes Brahms. The suitcase was opened and viewed and finally taken to Germany, where the letters were bought with public funds for an archive. Apart from the suitcase, there was a mahogany dresser containing letters, photographs, handwritten recollections, and, above all, concert programs and scores, including an album called *Das deutsche Lied*—a "Selection of German Songs from the Historical Song Recitals of Amalie Joachim, published by Heinrich Reimann"[2] (see fig. 6.1). This was a surprise! A sung history of German song over several recitals? Once home, I realized that I already owned the collection but just never connected it with Amalie Joachim, because the title page included only the publisher's name. Only the inside cover (fig. 6.2), which I had never noticed before, revealed that Reimann's edition was based on joint concerts with Amalie Joachim.

This tale reveals our unconscious selection mechanisms: information that is not linked to preexisting knowledge is easily lost. We then believe that people who were unknown were also insignificant. It also shows how women can vanish along with their work. Today it is not Amalie Joachim (see fig. 6.3), but Dietrich Fischer-Dieskau whose name is attached to the performance history of German song, and anyone looking for printed scores of the Lied will find the name of the male arranger Heinrich Reimann on the catalog entry, not that of the female singer.

From the prerecording era, we know only those singers who embody a legend, not necessarily because of their musical achievements, but because of the (male and female) fantasies connected with them. In reality, the work of female singers during this period could be transmitted only through singing schools. Operatic roles written for particular singers and the development and propagation of particular repertoire are generally understood only in relation to the composer—if at all.

Amalie Joachim, née Schneeweiss, grew up in Styria.[3] She made her debut at the age of fourteen in Graz and sang in Sibiu, Transylvania, and at the Vienna Kärntnertortheater before she was engaged at the Hanover Royal Court Opera in 1862 as first alto. She had hardly arrived before she met Joseph Joachim and married him in 1863. If marriage meant the end of her operatic career, it also marked the beginning of her career as a concert singer.

Why was she, like countless other female singers, confronted with the stark choice between marriage or the stage?[4] The reason was primarily legal: she could not marry without the consent of the theater director. Marriage generally meant a termination of the contract without notice. Such restrictions on marriage can be found in the contracts of many actresses and female singers into the twentieth century. The consequences were secret marriages and numerous illegitimate children sent to wet nurses in the countryside. Many of these children never knew who their parents were. In the best cases, they were taken into their parents' homes as putative siblings.

But this restriction merely reflected the prevailing belief that bourgeois marriage and a stage career were simply incompatible. Put bluntly, a woman who went onto the stage to earn money was selling her body. The only way for Amalie

Fig. 6.1. *Das deutsche Lied* (Berlin: Simrock, 1893), title page. *Source:* Author's own.

Fig. 6.2. *Das deutsche Lied* (Berlin: Simrock, 1893), inside cover. *Source:* Author's own.

Fig. 6.3. Amalie Joachim, photograph, ca. 1870. *Source:* author's own.

Schneeweiss to prove her "innocence" was by withdrawing from the stage. The "voluntary renunciation of the stage for love" became a motif in countless biographical representations of singers. Of course, there were some musical couples who performed together, such as the piano duo Marie Jaëll and Alfred Jaëll or occasionally Teresa Carreño and Eugen d'Albert and the violinist Wilma Neruda and pianist-conductor Charles Hallé. In vocal performance, there were examples dating from the second half of the nineteenth century, notably the married couple Lilian Henschel and George Henschel.

For a female singer, withdrawal from the stage thus did not necessarily mean a retreat from the public sphere altogether. In the second half of the nineteenth century, concerts and oratorio singing presented new employment opportunities for married women, giving them the prospect of an independent artistic and economic existence. Amalie Joachim seized these opportunities. Her married name marked a new chapter in her life, not only identifying her as the wife of a famous man but representing an explicitly antitheatrical aesthetic program. The concert hall in the second half of the nineteenth century increasingly resembled a sacred space, a counterspace to the theater, evident not least in the temple-like architecture of concert halls such as Berlin's *Sing-Akademie*. Here Amalie Joachim could appear, as it were, in the figure of a priestess next to her husband at the altar of art.

Seeking to live up to her new name, Amalie Joachim received instruction from the baritone Julius Stockhausen (1826–1906), which focused less on technical matters than on stylistic ones. Stockhausen's own operatic career had been cut short and his resulting specialization in oratorio and song had made him a pioneer in a new professional sphere of singing purely for the concert hall.[5] Thus legitimated by him as a man, this sphere also offered married women more and more chances to participate in public concert life. Amalie Joachim had met Stockhausen shortly before her marriage while learning Schumann's *Szenen aus Goethes Faust*, WoO3. Their meeting of February 16, 1863, prompted his observation "Miss Weiß, the most talented of them all."[6] Stockhausen, who had befriended Joseph Joachim in April 1859, conducted the Philharmonic Society concerts from October 1863, as well as the Hamburg Sing-Akademie, where he had been selected for appointment in preference to Brahms. He also founded a singing school in Hamburg in 1865. It was therefore natural that in November 1866, Amalie Joachim began lessons with Stockhausen as preparation for her new career. She took her first son with her to Hamburg,[7] while her second son Hermann, still less than a year old, remained in Hanover in the care of a housemaid.

Stockhausen's teaching methods have been described in wide-ranging, sometimes critical, accounts.[8] According to Amalie Joachim's letters, he worked predominantly on her articulation and studied repertoire with her, focusing above all on interpretive aspects.[9] As she was not required to pay for her lessons,[10] it seems that she was in not the position of a pupil but rather that of a colleague; indeed, Stockhausen performed with Amalie Joachim publicly as well as privately, an indication of the high esteem in which he held her.[11]

In late 1868, the Joachims moved to Berlin, where Joseph was appointed head of the newly founded *Königliche Hochschule für Musik*. Amalie Joachim's performances became sporadic while she bore six children. But after the couple's separation in 1884, Amalie was forced to reestablish an independent artistic existence. According to some reports, she was equally interested in acting and so, first, she attempted to return to the stage.[12] Now in her early forties, she was deemed too old. She began instead to develop her song repertoire systematically and soon became one of the most important oratorio singers and song interpreters of her time. In 1897, having briefly taught at the private Scharwenka Institute in Berlin, she founded her own vocal school.

Sources

An analysis of the material relating to Amalie Joachim's concerts can reflect only the portion of songs and choral works that can be definitely identified. Surviving accounts of her personality and singing are few, but descriptive letters provide some information about her artistic reflections and personal situation, and newspapers and magazines reveal much about her concert programs. The volume of her activity is surprising, because from the second edition of Joseph Joachim's biography by Andreas Moser, one would infer that Amalie Joachim disappeared after her separation. In the scholarly literature on Brahms, her name is associated mostly with the *Alto Rhapsody*, op. 53, or with the conflict between Brahms and Joseph on the couple's divorce. Only Max Kalbeck repeatedly emphasizes Amalie Joachim's role in Brahms's song composition and how Brahms supported her during her divorce. Meanwhile, she is no longer even mentioned in a compilation of Brahms interpreters, despite her crucial importance in the dissemination of Brahms's Lieder.[13] When we speak of Brahms singers of the past, female singers are mentioned only when he was allegedly in love with them, such as the soprano Louise Dustmann, the alto Hermine Spies, and the mezzo-soprano Alice Barbi. Dustmann was primarily an opera singer, Barbi solely a concert singer. Both Spies and Barbi withdrew from public life after their marriages and so were only briefly engaged in the performance of Brahms's Lieder. In contrast, Stockhausen and Amalie Joachim, and later Gustav Walter and George Henschel, continually brought Brahms's vocal music into the concert hall. Amalie Joachim sang Brahms's songs regularly wherever she traveled from their first meeting in May 1863 until his death in 1897—that is, for thirty-three years.[14] She even formed the Amalie Joachim Quartet, with whom she toured as far as Riga in 1890 in order to popularize his *Zigeunerlieder*, op. 103, and the *Liebesliederwalzer*, opp. 52 and 65. Yet obituaries noted her only as a Schubert or Schumann interpreter: in the late nineteenth century, Brahms was not yet considered a classic of German song. Thus, a reviewer in the *Vossische Zeitung* wrote the following about a cycle of concerts that Amalie Joachim presented in three evening performances, featuring works by Schubert (November 26, 1887), Schumann (January 11, 1888), and Brahms (February 1, 1888):

> The third concert given by Ms. Joachim was a Brahms recital. It did not quite reach the heights of a Schubert or Schumann recital: in the field of Lieder, Brahms does not possess the originality or naturalness that arises in Schubert and Schumann. With individual exceptions, Brahms's Lieder demand not only a more serious commitment on the part of the listener than Schubert's or Schumann's for the predominant sentiment to be accessible, but, what is worse, they do not even reward the listener for such engagement. That which is gloomy, bitter or raw, locked up in itself and pessimistic, typically dominates to the extent that only someone who glimpses the highest artistic ideal in the expression of such voices will be the equal of the previous great masters of this genre.[15]

Amalie Joachim's selection represents not only the Brahms Lieder for low female voice that are best known today, but also many relatively unknown settings. Furthermore, there was not necessarily any correspondence between her gender and that of the lyrical subject. She thus positioned herself in opposition to the contemporary opinion that Brahms's serious Lieder should be sung only by men.[16] According to this argument, it does not depend on the vocal possibilities or timbral requirements of a composition but rather a certain quality of expression supposedly accessible only to male experience. Even today, it is still widely argued that there are certain Lieder that only men or only women can (or should) sing. As a result, the song repertoire for women today is narrower and more gender-specific than in the past. In the nineteenth century, the singer could tailor the repertoire to his or her own voice. Another important criterion for the selection of repertoire came from the composition of the program: even within a single genre, more attention was paid to contrasts than today.

The review of a concert consisting solely of Brahms Lieder that Amalie Joachim gave on April 14, 1887, highlights the variety at the heart of the singer's conception of the program:

> The Brahms Concert given by Ms. Joachim on Thursday at the *Singakademie* took place before a sizable audience. . . . Ms. Joachim presented a total of thirteen Brahms Lieder. A number of these were well known and frequently heard, while others were still unfamiliar to most. By turns light and pleasant, poignantly serious and passionately affecting, one could delight in his unique creativity and invention everywhere, the warm, characteristic feeling, the

harmonic relationships of the melody and the rich piano accompaniment. If the point was to give the audience an idea of how much German song owes to Brahms, then this was surely made by these evening recitals.[17]

Space and Place

The concerts of *Das deutsche Lied* took place in the buildings of the Berlin Sing-Akademie (see fig. 6.4) under the auspices of the *Kunstverein für die heilige Musik*. With her recital consisting only of Brahms's—in other words, exclusively contemporary—music, Amalie Joachim represented the total breadth of Brahms's œuvre as a Lied composer. As the sole concert giver, who most likely bore the full financial risk of the evening, it was her task to give the public "an idea of how much German song owed to Brahms." Presented in a hall with almost eight hundred seats, a space reserved for "holy art," *das deutsche Lied* also had a national focus. In this hall, Joseph Joachim had organized a series of eight quartet recitals every winter season for almost forty years.[18] Her commitment to the formation of Lieder repertoire for the concert hall consisting of model composers in a Schubert-Schumann-Brahms series thus paralleled the formation of the string quartet repertoire through the choice of location. The performance space elevated the Lied to a genre equally appropriate for concert performance and, simultaneously, the singer as an interpreter. She distinguished herself from other female singers of her generation above all through these programming strategies. As with the Joachim quartet recitals, the public became something of a congregation.[19] Whether this public consisted largely of middle-class women cannot yet be established, but one may assume so because the Lied was not just connoted as female, but it was predominantly women who received singing lessons, acquired scores, and sang Lieder in the domestic sphere.[20]

Indeed, singers were important in the dissemination of literature intended for domestic use. The high proportion of popular songs in Amalie Joachim's repertoire therefore reflects not only her personal preferences but also publishers' interests: Amalie Joachim was a friend of Brahms's publisher Fritz Simrock. He often invited her to rehearse songs that Brahms sent him, in domestic circles or in matinées before a small audience. The possibility of a subsequent premiere served both her profile as a singer and the interest of the publisher. Amalie Joachim was therefore a mediator in the dissemination between concert hall and private spheres of the full span of the Lied, from historical to contemporary song compositions. This mediating function was also manifested in the song collections she edited and in her sung history of German Lieder in recitals. Both these phenomena have been extensively presented and discussed elsewhere.[21] Here I shall consider only those aspects that bear on the question of the concert hall as a gender-neutral place.

Fig. 6.4. The home of the Sing-Akademie, constructed from reports by Karl Friedrich Schinkel via Theodor Ottmer. *Source:* Aquatint, ca. 1830, Bildarchiv Preußischer Kulturbesitz.

From the postcard in fig. 6.5, which describes Amalie Joachim as "Schöpferin des historischen Cyklus 'Das deutsche Lied,'" we can recognize the importance she placed on her performance of the cycle. She developed the cycle with the organist, composer, and music editor Heinrich Reimann (1850–1906), who also initially served as her piano accompanist. The source material for the program was drawn from the Royal Library in Berlin. Commentaries published as brochures by Hermann Wolff were added to individual programs, and the booklet for each recital contained an introduction and the song texts. In addition, every individual song was prefaced by a short introduction with source references.

The recitals spanned four centuries, from 1475 until the contemporary. Reimann indicated in his preface that, for musical reasons, he did not follow a purely chronological order but rather grouped the selected material according to systematic criteria and then ordered them within the groups according to the date of composition. Thus, each program traced a historical arch. The assembling of the individual numbers and the overall program dramaturgy was thus oriented to the needs of a varied concert format and not gender considerations.

Fig. 6.5. Postcard with a portrait of Amalie Joachim, ca. 1899. *Source*: Author's own.

In an explicit distancing from the Italian vocal style, Amalie Joachim dedicated her first Lieder recital to folk-style songs from the fifteenth century to the contemporary. The evening began with the Innsbruck song ("Innsbruck, ich muss dich lassen" by Heinrich Isaac) and ended with Brahms's "Wiegenlied." The concert was divided into three parts. The first part included *Tenorlieder*, designated "old German folksongs" by Reimann. Alongside the Innsbruck song and Ludwig Senfl's "Ach Elslein," she sang Lieder in arrangements by Reimann or Wilhelm Tappert befitting the prevailing tastes. The historical consciousness displayed in the selection reflected not any intention of historical authenticity but rather the living appropriation of a valued song tradition.

Reimann wrote about this topic in the German-English edition of Lieder:

> This Lieder collection presents unknown treasures of the old Lied literature in a form that preserves the purity and authenticity of the melodies as carefully as possible. But this literature demands a well-formed artistic taste in Lied arrangements of any kind. Thus, two contradictory requirements must be satisfied: first, the preservation of historical fidelity, and second, a good artistic impression (not an effect!) on the audience. Both requirements were completely alien to the greater part of the musical literature for a long time but were fulfilled by Amalie Joachim. And this merit makes her a master of German song.[22]

For the next few years, the structure of the programs remained largely unchanged, but individual folk-style songs from the first evening in particular were altered by Joachim. Sometimes she reduced the four programs to three recitals, for example, in Vienna during the International Exhibition for Music and Theater in October 1892, or even to one recital. The overall concept of the four recitals corresponded to a draft of a history of the German Lied at a time when Kretzschmar's, Friedländer's, and Breslauer's extensive accounts of the history of the German Lied had not yet appeared.

These song recitals presented the history of the German Lied as the history of a genre, situated between the oral and the written, between noncomposed music created from the collective consciousness and the unique expression of an individual. All manifestations had a place as long as they corresponded to Reimann's and Joachim's aesthetic attitude. The high proportion of folk-style pieces certainly reflected the personal preferences of the singer, but Amalie Joachim and Heinrich Reimann also wanted to oppose the mass dissemination of parlor music with something valuable by reclaiming a forgotten repertoire of domestic music. This pedagogical impetus bound such performers and scholars with composers like Brahms or Robert Franz. With folk songs and songs written in a popular style, Amalie Joachim brought music into the concert hall that had been conceived in other social contexts and that, unlike piano or chamber music, had not taken permanent root in the concert hall.

Amalie Joachim's role as mediator absolutely corresponded to the idea of the bourgeois woman, as women were associated with the role of teachers. One could say that she performed with the intention of giving back to the people its own music, to galvanize it to singing as a communal act. The artlessness of popular song ostensibly required no professional vocal training and was linked to the maternal voice. The fact that the public performance of folk-style songs inherently called for a special kind of declamation did not disturb the image of the artless and maternal. Unlike the theatrical stage, the aim was not self-display,[23] but to provide a counterweight to the mass dissemination of so-called parlor music. Did folk songs transform the concert hall into a private space with feminine connotations, into a "home," or did the perception of Lieder change through their public presentation?

Amalie Joachim's focus on Lieder not originally intended for the concert hall occasionally provoked criticism. One example was at a concert on October 26, 1894, in the Berlin Sing-Akademie, where she performed solely Brahms's German folk songs recently published by Simrock:

> Folk song is made from very rough material: it strives with all its powers to be transplanted into the concert hall. It needs hardly to be stressed that Ms. Joachim has availed herself of the task masterfully. She sang the mournful

Lieder just as intimately as those that were light, cheerful, cheeky, or charming. Despite her consummate artistry, the Lieder recital as a whole was a little monotonous from the minor-mode character of the songs—Brahms only closes archaistically in the major. Perhaps it would have been better to sing the eighteen folksongs not one after another but to interpolate some of them in a concert of art songs. The concert organizer was supported superbly by the vocal quartet of the women Villa Whitney White and Klara von Senfft and the men Heinrich Grahl and Arthur von Eweyk.[24]

Her efforts in developing repertoire for both public and domestic performance were nevertheless thoroughly appreciated. Her sung history of the German Lied was received differently, not because of her underlying intention, but because of the question of how suitable the songs actually were for public performance. One Berlin critic declared Amalie Joachim's historical Lieder recitals to be "heroic deeds" ("Heldenthaten"), especially with respect to her variety of characterization, and noted the different kinds of applause lavished on her:

> Surveying Mrs. Joachim's whole achievement, one immediately recalls the heroic deeds executed by Bülow with his performance of Beethoven's complete sonatas or by Rubinstein with his seven historic piano recitals. In terms of the stamina that [Amalie Joachim] used in physical and intellectual respects, there is hardly any song recitalist to equal her. Still, it is not the same if someone presents a recital of, for example, the Müller Lieder one evening, *Winterreise* on the next, and *Schwanengesang* on the third. Just as one should not underestimate the physical effort such achievements require, one can also not underestimate the intellectual effort that Mrs. Joachim had to expend to characterize the styles of eras so distant from one another. In the art of individualization alone, Mrs. Joachim displayed a mastery that raised her far above all her singer colleagues whose voices are still so much more blooming and youthful than hers.
>
> The faithful congregation that Mrs. Joachim gathered around her for the four Lieder concerts fully appreciated the great artistic achievement as well as the unusual artistic gifts of the singer, and I note with particular pleasure this time that at the end the listeners gave thanks for the wealth of delights she had presented not only with thunderous shouts, but also with kerchief-waving, cheering, and all other signs of amazement.[25]

Meanwhile, the *Neues Wiener Tagblatt* scathingly deemed the concerts a failure, and as so often, one can learn more about the performance style of an artist from a bad review than from a good one:

> Already in September, during our music exhibition, Mrs. Amalie Joachim undertook the experiment of presenting the development of the German Lied in a cycle of three recitals, and she is about to repeat it. This time the podium has been relocated to the Great Hall of the Musikverein, and the first recital took place last Friday. That evening alone spanned four centuries. . . .

The similarity of the compositions from the slender first section out of which the emotional world of the songs in the second section extends, produced a certain monotony in the hall and a dangerous tendency toward boredom. Mrs. Joachim's whole manner of singing and declamation is realized by means of an affectation that becomes almost unbearable after some time. The certain underlining of every word, every syllable, the overacting, the laughter where there is nothing to laugh at, reduces the whole manner of performance to a thoroughly inartistic exaggeration. Mozart's "Wiegenlied," so moving and delightful in its simplicity, is inflated by Mrs. Joachim to a colossal dramatic scene, as is the folk song "Phyllis und die Mutter" and Schubert's "Haidenröslein" [sic], and thus each song that had ever become popular for its simplicity the singer manages to strip of its character. Mrs. Joachim coped better with the most modern Lieder, although even these suffered from the flaunting of a less-than-entirely refined taste.[26]

The Vienna critic regarded Amalie Joachim's theatrical style as an offense against the spirit of folk song—although the examples he named were without exception dramatic or scenic Lieder. Evidently, her performance transformed the concert hall in his eyes and ears, if only temporarily, into a theatrical space.

The Concert Hall as a Gender-Neutral Space? Spaces and Ways of Singing

With such devices of scenic interpretation as acting, laughter, theatrical declamation, outward-turned expressivity, the gender of the singer once again comes into play. Amalie Joachim's performance style can hardly have been gender-neutral, at least in the folk songs and scenic Lieder. She did not consistently theatricalize but rather modified her way of performance to suit the character of individual compositions, and from this we may gather that the "clarity of her objective representation" ("Klarheit der sachlichen Darstellung") had become widely reputed.[27] In the preceding discussion, objectivity as an interpretive ideal is placed in opposition to the use of theatrical means. Did the notion of "theater in the concert hall" amount to an offense against the sacralization of concert singing?

Defined against the stage as a space of spectatorship and of bodily representation, the concert hall was conceived as a potentially gender-neutral sacred place dedicated to art and to audition. This understanding corresponded to the aesthetic ideal propagated by art song and oratorio. For example, in reviews of Amalie Joachim's manner of performance, the "stylistic purity and objectivity" ("Stilreinheit und Objektivität") of her singing was held up as exemplary. "Style" in this instance meant above all oratorio style. "Calmness" ("Ruhe"), "warmth" ("Wärme"), "resounding voice" ("großer Ton") or "maestria" (Hans von Bülow's word), "sincere sacred solemnity" ("hoher heiliger Ernst"), and "dignified, noble restraint" ("würdevolles, edles Maßhalten") were all deemed essential characteristics of her performance manner.[28] In these descriptions, she assumes a gender-neutral, almost sacerdotal, figure singing at the altar of art. Hermine Spies provides another example, about whom it was said that "While the face of the singer maintained an ethereal, sibylline expression in communion with the eternal, the capacity of her voice grew in the course of her singing, becoming more and more beautiful with it. The objective and to an extent sexless quality, which lends the timbral character of her organ its uniqueness, allows Ms. Spies to represent the whole of human nature, as far as lyrical song goes."[29]

It was thanks to this very neutrality of gender—that is, the notion that the work could be performed by women as well as by men—that "the whole of human nature" could be represented. Thus, appearances on the concert hall stage did not contradict the widespread bourgeois feminine ideal, and women's public singing had no taint of prostitution. Hardly anyone expected singers to choose gender-specific repertoire. Just as it was self-evident for Amalie Joachim to sing Beethoven's *An die ferne Geliebte*, op. 98, Brahms's *Magelone* Romances, op. 33, and Schubert's cycles *Die schöne Müllerin*, D795, *Winterreise*, D911, and the Heine settings from *Schwanengesang*, D957, so Julius Stockhausen sang Schumann's *Frauenliebe und -leben*, op. 42. When Hans Christian Andersen met the Schumanns in Leipzig in 1844, it was Livia Frege née Gerhardt (1818–91) who performed Robert Schumann's opus 40 to him at the composer's behest.[30] Furthermore, Schumann's dedications of his song cycles opp. 24 and 25 to Pauline Viardot-Garcia (1821–1910) and Wilhelmine Schröder-Devrient (1804–60) respectively, even today regarded as almost exclusively for men, were not merely polite dedications but indications of the vocal character, not the gender, that Robert Schumann had composed into his Lieder.[31] Song in the concert hall also opened up new opportunities for female pianists, who could thus also present themselves as composers. Thus Mary Wurm, pupil of Clara Schumann and Charles Villiers Stanford, played Chopin's *Andante spianato et grande polonaise brillante* in E-flat as well as two pieces of her own composition, an Impromptu and a Barcarolle in this concert. (See table 6.1.)

In view of what has been said here, one could arrive at the following conclusion: the privileges and aura of chamber music as well as performers' self-image as servants of particular works, rather than in terms of their gender, shaped the way in which performance space was perceived as an antithesis to the notion of theater in the concert hall.[32] The question of place, whether a public concert hall or a room in a private residence, appeared relatively insignificant. It is the music that shapes the allegedly gender-neutral space as long as the audience's view is not intentionally directed at the bodies of the players, nor on the execution of the playing, but on the notes. Nevertheless, for female singers and female pianists, the halls in which these concerts took place remained spaces

Table 6.1. Program for an Alice Barbi and Mary Wurm concert.

Altes Gewandhaus
Sonnabend, den 6. Februar 1892, Abends 7½ Uhr:
Concert Von Alice Barbi K K. Oest. Kammersängerin Unter Mitwirkung von Fräulein Mary Wurm
Programm

1.	Variationen "The Harmonious Blacksmith"			G. F. Händel
2.	a.	Aria "Sospiri d'uscite"	a. d. 17. u. 18. Jahrhundert	G. Carissimi.
	b.	Arietta "Star vicini"		Sal. Rosa.
	c.	La Zingarella		G. Paisiello
3.	Andante spianato und Polonaise Es dur.			F. Chopin
4.	Lieder:			
	a.	Der Wegweiser		
	b.	Die Forelle		Franz Schubert
	c.	Trockne Blumen		
	d.	Heidenröslein		
5.	Lieder			
	a.	O versenk dein Leid		
	b.	Vor dem Fenster		Joh. Brahms
	c.	Immer leiser wird mein Schlummer		
	d.	Meine Liebe ist grün		
	e.	Wenn ich in deine Augen seh'		Rob. Schumann
	f.	Frühlingsnacht		
6.	a.	Impromptu. Barcarole		Mary Wurm
	b.	Valse-Caprice		A. Rubinstein
7.	Cavatine a "Tancred"			G. Rossini
	Concertflügel: Jul. Blüthner			

of cultural representation of a canon defined by men. When one inquires about women's places and spaces in urban musical culture, one notices that social inequality between the sexes through the ideological inscription of space and the interpretation of repertoire and "masculine" or "feminine" ways of playing endured not only well into the twentieth century but, to some extent, have even been sharpened since and that women's achievements have been marginalized through music historiography.[33] The example of Amalie Joachim demonstrates the importance of acknowledging the roles played by female artists in establishing performance conventions of repertoire, programming, and spaces.

Notes

1. Martina Löw, *The Sociology of Space: Materiality, Social Structures, and Action*, trans. Donald Goodwin (London: Palgrave Macmillan, 2016), 118. See also Martina Löw, *Raumsoziologie* (Frankfurt: Suhrkamp, 2001), 144; and Susanne Rode-Breymann, "Orte und Räume kulturellen Handelns von Frauen," in *History/Herstory: Alternative Musikgeschichten*, eds. Annette Kreutziger-Herr and Katrin Losleben (Vienna: Böhlau, 2009), 186–197.

2. Amalie Joachim and Heinrich Reimann, eds., *Das deutsche Lied: Eine Auswahl deutscher Gesänge aus dem XIVten bis XIXten Jahrhundert aus den Programmen der historischen Lieder-Abende der Frau Amalie Joachim*, 4 vols. (Berlin: Simrock, 1891–94).

3. See Beatrix Borchard, *Stimme und Geige: Amalie und Joseph Joachim; Biographie und Interpretationsgeschichte*, 2nd ed. (Vienna: Böhlau, 2007).

4. On the numerous biographies, see Beatrix Borchard and Nina Noeske, eds., *Musikvermittlung und Genderforschung: Lexikon und multimediale Präsentationen* (Hamburg: Hochschule für Musik und Theater Hamburg, 2003), http://mugi.hfmt-hamburg.de/.

5. See Julia Wirth, *Julius Stockhausen, der Sänger des deutschen Liedes: Nach Dokumenten seiner Zeit dargestellt* (Frankfurt: Englert and Schlosser, 1927).

6. "Fräulein Weiß, die talentvollste von allen." Letter from Julius Stockhausen to Frau Riggenbach-Stehlin, Basel, February 16, 1863. Cited in Borchard, *Stimme und Geige*, 239.

7. Letter from Amalie Joachim to Joseph Joachim, November 1866, Hamburg, Staats- und Universitätsbibliothek Hamburg: Briefe Joseph Joachim an Amalie Joachim Signatur BRA: Be3: 158-412 (unpublished), here: SUB, BRA: B3: 228, cited in Borchard, *Stimme und Geige*, 267–68.

8. See the preface to Renate Hofmann, ed., *Johannes Brahms im Briefwechsel mit Julius Stockhausen* (Tutzing, Ger.: Schneider, 1993), 12. Stockhausen's *Gesangsmethode* (Peters edition no. 2190; Leipzig: Peters, 1884) remains informative today. See also Monika Hunnius, *Mein Weg zur Kunst* (Heilbronn, Ger.: Eugen Salzer, 1925), 59ff; and Marie Gallison, *Aus meinem Leben in zwei Welten*, 4th ed. (Kaiserswerth, Ger.: Buchhandlung der Diakonissen-Anstalt, 1929), 78ff.

9. Letter from Amalie Joachim to Joseph Joachim, Hamburg, November 26, 1866, Hamburg, Staats- und Universitätsbibliothek Hamburg, BRA: B3: 230.

10. "Wie kann ich mich nur Stockhausen erkenntlich beweisen? Welchen Rath gibst Du mir?" (letter from Amalie Joachim to Joseph Joachim, December 1, 1866, Hamburg, Staats- und Universitätsbibliothek Hamburg, BRA: B3: 231).

11. Various examples of performances conducted by Stockhausen of works like Mendelssohn's *Elijah*, Beethoven's *Mass in C*, Gluck's *Orpheus*, and Schumann's *Das Paradies und die Peri* can be traced in the *Allgemeine musikalische Zeitung* in the mid-1860s. Private performances are documented in letters.

12. See Letter from Amalie Schneeweiss to Luise Scholz, September 9, 1862, Brahms-Institut an der Musikhochschule Lübeck, Sammlung Hofmann.

13. Christian Martin Schmidt, *Johannes Brahms und seine Zeit* (Laaber, Ger.: Laaber, 1983), 4.

14. See the analyses of the repertoire on the CD-ROM to Borchard, *Stimme und Geige*.

15. "Das dritte der von Frau Joachim gegebenen Konzerte war ein Brahms-Abend. Er konnte schon aus dem Grunde die Höhe eines Schubert- oder Schumann-Abend nicht erreichen, weil Brahms auf dem Gebiet des Liedes nicht die Ursprünglichkeit und

Natürlichkeit besitzt, durch die Schubert und Schumann sich so hoch emporschwangen. Brahms' Lieder verlangen—mit vereinzelten Ausnahmen—nicht nur eine viel ernstere Hingabe des Hörers als die Schubert'schen und die Schumann'schen, um überhaupt der Empfindung zugänglich zu werden, sondern sie gewähren, was schlimmer ist, für ein solches Entgegenkommen noch nicht einmal den hinlänglichen Lohn. Das Düstere, Herbe und Rauhe, das sich Verschließende, das Pessimistische überwiegt häufig in einem Maße, daß nur derjenige, der im Ausdruck solcher und ähnlicher Stimmungen das höchste Kunstideal erblickt, ihn auch in dieser Gattung als den großen früheren Meistern ebenbürtig betrachten kann" (*Vossische Zeitung* [Berlin], February 4, 1888).

16. See Philipp Spitta, "Johannes Brahms," *Zur Musik: Sechzehn Aufsätze* (Berlin: Paetel, 1892), 405. See also Heather Platt, "The Construction of Gender and Mores in Brahms's Mädchenlieder," in *Brahms in the Home and the Concert Hall: Between Private and Public Performance*, eds. Katy Hamilton and Natasha Loges (Cambridge: Cambridge University Press, 2014), 256–78; Marion Gerards, *Frauenliebe–Männerleben: Die Musik von Johannes Brahms und der Geschlechterdiskurs im 19. Jahrhundert* (Cologne: Böhlau, 2010); and Gerards, "Johannes Brahms," *MUGI: Musikvermittlung und Genderforschung; Lexikon und multimediale Präsentationen*, eds. Beatrix Borchard and Nina Noeske (Hamburg: Hochschule für Musik und Theater Hamburg), accessed June 22, 2017, https://mugi.hfmt-hamburg.de/Artikel/Johannes_Brahms.html. See further Marcia J. Citron, "Männlichkeit, Nationalismus und musikpolitische Diskurse. Die Bedeutung von Gender in der Brahmsrezeption," in *History/Herstory: Alternative Musikgeschichten*, eds. Annette Kreutziger-Herr and Katrin Losleben (Vienna: Böhlau, 2009), 352–74.

17. "Das von Frau Joachim am Donnerstag in der Singakademie veranstaltete Brahms-Konzert fand vor einem ansehnlichen Zuhörerkreis statt. . . . Frau Joachim brachte im Ganzen dreizehn Brahms'sche Lieder zum Vortrag, unter ihnen eine Anzahl der bekannten und oft gehörten, während andere den Meisten wohl noch fremd waren. Leichteres und Gefälliges, wehmütig Ernstes und Sinniges, leidenschaftlich Ergreifendes wechselten in fesselnder Weise miteinander ab, und überall konnte man sich der eigenthümlichen Erfindung, der warmen und charakteristischen Empfindung und des harmonischen Verhältnisses der Melodie und der reichen Klavierbegleitung in hohem Maße erfreuen. Kam es darauf an, den Zuhörern eine Vorstellung zu gewähren, wie viel auch das deutsche Lied Brahms verdankt, so mußte es durch die Vorträge dieses Abends geschehen" (*Vossische Zeitung* [Berlin], April 15, 1887). Because the reviewer does not name any titles, nor were they stated on the concert advertisements, we do not know in any detail which works Amalie Joachim sang.

18. Beatrix Borchard, "Quartettspiel und Kulturpolitik im Berlin der Kaiserzeit: Das Joachim-Quartett," in *Der "männliche" und der "weibliche" Beethoven: Bericht über den Internationalen musikwissenschaftlichen Kongress vom 31. Oktober bis 4. November an der Universität der Künste Berlin*, eds. Cornelia Bartsch, Beatrix Borchard, and Rainer Cadenbach (Bonn: Beethoven-Haus, 2003), 369–98.

19. See the review of a Lieder recital in *Allgemeine musikalische Zeitung*, December 4, 1891.

20. See Katharina Hottmann, ed., *Liedersingen: Studien zur Aufführungsgeschichte des Liedes* (Hildesheim, Ger.: Olms, 2013), 109–26.

21. See Beatrix Borchard, "Amalie Joachim und die gesungene Geschichte des deutschen Liedes," *Archiv für Musikwissenschaft* 4, no. 58 (2001): 265–99; and Reinhold Brinkmann, "Musikalische Lyrik im 19. Jahrhundert," *Musikalische Lyrik*, vol. 2, *Vom 19. Jahrhundert bis*

zur Gegenwart—außereuropäische Perspektiven, ed. Hermann Danuser (Laaber, Ger.: Laaber, 2004), *Handbuch der musikalischen Gattungen* 8, no. 2, 103-12.

22. "Danach sollte diese Liedersammlung unbekannte Schätze vorzugsweise der älteren Liedliteratur in der Form darbieten, welche einmal die Reinheit und Echtheit der Melodien so sorgsam als möglich bewahrt, sodann aber den Ansprüchen gerecht wird, die ein wohlgebildeter—also kein einseitiger—künstlerischer Geschmack an Lieder-Bearbeitungen jeder Art zu stellen genötigt ist. Somit waren zwei scheinbar sich widersprechende Forderungen zu erfüllen: Historische Treue zu wahren und eine gute künstlerische Wirkung (keinen Effect!) bei einem Publikum zu erreichen, welches zum weitaus grössten Teile der Musikliteratur einer entlegenen Zeit vollkommen fremd gegenüber stand. Dass dies schwierige Unterfangen gelang, ist, in allererster Reihe das hohe Verdienst der Meisterin des deutschen Sanges, Amalie Joachim" (Heinrich Reimann, *Das deutsche Lied*, vol. 3 [Berlin: Simrock, 1893], preface).

23. Andreas Moser, *Joseph Joachim: Ein Lebensbild*, exp. ed. (Berlin: Verlag der Deutschen Brahms-Gesellschaft, 1908–1910), 2: 413.

24. "Das Volkslied ist eben von sehr sprödem Stoff; es widerstrebt mit all seinen Kräften der Verpflanzung in den Konzertsaal. Es braucht kaum hervorgehoben zu werden, daß Frau Joachim sich ihrer Aufgabe mit Meisterschaft entledigte. Sie sang die schwermüthigen Lieder eben so innig wie die wenigen heiteren schalkhaft anmuthig. Trotz ihrer vollendeten Kunst war der Liederabend in seiner Gesammtheit wegen des vorherrschenden Mollcharakters der Gesänge—Brahms schließt archaistisch in Dur—ein wenig eintönig. Vielleicht wäre es besser gewesen, die achtzehn Volkslieder nicht hintereinander zu singen, sondern einem Konzert von Kunstliedern einige derselben einzufügen. Unterstützt wurde die Konzertgeberin in trefflicher Weise durch das Vokalquartett der Damen Villa Whitney White, Klara von Senfft, der Herren Heinrich Grahl und Arthur von Eweyk" (*Vossische Zeitung* [Berlin], October 27, 1894).

25. "Überschaut man die ganze Leistung der Frau Joachim, so wird man unwillkürlich an die Heldenthaten erinnert, die Bülow mit seinem Vortrag sämtlicher Beethoven'schen Sonaten und Rubinstein mit seinen sieben historischen Klavierabenden verrichtet haben. Die Ausdauer, welche die Künstlerin in physischer und geistiger Hinsicht bethätigt hat, dürfte unter Gesangskünstlern kaum ihres Gleichen haben. Es ist doch nicht dasselbe, ob Jemand z. B. an einem Abend die Müllerlieder, an einem andern die Winterreise, und an einem dritten den Schwanengesang öffentlich vortragen würde. So wenig die physische Anstrengung bei solchen Leistungen unterschätzt werden soll, so wenig könnte sich die geistige mit derjenigen messen, welche Frau Joachim aufwenden musste, um die Stylarten so fern auseinander liegender Epochen kunstgerecht zu charakterisiren. Gerade in der Kunst des Individualisirens bekundete Frau Joachim eine Meisterschaft, die sie weit über alle Sangeskolleginnen erhebt, mögen deren Stimmen auch um noch so viel blühender und jugendfrischer sein, als die ihrige. Die getreue Gemeinde, welche Frau Joachim während der vier von ihr gegebenen Liederkonzerte um sich versammelt hatte, würdigte in vollstem Maasse die große künstlerische That sowohl wie das ungewöhnliche künstlerische Vermögen der Sängerin, und mit besonderer Genugthuung verzeichne ich diesmal, dass die Zuhörer am Schluss nicht nur mit donnernden Zurufen, sondern auch mit Tücherwehen, gesungenen Hochrufen und allen anderen Zeichen der Bewunderung der Künstlerin Dank sagten für die Fülle von Genüssen, die sie ihnen dargeboten hat"

(*Allgemeine musikalische Zeitung*, December 4, 1891 [review of the first four historical Lieder recitals]).

26. "Frau Amalie Joachim hat das Experiment, die Entwicklung des deutschen Liedes in einem drei Abende umfassenden Zyklus praktisch zu demonstrieren bereits während der Septembertage unserer Musikausstellung durchgeführt und ist eben im Begriffe, dasselbe zu wiederholen. Diesmal ist das Podium in den großen Musikvereinssaal verlegt und am vergangenen Freitag hat der erste Abend stattgefunden. Gleich der erste Abend umfaßte vier Jahrhunderte. . . . Die Aehnlichkeit, ja Gleichartigkeit des Tonsatzes der Lieder aus der ersten Abteilung, der enge Kreis, in dem sich die Empfindungswelt der Gesänge aus der zweiten bewegt, brachten eine gewisse Monotonie in den Saal, der den gefährlichen Anstoß zur Langeweile bildet. Ueberdies ist die ganze Sing- und Deklamationsweise der Frau Joachim von einer Affektation erfüllt, die auf die Dauer geradezu unerträglich wird. Dieses gewisse Unterstreichen jedes Wortes, jeder Silbe, diese überladene Mimik, dieses Lachen, wo es nichts zu lachen gibt, stempeln die ganze Vortragsweise des Gastes zu einer fortwährenden und durchaus unkünstlerischen Uebertreibung. Mozart's Wiegenlied, in seiner Einfachheit so rührend und liebenswürdig, wird von Frau Joachim zu einer kolossalen dramatischen Szene aufgebauscht, ebenso wie das Volkslied "Phyllis und die Mutter" und Schubert's "Haidenröslein," und so gelingt es der Sängerin vollständig, jedes dieser durch ihre Einfachheit so volkstümlich gewordenen Lieder ihres Charakters zu entkleiden. Relativ besser gelang Frau Joachim das modernste Lied, doch litt auch dieses an den Exaltationen eines durchaus nicht geläuterten Geschmacks."—W. Fr. (*Neues Wiener Tagblatt*, February 5, 1893, 7).

27. This formulation comes from a review in the *Vossischen Zeitung* (Berlin) of February 19, 1884, "16.2.[18]84 Concert im Krollschen Theater."

28. See Heinrich Reimann, *Musikalische Rückblicke*, vol. 2, *Amalie Joachim: Ein Blatt der Erinnerung auf das Grab einer Unvergeßlichen* (Berlin: Harmonie. Verlagsgesellschaft für Literatur und Kunst, 1900), 125.

29. "Wie das Angesicht der Sängerin durch die Berührung mit dem Ewigen einen erdentrückten, sibyllischen Ausdruck erhält, so wachsen ihrer Stimme Schwingen während ihres Gesanges, und sie verschönt sich in und mit demselben. Das Objective und gewissermaßen Geschlechtslose, welches dem Klangcharakter ihres Organs eigenthümlich ist, erlaubt Fräulein Spies die gesamte Menschennatur, soweit sie im lyrischen Gesange sich erschöpfen läßt, zur Darstellung zu bringen." In reference to her Viennese debut in 1886, see Reimann, *Musikalische Rückblicke*, 2: 136.

30. Brigitte Richter, *Frauen um Felix Mendelssohn Bartholdy* (Leipzig: Eudora, 2014), 103.

31. See Rebecca Grotjahn, "Das Geschlecht der Stimme," in *Musik und Gender*, eds. Rebecca Grotjahn and Sabine Vogt (Laaber, Ger.: Laaber, 2010), 158–169.

32. See Beatrix Borchard, "Der Virtuose—ein 'weiblicher' Künstlertypus?," in *Musikalische Virtuosität*, eds. Heinz von Loesch, Ulrich Mahlert, and Peter Rummenhöller (Mainz, Ger.: Schott, 2005), 63–76.

33. Even in the new *Die Musik in Geschichte und Gegenwart* article on the topic of string quartet ensembles, only three of the women's quartets are listed as special ensembles to which "the early emancipation of women" is indebted. See Ludwig Finscher, "Streichqua-Ensemble," in *Die Musik in Geschichte und Gegenwart*, 2nd ed., ed. Ludwig Finscher, vol. 8 (Kassel: Bärenreiter Verlag, 1977–89), 98.

Bibliography

Borchard, Beatrix. "Amalie Joachim und die gesungene Geschichte des deutschen Liedes." *Archiv für Musikwissenschaft* 4, no. 58 (2001): 265–99.
———. *Clara Schumann: Musik als Lebensform. Neue Quellen. Andere Schreibweisen.* Hildesheim: George Olms, 2019.
———. "Quartettspiel und Kulturpolitik im Berlin der Kaiserzeit: Das Joachim-Quartett." In *Der "männliche" und der "weibliche" Beethoven: Bericht über den internationalen musikwissenschaftlichen Kongress vom 31. Oktober bis 4. November an der Universität der Künste Berlin*, edited by Cornelia Bartsch, Beatrix Borchard, and Rainer Cadenbach, 369–98. Bonn: Beethoven-Haus, 2003.
———. "Die Sängerin Amalie Joachim und *Die schöne Müllerin* von Franz Schubert." In *Frauen- und Männerbilder in der Musik*, edited by Freia Hoffmann, 69–80. Oldenburg, Ger.: Universität Oldenburg, 2000.
———. *Stimme und Geige: Amalie und Joseph Joachim; Biographie und Interpretationsgeschichte.* Vienna: Böhlau, 2007.
———. "Der Virtuose—ein 'weiblicher' Künstlertypus?" In *Musikalische Virtuosität* edited by Heinz von Loesch, Ulrich Mahlert, and Peter Rummenhöller, 63–76. Mainz, Ger.: Schott, 2005.
Borchard, Beatrix, and Nina Noeske, eds. *Musikvermittlung und Genderforschung: Lexikon und multimediale Präsentationen.* http://mugi.hfmt-hamburg.de/.
Brinkmann, Reinhold. "Musikalische Lyrik im 19. Jahrhundert." In *Musikalische Lyrik*. Vol. 2, *Vom 19. Jahrhundert bis zur Gegenwart—außereuropäische Perspektiven*, edited by Hermann Danuser, 9–124. Laaber, Ger.: Laaber, 2004.
Finscher, Ludwig. "Streichquartett-Ensemble." In *Die Musik in Geschichte und Gegenwart*, 2nd ed., edited by Ludwig Finscher. Vol. 8. Kassel: Bärenreiter Verlag, 1977–89.
Gallison, Marie. *Aus meinem Leben in zwei Welten.* 4th ed. Kaiserswerth, Ger.: Buchhandlung der Diakonissen-Anstalt, 1929.
Gerards, Marion. *Frauenliebe–Männerleben: Die Musik von Johannes Brahms und der Geschlechterdiskurs im 19. Jahrhundert.* Cologne: Böhlau, 2010.
———. "Johannes Brahms," MUGI: Musikvermittlung und Genderforschung; Lexikon und multimediale Präsentationen. Edited by Beatrix Borchard and Nina Noeske. Hamburg: Hochschule für Musik und Theater Hamburg. Accessed June 22, 2017. https://mugi.hfmt-hamburg.de/Artikel/Johannes_Brahms.html.
Grotjahn, Rebecca. "Das Geschlecht der Stimme." In *Musik und Gender*, edited by Rebecca Grotjahn and Sabine Vogt, 158–69. Laaber, Ger.: Laaber, 2010.
Hofmann, Renate, ed. *Johannes Brahms im Briefwechsel mit Julius Stockhausen.* Tutzing, Ger.: Schneider, 1993.
Hottmann, Katharina, ed. *Liedersingen: Studien zur Aufführungsgeschichte des Liedes.* Hildesheim, Ger.: Olms, 2013.
Hunnius, Monika. *Mein Weg zur Kunst.* Heilbronn, Ger.: Eugen Salzer, 1925.
Joachim, Amalie, and Heinrich Reimann, eds. *Das deutsche Lied: Eine Auswahl deutscher Gesänge aus dem XIVten bis XIXten Jahrhundert aus den Programmen der historischen Lieder-Abende der Frau Amalie Joachim.* 4 vols. Berlin: Simrock, 1891–94.
Löw, Martina. *Raumsoziologie.* Frankfurt: Suhrkamp, 2001.

———. *The Sociology of Space: Materiality, Social Structures, and Action*. Translated by Donald Goodwin. London: Palgrave Macmillan, 2016.
Moser, Andreas. *Joseph Joachim: Ein Lebensbild*. 2 vols. Berlin: Verlag der Deutschen Brahms-Gesellschaft, 1908–10.
Platt, Heather. "The Construction of Gender and Mores in Brahms's *Mädchenlieder*." In *Brahms in the Home and the Concert Hall: Between Private and Public Performance*, edited by Katy Hamilton and Natasha Loges, 256–78. Cambridge: Cambridge University Press, 2014.
Reimann, Heinrich. *Das deutsche Lied*. Berlin: Simrock, 1893.
———. *Musikalische Rückblicke*. Vol. 2, *Amalie Joachim: Ein Blatt der Erinnerung auf das Grab einer Unvergeßlichen*. Berlin: Harmonie. Verlagsgesellschaft für Literatur und Kunst, 1900.
Richter, Brigitte. *Frauen um Felix Mendelssohn Bartholdy*. Leipzig: Eudora, 2014.
Rode-Breymann, Susanne. "Orte und Räume kulturellen Handelns von Frauen." In *History/Herstory: Alternative Musikgeschichten*, edited by Annette Kreutziger-Herr and Katrin Losleben, 186–97. Vienna: Böhlau, 2009.
Schmidt, Christian Martin. *Johannes Brahms und seine Zeit*. Laaber, Ger.: Laaber, 1983.
Spitta, Philipp. *Zur Musik: Sechzehn Aufsätze*. Berlin: Paetel, 1892.
Wirth, Julia. *Julius Stockhausen, der Sänger des deutschen Liedes: Nach Dokumenten seiner Zeit dargestellt*. Frankfurt: Englert and Schlosser, 1927.

BEATRIX BORCHARD is Emeritus Professor of Musicology at the University of Music and Theater in Hamburg. She is author of *Clara Schumann: Ihr Leben*; *Fanny Hensel geb. Mendelssohn Bartholdy*; and *Stimme und Geige: Amalie und Joseph Joachim*.

JEREMY COLEMAN is Teaching Fellow of Music at the University of Aberdeen.

7 Nikolai Medtner
Championing the German Lied and Russian Spirit

Maria Razumovskaya

As IMPERIAL RUSSIA entered its final years, the Russian philosopher Ivan Ilyin (1883–1954) was full of hope that music would heal the world: "When our sickly generation is gone, the process of disintegration is over, and chaos is pushed back into the abyss whence it came, one of the musical thinkers of the future will [look back to the past] and give it new artistic meaning and depth, and reveal it to the world in fresh brilliance."[1] The composer in question was Nikolai Karlovich Medtner (1880–1951), the younger contemporary of Aleksandr Scriabin and Sergey Rachmaninoff. Unlike the latter two, who, according to Ilyin, had along with "all the Russian modernist musicians and poets" been unable to carry such a burden, and "lost their footing and fell," Medtner's Muscovite roots and German ancestry had put him in an altogether different league.[2]

Because Medtner graduated from the Moscow Conservatory at the age of twenty with the coveted Anton Rubinstein Prize and quickly garnered the respect of figures such as Arthur Nikisch and Wilhelm Furtwängler, it seemed that he would commit himself to the career of a virtuoso pianist. Medtner, however, turned his energies to composition. Medtner's output was prolific, focusing mainly on piano and chamber works. His lifelong search for what he called music's "internal song" led him to focus on this idea through the completion of just over a hundred Lieder. Like his friend Rachmaninoff, Medtner found his distinct voice in a style that delights in complex polyphonic textures and abandons itself in seemingly endless waves of melodic lines. Although his harmonic language always remained tonal—prompting accusations of being a neo-Brahmsian from some of his critics and, on the other hand (much to his annoyance and denial) praise that he embodied the best traits of Hugo Wolf—Medtner's harmonic inventiveness rewards the perseverance of listeners with a tapestry of luxurious, often meandering, chromaticism. With the harmonic material tending to define itself horizontally rather than vertically through the music's texture, Medtner's frequent use of chains of half-diminished chords, Neapolitan harmonic areas, chromatically altered dominants, and unresolved augmented sixths are often heard moving through intricate cross rhythms, passing across parts and leading on through inner voices.

Although Medtner's music seldom finds a place outside specialist circles today, and indeed suffered from various bans in Russia during the Soviet era for political reasons, in his day he was a messianic symbol of hope for many intellectuals living and working in Moscow in the final years of imperial Russia. This chapter will discuss how Medtner's task of healing a broken society through music fell on him at a time when artistic discourse on a Russian national identity had all but exhausted itself. Yielding only an inchoate but determined vision of otherness, Slavophile thinkers had sought to use Russian song to differentiate themselves from foreign German and French cultures. Against this context, Medtner's decision to look specifically to the German Lied to define Russian art in composition and performance was profoundly significant. Turning to Goethe as a symbol of the universal man, Medtner's numerous settings of Goethe's poetry ignited the enthusiasm of a dynamic intellectual community centered on the pre-Revolutionary Muscovite gatherings at the House of Song (*Dom pesni*), created by Maria Olenina-d'Alheim (1869–1970). Here, rather unexpectedly, Medtner's *Goethe Lieder* were presented as a labor of national love in a fight against "the world in which [Russia's rightful] ancestors [Beethoven, Goethe, Schumann, and Brahms] were stifled by the dark sins of their descendants." Their performance in concert was considered to bring about the long-awaited return of the singing Russian spirit to its rightful spiritual homeland.[3]

A National Background to the Russian Art Song Narrative

Staring at the chasm between Europe's erudite contribution to the arts and sciences and Russia's apparent slumber of indifference, Prince Vladimir Odoyevsky wrote in his 1844 magnum opus *Russian Nights* that "you will be astonished to learn that there exists a people who understand musical harmony naturally, without material study . . . and that an artist born from the Slav spirit, one of the triumvirate guarding the shrine of art, has found a fresh and untrodden path."[4] Thus, Odoyevsky, or the "Russian Hoffmann," conceived a landscape in which a young Russia stood at the "border of two worlds"—an "unbiased" country without a past and therefore not corrupted by the "crimes of the old Europe," but also a country whose future, although latent in "the depth of the Russian spirit," was still far from its moment of awakening.[5]

With the will to define Russianness gripping the Russian salons and intelligentsia in earnest from around the 1840s, the determination of Slavophiles to talk about the superiority of the Fatherland was thwarted by the lack of a clearly defined concept of their own national identity. This had the effect of limiting the narrative to drawing comparisons with Russian observations of neighboring cultures. The limits of such an exercise were clearly illustrated by the literary critic Pavel Annenkov, who, writing in the 1830s, observed that "since Russians as such did not exist," it was a futile activity for his intellectual compatriots to define themselves in any other way than through two options: becoming "a true, noble German" ("der treue, edle Deutsche") or a "vain, eccentric Frenchman" ("der eitle alberne Französe").[6]

French and German cultures, however, were never far away from Russia. In the minds of artists and thinkers, German culture, probably the most recurrent point of comparison for Slavophile thinkers, stretched back at least to the reforms of Peter the Great some one hundred and fifty years earlier in the 1700s. Indeed, the capital, Saint Petersburg, was home to a substantial and influential German community from its foundation, and its music scene was shaped by émigrés such as Adolf Henselt (1814–89) and Russian musicians sympathetic to Germanic ideas, such as Anton Rubinstein (1829–94) and Wilhelm von Lenz (1809–83). French culture, in contrast, was represented not so much by a tightly knit French community in Russia but rather by virtue of the hold that French culture had over the Russian aristocracy. French was the language adopted by the gentry and their salons, and Paris was regarded as the benchmark of good taste. Thus, Mikhail Glinka was reflecting common wisdom when he observed that "I have seen many young men of modern upbringing who speak and write beautifully in French without being able to write even a few lines in their native [Russian] language."[7]

The discourse on Russianness turned to the ideas of Herderian nationalism that Slavophile thinkers had begun to appropriate to fill the void and to rid themselves of a foreign *Volksgeist*. Transcending the confines of intellectual journals, issues of national identity quickly spread, clothed in literary and musical genres. The notion that folk song was the truest way of reconnecting with national character subsequently found itself in works like Ivan Turgenev's "The Singers" (1852), in which an aristocratic huntsman stops by a rural tavern and the folk songs he hears move him to tears as they awaken his Russianness: "A true, ardent Russian soul had sounded and breathed in [the song]. It gripped at your heart—gripped the very Russian heart-strings."[8] Folk song went on to achieve its most glittering portrayal in the large operatic and symphonic canvases of Mikhail Glinka (such as *A Life for the Tsar*, 1836, and *Ruslan and Lyudmila*, 1842), and the "Mighty Handful" (Nikolai Rimsky-Korsakov's 1881 *Snow Maiden*, 1900 *Tale of Tsar Sultan* and *Sadko*, op. 5, Alexander Borodin's 1887 *Prince Igor*, and Modest Mussorgsky's 1872 *Boris Godunov*).

These large-scale musical genres have long since attracted scholarly attention,[9] but from the middle of the nineteenth century to the Revolution it was the genre of art song—sung in the salons of Saint Petersburg and Moscow—where the discourse on Russianness would be hotly debated by a dynamic company of musicians, philosophers, writers, poets, theologians, artists, and aristocrats. Almost from the outset, art song challenged the marked divisions of the social order in imperial Russia. Art song's initial fast-paced evolution had its beginnings as the gentrified Russian *romans* in the generation of Glinka and Alexander Alyabiev and their older contemporaries, which was influenced by imitations of the melancholic *protyazhnaya* strophic Russian folk song genre. Its gradual favoring of settings in Russian rather than French came with the golden age poetry of Anton Delvig and Aleksandr Pushkin and caused the *romans* to become imbued with the symbolism of a change in society.[10]

Yet, as the *romans* became increasingly sophisticated, composers looked not to other Russian models but to the German Lied. Under the influence of Robert Schumann and Franz Liszt (who had both astounded Russian audiences during their tours in the mid-nineteenth century) the simplicity of the strophic *protyazhnaya* morphed into more complex forms that included extended *durchkomponiert* structures, and the adopted harmonic devices likewise pointed to the more advanced examples of the German Lied.[11] The arpeggio figuration or simple repeated chordal texture previously expected of the piano parts rapidly gave way to independent complicated and atmospheric commentaries with substantial introductions and postludes. Furthermore, despite the intention to promote a distinct national narrative through the arts, the publication of Heinrich Heine's poetry in Russian translation by Mikhail Mikhaylov in 1858 famously stimulated focus on significant numbers of Russian Heine settings, alongside other composers, by all the associates of the Mighty Handful, Pyotr Tchaikovsky, and Sergei Rachmaninoff. By the late nineteenth century, the desire of intellectuals to divorce Russian art from foreign cultures with the help of song had seemingly stalled, with an unmistakable reintegration of the genre back into Germanic culture, albeit in Russian translation. In a critique of the contemporary cultural situation, Sergei Taneyev wrote in 1879, "A Russian musician is like an architect who, on seeing a log house, would begin to build something similar out of stone, trying to lay the stones in such a way as to achieve the same curves. It is clear, that before long the architect would realize that nothing could come of his attempt."[12]

The feeling of lost direction that the twentieth-century musicologist Gerald Abraham ascribes to the period—which appears to characterize the vast corpus of Russian art song produced in the generation of Sergei Taneyev, Sergei Rachmaninoff, and Nikolai Medtner in the final decades of imperial Russian society—has led to the conspicuous absence of this repertoire in investigations of the continuing evolution of the Russian national narrative.[13]

The factors involved in this wavering between Russian and Germanic identities were acutely felt in intellectual circles. By the start of the twentieth century, the urgency of art or the intellectual salons to embrace and evolve an imperial Russian ("*rossiyskiy*") identity was simply no longer there. What Marina

Frolova-Walker has highlighted as the era's intricate network of contradictions forming the "myth of otherness" that was meant to differentiate Russia from Europe had found itself unresolved and met its failure.[14] Replacing this were broader shifts in favor of defining an ethnic Russian identity ("*russkiy*") that were beginning to take hold of society.[15] For many artists and thinkers it became imperative once more to focus, for different ideological reasons, on ridding the arts of their accumulated Germanic influence. With this movement to divorce from easily identifiable German traits, the circle of those interested in the interaction of the two cultures was growing ever narrower. Thus, just as Russia had lived through its first revolution in 1905, the music critic Boris Popov bleakly wrote that if Medtner had been born half a century earlier, "then his roses would have bloomed fully . . . the final luxury of a dying epoch. Today they are only November roses. Final, pale, and unnecessary."[16]

Medtner: Returning Russia to Goethe and the German Lied

Nikolai Medtner's role in the continuing evolution of Russia's national narrative might well have been a November rose had he not found himself living and working amid a unique intellectual movement that gripped many members of the artistic Muscovite salons in the last years of the empire—a time broadly referred to as Russia's renaissance or Silver Age.[17] This relatively short-lived epoch, eventually shattered by the onset of the Soviet regime, was one of the most productive and innovative cultural moments in Russian intellectual history. Although seeking a distinct Russian style of thought and art, the Silver Age gatherings of philosophers, musicians, publishers, critics, writers, poets, artists, and philanthropists—including Ivan Ilyin (1883–1954), Vyacheslav Ivanov (1886–1949), Andrei Beliy (1880–1934), and Sergei Durylin (1886–1954)—exhibited a particular sympathy for the Germanic philosophical tradition.

Unlike other attempts at defining a Russian national identity, in such company an apparent return to Germanic culture was not seen as the stagnation or failure of a national narrative, but rather as an opportunity to heal the rifts of an increasingly fractured society. Indeed, members of the Silver Age salons expressed grave intellectual concerns about the divisive nature of the narrow nationalism exhibited by those seeking to define an ethnic "russkiy" identity as opposed to a "rossiyskiy" one. By 1906 the philosopher Evgeny Trubetskoy (1863–1920), a core figure in these Muscovite gatherings, was instead writing of the urgency of finding a force of unification for the multiethnic empire where all its citizens (Russians, Poles, Jews, Baltic Germans, and the many other ethnic groups) would have equal rights and values, and where autocratic power was replaced by Christian morality that "unites fragmented classes and nationalities." This unifying force would be music.[18]

It is hardly accidental then, that the same year, the wealthy philanthropist and fellow founder (with Trubetskoy) of the Moscow Religious and Philosophical Society,[19] Margarita Morozova (1873–1958) hosted an entire evening at her salon on Moscow's Smolensky Boulevard dedicated to the musical vision of the young Nikolai Medtner—a Muscovite of Baltic German descent, and already heralded in 1903 as a "composer-theurgist" by the poet Andrei Beliy.[20] It was an introduction that brought Medtner a privileged place in the city's intellectual elite. His wife Anna recalled how she accompanied her husband regularly to the "Wednesdays at Vladimir Shmarovin's, the Artistic Literary Circle, the Religious-Philosophical Society, and [the meetings in the publishing houses] *Put'*, *Logos*, *Musaget*, and others."[21] Similarly, it was an introduction that soon placed on Medtner's shoulders the hopes of many who sought to identify his music as a force that would allow Russia to reunite the social and spiritual bonds, shattered by modern life, by embracing certain aspects of Romantic Germanic culture.

Medtner's standing in such gatherings was certainly enhanced by his elder brother's own activities. In fact, in his memoirs Andrei Beliy even went as far as to claim that Nikolai Medtner was "the creation coming from the hands of Emilii Karlovich"—a talented protégé of this masterful "conductor of souls."[22] Emilii Medtner's adolescent acceptance of his failure to express himself through music led him down a literary path as he established himself as a philosopher, editor, and critic (writing under the pseudonym "Vol'fing").[23] A staunch Wagnerian, Emilii Medtner believed that the resurrection of the great German culture of the past was Russia's only hope of salvation. Taking an active role in creating a forum for this debate both in person and in print (such as his recurring column in the journal *Trudï i dni* [Works and days], and *Zolotoye runo* [The golden fleece]), Emilii Medtner advocated his belief that engaging with Goethe (with whom his great-grandfather had actually been acquainted), Nietzsche and Schopenhauer would finally be the Siegfried who awakened Russia—the sleeping Brünnhilde.[24]

Although Beliy's remark is certainly less than complimentary and ignores Nikolai Medtner's fierce independence of conviction on many issues, Emilii did indeed devote considerable energy to promoting his younger brother's talent and to nurturing his knowledge of philosophy and aesthetics. It was largely due to Emilii's support that Nikolai forwent his initial ambition to pursue a promising concert career in order to devote his energies to composition. Thus, despite graduating in 1900 from the Moscow Conservatory with the gold medal for performance, and composition being a career of little material promise in imperial Russian society, Nikolai Medtner even turned down a professorship at the conservatory (with many reservations on the part of his parents) to avoid the distractions teaching would inevitably entail. Believing the act of composition to be a spiritually elevated task, for the rest of his life Nikolai Medtner would remain indebted to the patronage of his intellectual circles, writing, "I am unable to compose for the sake of earning money, and will never be able to do so."[25]

Early on, it was Medtner's songs that made the most striking impression on the frequenters of intellectual salons. In a series of awestruck letters sent to the composer, Sergei Durylin exclaimed that these songs were "true keys to living [artistic] creation ("*zhiznetvorchestvo*") and resurrection!"[26] The intimacy of the art-song genre made it particularly suitable for Muscovite salons, and the obvious advantages for dissemination in print made it one of the most powerful media that shared Emilii's public vision of an "awakened" Russia through the careful combination of German text and a carefully constructed abstract musical symbol. Emilii Medtner's great admiration for Goethe—as well as the brothers' mutual pride in the fact that their own great-grandfather had been an acquaintance of this literary genius—as the "universal man" who synthesized "life and work into an indivisible whole" (i.e. what Russian intellectuals termed "zhiznetvorchestvo") quickly became the primary focus of Nikolai's art songs.[27] Consequently, in August 1903, Nikolai Medtner wrote to his elder brother,

> Two weeks ago, I found in myself serious symptoms of my passion for Goethe. . . Exactly that—*passion*. . . . Recently I have forced myself to read poetry very diligently. First I read a little Tutchev, then the poetry in *Scorpion* and *Griffin* [*Grif*],[28] and then over the summer, an anthology of Fet. . . . I sweated trying to capture, understand, perceive in them at least something that resembles human form. . . . And so, now when I opened a volume of Goethe, I positively went mad from my amazement. If you take Tutchev or Fet—even though they are talented, one can feel nonetheless that poetic form is a burden for them. There is no art in the *form*, just in the thoughts and moods. . . . Russians have very little creativity in the artistic *form*. . . . it is just a burden, or a lesson which they have learnt—if they have even learnt it! Pushkin is an exception, . . . but Tutchev, Fet, and geniuses like Tchaikovsky or Dostoyevsky.[29]

The result of this formative interaction with Goethe's poetry emerged as the final song from the *Three Romances*, op. 3, set in Russian (translated by Fet), and over the next two decades a further twenty-nine Goethe settings would come into being, as well as cycles to texts by Nietzsche and Heine—all in German.

Although Medtner would later adopt the terms *poem* and *Lied* to describe most of his 103 songs, it is significant that, for his first efforts, he still adopted the title *romans,* thus refusing to sever the heritage arising from the evolution of Russian art song. Whatever Emilii's own agendas were in communicating the superiority of Germanic culture as the embodiment of universal values "capable of fertilizing the musical creation of kindred nations" such as Russia, Nikolai was less inclined to dismiss Russian artistic achievement and standing.[30] Despite making a point of practices such as giving his instrumental compositions German titles and performance directions, he nonetheless saw himself as first and foremost a Russian artist. This self-concept was reflected in his famous 1910 altercation with Wilhelm Mengelberg (1871–1951) in preparation for a performance of Beethoven's Fourth Piano Concerto, op. 58, hosted in the Saint Petersburg Koussevitsky Concerts. After a terse rehearsal that led to Medtner refusing to perform, the Russian press was ignited by his defiant explanation: "no one deserves the contempt with which Russian artists continue to be treated by foreign musical traveling salespeople. The incident with me is, so to speak, two-sided: a soloist, in the person of myself, was insulted by a conductor giving himself airs; more important, a *Russian* artist was insulted by a visiting foreigner."[31]

Nikolai Medtner's second attempt to set Goethe's poetry to music in 1906 was an altogether more ambitious undertaking. The *Nine Lieder von Goethe*, op. 6, dedicated to his brother Emilii, marked a substantial period of time in which Nikolai Medtner elected not to set any Russian poetry to music. Set in German, their harmonic writing, intricacy of texture and complex command of form marks them out as stylistic descendants of the German Lied tradition, more akin to Wolf (even though Medtner always remained indifferent to Wolf's Lieder) than to any developments in the romance. Their conservatism, in contrast both to modern German directions (namely Max Reger and Richard Strauss) and to the radical developments undertaken by his other contemporary and rival Scriabin, was seen as evidence of their genius in consolidating their position as part of the heritage of a true art. Indeed, here the choice to set Goethe to music was taken by Beliy as a deeply symbolic one: "The hub of the universe, for [modern] Europeans, is not Goethe, Nietzsche, or other luminaries of culture. . . . Goethe and Nietzsche are being experienced in Russia—they are ours, because we, Russians, are the only people in Europe who search and suffer and torment ourselves. In the West, they are happy growing flabby rosy-cheeked Mr. Bowler-Hat and ivory Mrs. Toothpick—the real bearers of culture ('*Kulturträger*') of the West."[32] Beliy quickly praised the cycle as the work of a "deeply modern" Russian artist who, unlike no other, was responding to contemporary Russian cultural needs by creating a "realm of the new religious consciousness of our days."[33] Thus, according to Beliy, Medtner's Goethe settings "truly heal the soul" and return to the "eternally known in all times . . . as previously expressed by Beethoven and Schumann" and was now "finally expressed by an imperial Russian citizen."[34]

This relative conservatism that saw Nikolai Medtner align his aesthetics with the musical heritage of German Romanticism and consciously turn away from modernist compositional practices that he believed were tearing society apart was rooted in a philosophical belief that the quest for an absolute truth in art would inevitably lead to a timeless spiritual foundation. Consequently, for both the Medtner brothers, concepts such as "tonality," "consonance," and "dissonance" were absolute values—and the abandonment of them was a reflection of the sickness and fragmentation of a self-obsessed contemporary society.[35]

Vitally, Nikolai Medtner believed that it was song that brought the spirit closer to absolute truth and in doing so healed and unified. As a genre, therefore, song remained an important symbol of spirituality throughout his life, as epitomized by later works such as his 1922 *Sonata-Vocalise mit einem Motto "Geweihter Platz" (Goethe)*, op. 41 no. 1, and op. 41 no. 2 for soprano and piano (1924 rev. 1927).

Nikolai Medtner maintained that all earthly music strives to approach a preexisting, eternal initial song that embodies a forgotten spiritual existence. This initial song resounded through the composer's "internal hearing," and Medtner believed that the calling of a composer was to give voice to this inspiration—this state of "being of song"—through his composition.[36] Such a process, according to Medtner, was perfectly demonstrated by Beethoven's compositional notebooks, which did not seek consciously to work out melody structurally but to find a more accurate embodiment of such divine inspiration. The religious nature of art was, therefore, not directed by the choice of subject matter but rather by its purpose. In this way, music itself that came from such a process had to first unify the present with a universal, timeless "spirit of music"—the very same sought by the greatest composers, like Beethoven, in previous generations, because "the final goal of all paths in essence is always the same." Second, such music's goal was to create the ideal spiritual harmony by unifying the experiential and cognitive beginnings of human endeavor: "The spirit is there, where thought feels, and feelings think. . . . The closer the balance between thought and feeling, the closer [one becomes] to the spirit . . . the root uniting us with the first days of God's creation."[37]

Medtner's idea that he was being brought back through his "internal hearing" to a spiritually rarefied atmosphere accessible in its entirety only to the great German Romantic composers who had absorbed Goethe was far from coincidental. Around the time of his composition of the op. 6 Goethe settings, Medtner had encountered a new congenial influence through his attendance and participation in the concerts and lecture recitals hosted and directed by Maria Olenina-d'Alheim. A professional singer, Olenina-d'Alheim had returned to settle in Moscow after spending several years in Paris with a mission to champion art song as society's ultimate unifying genre socially, as well as pointing to a universal spirituality common to all nationalities. Disillusioned with the Russian reception of art song at the end of the nineteenth century, Olenina-d'Alheim convinced herself that it was her duty to seek out and educate the Russian public to embrace the genre as a quasi-religious transformative experience in which they were active participants:

> All too often people wrongly regard song as a second-rate art form. . . . The main reasons, it seems to us, are the following: carelessness with which some composers "set to music" poems that randomly come their way . . . , lack of conscientiousness in compiling programs, and the strange inexplicable fact that many people perform songs not from a sense of vocation, but merely

because for one reason or another they failed to make their way on the [opera] stage. Be that as it may, such an erroneous understanding of the importance of song is inimical to the higher interests of art. It is through song that, most surely of all, there can arise a close spiritual union between creative artist, performer, and listener, which alone can bring works of art to life.[38]

With the support of her husband, the critic and musicologist Pierre [Piotr] d'Alheim, she put her mission into practice through her eight annual subscription concerts (usually in the Small Hall of the Moscow Conservatory), lecture recitals, bulletins (with program notes and translations of Lied sung in the vernacular), and songwriting and translation competitions expanded into a regular feature of Muscovite life, officially becoming known as the House of Song [*Dom pesni*] in 1908. From 1912, Olenina-d'Alheim's House of Song even took on the ambitious task of touring its programs across Russia, including the provinces, to present concerts to the working class, as well as internationally in Paris and London.[39]

To Beliy, Olenina-d'Alheim was not only the most captivating and expressive Russian singer in the period between 1902 and 1908, even in comparison with the legendary Fyodor Chaliapin, but she was also the "sword-bearer for the future of culture" who introduced Russians to an extraordinary amount of music they had previously known nothing about.[40] Bringing together Moscow's brightest intellectuals (including Beliy, the poet Aleksandr Blok [1880–1921], Vyacheslav Ivanov, and the poet Valeri Bryusov [1873–1924]) to join her as advocates for the ambitious cause, alongside the art song of her beloved Mussorgsky, Olenina-d'Alheim made the Lieder of Schubert, Schumann, and Brahms staples of her vision, often devoting entire programs to one of these composers' œuvres, a choice made all the more pronounced by her lack of interest in contemporary Russian art song.[41] Besides concerts, which presented what had until then been rarities (such as Schumann's *Dichterliebe*, op. 48; *Frauenliebe und -leben*, op. 42; and *Liederkreis*, op. 39; Beethoven's *An die ferne Geliebte*, op. 98; and Schubert's *Die schöne Müllerin*, D795), the House of Song organized extensive lectures on the genre, including a cycle of sixteen lectures in 1909 on German art song as an artistic form.[42] Chronicling her efforts, Beliy noted that the repertoire for each song recital unveiled a larger narrative "carved out of a single stone": "One song grew out of another, and disappeared into another; the significance and meaning grew; and somehow we were caught unaware with the assured realization that the *Winter Journey* [*Die Winterreise*], a song cycle, was no less significant than Beethoven's Ninth Symphony."[43]

Despite her avoidance of contemporary Russian art song, Olenina-d'Alheim found Nikolai Medtner's spiritual attitude to song particularly sympathetic with her own ideals, and he readily became a valued and prominent member of the House of Song. Not only did Olenina-d'Alheim turn to Medtner for counsel in matters of aesthetics and programming, but she provided him with an important platform before an eager and doting audience of intellectuals and enthusiasts to showcase and premiere his works—often with her as the soloist.[44] The admiration was mutual, with Medtner citing his close association with the House of Song in the role of regular accompanist and guest as one of the most significant influences on his own German songwriting. According to Medtner, hearing and performing the Lieder of Brahms and Schumann particularly stimulated and informed his composition in the genre and contributed to his fuller understanding of the "spirit of song" and its national element.[45]

Medtner's conviction that this environment and interaction with Olenina-d'Alheim proved fruitful in providing the necessary spiritual dimension for his activities as a composer brought about a further two substantial German song cycles, which were premiered and repeated at the House of Song's concerts at the Small Hall of the Moscow Conservatory: the *Twelve Lieder von Goethe*, op. 15 (1907), and the *Six Gedichte von Goethe*, op. 18 (1909). Both were set to German texts, and the former was dedicated to the institution. Building on the keen interest and knowledge that the regular intellectual core of the gatherings had now amassed with regard to German Lied thanks to Olenina-d'Alheim's efforts, it is striking to note that Medtner was confident enough to set poetry already in illustrious settings, but with deliberate stark differences. Among them are Medtner's "Meeresstille," op. 15 no. 7, which at the time would have been associated with the Schubert setting of the same name, D216; his "Mignon: Nur wer die Sehnsucht kennt," op. 18 no. 4, and "Wandrers Nachtlied," op. 15 no. 1, which would have been recognized from Schubert's and Wolf's settings;[46] "Die Spröde," op. 18 no. 1, and "Gleich und Gleich," op. 15 no. 11, from Wolf's; and his "Das Veilchen," op. 18 no. 5, instantly associated with Mozart's own setting, K476.

With the assurance that Olenina-d'Alheim's efforts had ensured for him an educated audience that now treated these original Lieder with reverence, Medtner knew that he could use his own miniature psychological dramas to tap into that shared knowledge and play on their expectations. In this way, his reimagination of "Das Veilchen" is an anguished human tragedy that is worlds apart from the delicacy of Mozart's. The violet's irreconcilable grief and longing to be cherished cannot be contained in words and overflows into dissonant outbursts in the piano, while the pain of unrequited love and incompatibility is literally alluded to by the enharmonic writing in the piano and vocal lines (see example 7.1). The darkness exuded by this harmonic displacement of piano and singer was a distinct technique that Medtner particularly honed within these German songs. In this respect, the Mignon setting typifies Medtner's growing fascination with harmonic dislocation in which the inconsolable weariness of the song's harmonic conflict sinks the music into defeat: its end unhinges from the home key of E-flat minor onto an F-flat (see example 7.2).

Example 7.1. Nikolai Medtner, "Das Veilchen," op. 18 no. 5, measures 24–26.

Example 7.2. Nikolai Medtner, "Mignon," op. 18 no. 4, measures 35–43.

Olenina-d'Alheim's respect for Medtner's opp. 15 and 18 was so great that her inaugural 1908–9 series at the House of Song—which promised to reunite audiences with "the eternal and pure source that produces the true phenomenon of art"—programmed them in the first week, preceded by lectures on spirituality and the arts by Beliy and discussions about national identity in art.[47] Giving Medtner the honor of being the only living composer on her program for the entire season, Olenina-d'Alheim astutely encouraged the composer to contribute an essay on Goethe for the published notes, knowing full well that its content would resonate with her own vision of art song's spiritual significance: "not entertainment, but the education of spiritual experience" in the audiences, performers, and other participants.[48]

Medtner's essay shows that it is the complexity of the envisioned programming that is particularly striking. Falling very much in line with the House of Song's policy that a recital, if not an entire season of concerts, should be linked through common thematic purpose, Medtner devoted his inaugural performance to the exploration of Goethe as the symbol of man's admittance into spiritual consciousness and his "struggle for worldview."[49] Answering the Silver-Age urgency to imbue art with theological significance that would awaken Russian national and moral identity, Medtner assured his audience that the door to great art, which Russia was on the cusp of beholding, was Goethe's notion that "the more you feel yourself a man, the closer you are to the gods."[50] The earth, Medtner exclaimed, is "God's temple," and "Earthly life—the symbol of Divine life."[51]

Medtner set about devising an elaborate melding from his various Goethe settings, ordered in such a way as to narrate the spiritual journey of becoming. Thus, the setting of "Wandrers Nachtlied," op. 15 no. 1, was to be understood as the expression of the "weary soul who is tired of this wandering life as a guest" on the earth, and the following song "An die Thüren will ich schleichen," op. 15 no. 2, as the "melancholy but aimless soul that meanders near the thresholds that lead into life, but is unable to cross them." The soul's "aesthetic contemplation" of the possibilities of life, in which it has never participated, form the symbolism of "In Vorübergehen," op. 6 no. 4. The following "Die Spröde," op. 18 no. 1, "Der untreue Knabe," op. 15 no. 10, and "Die Bekehrte," op. 18 no. 2, were to represent the other, equally spiritually impoverished, existence—that of the "soul which takes, but never gives itself back."[52]

"Vor Gericht," op. 15 no. 6, provides the turning point, the vow to turn away from such a "harlot life." No doubt Medtner chose to program it for its striking resistance against reaching the tonic, C minor, from what should be such an obvious and indeed inevitable upbeat, the determined progress being impeded by the insistent appearances of A-flat (see example 7.3). This combination of determination to move ahead with the struggle to push past distraction is an integral facet

Example 7.3. Nikolai Medtner, "Vor Gericht," op. 15 no. 6, measures 1–2.

Example 7.4. Nikolai Medtner, "Vor Gericht," op. 15 no. 6, measures 8–11.

of Medtner's idiosyncratic compositional language. In this case, the program's evocation of the difficult escape from a "harlot life," represented by the tempting modulatory passages in the expansive piano accompaniments, is signified by the arrival of a German augmented 6th over a fermata prior to the singer's entry (see example 7.4).

This tension of two existences, the desired and the present, which fascinated Medtner as a topic for musical narration, gives rise to the unmistakable (vertical) misalignment of harmonic time that can make his music so difficult to perform and that can require a level of perseverance from his listener.[53] Here, in measure 38, this is demonstrated as the vocal line arrives demonstrably in C minor with the words "leave me in peace!" ("laßt mich in Ruh!"). It is a moment of dissonance provided by the C being encased within a brief clashing diminished seventh as the piano is still working its way through F minor (see example 7.5); and which will continue to search frantically and alone for the tonic for several bars yet to come.

Example 7.5. Nikolai Medtner, "Vor Gericht," op. 15 no. 6, measures 35–38.

Following on from this, "Meerestille," op. 15 no. 7, brings the soul to witness the complete lack of all that which it had thought defined life: "With the sensation of nothing under the feet . . . all sadness and joy is gone." The opening harmony has the tonic, F sharp minor, the tonic hidden within its core. Coexisting with it, the outer parts bring a strongly delineated major subdominant seventh (see example 7.6). It is a moment harmonically representing this nothingness; even the pull of the dominant, falling at the end of the bar, cannot resolve back to the tonic. Instead it hangs on a chromatically altered fifth that is reached from an enharmonically spelled Neapolitan sixth. Melodically, the piano accompaniment seems completely devoid of the motifs that will form the fluidly rocking vocal line. The soul is frozen by this lifeless emptiness. Harmonically, it is one of Medtner's most static works with the simple but widely spaced triadic accompaniment contributing to its bleakness. The unusual choice of 8/8 time signature never allows the bars to settle into equal divisions of halves or quarters. Instead, a funeral-march rhythm over a dotted crotchet is interspersed with four lilting semiquavers, so that neither performers nor listeners rhythmically feel there is something "under the feet."

Man acknowledges his weakness—the meandering accompaniment through diminished seventh harmonies and chromatically altered chords over a chromatically rising bass from E to G-sharp refuses to allow the voice to settle in A, and the vocal line makes no further attempt to break from the tonic key of F-sharp minor (see example 7.7). Out of this recognition, however, standing for a moment face to face with death, the soul finds strength "to find communion with true life."

As the voice enters for its last stanza, it is the first time that the melodic line finds itself at one, in terms of pitch, with the accompaniment's chordal texture. Only as the music returns to the initial vocal melodic fragment are the listeners and performers extended the opportunity to reflect on just how intricately derivative the voice had always been of that seemingly detached piano accompaniment, coming into being from what appeared to be the harmonic dissonances. With the final stanza, we are reminded once more of the opening vocal motif (refer back to example 7.6) being a direct echo of the piano's left hand of C-sharp in bar 3; descending to the A and G-sharp (reconciling the piano's G natural) of bar 4; and finally to the F-sharp minor triad of measure 5.

Arriving at this profound moment, the fog is broken to reveal the earth in all its glory in "Glückliche Fahrt," op. 15 no. 8. Having renounced a barren and selfish life and turned faithfully to the path of true life, the soul is admitted to eternal life in "Gleich und gleich," op. 15 no. 11, and with the joyful strains of "Gefunden," op. 6 no. 9, is finally at one with the earth, and hence divinity—and Medtner asks, "Is not Earth in the Heavens?" The second "Wandrers Nachtlied," op. 6 no. 1, sees the soul finding comfort in the death that freed it from its previous false life

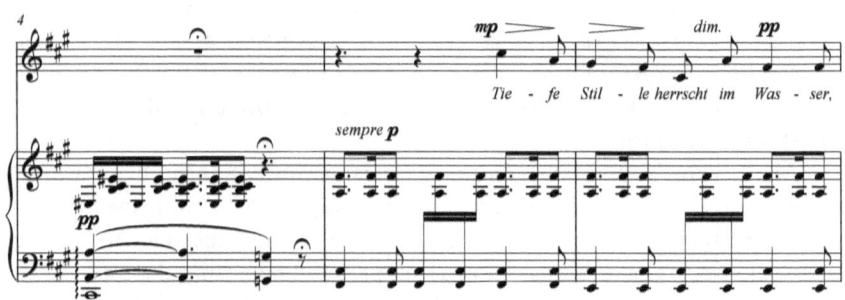

Example 7.6. Nikolai Medtner, "Meerestille," op. 15 no. 7, measures 1–8.

Example 7.7. Nikolai Medtner, "Meerestille," op. 15 no. 7, measures 9–12.

and returning to its "rightful homeland," and it "sends its greetings to all who are living" ("Geistesgruß," op. 15 no. 12).[54]

These efforts that sought to minister to the hopes of spiritual salvation through art gained unprecedented praise from the intellectual circles who had placed their hopes in Medtner as the living symbol of a new spiritual Russian culture.[55] Indeed, the stature of Medtner's Goethe settings was of such significance that the coveted 1912 Glinka Prize for the most outstanding contribution to Russian music—previously held by Tchaikovsky, Rimsky-Korsakov, Scriabin, and Rachmaninoff, and usually awarded for works in the large-scale symphonic genre—was awarded to the three Goethe cycles (opp. 6, 15, and 18). Subsequent performances of such works in 1913 garnered lavish praise from critics, with Yuliy Engel' claiming that among all German art since the time of Brahms, there "was not one in whom the 'holy flame' of these hereditary testaments burned as cleanly and purely as in Medtner—and his homeland is Moscow."[56]

Thus, Nikolai Medtner's close association with the House of Song contributed to his persona becoming something of a cult for those Muscovite intellectuals seeking to present true "Russianness" as whatever would take the mantle from a Germanic heritage and bring it into a distinctly Russian spiritual realm.

By 1913, Durylin joined the praises of Ilyin to proclaim Medtner's songs the greatest achievements of the Russian spirit—finally giving it freedom from its previous heavy burden of foreign influence and failures.[57] For Durylin in particular, Medtner's ability to forge a spiritual territory out of necessity, rather than subject matter, encouraged him to see the composer as the rightful heir to continue what he believed was the uncompleted mission of Wagner's *Parsifal*, which had been doomed by Germany's loss of its Christian foundations. Medtner, by contrast, had shown an innate calling to absorb the significance of *Parsifal* to demonstrate that the destiny of the true Christian mystery lay in the saving hands of Russia.[58]

Emilii Medtner too was anxious to promote his younger brother's unification of the German and Russian in a quest for absolute truth as one of significance not just to Russian society but to European society as a whole. It similarly brought him to the issue of the symbolic inheritance of *Parsifal*. Full of emotion, Emilii Medtner wrote in September 1912 to Margarita Morozova that

> It was there [during the Bayreuth performance of *Parsifal*] that the greatness of Kolya [Nikolai] as a human became clear to me. . . . Gasping from the unbearable excitement, he spoke words that were unbelievable in their depth and appropriateness and, I repeat, I could not decide where there was more greatness: on the stage, or here in this experience that was so congenial that Wagner, if he had arisen from his grave, would have welcomed Kolya as a brother. . . . This is the secret, brought about through art—this is the Mystery of communion through art. This is the true Mystery that seized Kolya through *Parsifal*.[59]

Despite Nikolai Medtner's insistence that his close association with the House of Song had been a vital catalyst for his finding the spirit of Russianness, Emilii was unsatisfied that the organization was Germanic enough to support the vision he had for Nikolai's art. Despite the emphasis that the House of Song and Olenina-d'Alheim placed on presenting German art song, Emilii Medtner considered the salon's growing cosmopolitan outlook to be a "poisonous influence" for his younger brother's activities, a "trap for Siegfrieds of the twentieth century who should be following Goethe, Beethoven, and Kant," and the d'Alheims—Hagen (Siegfried's killer), whose ideas arose from the corruption of Mime (Liszt).[60] Likewise, he felt increasingly that Nikolai Medtner's preoccupation with the composition and performance of Lieder stifled his potential to express himself in larger genres.

Notwithstanding Emilii Medtner's reservations, Nikolai chose to retain close ties with the House of Song until its dissolution in 1918 and was deeply encouraged by Olenina-d'Alheim's unfortunately futile plans to reestablish it in Paris in 1935.[61] Although these ties afforded him a messianic status as a truly Russian creator in the eyes of many of the Silver Age intellectuals who had engaged in the discourse of national narrative in the Muscovite salons, beyond this a larger contemporary anxiety that sought to sweep away imperial Russian identity began taking hold of prerevolutionary society. German culture proved a convenient contrast, reinforced by gathering anti-German sentiment with the outbreak of World War I. Medtner's "Russianness" also became subject to questioning, with the composer and critic Vyacheslav Karatygin (1875–1925) offering a typical and increasingly common view:

> One can hardly name another composer occupying a more isolated place in the family of Russian musicians [than Medtner]. We have many "pupils" of Rimsky-Korsakov, not a few followers of Tchaikovsky, and there are composers attracted to Glazunov and Scriabin, while others keep a watchful eye of Strauss and Debussy, but, with one sole exception, we have no followers of orthodox Germanism . . . Taneyev being merely an analogue of Brahms. The only typical "Russian German," native Brahmsian, is the Muscovite Medtner.[62]

Nikolai Medtner's music—with its conservative use of form, respect for tonal harmony, settings of Goethe's poetry in German, and tempered Dionysian emotional impulses—which had served as a beacon for Russia's new identity of spiritual existence, which transcended ethnic social divisions of the empire by its integration of German and Russian cultures, was now criticized for corrupting the Slavic with "German blood."[63]

The news of the war's outbreak left Nikolai in a condition that he described as "paralyzed," with his wife, Anna, fearful for his physical and mental state.[64] Writing to the poet and literary critic Marietta Shaginian (1888–1982), Anna despaired. "Our love for Russia . . . has grown all the keener over these past days . . . and so it is painful that we are foreigners to our own beloved Mother. Kolya says that because he can only feel himself to be a Russian citizen, and Russia does not seem to want him (or so it appears these days), then all that is left, is to take on heavenly ("nebesnoye") citizenship."[65] Whether Germany or Russia would claim victory had almost become irrelevant for Medtner. It was a war between the two very cultures his art had sought to unite into a higher spiritual identity. For whoever won, it would be a victory that was not built on the dream of unity but focused on the destruction of an enemy. Whoever won, the war was a victory for the divisive impulse of modernity that Medtner had so vividly seen as the root of society's cultural and sociopolitical chaos and loss of spirituality.

The 1917 Revolution was a further blow. Having collected a notebook of melodic fragments—recorded moments of divine inspiration for the initial song resonating in his inner hearing—they turned into a recurring nightmare. By 1918, Medtner would "wake at night in a fever" as these numerous fragments would "enter the room, clustered threateningly in the corner, mocking him." Surrounded by these ghosts he would cry out aghast at their unruly disunity.[66] Unlike Emilii, who left Russia and, after a brief internment in Germany after the outbreak of World War I, eventually settled in Switzerland, Nikolai Medtner did not commit to emigration until 1921. In late 1935, he settled in London, where he lived in near-complete obscurity, never to write a German song again. These cataclysmic political events shattered the Silver-Age dreams of the Muscovite intellectual salons. A vision of a Russian healing spirit, stemming from the sanctity of a great Germanic culture, had come to a disillusioned end. As proclaimed by Igor Stravinsky, it was a new epoch: "a new peasant Russia . . . a Russia rid of her parasites: the bureaucracy imported from Germany . . . , her 'intellectuals,' and Europeanism."[67] It was, however, a new epoch that, like the short-lived Silver Age, was too soon to give way to the new discourses of the Soviet Union.

Although Medtner's German songs may have increasingly become rarities—the "pale and unnecessary November roses"—their composition and performance in the final decade of imperial Russia was indebted to the efforts of advocates like Olenina-d'Alheim's House of Song, which championed the previously unheard Lieder of Schubert, Schumann, and Brahms in Russia as a necessary cultural and spiritual foundation, and their importance equal to that of any symphonic work. Although the House of Song's Silver Age vision of spiritual salvation through Germanic art never found a comparably fertile ground, a rich body of works entered the standard repertoire of concert halls across Russia and the Soviet Union. The performance of German Lieder would, in time, inspire many new directions for the Russian composers and poets to come.

Notes

1. Ivan Ilyin, "Sonata Form in Medtner," in *Nicholas Medtner (1879–1951): A Tribute to His Art and Personality*, ed. Richard Holt (London: Dennis Dobson, 1955), 180. All translations from Russian texts, presented in transliterated form in footnotes, are by the author unless otherwise stated. The transliteration is presented in a modified *New Grove*, which omits soft and hard signs in proper nouns in the main text (restored in the references). Titles of commonly found Russian works are given in English in the text. Russian names in the main text are given following their widely used Western spelling.

2. Ilyin, "Sonata Form," 167.

3. Ivan Ilyin, "A Study of Medtner," in *Nicolas Medtner (1879–1951): A Tribute to His Art and Personality*, ed. Richard Holt (London: Dennis Dobson, 1955), 167.

4. Vladimir Odoyevskiy, *Russkiye nochi* (Leningrad: Nauka, 1975), 182.

5. Odoyevskiy, *Russkiye nochi*, 148.

6. Quoted in Kseniya Kasyanova, *O russkom natsional'nom kharaktere* (Moscow: Akademicheskiy Proekt, 1994), 36–37.

7. Ol'ga Levashova, *M. Glinka* (Moscow: Muzïka, 1987), 1: 27–28.

8. Ivan Turgenev, "Pevtsï," in *Sochineniya*, vol. 3, ed. M. P. Alekseyev (Moscow: Nauka, 1979), 222.

9. Including Marina Frolova-Walker, *Russian Music and Nationalism from Glinka to Stalin* (New Haven, CT: Yale University Press, 2007); Richard Taruskin, *Defining Russia Musically: Historical and Hermeneutical Essays* (Princeton, NJ: Princeton University Press, 1997); Taruskin, *On Russian Music* (Los Angeles: University of California Press, 2009).

10. For a more detailed exploration on the beginnings of Russian romance, see Gerald Abraham, *Essays on Russian and East European Music* (Oxford, UK: Clarendon, 1985), 5; and Frolova-Walker, *Russian Music*, 29–43.

11. Mili Balakirev considered his own interest in Liszt to be one of the pivotal influences on his compositional voice (Francis Maes, *A History of Russian Music: From Kamarinskaya to Babi Yar*, trans. Arnold J. Pomerans and Erica Pomerans [Los Angeles: University of California Press, 2002], 66). Rimsky-Korsakov's appreciation of Liszt and Schumann is reflected in a particularly striking manner with their portraits taking pride of place in his study in the Saint Petersburg apartment on Zagorodnïy Prospect (now the Rimsky-Korsakov Museum).

12. Sergei Taneyev, *Personality, Works and Documents* (Moscow: 1925), quoted in Victor Seroff, *Rachmaninov* (London: Cassell, 1951), 25–26.

13. Abraham, *Essays*, 30–31.

14. Frolova-Walker, *Russian Music*, 18–25.

15. Rebecca Mitchell, *Nietzsche's Orphans: Music, Metaphysics, and the Twilight of the Russian Empire* (New Haven, CT: Yale University Press, 2016), 106.

16. Boris Popov, "Pis'ma o muzïke: Noyabr'skiyi rozï," *Pereval* no. 2 (1906): 61.

17. Medtner's role is absent in key texts such as Frolova-Walker, *Russian Music*; Taruskin, *Defining Russia Musically*; and Maes, *History of Russian Music*. Because of the short span of Silver Age activity, and the complexity of its aesthetics, its broad scope has been largely ignored in Anglophone musicology, which has tended to focus on the beginning of the Soviet era.

18. This can be seen for instance in Evgeny Trubetskoy, "Gde zhe nakonets, Rossiya?," *Moskovskiy Yezhenedel'nik* no. 24 (September 2, 1906); here cited from Evgeny Trubetskoy, "Minornïye i mazornïye notï," *Moskovskiy Yezhenedel'nik* no. 4 (January 23, 1910): 14–15.

19. The other founders included Sergei Bulgakov and Nikolai Berdyayev.

20. Zaruy Apetyan, *N. K. Metner: Pis'ma* (Moscow: Sovetskiy Kompozitor, 1973), 42–52.

21. Mitchell, *Nietzsche's Orphans*, 13.

22. Andrei Belïy, *Nachalo veka* (Moscow: Khudozhestvennaya literatura, 1990), 89.

23. Emilii Medtner struggled with music theory, although, as shown by his correspondence with Nikolai, he sought Nikolai's help and instruction. Emilii also seems to have had an acute problem with his nerves as a performer.

24. Vol'fing, "Vagneriana: Nabroski k kommentariyu," *Trudï i dni*, nos. 4–5 (1912): 23–37.

25. Letter to Boris Jurgenson (son of Peter Jurgenson, who inherited his father's publishing house, P. Jurgenson), September 1907 (Apetyan, *N. K. Metner*, 110).

26. From an unpublished series of letters as quoted in Mitchell, *Nietzsche's Orphans*, 108.

27. Magnus Ljunggren, *The Russian Mephisto: A Study of the Life and Work of Emilii Medtner* (Stockholm: Almqvist and Wiksell, 1994), 12.

28. Symbolist poetry published by Russian journals included that of Valeri Bryusov, Aleksandr Blok, Andrei Belïy, Konstantin Balmont, and Fyodor Sologub.

29. Apetyan, *N. K. Metner*, 48–49.

30. Vol'fing, "Invektivï na muzïkal'nuyu sovremennost'," *Trudï i dni* no. 12 (1912): 29.

31. As cited in Barrie Martyn, *Nicolas Medtner: His Life and Music* (Aldershot, UK: Ashgate, 1995), 79.

32. Andrei Beliy, *Peterburg* (Moscow: Nauka, 1981), 594.

33. Andrei Beliy, "O teurgiyi," *Novij put'* no. 9 (September 1903): 100–124.

34. Beliy, "O teurgiyi."

35. Apetyan, *N. K. Metner*, 307–12.

36. Nikolay Medtner, *Muza i Moda* (Paris: Vozrozhdenye, 1935), 23.

37. As quoted from Medtner's notebook of musical thoughts held at the Moscow State Central Museum of Culture in Mitchell, *Nietzsche's Orphans*, 116.

38. From the 1912 bulletin from the *Dom pesni* (House of Song) presented in Aleksandr Tumanov, *The Life and Artistry of Maria Olenina-d'Alheim*, trans. Christopher Barnes (Alberta, Can.: University of Alberta Press, 2000), 167–68.

39. The House of Song expanded its objectives further, becoming the House of Song Society in 1912.

40. Beliy, *Nachalo Veka*, 427–428.

41. Tumanov, *Life and Artistry*, 150.

42. Tumanov, *Life and Artistry*, 173–75.

43. Beliy, *Nachalo Veka*, 428.

44. Apetyan, *N. K. Metner*, 119.

45. Apetyan, *N. K. Metner*, 16–17.

46. The words of "Nur wer die Sehnsucht kennt" would also have been familiar to Medtner and his audiences through Tchaikovsky's famous setting of Lev Mei's translation of the poem.

47. House of Song 1908–9 program booklet no. 21, 5. Bibliothèque nationale de France. 8-VM PIECE-1176.

48. House of Song 1908–9 program booklet no. 21, 5. Bibliothèque nationale de France. 8-VM PIECE-1176.

49. House of Song 1908–9 program booklet no. 8, 7. Bibliothèque nationale de France. 8-VM PIECE-1176.

50. House of Song 1908–9 program booklet no. 8, 7. Bibliothèque nationale de France. 8-VM PIECE-1176.Most likely referring to Goethe's *Faust*.

51. House of Song 1908–9 program booklet no. 8, 7. Bibliothèque nationale de France. 8-VM PIECE-1176.

52. House of Song 1908–9 program booklet no. 8, 7–8. Bibliothèque nationale de France. 8-VM PIECE-1176.

53. As an example of this, in his notes to the booklet for his recording of Medtner's songs, the pianist Iain Burnside remarked how often in rehearsal for this repertoire the singers he was working with cried out, "It all makes sense until you start playing" (*Medtner Songs*, Delphian DC 4177, compact disc, 2018 [liner notes, p. 5], https://www.chandos.net/chanimages/Booklets/DC4177.pdf).

54. House of Song 1908-9 program booklet no. 8, 8—9, i.e. N.51. Bibliothèque nationale de France. 8-VM PIECE-1176.

55. Apetyan, *N. K. Metner*, 16.

56. Yuliy Engel', "Kontsert N. Metnera," *Russkiye Vedomosti*, February 12, 1913, 4.

57. As quoted from Durylin's correspondence in Mitchell, *Nietzsche's Orphans*, 133.

58. Sergei Durylin, *Vagner i Rossiya* (Moscow: Musaget, 1913), 16.

59. Letter as quoted in Mitchell, *Nietzsche's Orphans*, 123–24.
60. Beliy, *Nachalo Veka*, 90.
61. Apetyan, *N. K. Metner*, 470.
62. From a 1913 review quoted in Martyn, *Nicolas Medtner*, 98.
63. Popov, "Pis'ma o muzïke," 61.
64. Martyn, *Nicolas Medtner*, 112. Anna Bratenskaya (1877–1965) had been married to Emilii Medtner and Nikolai married her in 1919, after Emilii granted a divorce in 1915 while interned in Germany. The two brothers had essentially been living together with her until then.
65. Anna Beliy to Marietta Shaginian, May 30, 1915, fond 132, no. 4730, State Central Museum of Musical Culture, Moscow.
66. Zaruy Apetyan, ed., *N. K. Metner: Vospominaniya, Stat'i, Materialï* (Moscow: Sovetskiy Kompozitor, 1981), 41.
67. Charles Ferdinand Ramuz, *Souvenirs sur Igor Strawinsky* (Lausanne: H. L. Mermod, 1941), 14: 68.

Bibliography

Abraham, Gerald. *Essays on Russian and East European Music*. Oxford, UK: Clarendon, 1985.
Apetyan, Zaruy, ed. *N. K. Metner: Pis'ma*. Moscow: Sovetskiy Kompozitor, 1973.
———, ed. *N. K. Metner: Vospominaniya, Stat'i, Materialï*. Moscow: Sovetskiy Kompozitor, 1981.
Beliy, Andrei. *Nachalo veka*. Moscow: Khudozhestvennaya literatura, 1990.
———. "O teurgiyi," *Novïj put'* no. 9 (September 1903): 100–124.
———. *Petersburg*. Moscow: Nauka, 1981.
Durylin, Sergei. *Vagner i Rossiya*. Moscow: Musaget, 1913.
Engel', Yuliy. "Kontsert N. Metnera." *Russkiye Vedomosti*, February 12, 1913, 4.
Frolova-Walker, Marina. *Russian Music and Nationalism from Glinka to Stalin*. New Haven, CT: Yale University Press, 2007.
Ilyin, Ivan. "Sonata Form in Medtner." In *Nicholas Medtner (1879–1951): A Tribute to His Art and Personality*, edited by Richard Holt, 180–88. London: Dennis Dobson, 1955.
———. "A Study of Medtner." In *Nicolas Medtner (1879–1951): A Tribute to His Art and Personality*, edited Richard Holt, 163–74. London: Dennis Dobson, 1955.
Kasyanova, Kseniya. *O russkom natsional'nom kharaktere*. Moscow: Akademicheskiy Proekt, 1994.
Levashova, Ol'ga. *M. Glinka*. 2 vols. Moscow: Muzïka, 1987.
Ljunggren, Magnus. *The Russian Mephisto: A Study of the Life and Work of Emilii Medtner*. Stockholm: Almqvist and Wiksell, 1994.
Maes, Francis. *A History of Russian Music: From Kamarinskaya to Babi Yar*. Translated by Arnold J. Pomerans and Erica Pomerans. Los Angeles: University of California Press, 2002.
Martyn, Barrie. *Nicolas Medtner: His Life and Music*. Aldershot, UK: Ashgate, 1995.
Medtner, Nikolay. *Muza i Moda*. Paris: Vozrozhdenye, 1935.
Mitchell, Rebecca. *Nietzsche's Orphans: Music, Metaphysics, and the Twilight of the Russian Empire*. New Haven, CT: Yale University Press, 2016.

Odoyevskiy, Vladimir. *Russkiye nochi*. Leningrad: Nauka, 1975.
Popov, Boris. "Pis'ma o muzïke: Noyabr'skiyi rozï." *Pereval* no. 2 (1906): 61.
Ramuz, Charles Ferdinand. *Souvenirs sur Igor Strawinsky*. Lausanne: H. L. Mermod, 1941.
Seroff, Victor. *Rachmaninov*. London: Cassell, 1951.
Taneyev, Sergei. *Personality, Works and Documents*. Moscow, 1925.
Taruskin, Richard. *Defining Russia Musically: Historical and Hermeneutical Essays*. Princeton, NJ: Princeton University Press, 1997.
———. *On Russian Music*. Los Angeles: University of California Press, 2009.
Trubetskoy, Evgeniy. "Gde zhe nakonets, Rossiya?" *Moskovskiy Yezhenedel'nik* no. 24 (September 2, 1906): 1–9.
———. "Minornïye i mazornïye notï." *Moskovskiy Yezhenedel'nik* no. 4 (January 23, 1910): 14–15.
Tumanov, Aleksandr. *The Life and Artistry of Maria Olenina-d'Alheim*. Translated by Christopher Barnes. Alberta, Can.: University of Alberta Press, 2000.
Turgenev, Ivan. *Sochineniya*. Vol. 3. Edited by M. P. Alekseyev. Moscow: Nauka, 1979.
Vol'fing. "Invektivï na muzïkal'nuyu sovremennost'," *Trudï i dni* no. 12 (1912): 29–45.
———. "Vagneriana: Nabroski k kommentariyu." *Trudï i dni* nos. 4–5 (1912): 23–37.

MARIA RAZUMOVSKAYA teaches at the Guildhall School of Music and Drama, London, and is a pianist. She is author of *Heinrich Neuhaus: A Life beyond Music*.

8 From the Benefit Concert to the Solo Song Recital in London, 1870–1914

Simon McVeigh and William Weber

Sacralization, Professionalization, and Miscellany in the British Context

Writing about a vocal recital at the Bechstein Hall in 1908, a journalist for the London *Standard* declared that everyone assumed that "no song recital would be seriously considered that did not open with a group of German Lieder."[1] Four years later the critic from the *Daily Telegraph* wrote that "programmes are rare that do not contain the names of Schumann, Schubert, and Brahms," and for that reason, "the ordinary concert-singer rings the changes everlastingly upon some half-dozen examples of each composer."[2] Thus did German Lieder take on a high aesthetic status in London's song recitals, no longer functioning as *Hausmusik*.[3] Natasha Loges defined this change as coming from the professionalization of the singing of Lieder, a change that endowed Lieder with a quasi-religious sanctity. Such a sensibility appeared in the statement by the *Musical News* in 1908 that fans of the singer Hugo Heinz had begged him to sing *Dichterliebe*, op. 48, because Schumann had "enshrined the poem in music."[4] Apparently, Heinz asked that there be no applause until the end of the cycle, "making it possible to hear the lovely sequence undisturbed by distracting interruption." Thus, the musical ability of a singer was often gauged by successfully performing canonic Lieder in a style appropriate to the genre.

Yet not that many vocal concerts followed so strict a line of taste, since it had long been conventional to offer a variety of countries and periods on a program. In reality, not that many concerts opened with Lieder, and solo vocal concerts in London's three main recital halls offered a rich variety of periods and tastes. Despite the centrality of songs by Schubert, Schumann, and Brahms, German composers did not dominate vocal recitals as much as they did at concerts by symphony orchestras or string quartets.[5] French, Italian, and British music played strong roles in these events in the time devoted to them and the significance such music claimed; indeed, a few concerts were devoted to songs from just one of these three countries.

Moreover, song concerts such as were pioneered by George Henschel (1850–1934) created a much more sympathetic relationship between recent and canonic repertoire than existed in concerts by orchestras or chamber-music ensembles. The numerous recitals that offered new works accomplished a countertrend to the declining prominence and popularity of such a repertoire in the mainstream of classical-music events. A singer would juxtapose pieces by Schubert and Brahms with those by major living composers such as Richard Strauss and Claude Debussy, or indeed Roger Quilter and Ralph Vaughan Williams. The programs brought about an intimate mingling of epochs and nationalities in listeners' ears, thereby serving as a mediator among diverse areas of concert life, sometimes ending with popular parlor songs. In this way, the tradition of concert miscellany continued to define programming in London's recital halls prior to World War I.

Canon and Programming Strategies

Table 8.1 suggests what can be seen as the canon of song composers represented on London programs by 1910, listed in order of year of birth and divided into four periods. Yet these composers were regarded differently in informed opinion at that time, and it is therefore vital to inquire into the nature of canon and the diverse ways in which composers held such status. One might adapt the historically based thinking of Hans Robert Jauss to studying musical culture, specifically his concept that a canonic work offers a new *horizon of expectations*. Thus did such a standing arise "only through the horizon-of-experience of a continuity in which the perpetual inversion occurs from simple reception to critical understanding, from passive to active reception, from recognized aesthetic norms to a new production that surpasses them."[6] This analytical tool helps us to discern how works successively by Schubert, Schumann, and Brahms captured the attention of the public and the critical press, in the process developing the fundamental canon for Lieder. Indeed, a broader group of composers, such as are given in table 8.1, was deemed to share in the new horizon that had been established by the three great figures.

Nonetheless, canonic recognition must be viewed as unstable by nature during and for some time after the lifetime of a composer, since they faced the threat of changing taste and loss of high status within public or critical commentary. Therefore, let us speak of an *incipient* canonic status, and also look for continuing problematic aspects of the composer's reputation. A composer might either lose canonic status altogether (rather as did Spohr and Meyerbeer) or be less recognized than figures seen to reside in the high canon. The case of Hugo Wolf is particularly important, especially considering the lavish praise Ernest Newman bestowed on him in a book published in 1907.[7] It is clear that Wolf's status was still a matter of debate: for example, in 1909 the *Musical Standard* declared that "some

Table 8.1. The leading composers in London's vocal recitals ca. 1910, by birth year.

Carl Loewe (1796–1869)
Franz Schubert (1797–1828)

* * *

Felix Mendelssohn (1809–47)
Robert Schumann (1810–56)
Franz Liszt (1811–86)
Robert Franz (1815–92)
Peter Cornelius (1824–74)

* * *

Johannes Brahms (1833–97)
Adolf Jensen (1837–79)
Pyotr Ilyich Tchaikovsky (1840–93)
Antonin Dvořák (1841–1904)
Edvard Grieg (1843–1907)
Gabriel Fauré (1845–1924)
Arthur Goring Thomas (1850–92)

* * *

Hugo Wolf (1860–1903)
Alexander von Fielitz (1860–1930)
Claude Debussy (1862–1918)
Richard Strauss (1864–1949)
Ralph Vaughan Williams (1872–1958)
Max Reger (1873–1916)
Roger Quilter (1877–1953)
Cyril Scott (1879–1970)

say Wolf's prominence is only the result of a passing fashion.... [Yet] it requires the rashness of a Bernard Shaw to declare with conviction that Hugo Wolf will not eventually take rank."[8] We should also view Richard Strauss from such a perspective, since by 1910 he had established new parameters with his songs and symphonic poems, but controversies continued to surround his operas.[9]

With this in mind, we can see how certain composers active in earlier periods gained different levels of standing. For one thing, in many programs around 1910 Brahms played a more central role than either Schubert or Schumann. Moreover, in comparison with Schubert, Schumann, and Brahms, songs of Mendelssohn did not appear often in programs focused on German Lieder, but rather formed part of larger Victorian song culture. They were often performed at popular ballad concerts during the late nineteenth century, but by 1910 they did not appear as frequently. Instead, the larger canon of Lieder composers included Loewe, Peter

Cornelius, and Robert Franz, enjoying a distinct if less elevated level of respect. Franz occupied an important position; he was respected for devising an appealing conservative style that did not seem passé in 1910. Indeed, his songs outnumbered those by the great masters on some programs.[10] Furthermore, composers such as the Königsberg-born Adolf Jensen or the Norwegian Christian Sinding continued to hold not insignificant canonic status. Alexander von Fielitz likewise drew particular attention in London, most notably for his 1902 song cycle *Eliland: Ein Sang vom Chiemsee*.[11] Other countries also were represented in the broader canon: songs by Tchaikovsky, Grieg, and Dvořák were widely performed, translated into either German or English, achieving a close relationship with the German canon. And then, Max Reger was deeply respected in Germany but not in Britain. Even though his songs were widely performed in London, they were usually seen as unattractively overcomplicated and therefore alien to the warmth considered special to the Lieder tradition.[12]

Part 1: The Early Development of the Vocal Recital in London

Miscellaneity

London's eighteenth-century practice of mixing vocal and instrumental music, along with contrasting national genres, extended right into the twentieth century, with Italian opera arias and English theater songs being supplanted throughout the nineteenth by ballads and art songs of all countries.[13] Miscellaneous concerts were generally focused on the primary genres of domestic music making: English song and piano music, with their close relationship to the lucrative publishing industry. Indeed, the ballad concert—promoted by publishers Boosey and Chappell from 1867, associating individual songs with specific singers, who received a royalty on sales—explicitly reified this link.[14] In such an environment, German song (often in translation) joined an essentially home-grown repertory, accelerated by publications such as those of Novello.

There was also a much more direct route by which German song reached London audiences, through musicians visiting from Germany and Austria. The Monday and Saturday Popular Concerts at St. James's Hall—popular only in the sense that they reached large audiences at low prices—were focused on serious classical chamber music, with regular appearances by Joseph Joachim and Clara Schumann.[15] It was here that the celebrated baritone Julius Stockhausen first appeared in 1870 (table 8.2). Assuredly, vocal music was subsidiary at such concerts, but it was starting to gain a presence, with texts provided in both German and English, and the occasional program note. A second, related, concept was the classical piano recital, of which Clara Schumann was a pioneer. Her programs typically interleaved German song between large canonic works of the piano repertoire (table 8.3).

Table 8.2. Monday Popular Concert, St. James's Hall, November 21, 1870: Beethoven centenary program.

String quartet in D, op. 18 no. 3	Mme. Norman-Néruda [later Lady Hallé], Ries, Zerbini, Piatti
Liederkreis [*An die ferne Geliebte*]	Stockhausen
Piano sonata in D, op. 10 no. 3	Charles Hallé
...	
Piano trio in Eb, op. 1 no. 1	Charles Hallé, Mme. Norman-Néruda, Piatti
Songs "Wonne der Wehmuth" "Neue Liebe, neues Leben"	Stockhausen
String quartet in C minor, op. 18 no. 4	As above

Source: British Library, Music Collections, d.480.

Table 8.3. First of Clara Schumann's two recitals of pianoforte music, St. James's Hall, February 1, 1871, with Stockhausen.

Beethoven	Piano sonata in Eb, op. 31 no. 3
Schumann	"Wiegenlied"
Mendelssohn	"Frühlingslied"
Schumann	*Davidsbündlertänze*
Brahms	"Von ewiger Liebe"
Bach	Italian Concerto
Schubert	"Liebe Farbe" and "Böse Farbe" [*Die schöne Müllerin*]
Mendelssohn	Prelude in E minor
Chopin	Nocturne in G minor
Chopin	Impromptu in C# minor

Source: Daily Telegraph, February 1, 1871.

Lieder also had a strong presence at high-minded private salons such as those of the artist Frederic Leighton (where repertoire and performers resembled those just described), or those of the more progressive Edward Dannreuther, at which Liszt and Wagner's *Wesendonck Lieder* were admired.[16] Modeled on house concerts of the kind that flourished in midcentury Germany, these salons were meeting places for London's literary and artistic elite in the 1870s: although such intensely serious private concerts were no doubt unusual in Britain, they still contributed to the enhanced status that German song was beginning to acquire.[17]

Initially, singers themselves were not primary agents in the development of the song recital in London. There were no equivalents to Stockhausen's famous concerts across Germany focusing on song cycles, which began in 1856, nor the

Schubert song recitals given by Gustav Walter in Vienna twenty years later.[18] This was all to change in the 1880s.

George Henschel and Early Vocal Recitals in London

First, let us dispose of a myth. It is commonly stated that the tenor Raimund von Zur Mühlen (1854–1931) gave the first public Liederabend in England, perhaps in 1882. But no such record has surfaced in any newspapers or periodicals of the 1880s, though he did indeed sing Lieder at the Popular Concerts in 1881. The person who really established the genre in London was George Henschel, the famous baritone, composer, and first conductor of the Boston Symphony Orchestra.[19] A close friend of Brahms, Henschel brought to London his experience both of Austro-German public music making and of *Hausmusik*. He had already appeared at the Popular Concerts in 1877, making a strong impression:

> It is not often that there is much temptation to call attention to the vocalists at these concerts; but there was a *début* last Monday, the importance of which cannot be rated too highly. His songs on the 19th were from Handel's opera *Rinaldo*, "Sibillar," and two Lieder by Schubert, "Die Neugierige" (No. 6 of the set in the series "Die schöne Müllerin" Op. 25, introduced here by Miss S. Löwe at her concert) and the "Ganymied" [sic] Op. 19, of Goethe, dedicated to the poet. The auditory was taken by surprise by the sympathetic quality and expressive style of Herr Henschel, who was twice recalled after Handel's air, and equally applauded after Schubert's songs.[20]

Two years later, Henschel attained still more prominence when the same series unusually devoted a half-program to his *Serbisches Liederspiel*, op. 32, for four individual singers (on the lines of Schumann's *Spanisches Liederspiel*, op. 74, as well as Brahms's sets of *Liebeslieder-Walzer*, opp. 52 and 65).[21] But the big change came on June 13, 1883, when Henschel and his wife (the US soprano Lillian Bailey [1860–1901]) gave their first vocal recital, with no piano pieces or other instrumental contrast. Evidently this was a new concept: "far less monotonous than might have been anticipated," and an opportunity to hear a variety of neglected composers, according to one review.[22] It was the first of many similar programs, mixing German Lieder with (often older) songs and duets by French and Italian composers (table 8.4).

Two other features are worth highlighting. First, Henschel habitually accompanied both himself and his wife, usually "without book" (that is, from memory), which was seen as an impressive feat even if it reduced the dramatic effect of his own singing because "the singer [was] invisible behind the piano."[23] A second, and related, feature was that the atmosphere in the Prince's Hall deliberately evoked the informal salon or the literary academy:

> The title of Drawing-room Meetings would, but for the locality in which they are held, perhaps more accurately describe the character of these delightful

Table 8.4. Mr. and Mrs. Henschel's vocal recital, Prince's Hall [1887].

Marco da Gagliano	[Italian early seventeenth century] Duet
Grétry	[French late eighteenth century] Duet
Schubert	Five Lieder (from *Die schöne Müllerin*)
Liszt	"The Loreley"
Weber	Lullaby
Brahms	"Meine Liebe ist grün"
Henschel	[German] Duets
Schumann	"Flutenreicher Ebro," "Ich grolle nicht," "Frühlingsnacht"
Gounod, Bizet, Liszt	Three French songs
Boieldieu	[French early nineteenth century] Duet

Source: British Library, London, Music Collections, item c.374.a.(2.).

rencontres, where the usual formalities are almost entirely dispensed with, Herr Henschel acting both as his own "conductor" and accompanist on these occasions.[24]

The almost social character of these entertainments has served to establish friendly relations between the performers and their audiences, with the best results for both; and the programmes furnished each night prove how much good vocal music there is in existence, and how unnecessary it is to descend to the nether depths of the Royalty Song.[25]

Henschel's concerts thus referenced the domestic origins of singing with the piano; and indeed, the way the format was discussed precisely recalls the familiar German question of whether it was appropriate to perform Lieder on the public concert platform.[26]

Reviews consistently supported Henschel's risky venture by stressing the artistic, intellectual, and educational aspects of his presentations, using the critical language applied to the serious classical chamber concert: "These excellent artists rigorously exclude from their programmes everything vulgar or commonplace, and were it only for that reason their performances have a distinct educational value."[27] Programs of this sort marked a drastic departure from the way in which ballad concerts were typically dispatched by serious critics: "Madame Lemmens-Sherrington, accommodating herself without scruple to the tastes of her hearers, exhausted the resources of claptrap in Home, Sweet Home, Comin' thro' the Rye, and a couple of modern songs, on the sale of which she probably has the customary royalty, as it is not otherwise conceivable that she or anyone else would sing them."[28] Henschel thus brought to the London concert hall an entirely new status for serious vocal music, and for the Lied in particular, drawing on his reputation for sensitive vocal interpretation, as well as his association with the Austro-German symphonic repertoire—something he exploited directly in his founding of the London Symphony Concerts in 1886.

The Explosion of Vocal Concerts: The Profession of Concert Singer

What the Henschels offered as a concert format seemed at first to be "peculiarly their own," as London lagged distinctly behind continental practice;[29] but others soon followed and the later profusion of vocal concerts and recitals certainly reflected what Hugo Wolf in Vienna described as an epidemic.[30] Once the notion of the song or Lieder recital became established in the calendar in the 1890s, specialist concert singers emerged, whether home-grown, as with Harry Plunket Greene (1865–1936) and Muriel Foster (1877–1937), or European Lied specialists such as Dr. Theodor Lierhammer (1866–1937) and Dr. Ludwig Wüllner (1858–1938) among the men (the titles are surely significant for the serious authority they added, although Lierhammer was also a trained physician and Wüllner a Germanist), or Elena Gerhardt (1883–1961), Tilly Koenen (1873–1941), and Julia Culp (1880–1970) among the women.

The career of Elena Gerhardt has been discussed often in the scholarly literature: born in Leipzig and having studied at the Conservatorium, she gave her London debut in 1906, accompanied by her teacher Arthur Nikisch (1855–1922). Said to have a pure though not powerful voice, she abstained from opera, as was done by several other female singers at that time.[31] For women in particular, to quote Paula Gillett, this world of "restrained gestures and distilled emotion" was indeed a respectable way to enter the music profession[32] (even if the fashionable low-cut dress may still have been a barrier for the strict Quaker Antoinette Sterling). The concert platform even attracted upper-class rebels such as "Elsie" (Elizabeth) Swinton (née Ebsworth, 1874–1966) or Gervase Elwes (1866–1921), leading exponents of Brahms and English song during the 1900s.[33] Most popular of all in this decade was the booming contralto of Clara Butt (1872–1936), though, like Sterling, she increasingly leaned toward ballad repertoire, making vast profits on world tours with her husband Kennerley Rumford (1870–1957).[34] But even those closely associated with opera looked to advance their reputation as serious artists through the recital platform—including Wagnerians such as Marie Brema (1856–1925), Anton van Rooy (1870–1932), Louise Kirkby Lunn (1873–1930), and many others.

Indicative of the importance of the vocal recital in the concert season, and in the perceptions of audiences, are the annual series promoted by the German Wagnerian agent Alfred Schulz-Curtius—admittedly in the cause of his own artists. The schedules demonstrate a clear planning principle, imposing some balanced variety on the season as a whole, as the list from 1899–1900 suggests (table 8.5). Such a schedule contrasted markedly with the comparatively uniform patterning of the Popular Concerts, where variety was perpetuated within

Table 8.5. Schedule of the Curtius Concert Club, 1899–1900.

October 25, 1899	Madame Blanche Marchesi's Song Recital
November 1, 1899	Mr. Ben Davies's Evening [voice and piano]
November 8, 1899	Mdlles. Eissler's Evening [harp, violin]
November 15, 1899	Herr Anton Van Rooy's "Lieder Abend"
November 22, 1899	The Willi Hess String Quartet
November 29, 1899	Busoni's Pianoforte Recital
December 6, 1899	Herr Schönberger and Mr. Hugo Heinz's Pianoforte and Vocal Recital
December 13, 1899	Miss Marie Brema's "Lieder Abend"
January 10, 1900	The Kruse String Quartet
January 17, 1900	Herr Schönberger and Mr. Hugo Heinz [as before]
January 24, 1900	Madame Blanche Marchesi's Vocal Recital
January 31, 1900	Mr. A. Dolmetsch's Evening [lecture on old instruments]

Source: British Library, London, Music Collections, item b.622.(a.).

each program, but always in a similar way—with three chamber works surrounding songs and piano music in rigid succession (refer back to table 8.2).

Aura and Audiences

Though rarely publicized explicitly, the artistic recital was increasingly recognized as an experience that would prove "popular with amateurs of a cultivated class," thereby distinguished from the commonplace miscellaneous concert and the commercial world of the ballad concert.[35] Singers' memoirs take pains to emphasize both their disdain for grasping publishers and their own personas as serious artists. As David Bispham, one of those who made the transition from Wagner opera to the recital platform, articulated (albeit retrospectively):

> In concerts I was a new quantity to the purveyors of music, who declared that I almost invariably sang over the heads of my audiences, [choosing] airs by Handel, selections from Purcell, ballads by Loewe, pieces by Schubert and Schumann, and advanced works by contemporary Englishmen. My reply, when somewhat taken to task for the severity of my selections, was, "I prefer breaking new ground to competition with every other barytone in London in a repertoire which is common property." I believed then as now, that the artist with courage to climb high upon the ladder gets into a different atmosphere.[36]

Reviews suggest that audience behavior at serious song recitals was closer to that enforced at Ella's Musical Union chamber music concerts than at a typical ballad concert: at one given by the Henschels, "the gratification of the audience was, apart from plaudits and encores, best shown by that rapt attention which seemed to follow every note."[37] Certainly by the turn of the century, audiences were expected to listen in silence, a practice that had extended across all types of concert. Shaw is quite explicit on this, writing in 1894 that "We do not all realize how modern an institution the silent audience is. Even in the dreariest moments in a bad concert nowadays we do not talk, or go in and out noisily, or beat time with our boots."[38] He goes on to say that critics no longer had to point out tritely that "the vast audience was hushed" because "audiences always are hushed." Furthermore, by this time, program booklets routinely print both text and translation, sometimes with a program note, suggesting a close attention to the setting of the words. But there is also the question of language: Bispham passionately advocated singing Lieder in translation, even if it is often hard to tell whether that was done.[39]

Singers' deportment reflected a similar change in aura. As Laura Tunbridge has shown, Stockhausen suppressed theatrical gestures,[40] and in London too there was debate over how far the recitalist should exaggerate or dramatize emotions—or alternatively maintain a calm, self-contained exterior. Two further reviews by Shaw from 1894 piquantly contrasted two approaches to recital projection, at the same time casting characteristic barbs at audiences of every kind (even backhandedly at those of refined taste). First, a description of the sensitive recitalist, focusing on a single composer: "Mr Bispham's Schumann concert was so prodigiously successful . . . [with] his own fine singing, which is getting almost too gentle in its touch for large popular audiences, and will probably be all the better for the greater sharpness of definition and vigor of stroke which Drury Lane will demand from him in the forthcoming German Opera season there."[41] And second, of the inflated theatrical manner of the opera tenor:

> Having already heard Clément at St James's Hall, I had great hopes he would break the windows [of the Salle Érard] with one of those strident notes of which he is so proud. I must own that he did his best. . . . I would ask Clément whether he thinks that the English people have built up their nation through all these centuries only to sit down now and hear a young man yell at the top of his voice. That may do very well for the gallery at the Opéra Comique, for the suburbs, for the provinces, for Australia, for South Africa, for City dinners, for smoking concerts, and other barbarous places; but in the true artistic centre of London "people dont do such things."[42]

There is a telling passage in Elwes's biography referring to his attitude on the concert platform, eventually resolved by his holding in both hands a small piece of paper with the song texts.[43] It was further decided that he ought "to hold both the posture and the expression with which he finished his song unchanged until the last note of the accompaniment had been played," evidently an exceptional practice.[44]

The shift toward a recognizable recital culture was most strikingly characterized by the building of a comparatively grand new piano manufacturer's hall, the Bechstein Hall (now called the Wigmore). It was by then entirely to be expected that the miscellaneous opening concert in May 1901 should include German Lieder, in this case by Schubert and Schumann sung by von Zur Mühlen. The hall was set up much as it has been restored today: the managers promulgated a carefully constructed aura of attentive listening, thereby bringing about a clear separation between symphonic concerts at Queen's Hall and the highest-class recitals at the Bechstein.[45] It was certainly the venue of choice for pure Lieder programs, such as those of Julia Culp or of Elena Gerhardt with Nikisch, as will be discussed in more detail in the next section.

Part 2: Programming in 1910

Programming Vocal Recitals

By 1910, German Lieder had become less common at ballad concerts than they had been around 1880, edged out by contemporary songs among the thirty or forty numbers on a program. These events increasingly served to advertise the most recently published songs, at the expense of both German Lieder and old English songs. Whereas in 1883 one ballad concert offered two pieces by Schubert and one by each Mendelssohn and Franz,[46] after 1900 basically only songs by Mendelssohn survived. There was some compensation in the vogue for serious songs by living British composers, but the ballad concert was by now more consistently distinguished from song recitals.

By contrast, an increasing number of singers put on high-minded vocal recitals in the years around 1910. The profusion of recitals related to the explosion in culture generally, driven by economic expansion and social changes that were opening up cultural life to a wider public. The press was likewise expanding both in the number and in the scale of publications. Music teachers seem to have believed that presenting a recital in a prominent hall was necessary to attract students in the expanding population within the metropolitan area and beyond, as provincial teachers took back home the accolade of a Bechstein recital review. Moreover, singers and pianists generally must have been looking for invitations to perform with local orchestras, since such ensembles almost always included vocal or instrumental pieces in their programs. For example, in Liverpool around 1910, the Societa Armonica normally featured solos of both kinds; on October 29, 1910, Henriette Engelhard sang Grieg's "Ich liebe dich" from his *Melodies of the Heart*, op. 5.[47]

The result was, as with everything else in Edwardian musical life, overprofusion. Just one day after the funeral of Edward VII, Elena Gerhardt's Bechstein Hall recital on May 21, 1910 (table 8.6) was succeeded by a torrent of concerts in the following week alone: at least thirty recitals, of which more than half were put on by singers, either solo or collaboratively (not to speak of a dozen choral or orchestral concerts, one promoted by the soprano Pauline Donalda). In a battle of centenaries, Gerhardt came up directly against Vladimir de Pachmann's Chopin at Queen's Hall; and, a week later, her Schumann program competed against another Chopin recital, this time by Wilhelm Backhaus. To stand out from the crowd, a recitalist needed both to establish a reputation for international excellence and to develop a distinctive product that could be sustained for many years or even decades.

As we have seen with Bispham, some recitalists deliberately built an audience by cultivating a more sophisticated taste for German Lieder, which was extended by public familiarity with the earliest gramophone recordings. (He himself recorded several Schubert songs—some in English—in 1906.) As in German cities and Vienna, many recital formats were attempted, trying to give coherence to the overall program while admitting variety, and thereby laying down a marker of serious intent. Typically, this meant avoiding the miscellaneous ragbag that was by then limited to lesser performers: only the shared piano and vocal recital maintained high status, the two now on an equal footing, as with the programs of Plunket Greene and the classically oriented pianist Leonard Borwick (1868–1925), mixing substantial piano works with large groups of Lieder and British folk settings.

The basis for the following discussion is the set of programs of all the concerts given at the Bechstein Hall in the year 1910:[48] sixty-four recitals involving a singer, sometimes also an instrumentalist, and twenty programs offered by chamber-music societies, which always included some songs. The programs generally followed certain basic principles. Among the song recitals, twelve were devoted to canonic German Lieder, five featured modern music, and five were focused narrowly on a historical sequence; the others were mixed and matched among these options. Indeed, a rough historical sequence was conventional in at least half of the programs; it was common to open with songs from the eighteenth century, proceed to the German canon, and conclude with operatic and modern pieces.

The Canonic Lieder Specialist

A major exception to the traditional miscellaneous concert was the dedicated German Lied recital, since it was closely related to the highly specialized repertoire offered in concerts led by string quartets. Thus the Classical Chamber Concert Society (formerly the Joseph Joachim Concerts) enlisted a vocal quartet to sing Brahms's *Zigeunerlieder*, op. 103, and also offered songs for alto voice composed by Schubert and Brahms.[49] Such programs grew directly out of the

Table 8.6. German canonic programs: Elena Gerhardt, Bechstein Hall, May 21, 1910.

1. Schubert	"Heiss mich nicht reden," D877/2; "Wohin?" (*Die schöne Müllerin*); "Du bist die Ruh," D776; Romanze (*Rosamunde*), D797; "Erlkönig," D328
2. Brahms	*Zigeunerlieder*, op. 103, six songs arranged for solo voice
3. Adolf Jensen	"Klinge, klinge, mein Pandero," op. 21 no. 1 (1864); "Am Ufer des Flusses," op. 21 no. 6 (1864)
4. Wolf	"Und willst du" (*Italienisches Liederbuch*); "Der Gärtner" and "Lied vom Winde" (*Mörike-Lieder*); "Bescheidene Liebe" (*Lieder aus der Jugendzeit*); "Liebesglück" (*Eichendorff-Lieder*)

Source: Program in Wigmore Hall Archive, 1910.

Popular Concerts (table 8.2 above), a tradition also perpetuated in canonic concerts by the pupils of Clara Schumann and others from the Brahms circle, involving singers such as Amalie Joachim (1839–99), Hermine Spies (1857–93), or Marie Fillunger (1850–1930).[50] Occasionally a singer would devote a program entirely to German Lieder, usually taking on challenging works such as Brahms's *Vier ernste Gesänge*, op. 121. It is interesting that Brahms was represented significantly more often than Schubert, followed by Wolf and Strauss. This suggests that song programs included many pieces by fairly recent composers holding incipient canonic reputations, and we shall see that quite a few new works were included as well.

Notably, women singers were taking strong leadership at this time in both Lieder recitals and, separately, the opera world. In 1910 three women musicians who had avoided careers in opera stood out as the main exponents of the Lieder repertoire. Elena Gerhardt was the most prominent, managing to familiarize an unusually large public with challenging pieces, as we see in table 8.6.

This program differs from the more usual practice of offering variety in period, region, and musical character. In this program, Gerhardt introduced German composer Adolf Jensen, who was relatively unknown but respected by specialists of Lieder.[51] Her choice probably arose from the accusation made by the acerbic critic of the *Times* of London two years before that she kept offering only songs the public liked the most, "over and over again," tending to devote herself to "sentimental lingering over certain notes."[52] More than any other critic, the man at the *Times* in this period—possibly John Alexander Fuller Maitland— articulated a lofty, idealistic sense of the Lied, frowning on any tendency by which performative manipulation of the music might conflict with high canonic principles.[53] In that respect, he differed from critics writing for the magazines, who were more tolerant of appealing to a wider public. Another journalist remarked more politely that one of her programs amounted to "a confessedly popular programme," perhaps hinting that the singer was veering toward the "royalty ballad" system supported by major music publishers.[54] Still, on another occasion the *Times* critic made a backhanded criticism of Gerhardt by referring to her practice of offering the same songs time after time, while noting that in this case she had "avoided the more hackneyed songs of her repertory" by singing Brahms's *Zigeunerlieder* and six songs by Tchaikovsky.[55]

The Dutch singer Julia Culp had less commanding vocal skills but became known as a connoisseur's singer thanks to her musical sophistication. Her all-German program on November 26, 1910, offered unusual composers—Loewe and Cornelius alongside Beethoven, choosing "Adelaide" and two pieces from *Egmont*. A more forward-looking program was chosen by the least prominent of the three singers: Julia Hostater (ca. 1877–1917), a US native living in Paris and a pupil of Henschel and Madame Nikisch (Amélie Heussner), who offered pieces by Wolf, Strauss, and Liszt, and then Brahms and Franz.[56]

The Historical Program

The historically defined programs differed significantly from those focused on canonic German song. The sections in such a program progressed roughly in chronological order and usually included composers who were little known and had acquired what we might call a *historical* rather than *canonic* reputation. It commonly opened with pieces from the seventeenth or eighteenth century, most often of French or Italian origin. As can be seen in table 8.7, such a model was followed by the opera diva Agnes Nicholls, who was known at the time chiefly for her interpretation of Sieglinde in *Die Walküre*. The *Times* critic was impressed that she chose songs by Schumann that were not familiar to the average audience and were therefore "well worth reviving."[57]

Historical programs could be wildly diverse in their choices. On one occasion Jean Waterston (1881–1948), a well-known performer at recitals and orchestral concerts, included twenty-six songs stretching from Monteverdi to Debussy by way of pieces by Brahms, Arne, César Franck, and Granville Bantock. Perhaps the least well known piece was Albert Fuchs's *Balladen und Romanzen für mittlere Singstimme*, composed in the 1890s.[58] Likewise, the prominent opera singer Louise Kirkby Lunn (1873–1930) surveyed French songs from the thirteenth to the sixteenth century, touched base with Brahms, Reger, Strauss, and Wolf, and ended with songs by Roger Quilter, Hamilton Harty, and Edward MacDowell.[59] In his memoirs Bispham set out his own ideal program, the four sections (early, classical, new, and lighter modern) providing a foretaste of much that might be familiar in today's programming (table 8.8).[60]

The frequent appearance of opera selections in historically organized programs stimulated critical comments about the aesthetic tension between such

Table 8.7. Historical programs: Agnes Nicholls, Bechstein Hall, April 21, 1910.

1. †J. S. Bach	"Laßt der Spötter Zungen schmähen" (*Wachet! betet!* BWV 70)
†Giovanni Bononcini	Arietta, "Non posso disperar" (*Eraclea*, 1692)
†Raffaello Rontani	Canzonetta, "Se bel rio"
†Giovanni Legrenzi	Aria, "Che fiero costume"
2. †Mendelssohn	"Auf Flügeln des Gesanges" (op. 34 no. 2)
†Schubert	"Memnon" (D541); "Eifersucht" (*Die schöne Müllerin*), D795
†Schumann	"Geisternähe" (op. 77 no. 3); "Mein Garten" (op. 77 no. 2); "Die Kartenlegerin" (op. 31 no. 2)
3. Arthur Somervell	Song cycle, *Love in Springtime* (1901)
4. †Wolf	*Mörike-Lieder*: "Um Mitternacht," "Elfenlied," "Auf ein altes Bild;" *Eichendorff-Lieder*: "Waldmädchen," "Seemanns Abschied"

Source: Program in Wigmore Hall Archive, 1910.

Table 8.8. David Bispham's ideal male program.

Songs by Handel, Purcell, Haydn, Mozart	
Beethoven	"Creation's Hymn"
Schubert	"The Wanderer"
Schumann	"The Hidalgo"
Brahms	"May Night"
Loewe	"Edward"
Verdi	"When I Was Page" (*Falstaff*)
Hahn	"At Evening's Hour"
Grieg	"Autumnal Gale"
Wolf	"Secrecy"
Strauss	"The Stonebreaker's Song"
Songs by MacDowell, Chadwick, Gilbert, Branscombe, Damrosch	

Source: Bispham, *Quaker Singer's Recollections*, 350.

pieces and German Lieder. Reviewers often complained that recitalists wrongly delivered the emotions of the sacrosanct German repertoire in excessively theatrical fashion. Stephen Banfield has noted the "almost ethical aversion to melismatic or virtuoso vocal writing," which caused a strict—perhaps false—distinction between song and Italian opera.[61] A London critic complained that a Swedish singer "belongs to that class of vocalist that is best described as *operatic* . . . that is, she apparently has great difficulty in adapting that vocal quality to the requirements of the concert hall."[62] By the same token, selections from the operas of Richard Wagner were more often grouped with French or Italian pieces, involving either songs or opera numbers, rather than German Lieder, suggesting that a prejudicial sense of theatricality existed in both countries. We can see aesthetic lines drawn in the program given by Hans Lissmann (1885–1964) and his sister Eva Katharina Lissmann (1883–?), who divided their programs by countries, probably because of their contrasting voice types and previous training. Whereas she opened with five well-known Schubert Lieder and went on to sing Russian selections, he offered numbers from *La traviata* and *Rigoletto* alongside others by Massenet and Gounod. But they concluded the concert with Schumann's duet "Liebhabers Ständchen," op. 34 no. 2.[63]

These examples illustrate how the traditional principle of miscellany still survived in vocal recitals, offering diverse genres and tastes within patterned frameworks—as it had indeed in private performances.[64] The main source of division among vocal recitals came, of course, from the separate national traditions of songs. Despite the claims of the reviewer quoted at the beginning of this chapter, German Lieder most commonly appeared prominently in the middle of a program, implying the centrality of such music. Pieces by eighteenth-century British composers, particularly Thomas Arne, became common but might earn rebuke, as happened with a piece from one of his English operas: "The music was quite of a light order, too light, it may be, for those who enjoy the Lieder of Schubert, Schumann, and Brahms."[65]

Modernity and Contemporary Music

As elsewhere, there was a striking shift during the 1900s toward recent music. Thus, in 1906, the US bass Ernest Sharpe gave two recitals of Lieder by Wolf and Reger, accompanied by the forward-looking pianist Hamilton Harty (1879–1941), whose wife Agnes Nicholls (1877–1959) also specialized in the Lieder of Strauss and Wolf.[66] But a larger agenda can be seen taking place in the years leading up to 1914. Singers began working closely with composers to help them make their names at a time when the public was recognizing British music more actively than had usually been the case. The tendency did not impute a rejection of the canonic repertory; instead, it amounted to expansion of the practice, already common, of devoting the final section of a concert to new works. Such events were not organized by composers or called "new music" concerts, and indeed they always included canonic pieces seemingly to legitimize their focus on recent works. Nevertheless, they provided a more sympathetic and open-ended vehicle for contemporary music than was the case in orchestral or chamber-music concerts. Table 8.9 shows a particularly interesting program given by Gertrude Lonsdale, a singer holding a limited reputation at that point.[67] The most significant

Table 8.9. Contemporary music programs: Gertrude Lonsdale, Bechstein Hall, June 27, 1910.

1. †Peter Cornelius	Song cycle, *Brautlieder* (1856)
2. †César Franck	Mélodie, "La procession" (1893)
Eva Dell'Acqua	"Les étoiles filantes" (1884)
†Arthur Goring Thomas	"The Willow" (1889)
Walter Morse Rummel	"Ecstasy" (1907)
3. Richard Strauss	"Befreit" (op. 39 no. 4, 1898)
Theodor Streicher	"Ein Kinderlied" (*Weinsüppchen*, 1903)
Franz Ries	"Vergebens" (op. 41 no. 2); "Himmlische Zeit" (op. 39 no. 2, 1890s)
4. Ralph Vaughan Williams	"The Roadside Fire" (*Songs of Travel*, 1904)
Carl Weber	"A Tale of Old" (1910)
Frederick Delius	"In the Garden of the Seraglio" (1897)
†Garnet Wolseley Cox	"Morning" (early 1900s)

Source: Program in Wigmore Hall Archive, 1910.

piece among them was "In the Garden of the Seraglio" by Delius, who lived near Paris but whose music had recently become prominent in London. Likewise, Vaughan Williams's *Songs of Travel*, which opened the final section, had made quite a sensation at its Bechstein premiere six years earlier, a concert he organized with Gustav Holst.[68] It is interesting to see how two different kinds of musical events—a singer's recital and a composer's concert—interacted in the promotion of rising young composers. The song by Garnet Wolseley Cox that concluded the recital followed the convention of ending with light-hearted parlor songs, a genre in which Cox had specialized.

By 1900 the growing frequency of concerts devoted to Lieder at the Bechstein, Aeolian, and Steinway halls was internationally significant, since the repertoire was linked implicitly with comparable concerts in Vienna and Berlin. Moreover, in London songs from Northern and Eastern Europe—most prominently by Grieg and Tchaikovsky—frequently appeared in concerts, expanding the geographical range of compositions related in some fashion to the German example. The cosmopolitan repertoire of song recitals also often included songs and piano pieces by US composer Edward MacDowell and by Claude Debussy. Political resistance to German culture probably affected Lieder programming in France and in Britain in the years leading up to World War I. This tendency reinforced the growing focus on contemporary pieces, making new pieces by natives a strong alternative to the German canon (still, it would be misleading to exaggerate opposition to German music during the first decade of the century, at least among elite musical circles).

We have seen how after about 1900, song recitals began to integrate the past and the present through a new kind of forward-looking perspective, combining the canon of German song sympathetically with new music. The tradition of patterned miscellany contributed to this tendency, since it was founded on the assumption that a program would derive from contrasting tastes and epochs. Such programming played a central role as the vocal recital became central to concert life as a whole. By contrast, conservative assumptions about the primacy of long-standing old repertoire prevailed in orchestral and chamber-music concerts, indeed increasingly also in opera houses, making new works seem an imposition upon good taste. As Edward Kravitt put it, during the fin-de-siècle, a process unfolded that in both music and musical life "fused modernity and tradition, permeating old Lied forms with the late-romantic inclination for perpetual growth, [and] continual development."[69] By integrating German canon with forward-looking British music, song recitals took on a strong positive role within the country's musical life, giving a sense of how music of the past and the present could strengthen one another mutually.

Notes

1. "Mlle Holmstrand's Recital, Bechstein Hall," *The Standard*, November 7, 1908, 9.
2. *Daily Telegraph*, May 20, 1912, 5.
3. Natasha Loges, "The Limits of the Lied: Brahms's *Magelone-Romanzen* Op. 33," in *Brahms in the Home and the Concert Hall: Between Private and Public Performance*, ed. Katy Hamilton and Natasha Loges (Cambridge: Cambridge University Press, 2014), 300–23.
4. "London Concerts," *Musical News*, December 25, 1909, 599.
5. William Weber, *The Great Transformation of Musical Taste: Concert Programming from Haydn to Brahms* (Cambridge: Cambridge University Press, 2008); Simon McVeigh, "The London Symphony Orchestra: The First Decade Revisited," *Journal of the Royal Musical Association* 138, no. 2 (2013): 313–76.
6. Hans Robert Jauss, *Toward an Aesthetic of Reception*, trans. Timothy Baht (Minneapolis: University of Minnesota Press, 1982), 19; Mark Everist, "Reception Theories, Canonic Discourses, and Musical Value," in *Rethinking Music*, ed. Nicholas Cook and Mark Everist (Oxford: Oxford University Press, 1999), 382–84; Robert Holub, *Reception Theory: A Critical Introduction* (London: Methuen, 1984), 52–82.
7. Ernest Newman, *Hugo Wolf* (Mineola, NY: Dover, 2012). See the review in *Musical Times*, December 1, 1907, 800: "It is questionable whether his cause will be advanced by any depreciation of Schubert such as is given on p. 154." Contrariwise, see "Vocal Recitals," *Musical Times*, December 1, 1906, 833, making the point that Wolf "is regarded by some German musicians as a second Schubert."

8. "Music in London," *Musical Standard*, January 30, 1909, 74–75.

9. William Weber, "Beyond the Classics: Welche neue Musik hörte das deutsche Publikum im Jahre 1910?," in *Kommunikationschancen: Entstehung und Fragmentierung sozialer Beziehungen durch Musik im 20. Jahrhundert*, ed. Sven Oliver Müller, Jürgen Osterhammel, and Martin Rempe (Göttingen, Ger.: Vandenhoeck and Ruprecht, 2014), 79–81.

10. Walter Frisch, "The 'Brahms Fog': On Analyzing Brahmsian Influences at the *fin-de-siècle*," in *Brahms and his World*, 2nd ed., ed. Walter Frisch and Kevin C. Karnes (Princeton, NJ: Princeton University Press, 2009), 117–36.

11. *Eliland* was performed by Robert Charlesworth at his recital at the Bechstein on February 3, 1910; the only other Lieder were by Brahms ("Wie bist du, meine Königin") and Wolf ("Verborgenheit").

12. For his first visit to London, see "Occasional News," *Musical Times*, May 1, 1909, 312; and "Herr Reger," *Musical Times*, June 1, 1909, 287–88: "His tendency to view the task of composition almost in the light of a mathematical problem."

13. Simon McVeigh, "The Benefit Concert in Nineteenth-Century London: From 'Tax on the Nobility' to 'Monstrous Nuisance,'" in *Nineteenth-Century British Music Studies*, ed. Bennett Zon (Aldershot, UK: Ashgate, 1999), 1: 242–66.

14. The "pernicious system" was scathingly described by George Bernard Shaw on January 17, 1877 (Dan Laurence, ed., *Shaw's Music: The Complete Musical Criticism* [London: Max Reinhardt, 1981], 1: 80–81).

15. Therese Ellsworth, "'Caviare to the Multitude': Instrumental Music at the Monday Popular Concerts, London," in *Instrumental Music and the Industrial Revolution*, ed. Roberto Illiano and Luca Lévi Sala (Bologna: Ut Orpheus, 2010), 121–42. Lieder were less frequently selected among the vocal items at Ella's Musical Union (Christina Bashford, *The Pursuit of High Culture: John Ella and Chamber Music in Victorian London* [Woodbridge, UK: Boydell and Brewer, 2007], 236, 357–60).

16. Michael Musgrave, "Leighton and Music," in *Frederic Leighton: Antiquity, Renaissance, Modernity*, ed. Tim Barringer and Elizabeth Prettejohn (New Haven, CT: Yale University Press, 1999), 299–306; Jeremy Dibble, "Edward Dannreuther and the Orme Square Phenomenon," in *Music and British Culture, 1785–1914: Essays in Honour of Cyril Ehrlich*, ed. Christina Bashford and Leanne Langley (Oxford: Oxford University Press, 2000), 294. Pianist and writer Dannreuther founded the London Wagner Society in 1872.

17. Hamilton and Loges, *Brahms in the Home and the Concert Hall*. By contrast, a singer named Mme. Puzzi gave many private concerts of strictly Italian repertoire, which illustrates how learned in their own right the connoisseurs of that music were, as is found in the collection of Puzzi programs, Special Collections, Royal College of Music.

18. Kravitt, *The Lied: Mirror of Late Romanticism* (New Haven, CT: Yale University Press, 1996), 18. See also "From Miscellanies to Musical Works," chapter 3 by Natasha Loges in this volume.

19. Georges Bozarth, *Johannes Brahms & George Henschel: An Enduring Friendship* (Sterling Heights, MI: Harmonie Park, 2008).

20. *Athenaeum*, February 24, 1877 (on the concert at St. James's Hall on February 19). The author was probably Charles L. Gruneisen (Meirion Hughes, *The English Musical Renaissance and the Press, 1850–1914* [Aldershot, UK: Ashgate, 2002], 74–76, 190).

21. Dedicated to Brahms (St. James's Hall, March 24, 1879).

22. *Athenaeum*, June 23, 1883. A second concert followed on June 16. No printed programs have yet been found, but composers represented included Paisiello, Boieldieu, Carissimi, Cimarosa, Bizet, Méhul, Monsigny, and Haydn, as well as Schubert, Schumann, and Henschel himself (*Athenaeum*, June 23, 1883; *Academy*, June 23, 1883).

23. *Musical World*, March 12, 1887; *Monthly Musical Record*, March 1, 1888.

24. *Musical Times*, December 1, 1885. "Conductor" in this context appears to mean the concert organizer or master of ceremonies.

25. *Musical World*, March 20, 1886. "Royalty Song" is a reference to the kind of parlor song marketed at the Ballad Concerts.

26. Kravitt, *The Lied*, 18–26.

27. *Musical World*, February 19, 1887.

28. Laurence, *Shaw's Music*, 1: 101 (March 14, 1877).

29. *Musical World*, March 6, 1886; *Monthly Musical Record*, March 1, 1888 ("their exclusive practice").

30. Kravitt, *The Lied*, 20.

31. "London Concerts," *Musical Times*, May 1, 1907, 319: "Miss Gerhardt's vocal means are not exceptionally great, but the voice is never strained, as is too often the case with German vocalists." For a later reflection on this high-canonic tradition, see Elizabeth Schumann, *German Song* (London: Max Parrish, 1948).

32. Paula Gillett, *Musical Women in England, 1870–1914*: "Encroaching on All Man's Privileges" (Basingstoke, UK: Macmillan, 2000), 178.

33. David Greer, *A Numerous and Fashionable Audience: The Story of Elsie Swinton* (London: Thames, 1997): even more surprising, she continued her career as a married woman (though painted by Sargent as Mrs. George Swinton); Winefride Elwes and Richard Elwes, *Gervase Elwes: The Story of His Life* (London: Grayson and Grayson, 1935).

34. Sophie Fuller, "'The Finest Voice of the Century': Clara Butt and Other Concert-Hall and Drawing-Room Singers of Fin-de-Siècle Britain," in *The Arts of the Prima Donna in the Long Nineteenth Century*, ed. Rachel Cowgill and Hilary Poriss (Oxford: Oxford University Press, 2012), 308–27.

35. "Messrs. Borwick and Plunket Greene," *Monthly Musical Record*, April 1, 1897, 88.

36. David Bispham, *A Quaker Singer's Recollections* (New York: Macmillan, 1920), 124.

37. *Musical World*, March 12, 1887.

38. Laurence, *Shaw's Music*, 3: 205 (May 9, 1894).

39. Bispham, *Quaker Singer's Recollections*, 224–26, 235.

40. Laura Tunbridge, *The Song Cycle* (Cambridge: Cambridge University Press, 2010), 44–45.

41. Laurence, *Shaw's Music*, 3: 241 (June 13, 1894).

42. Laurence, *Shaw's Music*, 3: 296–97 (July 25, 1894).

43. Elwes and Elwes, *Gervase Elwes*, 149.

44. Elwes and Elwes, *Gervase Elwes*, 150.

45. Cyril Ehrlich, "The First Hundred Years," in *Wigmore Hall 1901–2001: A Celebration*, ed. Julia MacRae (London: Wigmore Hall Trust, 2001), 31–65.

46. St. James's Hall, May 26, 1883.

47. We are indebted to Janet Hilton for the loan of her family's scrapbook of programs of that period.

48. We are indebted to the staff of Wigmore Hall for allowing us to copy the programs of the year 1910.

49. On the rarity of vocal quartets in concerts, see Katy Hamilton, "Music inside the Home and outside the Box: Brahms's Vocal Quartets in Context," in *Brahms in the Home and the Concert Hall: Between Private and Public Performance*, ed. Katy Hamilton and Natasha Loges (Cambridge: Cambridge University Press, 2014), 279–99. On the intimacy of Brahms's compositional life, see Paul Berry, *Brahms among Friends: Listening, Performance, and the Rhetoric of Allusion* (New York: Oxford University Press, 2014).

50. See, for example, the Grand Morning Concert of Clara Schumann's pupil Fanny Davies, Prince's Hall, June 11, 1890 (with Marie Fillunger), the program consisting entirely of piano music and Lieder by Clara and Robert Schumann.

51. "London Concerts," *Musical News*, May 28, 1910, 367.

52. "Elena Gerhardt Concert," *The Times* (London), November 22, 1909, 10.

53. Hughes, *English Musical Renaissance*, 29–38, 190.

54. *The Times* (London), June 11, 1910, 2.

55. *The Times* (London), March 7, 1910, 8.

56. *The Times* (London), November 24, 1910, 13; *Musical News*, June 12, 1909, 620; and "Two Deaths in the American Colony of Paris," *Musical Courier*, September 27, 1917, 34.

57. *The Times* (London), April 22, 1910, 12.

58. *The Times* (London), May 3, 1909, 13.

59. *The Times* (London), December 4, 1899, 9.

60. Bispham, *Quaker Singer's Recollections*, 350 (he also gives a female program).

61. Stephen Banfield, *Sensibility and English Song: Critical Studies of the Early 20th Century* (Cambridge: Cambridge University Press, 1985), 325.

62. "Mlle Holmstrand's Recital," *Daily Telegraph*, November 27, 1908, 9. See also "Miss Freund's Recital," *London Standard*, June 3, 1909, 13. Compare Shaw's review of Clément quoted above.

63. *The Times* (London), June 30, 1910, 12.

64. Loges, "Limits of the Lied," 302–3; William Weber, "From Miscellany to Homogeneity: Concert Programmes at the Royal Academy and Royal College of Music in the 1880s," *Music and British Culture, 1785–1914: Essays in Honour of Cyril Ehrlich*, ed. Christina Bashford and Leanne Langley (Oxford: Oxford University Press, 2000), 299–320.

65. "Aeolian Hall," *Daily Telegraph*, November 23, 1908, 6; Weber, "The Survival of English Opera in Nineteenth-Century Concert Life," in *The Oxford Handbook of the Operatic Canon*, ed. William Weber and Cormac Newark (New York: Oxford University Press, forthcoming).

66. October 25 and November 1, 1906; compare Jeremy Dibble, *Hamilton Harty: Musical Polymath* (Woodbridge: Boydell, 2013), 52.

67. Miss Lonsdale sang in subordinate roles in several prominent concerts. For other mentions of her, see "Music in Yorkshire," *Musical Times*, January 1, 1908, 49; "Exposition Internationale de Gand," *Musical Times*, June 1, 1913, 1; and "Miss Gertrude Lonsdale's Concert," *The Times* (London), May 29, 1914, 5.

68. Michael Kennedy, *The Works of Ralph Vaughan Williams* (Oxford: Oxford University Press, 1964), 50–62, 90–9.

69. Kravitt, *The Lied*, 244.

Bibliography

Banfield, Stephen. *Sensibility and English Song: Critical Studies of the Early 20th Century.* Cambridge: Cambridge University Press, 1985.

Bashford, Christina. *The Pursuit of High Culture: John Ella and Chamber Music in Victorian London.* Woodbridge, UK: Boydell and Brewer, 2007.

Berry, Paul. *Brahms among Friends: Listening, Performance, and the Rhetoric of Allusion.* New York: Oxford University Press, 2014.

Bispham, David. *A Quaker Singer's Recollections.* New York: Macmillan, 1920.

Bozarth, George. *Johannes Brahms and George Henschel: An Enduring Friendship.* Sterling Heights, MI: Harmonie Park, 2008.

Dibble, Jeremy. "Edward Dannreuther and the Orme Square Phenomenon." In *Music and British Culture, 1785–1914: Essays in Honour of Cyril Ehrlich*, edited by Christina Bashford and Leanne Langley, 275–98. Oxford: Oxford University Press, 2000.

———. *Hamilton Harty: Musical Polymath.* Woodbridge, UK: Boydell, 2013.

Ehrlich, Cyril. "The First Hundred Years." In *Wigmore Hall 1901–2001: A Celebration*, edited by Julia MacRae, 31–65. London: Wigmore Hall Trust, 2001.

Ellsworth, Therese. "'Caviare to the Multitude': Instrumental Music at the Monday Popular Concerts, London." In *Instrumental Music and the Industrial Revolution*, edited by Roberto Illiano and Luca Lévi Sala, 121–42. Bologna: Ut Orpheus, 2010.

Elwes, Winefride, and Richard Elwes. *Gervase Elwes: The Story of His Life.* London: Grayson and Grayson, 1935.

Everist, Mark. "Reception Theories, Canonic Discourses, and Musical Value." In *Rethinking Music*, edited by Nicholas Cook and Mark Everist, 378–402. Oxford: Oxford University Press, 1999.

Frisch, Walter. "The 'Brahms Fog': On Analyzing Brahmsian Influences at the *fin-de-siècle*." In *Brahms and His World*, 2nd ed., edited by Walter Frisch and Kevin C. Karnes, 117–36. Princeton, NJ: Princeton University Press, 2009.

Fuller, Sophie. "'The Finest Voice of the Century': Clara Butt and Other Concert-Hall and Drawing-Room Singers of Fin-de-Siècle Britain." In *The Arts of the Prima Donna in the Long Nineteenth Century*, edited by Rachel Cowgill and Hilary Poriss, 308–27. Oxford: Oxford University Press, 2012.

Gillett, Paula. *Musical Women in England, 1870–1914: "Encroaching on All Man's Privileges."* Basingstoke, UK: Macmillan, 2000.

Greer, David. *A Numerous and Fashionable Audience: The Story of Elsie Swinton.* London: Thames, 1997.

Hamilton, Katy. "Music inside the Home and outside the Box: Brahms's Vocal Quartets in Context." In *Brahms in the Home and the Concert Hall: Between Private and Public Performance*, edited by Katy Hamilton and Natasha Loges, 279–99. Cambridge: Cambridge University Press, 2014.

Hamilton, Katy, and Natasha Loges. *Brahms in the Home and the Concert Hall: Between Private and Public Performance.* Cambridge: Cambridge University Press, 2014.

Holub, Robert. *Reception Theory: A Critical Introduction*. London: Methuen, 1984.
Hughes, Meirion. *The English Musical Renaissance and the Press, 1850–1914*. Aldershot, UK: Ashgate, 2002.
Jauss, Hans Robert. *Toward an Aesthetic of Reception*. Translated by Timothy Baht. Minneapolis: University of Minnesota Press, 1982.
Kennedy, Michael. *The Works of Ralph Vaughan Williams*. Oxford: Oxford University Press, 1964.
Kravitt, Edward. *The Lied: Mirror of Late Romanticism*. New Haven, CT: Yale University Press, 1996.
Laurence, Dan, ed. *Shaw's Music: The Complete Musical Criticism*. 3 vols. London: Max Reinhardt, 1981.
Loges, Natasha. "The Limits of the Lied: Brahms's *Magelone-Romanzen* Op. 33." In *Brahms in the Home and the Concert Hall: Between Private and Public Performance*, edited by Katy Hamilton and Natasha Loges, 300–23. Cambridge: Cambridge University Press, 2014.
McVeigh, Simon. "'An Audience for High-Class Music': Concert Promoters and Entrepreneurs in Late-Nineteenth-Century London." In *The Musician as Entrepreneur, 1700–1914: Managers, Charlatans, and Idealists*, edited by William Weber, 162–82. Bloomington: Indiana University Press, 2004.
———. "The Benefit Concert in Nineteenth-Century London: From 'Tax on the Nobility' to 'Monstrous Nuisance.'" In *Nineteenth-Century British Music Studies*, edited by Bennett Zon, 1: 242–66. Aldershot, UK: Ashgate, 1999.
———. "The London Symphony Orchestra: The First Decade Revisited." *Journal of the Royal Musical Association* 138, no. 2 (2013): 313–76.
Musgrave, Michael. "Leighton and Music." In *Frederic Leighton: Antiquity, Renaissance, Modernity*, edited by Tim Barringer and Elizabeth Prettejohn, 299–306. New Haven, CT: Yale University Press, 1999.
Newman, Ernest. *Hugo Wolf*. Mineola, NY: Dover, 2012.
Schumann, Elizabeth. *German Song*. London: Max Parrish, 1948.
Tunbridge, Laura. *The Song Cycle*. Cambridge: Cambridge University Press, 2010.
Weber, William. "Beyond the Classics: Welche neue Musik hörte das deutsche Publikum im Jahre 1910?" In *Kommikationschancen: Entstehung und Fragmentierung sozialer Beziehungen durch Musik im 20. Jahrhundert*, edited by Sven Oliver Müller, Jürgen Osterhammel, and Martin Rempe, 79–81. Göttingen, Ger.: Vandenhoeck and Ruprecht, 2014.
———. "The Survival of English Opera in Nineteenth-Century Concert Life," In *The Oxford Handbook of the Operatic Canon*, edited by William Weber and Cormac Newark. New York: Oxford University Press, forthcoming.
———. "From Miscellany to Homogeneity: Concert Programmes at the Royal Academy and Royal College of Music in the 1880s." In *Music and British Culture, 1785–1914: Essays in Honour of Cyril Ehrlich*, edited by Christina Bashford and Leanne Langley, 299–320. Oxford: Oxford University Press, 2000.
———. *The Great Transformation of Musical Taste: Concert Programming from Haydn to Brahms*. Cambridge: Cambridge University Press, 2008.

SIMON McVEIGH is Professor of Music at Goldsmiths, University of London, and President of the Royal Musical Association. He is author of *Concert Life in London from Mozart to Haydn* and coauthor of *The Italian Solo Concerto 1710–1760: Rhetorical Strategies and Style History*.

WILLIAM WEBER is Emeritus Professor of History at California State University, Long Beach. He is author of *The Musician as Entrepreneur, 1700–1914*; *Music and the Middle Class: The Social Structure of Concert Life in London, Paris and Vienna between 1830 and 1848*; *The Rise of Musical Classics in Eighteenth-Century England: A Study in Canon, Ritual, and Ideology*; and *The Great Transformation of Musical Taste: Concert Programming from Haydn to Brahms*.

9 German Song and the Working Classes in Berlin, 1890–1914

Wiebke Rademacher

Research into German song is still almost exclusively concerned with how songs were performed in bourgeois milieus, in keeping with the nineteenth-century conception of song as art music.[1] In the present chapter, I will challenge this focus and show that the songs performed in such milieus in fact also played a big role in the concert life of the working classes. In what follows, I will explore a range of contexts in which members of the Berlin working classes between the end of the Anti-Socialist Laws in 1890 and the beginning of World War I listened to and performed songs on the concert stage. The narrow focus on one city and one short period will allow us to take a closer look at the various concert formats and performance contexts that proliferated there at the time. Still, the results of this examination could apply to some extent also to other cities in Europe, for previous research has shown that the development of concert life in various European cities proceeded in a similar way.[2]

The examples discussed in this chapter suggest that there was an extensive performance culture beyond concert halls and bourgeois societies. Even though Dave Russell noted as early as 1987 that "it seems likely that a greater popular base for art music existed between 1840 and 1914 than before or since,"[3] research that focuses on these contexts remains comparatively rare up to now—at least with regard to Germany.[4] Yet Schumann song cycles in small theaters, Mendelssohn choirs at socialist party conferences, and Rossini arias in variety shows were part of the everyday experience of many working-class Berliners around the turn from the nineteenth to the twentieth century. By examining the role songs played in working-class milieus, we can gain a better understanding of late-nineteenth- and early-twentieth-century performance culture as a whole. This chapter will consider the various concert formats, musical institutions, and pedagogical methods that shaped the reception and performance of German song at the time, and it will attempt to complete the rather hazy picture we still have of these performances. In which contexts did working-class people listen to and sing German songs? What role exactly did the songs themselves play in these concerts?

What motivated concert organizers and audiences? And finally, what social and political questions might have been negotiated through these events?

The opening of the chapter will discuss song concerts that were held by musical or pedagogical institutions and societies in order to educate the working classes. The second part will discuss several examples in which members of the working classes performed songs on stage for working-class audiences. The final section will illustrate the role of songs in the recreational programs of working-class associations that initially had another purpose.

"Art for the People": Educational Concerts for the Working Classes

A large number of public concerts featuring German songs were organized by associations that aimed to educate the working classes and make "high art" accessible for them. Their activities stood in the tradition of the *nationale Volkserziehung* (national education for the people), which had existed since the Enlightenment. The belief underpinning such initiatives was that music has a positive impact not only on people as individuals but on society as a whole, and that concerts could be used as a medium for building the nation and spreading bourgeois ideals. Such self-righteous idealism was the prerogative of the fin-de-siècle bourgeoisie: art music was assumed to have superior, universal value. It was therefore thought to be desirable to teach all humans to appreciate this kind of music and to help them attain the levels of refinement and connoisseurship required for them to understand the classical works.[5]

For bourgeois associations, then, Lieder were an educational weapon in the greater struggle for the establishment of high art. A quotation by the progressive educator Heinrich Wolgast illustrates the force of this conviction quite crudely: "If we manage to bring the real folk songs to life for our children, as we do with Dürer and Holbein, then they will have something to protect themselves with against the pernicious effects of the cloying, slippery excrements that more than ever before pass for poetry and art nowadays, crowding the pages of the so-called family magazines and cheapening the popular taste."[6] This quotation must be read against the background of a larger ongoing debate in the outgoing nineteenth century on *Schund* (trash); that is, the popular literature, music, and theater considered to be lewd.[7] Traditional German folk song, especially in the form of art songs, has been seen as a valuable substitute for such popular entertainment. It might be one of the reasons why German art songs were deemed to be especially suitable for educational concerts for both pragmatic and pedagogical reasons.

The Schiller-Theater company, which was founded in 1894, had strong ties to the *Freie Volksbühne* association and shared the latter's motto "Die Kunst dem Volke," "[bringing] art to the people." Indeed, the Schiller-Theater was instrumental in providing access to cultural events (mostly theater performances, but also literary and musical events), to the Berlin working classes of the period. Yet its founders were often impeded in their mission by financial and artistic difficulties. The performance of German songs on the company's stage during *Dichter- und Tondichter-Abende* played a crucial role in helping them overcome such difficulties.

The main aim of the *Dichter- und Tondichter-Abende* was, in the words of Raphael Löwenfeld, the founder of the Schiller-Theater, to offer an "appropriate educational entertainment program for a particularly low entrance fee" for those "who, tired from the work of the week, would like to take part in a ceremony with the greatest minds."[8] The program was meant to complement the core repertoire of the Schiller-Theater, which mainly consisted of theater plays, and appeal to new audiences that could otherwise not have afforded high ticket prices.[9] The series started in 1894, the year the Schiller-Theater was founded, with *Dichter-Abende*, weekly evening performances dedicated to a poet each. They were divided into two equal parts with a break halfway through, and they always began with a twenty-minute introductory talk about the life and work of the poet being presented in each case, after which came a recital of several of the poet's works. After the break, four to six songs were performed, the lyrics of which were taken from the poet's work, followed by another recital of poems. On September 23, 1894, for instance, there was an evening on Goethe with this structure, the program for which is shown in figure 9.1.

Coming from the world of drama, the artistic directors of the Schiller-Theater initially intended to offer events with an emphasis on the spoken word. The songs were simply meant as an alternative, more accessible way of presenting the poetry with which the directors hoped to inspire in listeners a greater and more general interest in drama and poetry. The use of song and music, however, ended up being a successful strategy. It was notably this intermediality that made the *Dichter-Abende* popular with contemporary audiences: a survey from 1907 conducted at a very similar series of events in Hamburg showed that almost all visitors preferred the musical parts and wished that they were extended.[10] It was the quick alternation between lecture, recital, and music, then, rather than the poetry itself, that helped keep the audience's attention.

Probably as a result of the great popularity of the musical elements of these events, the *Tondichter-Abende*, or composers' evenings, were introduced to complement the *Dichter-Abende* in the second year of the Schiller-Theater. In the *Tondichter-Abende*, the poetry recitals in both parts were replaced by the performance of opera arias or short instrumental compositions. At a Mozart evening in 1895, for instance, eight songs and eight aria duets were performed. In total, the musical parts represented more than two-thirds of the program.[11] The choice and order of the songs and compositions did not follow a recognizable pattern or artistic rationale. What gave the evenings unity was that the pieces performed

Fig. 9.1. Program of the "Dichter- und Tondichter-Abende," September 23, 1894. *Source:* Program of the "Goethe-Abend," September 23, 1894, Theaterhistorische Sammlung Walter Unruh, Freie Universität, Berlin, Germany, box "Schiller-Theater," folder 5.1.

in each instance were always by the same composer or poet. In order for people with a low income to be able to afford them, the entrance fee did not exceed 30 Pfennig.[12] The municipal administration allowed the Bürgersaal des Rathauses, a designated room in the city hall, to be used as the concert venue free of charge in order to support the philanthropic aims of the endeavor, and the company often resorted to its own in-house actors for the poetry recitals. But the expenses for the commissioned musicians and lecturers were consistently higher than the gains made through the ticket sales. The resulting financial limitations of the Schiller-Theater meant that the singers employed were mediocre at best. Moreover, the organizers could not be very selective about the choice of the songs and were mostly forced to program songs that were part of the singers' repertoire. Because of this, the theater invited harsh criticism from the cultural establishment,[13] which Löwenfeld tried to silence by commenting, "Should we prefer to give the hungry people nothing, just because we cannot give them the best?"[14]

Löwenfeld's pragmatic approach helps us understand the role the performance of songs in the *Dichter- und Tondichter-Abende* played for all involved. We can say with some certainty that everyone involved in these events benefited from having Lieder on the program. For the idealistic bourgeois philanthropists, they were part of the *Bildungskanon* and therefore a valuable medium for the education of the working class. For the Schiller-Theater, they were a relatively affordable way of programming; for the actors and dramatists, they offered a platform to present poetry and literature; and for the audiences, which indeed regularly attended these events for decades, songs were interesting and entertaining.

But for Johannes Velden, a music teacher and violinist working at the Pestalozzi-Fröbel-Haus in Berlin, such a pragmatic approach was pedagogically and artistically insufficient. He criticized the somewhat arbitrary programming as well as the low quality of the performances. In his opinion, a carefully developed, consecutively structured, modular concert curriculum that was transferable to rural areas would increase the pedagogical value and the artistic quality of the popular concerts as well. The name of the concert series he set up, *Künstlerische Volkskonzerte*, roughly translated as "people's art concerts," incorporated both his aims. Velden's pedagogically and artistically more elaborate vision is also reflected in the process of programming, which involved a committee of important music directors, professors, and musicians.[15] This committee devised a series of seven concert evenings, each of which offered several instrumental and vocal works. The titles of the seven concerts, with their approximate English translations, are presented in table 9.1. Each concert was complemented by an introductory talk and a preface to each piece, as well as program notes, which were distributed with the tickets long before the concerts started so that the audience had the chance to read the notes in advance.[16]

Table 9.1. Joachim Velden's *Künstlerische Volkskonzerte*.

1.	"Volkslied und Volkstanz" ("Folk song and folk dance")
2.	"Das Volk in Lied und Tanz" ("The people in singing and dancing")
3.	"Alt-Berlin in Sang und Klang" ("Old Berlin through song and sound")
4.	"Ein Wiener Haus-Musikabend um 1800" ("A Viennese home concert evening around 1800")
5.	"Kunstlied und Kammermusik: Die Variation" ("Art song and chamber music: The variation")
6.	"Der jüngste Wiener Klassiker: Franz Schubert" ("Franz Schubert: the latest of the Viennese classics")
7.	"Weihnachtskonzert" ("Christmas concert")

Source: The table was constructed by the author from Johannes Velden, Die "Künstlerischen Volkskonzerte." Berlin: Hansa-Druck, 1912, 12–36.

Significantly, the first concert of the series was dedicated to folk songs. Velden was a great admirer of the form, writing in 1913 that "if we literally dig into German folk song, we'd find enough gold in it to throw out the window by the handful."[17] But folk songs were not only seen as valuable objects in and of themselves; they were considered to be stepping stones toward a better understanding of more elaborate art music. The fifth evening, "Kunstlied und Kammermusik: Die Variation" (table 9.2), exemplifies Velden's method well. The juxtaposition of songs and instrumental works in this concert was meant to promote in the audience an intuitive understanding of the variation form and provide them with an accessible introduction to the world of chamber music. To this end, Velden chose pieces such as the second movement of Haydn's String Quartet, op. 76 no. 3, a variation based on the song "Gott erhalte Franz den Kaiser," which was broadly known at the time as the Austro-Hungarian imperial anthem. Velden reflects in his program notes: "May anyone who knows this tune—and is there anyone in Germany who does not?—also become familiar with its artistic rendition."[18]

By choosing to alternate songs with lyrical chamber music pieces, Velden's committee tried to fight the common prejudice that chamber music was too complex for the musically uneducated ear to understand. A board member of a craftsmen's society from the little village Pritzwalk near Berlin who decided to book the art song and chamber music concert for the society praised the concerts without hiding his initial skepticism about their appeal: "Though there had long been concerns that an evening exclusively consisting of art music, that is, only with songs, piano, and a string quartet, would not be met with sufficient interest," he wrote, "we went ahead with organizing the concerts. The choice and order of the

Table 9.2. Velden's fifth *Künsterisches Volkskonzert*: "Kunstlied und Kammermusik: Die Variation."

	Kunstlied und Kammermusik. **Die Variation.** (Haydn—Mozart—Beethoven) Ausgeführt von Gesang, Streichquartett, Klarinette (6 Mitwirkende)		
1.	Serenade für Streichtrio (Violine, Viola, Violoncell), op. 8, D-Dur	Marsch (Allegro) Adagio Menuett (Allegretto) Adagio—Scherzo (Allegro molto)—Adagio (tempo primo)—Allegro molto—Adagio—Allegretto alla Polacca Andante quasi Allegretto mit Variationen—Allegro—Andante Marsch (Allegro)	Ludwig van Beethoven (1770–1827)
2.	Lieder	a. Mailied b. Marmotte c. Wonne der Wehmut	Beethoven
3.	Variationen (2. Satz) aus dem Streichquartett, op. 76 Nr. 3, C-dur	(Poco adagio cantabile)	Joseph Haydn (1732–1809)
4.	Lieder	a. Heller Blick b. Jeder meint, das holde Kind c. Lob der Faulheit	Haydn
5.	Lieder	a. An Chloe b. Das Veilchen	Wolfgang Amadeus Mozart (1756–1791)
6.	Quintett A-Dur für Klarinette, 2 Violinen, Viola und Violoncell	Allegro—Larghetto—Menuetto—Allegretto con Variazioni—Adagio—Allegro	Mozart

Source: The table was constructed by the author from Johannes Velden, Die "Künstlerischen Volkskonzerte." Berlin: Hansa-Druck, 1912, 23.

pieces and the artistically masterful, gripping performances of both programs have refuted all previous concerns."[19]

It is certain that Velden used German song as a pedagogical tool to introduce and contextualize other genres and compositional styles for their audiences: "We should absolutely start with folk music," he states in his writings, "insist on them, and only then proceed with our education toward art music."[20]

He regarded songs as suitable for that purpose for several reasons. First, the lyrics added a semantic layer to the instrumental structure that was more readily intelligible to the audience and thus functioned as a starting point for an appreciation of the music. On top of that, the melodic structure of the songs was often easy to understand and to memorize, and some of them were even already well-known among the less educated classes. This popular character of the songs, their *Volkstümlichkeit*, made them a useful tool for Velden and the committee.[21]

"One Does Not Sing with the Bourgeoisie": Working Class Choirs in (Non-)Bourgeois Contexts

Educational concerts were not the only occasions on which the urban working classes could become acquainted with highbrow performances of German songs. The idea that collective musical activities and mass participation in cultural events could promote a more democratic, less divided, society was quite common in the late nineteenth century. As a commentator suggests, "it was not without good reason that music was described as the most popular of the arts, because its tools and instruments are given to *all* human beings. . . . Even the poorest and most disadvantaged man in our nation has ears to listen and a voice to sing with and speak, and he uses it."[22] Collective singing promoted social cohesion not only at leisure events but also, significantly, in people's political engagement. In what follows, two examples will be discussed: the first one is of an educational initiative similar to the ones discussed in the previous sections, with the difference that it follows an approach that is more participatory. The second example, discussed in some detail, is that of an umbrella organization for working-class music associations, which shows that recreational songs had uses in working-class milieus that went beyond the merely educational.

The Berliner Volkschor, or Berlin people's choir, was both an ambitious workers' choir and an organization for working-class education that did much to bridge the divide between bourgeois ensembles and the working-class movement.[23] Its active members and their families had access to a music library, were granted free entrance to chamber music and orchestra concerts—as well as to exclusive concert talks before these concerts—and met for weekly choir rehearsals, which included members' individual voice training. For a monthly fee of 50 Pfennig, the members could get a well-rounded, high-quality introduction to the sophisticated world of classical music.

In almost all concerts in a season, the choir would perform German songs or large-scale choral works and oratorios together with professional musicians, as for instance the Joachim string quartet, represented by major concert agencies

 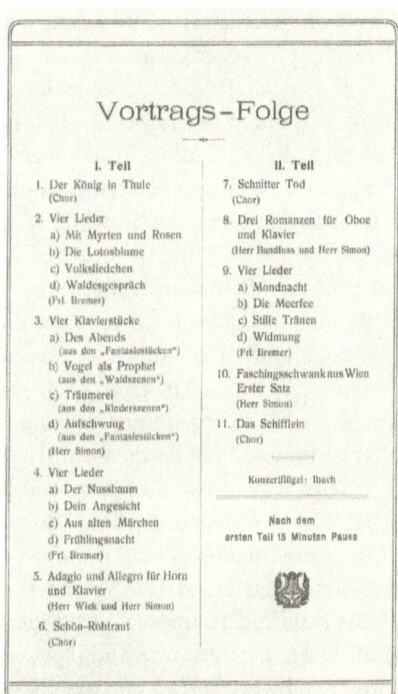

Fig. 9.2. Program of a "Schumann-Abend" in Happolts neuer Konzertsaal in 1910. *Source:* Arbeiterlied-Archiv, Akademie der Künste, Berlin, Germany, ALA 1942.

such as Concert-Direction Hermann Wolff. It is clear that, despite their common educational mission and bourgeois origins, these concerts and the concerts organized by the Schiller-Theater and Velden concerts discussed in an earlier section differed significantly: while in the latter, the working-class target group were the audience, in the former, they took on the role of performers as well. German songs served in this case not only as a pedagogically valuable object but also as the link between professional musicians and an amateur choir, as the program of a Schumann-Abend (figure 9.2), held in a venue referred to as "Happolts neuer Konzertsaal" in 1910, exemplifies. The members of the choir engaged with Schumann songs in the course of this evening on four levels: during the introductory talk; by actively performing the songs; by listening to the performance of the songs in their original version; and, finally, by being encouraged to compare them to songlike instrumental works that followed the performance. All instrumental works, and especially the "Charakterstücke" for piano, are characterized by a lyrical melodic structure that connects them with the songs on the program.

The arrangements of songs for choir facilitated a comparably undemanding involvement of the working-class members in the concerts. Choral singing was regarded as a more valuable and effective means of music education than the passive reception of performances, and some contemporaries even deemed it to be the only real way in which a deep understanding of music could be cultivated.[24] The choice and the order of the works performed by musicians, as well as the framing of both concert parts by choir arrangements, guaranteed a program without gaps between the amateurs and the professionals. Finally, the involvement of an amateur choir in these concerts also had an effect on the audiences. Listening to musicians from their own peer group perform well-known songs alongside professional musicians may have countered, to some extent, the audience's impression of being administered an education "from above."

With its musical ambition and high-brow cooperation, the Berliner Volkschor was a rather exceptional initiative, but it should be viewed within the larger phenomenon of working-class choirs in Berlin belonging to the Deutscher Arbeiter-Sängerbund (DAS), the German workers' singer association. These choirs acquired an important political dimension in the years after the German unification. Between 1878 and 1890, when the political activities of socialists were forbidden by Bismarck's antisocialist laws, working-class choirs served as undercover organizations for political agitation. After the suspension of the laws in 1890, choir membership numbers increased exponentially, going from 9,150 in 1882 to 108,000 in 1914.[25]

The DAS was an umbrella organization for working-class choirs throughout Germany, but their administration and largest regional branch were in Berlin. The DAS published a monthly journal with articles on subjects ranging from singing techniques and reports on members' cultural activities to politics, and it also organized concerts that their members could attend or perform in. The leaders of the DAS spared themselves no effort to distinguish themselves from their bourgeois competitors. In almost every volume of the monthly journal *Lieder-Gemeinschaft deutscher Arbeitersänger*, one can find statements such as "The vast majority of musical numbers in the concerts are completely disconnected from the reality of the struggling proletariat. Rather, their sickly sentimentality has trickled down from the bourgeoisie to the proletariat, causing urgent need to build a solid dam between them."[26] This tendency to distinguish themselves from bourgeois choirs applied not only to the repertoire but also to the members of the choirs. A manifesto from a 1906 *Lieder-Gemeinschaft* issue reads, "if our women have now learned that you do not dance with strikebreakers, we have learned that you do not sing with the bourgeoisie!"[27]

Nevertheless, even though authors who wrote for the journal stressed the differences between *Liedertafeln* and working-class choirs, the organizational structure, events, musical aims, and even the repertoire of DAS choirs had a very significant overlap with those of their bourgeois counterparts. One reason is that composers, rehearsal venues, and well-educated conductors for working-class choirs were hard to find. Good-quality agitational (*agitatorisch*) songs were therefore rare and, as a result, the working-class choir concerts most often had to combine agitational songs with art or folk songs.

A good example of such a concert is the 15th DAS Stiftungsfest in December 1905, which celebrated the fifteenth year of the organization's existence in the fully booked Brauerei Friedrichshain, which was built to seat around three thousand people.[28] In the first part of the event, the orchestra performed several symphonic works by Carl Maria von Weber, Richard Wagner, and Giuseppe Verdi. In the second part, six choirs presented arrangements of Lieder of their own choice. It is worth noting that the choirs chose mostly songs about nature or love, such as Mendelssohn's "Zwei Volkslieder." Only the last two songs on the program, which were performed by all six choirs together and probably chosen by the DAS, had a political subject. These were "Empor zum Licht" and "Dem Lenz entgegen" by Gustav Adolph Uthmann, the most successful composer of agitational songs.

The program of this event suggests that folk songs must have made up a significant percentage of the pieces rehearsed weekly by the choirs. It also shows that they coexisted unproblematically with agitational songs.[29] Many working-class people were therefore quite well acquainted with the standard repertoire of German song, whether by singing in one of the numerous choirs under the DAS—as, according to an estimate from 1905, about one in three urban workers did—or by attending concerts as part of the audience.[30]

But not only were German songs popular music to be sung in working-class choirs, they had also a place in the mass commercial entertainment culture emerging at the time. The DAS Sängerfest, or singers' festival at the Berlin Weißensee in 1912, for instance, was attended by more than ten thousand people. German songs were performed there in a very different setting from the intimate contexts in which they usually featured. Schubert's "Ave Maria," D839, and Mozart's "Weihe des Gesangs" (an arrangement of "O Isis und Osiris," no. 18 from *Die Zauberflöte*, K620) for instance, were presented in arrangements for brass orchestras.[31] Apart from these, popular German folk songs such as "Märzluft," "Frühling im Herbst," or "Morgenlicht," which again mostly dealt with the subjects of nature and romance, were performed on an open-air stage by various choirs. These massive festivals, such as the Sängerfest, had neither an educational nor a strong political focus, and only a fraction of the pieces on their program had a political intention. Rather, they were meant to offer recreation for the workers and their families with performances of popular music, which at the time included German songs.

Between Agitation and Recreation: The Political and Social Dimension of German Songs in Nonmusical Working-Class Societies

The initiatives discussed so far, whether coming "from above" or from workers' leaders themselves, were all organized by associations and ensembles with a specifically musical purpose. Yet music, and especially German song, also played a significant role in events organized by nonmusical working-class associations. The examples that follow illustrate how the sports club Turnverein Fichte and the Arbeiterbildungsschule, a center for workers' education, used music to further their own aims.

In early twentieth-century Germany, it was less of an oddity for a sports club also to offer musical events than it is today. The Berlin-based Turnverein Fichte, for example, the biggest working-class sports club at the time, regularly offered concerts for their members. They were embedded in the broader recreational, educational, and political program the club offered, which included excursions to other cities, lectures about politics, hygiene, sexuality, or history, and participation in agitprop activities.[32] The concerts on the program primarily addressed the workers' recreational needs, besides aiming to edify them.

One particular event organized by the Fichte sports club was characteristic of an event type which flourished at the time and appeared also in many other nonmusical associations:[33] On Saturday, November 5, 1910, a *Kunstabend*, an evening dedicated to the arts, took place in the large hall of the Brauerei Friedrichshain.[34] The tripartite program of the evening included a great variety: orchestral works such as "Feierlicher Aufzug" from *Die Königin von Saba* by Charles Gounod, "Ungarischer Marsch" from Hector Berlioz's *The Damnation of Faust*, two string quintets, recitals of nineteenth-century poetry, and several songs. Among the works performed that night were Robert Schumann's "Frühlingsnacht," op. 39 no. 12; Carl Loewe's "Prinz Eugen der edle Ritter," op. 92; "Gesegnet seid mir Wald und Au" by Pyotr Tschaikovsky; and the prologue from the opera *Bajazzo* by Ruggiero Leoncavallo.

The choice of the pieces did not really reflect any specific artistic principle; the program was simply a compilation of popular pieces of that time, and the great variety of the songs was thought to guarantee the entertainment of the audience. From a financial perspective, it is rather surprising that the organizers decided to engage both an orchestra as high-class as the Berliner Sinfonie-Orchester and several famous soloists and actors for the recitals and songs.[35] The different sound of German songs with piano accompaniment was obviously regarded as a worthwhile addition to the sound of a full orchestra.

Instead of introductory talks, a ball was held directly after the concert, for which the men had to pay an extra fee of 50 Pfennig, which indicates that there must have been high demand for this element of the program. Even if the concert was not designed to appeal to or require of the audience a refined bourgeois taste for art, its program bears several traces of that culture. At least the concert parts presupposed an attentive, serious audience. The bottom of the printed program leaflet reads, "Beginning Precisely at 8 1/2. Smoking Permitted," a reminder that regularly appeared on the programs of reputable concert halls and bourgeois societies.[36]

German songs functioned on two levels at these concerts. As previously mentioned, audiences were familiar with them because they constituted contemporary popular music. A program that included them was helpful in order for the event to attract large audiences. At the same time, they were also associated with highbrow cultural life, and thereby were bearers of bourgeois aesthetic ideals. By using the same repertoire, behavioral rules, layout of concert programs, and even musicians, the organizers offered an occasion for the workers to receive music in a bourgeois way. The appreciation of this music by working-class audiences, in other words, was a token of upward social orientation.[37]

The Arbeiterbildungsschule in Berlin, which Joseph Olbrich described as "the most important educational institution for the party before the turn of the century,"[38] offered song recital evenings of a similar type.[39] What makes the musical events of this working-class school particularly interesting, however, is the fact that they used German songs to promote the school's political agenda. After the end of the socialist ban, the Arbeiterbildungsschule was a space where workers could attend talks and lectures on various subjects for a low monthly fee. In contrast to the rather apolitical and art-focused societies already discussed, the Arbeiterbildungsschule was founded by and remained strongly connected to the Social Democratic Party. The school aimed not only to educate the workers in general, but also to prepare them for the class war. As music and the fine arts did not seem to promote that aim directly, they did not play a significant role in the weekly school curriculum. The topics of the weekly talks, which included economics and history, rhetoric and law, are documented in detail in the school's annual reports.[40]

Nevertheless, music played a significant extracurricular role in the life of the Arbeiterbildungsschule. In events such as the *Revolutionärer Dichter-Abend*, a revolutionary poetry evening in 1906, for instance, songs and poems were interwoven with an overt political agenda.[41] The annual anniversaries and the March festivals, which attracted 1,500 to 3,000 people,[42] always included musical performances. These events strove above all for political impact and so revolved around an official speech by one of the famous leaders of the working-class movement.[43] The speech was followed by recitals, songs, and instrumental music.

All the poems and lyrics of songs included in the program were about class struggle and the proletarian revolution. "Vor der Fahrt" by Ferdinand Freiligrath, for instance, was sung to the historically and symbolically charged melody of the "Marseillaise."

Despite the clear predominance of songs for political agitation, some specimens of art music did make their way into the program. The last song of the *Revolutionärer Dichter-Abend* was, for example, the "Aria of Adriano" from the opera *Rienzi* by Richard Wagner. In this aria, the desperate Adriano begs for help against the armed nation pursuing him and finally decides to flee. The plot was most likely presented in this context as a metaphor for the power of the working classes. The integration of originally apolitical or specifically nonsocialist music into the working-class empowerment discourse was quite common a practice at the time.[44] German songs were appropriated by the Arbeiterbildungsschule for the communication of political messages and thus became an object of cultural negotiation between the classes.

By way of conclusion, some general observations can be made, even if each of the examples explored in this chapter could supply enough material for a separate study, and, indeed, such a study would be necessary in order for us to further determine the extent of the social, political, and artistic impact of each initiative. First, it is certain that performances of German songs and instrumental works in working-class milieus were anything but a marginal phenomenon. Almost all events discussed in the previous sections formed part of regular concert series, many of them held every week, which means that workers must have had the chance to attend concerts for a low entrance fee in venues all over the city more than once a week. The durability of these concert formats over the decades is evidence of the high demand the concerts generated. Indeed, sources record consistently large audiences at these events, and the venues where they were held were chosen for their capacity to accommodate sizable crowds.

Apart from the success of the events, the examples show the various ways in which the workers engaged with German song. This engagement was either passive—that is, when people listened to the songs in their original versions, in instrumental or choir arrangements as part of the audience—or active, when they sang them themselves and learned about them in libraries and lectures. The meanings attached to the songs by the various groups were similarly various. As we have shown, they sometimes functioned as a medium for a top-down education of the proletariat by their social superiors, but just as often they were used by bottom-up movements such as the rapidly expanding working-class choir movement. In fact, they proved to be quite versatile, useful as a pedagogical tool to exemplify compositional structures but useful also to create a festive atmosphere at special events or to support a political agenda. Their versatility means that

German songs could be used on all levels of working-class mobilization to different ends.[45]

Moreover, what makes these songs a particularly interesting object of study is the fact that they occupy a specific position between popular music and art music, which was controversial in the musicological and pedagogical discourses of the time. As the effects of the dichotomy established in the eighteenth and nineteenth centuries are still influential in recent musicological discourses and present-day concert culture—as they are in relation to the wider repertoire of classical music—an examination of their historical appearance on both a discursive and an artistic level is a very interesting endeavor. The examples discussed here show that the dichotomy was far less unambiguous at the turn from the nineteenth to the twentieth century than the common narrative suggests. The quoted text sources often highlighted the intellectual dimension of art music, but the contexts of art music performance reached far into the spheres of recreational popular entertainment culture and political agitation. The very same songs were performed for socially completely heterogeneous audiences, at highly different venues and for equally different purposes. The observation applies not only to songs: As we have seen, the songs were performed in combination with orchestral and instrumental works—including Mozart's Clarinet Quintet, K581, Mendelssohn's *Walpurgisnacht*, op. 60, and Berlioz's *La Damnation de Faust*, op. 24.[46] In order to better understand the role of music in its historical context, we should keep in mind that the narratives of social distinction within the music-related discourses of a time do not necessarily mirror the historical realities of the contemporary performance contexts. Previous research on the nineteenth century has often focused on the former. But especially by considering the social and cultural dimension of the performances themselves, the musicological discipline can—as we hope this chapter has shown—contribute significantly to a better understanding of the cultural negotiations between the classes of the late-nineteenth and early-twentieth-century society.

Notes

1. I wish to thank Jonas Löffler and Myrto Aspioti for most helpful comments and stylistic advice. Thanks also to Andreas Domann and Frank Hentschel for suggesting interesting sources and methodological ideas, and to Peter Jammerthal of the Theaterwissenschaftliche Sammlung of the Free University Berlin as well as Peter Deeg from the Akademie der Künste of Berlin for their support during my archival research.

2. See, for instance, Tobias Becker, *Inszenierte Moderne: Populäres Theater in Berlin und London, 1830–1930* (Munich: De Gruyter, 2014); Friedrich Lenger, *Metropolen der Moderne: Eine europäische Stadtgeschichte seit 1850* (Munich: C. H. Beck, 2013); Sven Oliver Müller,

Das Publikum macht die Musik: Musikleben in Berlin, London und Wien im 19. Jahrhundert (Göttingen, Ger.: Vandenhoeck and Ruprecht, 2014).

3. Dave Russell, *Popular Music in England, 1840–1914: A Social History* (Manchester, UK: Manchester University Press, 1987), 7.

4. The situation in Great Britain has been scrutinized by researchers much more often. See, for instance, Alan P. Bartley, *Far from the Fashionable Crowd: The People's Concert Society and Music in London's Suburbs* (Newbury, UK: Whimbrel, 2009); Peter Bailey, *Popular Culture and Performance in the Victorian City* (Cambridge: Cambridge University Press, 1998); Jim Davis and Victor Emeljanow, *Reflecting the Audience: London Theatregoing, 1840–1880* (Iowa City: University of Iowa Press, 2001), 41–95; Simon McVeigh, "'An Audience for High-Class Music': Concert Promoters and Entrepreneurs in Late-Nineteenth-Century London," in *The Musician as Entrepreneur, 1700–1914: Managers, Charlatans, and Idealists*, ed. William Weber (Bloomington: Indiana University Press, 2004), 162–182; Paul Watt and Alison Rabinovici, "Alexandra Palace: Music, and the Cultivation of 'Higher Civilization' in the Late Nineteenth Century," *Music and Letters* 95, no. 2 (May 2014): 183–212; Trevor Herbert, "The Repertory of a Victorian Provincial Brass Band," *Popular Music* 9, no. 1 (1990): 117–32.

5. See, for instance, Hermann Kretzschmar, *Musikalische Zeitfragen: Zehn Vorträge* (Leipzig: C. F. Peters, 1903), 120.

6. "Wenn es gelingt, im Kinde das echte Volkslied, sowie Dürer und Holbein lebendig zu machen, so ist ihm damit ein Schutzmittel gegeben gegen die verderbliche Wirkung der süßlichen und glattgeformten Afterdichtkunst und Afterbildkunst, wie sie gerade jetzt mehr denn je in den sogen. Familienblättern sich breit machen und den Geschmack des Volkes veräußerlichen" (Heinrich Wolgast, *Die Bedeutung der Kunst für die Erziehung* [Leipzig: Wunderlich, 1903], 13). Unless stated otherwise, all translations are by the author.

7. See Kaspar Maase, *Die Kinder der Massenkultur: Kontroversen um Schmutz und Schund seit dem Kaiserreich* (Frankfurt: Campus, 2012).

8. Raphael Löwenfeld, *Die Dichter-Abende des Schiller-Theaters* (Berlin: Hermann Paetel, 1895), 6, 10.

9. Many other institutions all over Germany had a similar approach. The journal *Die Volksunterhaltung. Zeitschrift für die gesamten Bestrebungen auf dem Gebiete der Volksunterhaltung* offers a good overview of activities in this field undertaken across Germany.

10. "Vermischtes," *Die Volksunterhaltung* 8, nos. 7–8 (1906): 112–13.

11. Program of the Mozart-Abend, November 10, 1895, Theaterhistorische Sammlung Walter Unruh, Freie Universität Berlin, box Schiller-Theater, folder 5.4: Part I: "Das Veilchen," "Abendempfindung," "An Chloe," "Wiegenlied," "Das Traumbild," "Lied der Freiheit," "Meine Wünsche," "Sehnsucht nach dem Frühlinge" | Break | Part II: From *Figaros Hochzeit*, "Arie des Cherubin," "Arie des Figaro," "Recitativ und Arie der Susanne"; from *Don Juan*, "Duett Zerline und Don Juan," "Ständchen," "Champagnerlied"; from *Die Zauberflöte*, "Arie des Tamino," "Lied des Papageno."

12. A one-kilogram loaf of bread, for comparison, was 41 Pfennig in 1900 (Gustav Brutzer, *Die Verteuerung der Lebensmittel in Berlin im Laufe der letzten 30 Jahre und ihre Bedeutung für den Berliner Arbeiterhaushalt*. Schriften des Vereins für Socialpolitik 139/2 [Munich: Duncker and Humblot, 1912], 46–47).

13. Kongreß für Volksunterhaltung, November 13 and 14, 1987, Berlin (Raphael Löwenfeld, ed., *Die Volksunterhaltung: Vorträge und Berichte; Stenographischer Bericht über den Ersten*

Kongreß für Volksunterhaltung am 13. und 14. November 1987 zu Berlin [Berlin: Dümmlers, 1898]).

14. "Sollen wir den Hungernden, weil wir ihnen nicht das Beste geben können, garnichts geben?" Löwenfeld, *Dichter-Abende*, 10.

15. For a list of the committee members, see Johannes Velden, *Die "Künstlerischen Volkskonzerte"* (Berlin: Hansa-Druck, 1912), 1.

16. The school system was improving, and literacy rates were very high by the end of the nineteenth century (Christa Berg, ed., *Handbuch der deutschen Bildungsgeschichte*. Vol. 4, *1870–1918, von der Reichsgründung bis zum Ende des Ersten Weltkrigs* [Munich: C. H. Beck, 1991], 193).

17. "Im deutschen Liede können wir förmlich wühlen und mit vollen Händen das Gold auf die Straße werfen" (Johannes Velden, "Musikalische Kulturfragen: Organisation musikalischer Bildungsarbeit," in *Bildungsfragen der Gegenwart* [Berlin: Protestantischer Schriftenvertrieb, 1913], 16).

18. "Und so möge denn auch jeder, der die Weise kennt—und wer kennt sie in Deutschland nicht?—auch mit der künstlerischen Bearbeitung vertraut werden." (Velden, *Die "Künstlerischen Volkskonzerte,"* 27).

19. "Obwohl schon seit Zeiten die Befürchtung bestand, daß ein nur durch Kunstmusik ausgefüllter Abend (Gesang, Klavier, Streichquartett) keinem genügenden Interesse begegnen würde . . . , wagten wir doch die Veranstaltung der Konzerte. Die Auswahl und Anordnung der Piecen und die künstlerisch hochstehende und packende Durchführung beider Programme haben alle Befürchtungen widerlegt" (M. Petschelt, "Handwerker-Verein Pritzwalk, 2. Februar 1914," in Johannes Velden, *Die "Künstlerischen Volkskonzerte,"* 7).

20. See Velden, *Musikalische Kulturfragen*, 16.

21. Velden, *Musikalische Kulturfragen*, 16.

22. M. Wittich, "Vom Volkslied und vom Kunstgesang," *Lieder-Gemeinschaft der Arbeiter-Sängervereinigung* 1, no. 1 (1899): 1–2.

23. The concert venues of the seasons 1904–7 illustrate the heterogeneous spheres in which the choir was present: Sing-Akademie, Gewerkschaftshaus (House of the Workers' Union), Sophien-Säle, Königliche Hochschule für Musik, and the Deutscher Hof. See the third annual report of the Berliner Volkschor, 1907, Arbeiterlied-Archiv, Akademie der Künste, Berlin, Germany, ALA 1942. (All following archival materials with the ALA locator number belong to the Arbeiterlied-Archiv.) Moreover, the choir was invited to perform at the most important occasions for organized labor. At the Fourth Prussian Social Democratic Party Conference in 1913, for instance, they performed Mendelssohn's *Walpurgisnacht* (Program of the Festkonzert anlässlich des vierten Parteitages der sozialdemokratischen Partei Preussens in der Neuen Welt, January 6, 1913, ALA 2164).

24. See, for instance, Kretzschmar, *Musikalische Zeitfragen*, 120.

25. Dietmar Klenke, Peter Lilje, and Franz Walter, *Arbeitersänger und Volksbühnen in der Weimarer Republik* (Bonn: Dietz, 1992), 56.

26. "Die überwiegende Mehrzahl der üblichen Programmnummern hat mit der Gefühlsstimmung des im Kampfe stehenden Proletariats auch nicht das geringste zu thun. Aus dem Bürgerthum sind diese Gefühlsduseleien bis ins Proletariat durchgesickert, und es thut noth, daß hier ein fester Damm aufgeworfen wird" (Hermann Duncker, "Was sollen wir singen?" *Lieder-Gemeinschaft der Arbeiter-Sängervereinigung Deutschlands* no. 2 [October 1900]: 4).

27. "Wenn Arbeiterinnen schon wissen: mit Streikbrechern tanzt man nicht, so wissen wir: mit Bourgeois singt man nicht!" Eugen Thari, "Kulturelle Aufgaben

der Arbeitergesangvereine," *Lieder-Gemeinschaft der Arbeiter-Sängervereinigung* 13 (March 1906): 3.

28. f., "Das 15. Stiftungsfest des Arbeiter-Sängerbundes Berlins und Umgebung," *Die Tonkunst* 9 (December 1905): 267–68.

29. Hermann Duncker, "So, Mann der Arbeit, sollst du Feste feiern," *Lieder-Gemeinschaft der Arbeiter-Sängervereinigung* no. 5 (November 1902): 1–2.

30. "Der Arbeiter-Sängerbund Berlins und Umgebung," *Die Tonkunst* 9, no. 12 (June 1905): 141.

31. Program of the DAS Sängerfest 1912 in Berlin Weißensee, July 28, 1912, ALA 2268.

32. For information about the history of the Turnverein Fichte, see Günter Möschner, "5. August 1890. Erster Berliner Arbeiterturnverein," *Berlinische Monatsschrift, Edition Luisenstadt* 8 (August 1996): 86–87.

33. See, for instance, announcements from the Deutscher Arbeiter-Abstinenten-Bund: "Kunst-Abend" (November 11, 1906), "Goethe-Beethoven-Abend" (October 22, 1911), "Volkslieder-Abend" (March 10, 1912), ALA 2163; and from the Verein der Lehrlinge, jugendlichen Arbeiter und Arbeiterinnen Berlins und Umgegend: "Stiftungsfest" (September 7, 1907), ALA 2155.

34. Program of the Kunstabend organized by the Turnverein Fichte, ALA 2183.

35. The poems were recited by the famous actor Adele Sandrock, the songs by Wilhelm Kaiser, part of the opera ensemble of the Volkstheater.

36. Indeed, there was a broad discussion about drinking, smoking, and leaving the concert venue during the musical presentations in the (working-class) press. See, for instance, "Konzertberichte aus den Vereinen," *Die Tonkunst* 8, no. 22 (1905): 267–68; "Märzfest der Freien Volksbühne," *Vorwärts*, 2. *Beilage* 21, no. 69 (March 22, 1904), unpaged.

37. This dimension was already noted by contemporary authors; see, for instance, "Welche Volksschichten erreicht unsere Arbeit und wie wirkt sie?," *Die Volksunterhaltung* 8, no. 10–11 (May 1907): 157–58.

38. Joseph Olbrich, *Geschichte der Erwachsenenbildung in Deutschland* (Opladen, Ger.: Leske and Budrich, 2001), 111.

39. März-Dichter-Feier (March 20, 1897); Heinrich Heine-Abend (March 22, 1903); Volks-Lieder-Abend (March 20, 1904); 15. Stiftungs-Fest (January 21, 1906); Eichendorff-Abend (November 10, 1907), all in ALA 2158. These examples will not be discussed here in detail because they are similar to the examples just discussed.

40. See for instance the annual reports of the Arbeiterbildungsschule from 1897/98 to 1913/14, Bibliothek des Bundesarchivs, Berlin Lichterfelde, Germany, Magazin 56/5992 and 61/10254.

41. Arbeiterbildungsschule, Revolutionärer Dichter-Abend, March 4, 1906, ALA 2158.

42. Wolfgang Bagger, "Untersuchungen zur Geschichte des Berliner Arbeiter-Bildungs-Instituts von 1878 und der Arbeiter-Bildungsschule Berlin 1891 bis 1914," PhD diss., Humboldt Universität Berlin, 1983, 86–101.

43. Duncker, "So, Mann der Arbeit," 1–2.

44. As an example of this sort of adaptation, see, for instance, Kurt Eisner, "Die Heimat der Neunten," *Die Neue Gesellschaft* 1 (1905): 9–10.

45. Peter Friedemann names three levels that are interestingly congruent with the three parts of this article. "Feste und Feiern im rheinisch-westfälischen Industriegebiet 1890–1914," in *Sozialgeschichte der Freizeit*, ed. Gerhard Huck (Wuppertal, Ger.: Peter Hammer, 1980), 177.

46. My most recent research on four performance contexts of Beethoven's Leonore Overture no. 3 gives further evidence for this hypothesis. See Wiebke Rademacher, "Beethoven's Leonore in Berlin around 1900: On Contextual Factors of Music Performances as Source Material for Past Emotional Practices," *Cultural History* 7, no. 2 (2018): 167–86.

Bibliography

Bagger, Wolfgang. "Untersuchungen zur Geschichte des Berliner Arbeiter-Bildungs-Instituts von 1878 und der Arbeiter-Bildungsschule Berlin 1891 bis 1914." PhD diss., Humboldt Universität Berlin, 1983.
Bailey, Peter. *Popular Culture and Performance in the Victorian City*. Cambridge: Cambridge University Press, 1998.
Bartley, Alan P. *Far from the Fashionable Crowd: The People's Concert Society and Music in London's Suburbs*. Newbury, UK: Whimbrel, 2009.
Becker, Tobias. *Inszenierte Moderne: Populäres Theater in Berlin und London, 1830–1930*, Munich: De Gruyter, 2014.
Berg, Christa, ed. *Handbuch der deutschen Bildungsgeschichte*. Vol. 4, *1870–1918, von der Reichsgründung bis zum Ende des Ersten Weltkriegs*, Munich: C. H. Beck, 1991.
Brutzer, Gustav. *Die Verteuerung der Lebensmittel in Berlin im Laufe der letzten 30 Jahre und ihre Bedeutung für den Berliner Arbeiterhaushalt*. Schriften des Vereins für Socialpolitik 139/2. Munich: Duncker and Humblot, 1912.
Davis, Jim, and Victor Emeljanow. *Reflecting the Audience: London Theatregoing, 1840–1880*, Iowa City: University of Iowa Press, 2001.
Duncker, Hermann."So, Mann der Arbeit, sollst du Feste feiern." *Lieder-Gemeinschaft der Arbeiter-Sängervereinigung* no. 5 (November 1902): 1–2.
———. "Was sollen wir singen?" *Lieder-Gemeinschaft der Arbeiter-Sängervereinigung Deutschlands* no. 2 (October 1900): 2–4.
Eisner, Kurt. "Die Heimat der Neunten." *Die Neue Gesellschaft* no. 1 (1905): 9–10.
f. "Das 15. Stiftungsfest des Arbeiter-Sängerbundes Berlins und Umgebung." *Die Tonkunst* 9 (December 1905): 267–68.
Friedemann, Peter. "Feste und Feiern im rheinisch-westfälischen Industriegebiet 1890–1914." In *Sozialgeschichte der Freizeit*, edited by Gerhard Huck, 161–85. Wuppertal, Ger.: Peter Hammer, 1980.
Herbert, Trevor. "The Repertory of a Victorian Provincial Brass Band," *Popular Music* 9, no. 1 (1990): 117–32.
Klenke, Dietmar, Peter Lilje, and Franz Walter. *Arbeitersänger und Volksbühnen in der Weimarer Republik*. Bonn: Dietz, 1992.
"Konzertberichte aus den Vereinen." *Die Tonkunst* 8, no. 22 (1905): 267–68.
Kretzschmar, Hermann. *Musikalische Zeitfragen: Zehn Vorträge*. Leipzig: C. F. Peters, 1903.
Lenger, Friedrich. *Metropolen der Moderne: Eine europäische Stadtgeschichte seit 1850*. Munich: C. H. Beck, 2013.
Löwenfeld, Raphael. *Die Dichter-Abende des Schiller-Theaters*. Berlin: Hermann Paetel, 1895.
———, ed. *Die Volksunterhaltung: Vorträge und Berichte; Stenographischer Bericht über den Ersten Kongreß für Volksunterhaltung am 13. und 14. November 1987 zu Berlin*. (Berlin: Dümmlers, 1898).

Maase, Kaspar. *Die Kinder der Massenkultur: Kontroversen um Schmutz und Schund seit dem Kaiserreich*, Frankfurt: Campus, 2012.
"Märzfest der Freien Volksbühne." *Vorwärts*, 2. Beilage 21, no. 69 (March 22, 1904), unpaged.
McVeigh, Simon. "'An Audience for High-Class Music': Concert Promoters and Entrepreneurs in Late-Nineteenth-Century London." In *The Musician as Entrepreneur, 1700–1914: Managers, Charlatans, and Idealists*, edited by William Weber, 162–82. Bloomington: Indiana University Press, 2004.
Müller, Sven Oliver. *Das Publikum macht die Musik: Musikleben in Berlin, London und Wien im 19. Jahrhundert*. Göttingen, Ger.: Vandenhoeck and Ruprecht, 2014.
Olbrich, Joseph. *Geschichte der Erwachsenenbildung in Deutschland*. Opladen, Ger.: Leske and Budrich, 2001.
Rademacher, Wiebke. "Beethoven's Leonore in Berlin around 1900: On Contextual Factors of Music Performances as Source Material for Past Emotional Practices." *Cultural History* 7, no. 2 (2018): 167–86.
Russell, Dave. *Popular Music in England, 1840–1914: A Social History*, Manchester, UK: Manchester University Press, 1987.
Thari, Eugen. "Kulturelle Aufgaben der Arbeitergesangvereine." *Lieder-Gemeinschaft der Arbeiter-Sängervereinigung* 13 (March 1906).
Velden, Johannes. *Die "Künstlerischen Volkskonzerte."* Berlin: Hansa-Druck, 1912.
———. "Musikalische Kulturfragen: Organisation musikalischer Bildungsarbeit." In *Bildungsfragen der Gegenwart*. Berlin: Protestantischer Schriftenvertrieb, 1913.
"Vermischtes." *Die Volksunterhaltung* 8, nos. 7–8 (July-August 1906): 112–13.
Watt, Paul, and Alison Rabinovici. "Alexandra Palace: Music, and the Cultivation of 'Higher Civilization' in the Late Nineteenth Century." *Music and Letters* 95, no. 2 (May 2014): 183–212.
"Welche Volksschichten erreicht unsere Arbeit und wie wirkt sie?" *Die Volksunterhaltung* 8, nos. 10–11 (May 1907): 157–58.
Wittich, M. "Vom Volkslied und vom Kunstgesang." *Lieder-Gemeinschaft der Arbeiter-Sängervereinigung* 1, no 1 (1899): 1–2.
Wolgast, Heinrich. *Die Bedeutung der Kunst für die Erziehung*. Leipzig: Wunderlich, 1903.

WIEBKE RADEMACHER is Research Fellow at the a.r.t.e.s. Graduate School for the Humanities at the University of Cologne.

10 Lilli Lehmann's Dedicated Lieder Recitals

Rosamund Cole

"The audience must without exception have realized that this is one of the greatest, most exquisitely perfect singing artists of our time," wrote Paul Gerhardt about the opera singer Lilli Lehmann's performance of her new program of Lieder by August Bungert (1845–1915) in the Theatersaal of the Krystallpalast in Leipzig on January 11, 1893.[1] The year 1892 had marked a turning point in Lehmann's career: she had collapsed from overwork while on tour in the United States and had had to return home to Berlin to rest and recover.[2] Realizing that she needed a new way forward, she devised a fresh strand to her performing career and, during a nine-month break, prepared an innovative recital program consisting solely of Lieder composed by her friend Bungert. This very unusual decision to create a Lieder recital dedicated to one composer, with the focus on the relatively little known Bungert, could have been controversial, but the bold plan allowed Lehmann both to recover physically and to reinvent her art, providing her with a new form of artistic expression and source of income that would sustain her until she finally gave up singing in 1920, at the age of seventy-two.

Lehmann (1848–1929) maintained a handwritten record of all her performances in a book; the book has recently come to light and forms the basis of information presented for the first time in this essay.[3] Her list describes where, when, and what she performed, often with whom, and even other details, such as what she wore and references to important current events. From her diaries, letters, newspaper reviews, and writings, further practical details emerge that enrich our understanding of her performances of German song.

From her autobiography, we learn that in her early career Lehmann appears to have enjoyed Lieder primarily as a form of entertainment at home, as was typical in the 1850s and 1860s.[4] Her childhood friend Käthe Damm, in a newspaper article about Lehmann, also recalled Lilli as a young adult accompanying herself singing Lieder at the piano.[5] Her professional career began in 1865 and spanned more than half a century. She gave her first concert containing Lieder in 1872, singing Schubert's "Heidenröslein" and Robert Franz's "Stille Sicherheit."[6] For the first twenty years, she performed only about twenty Lieder professionally, which she tended to repeat in various combinations of three or four, usually prefaced with one aria—often, at this point in her career, a bravura piece such as "Flamme vengeresse" from *Le domino noir* by Auber or "La diva" by Visetti. Each year, typically during the summer break, she added a few more carefully chosen songs to her repertoire. Thus, by the time she ceased performing in 1920, her performed repertoire had expanded from 2 to more than 469 Lieder.[7]

Between the pages of the Repertoire book that relate to concerts in February 1914 is a handwritten note on a slip of paper that details a booking for some of her last series of recitals:

Wien Liederabende 1920
2. Dez, 6. 8. Tonkünstlerverein
11 Dez 1920 Arie D. A. 1 Don Ott.
Arie D. A. II Ach Grausame.
Hof Oper Berlin, 4 Mai 1916
Fidelio Ehrengastspiel 50 Jahre Theater.

The date of the performance at the Hofoper Berlin implies that the later performances were booked prior to 1916, suggesting that Lehmann at sixty-eight years old was still in demand for bookings four years in advance. In the relevant pages of the Repertoire book she notes "Konzertdirektion: Hugo Heller," suggesting that these notes may have been made in a telephone call with Heller's concert agency.

Lehmann evidently did make use of the services of concert agents, but it seems that she undertook many of the practicalities associated with organizing her work herself. There are occasional references to concert agencies such as Habelmann, Keller and König, and she also used the help of Dr. Max Goldschmidt to collate her reviews. It seems, however, that she herself was mostly in charge: her diaries mention writing to people to cancel performances, to negotiate her fees, and occasionally even to newspapers to explain her cancelations. One letter from Reynaldo Hahn to Lehmann indicates that, to his dismay, she had booked a hotel herself instead of waiting for him to do so, causing her needless expense.[8] Her financial autonomy is also evident; her papers reveal that she earned far more than her husband Paul Kalisch and managed that money herself. For example, on February 13, 1896, she noted in her diary that she had set up a pension fund for Kalisch.[9]

From Lehmann's letters it becomes clear that she had not always been so independent in choosing recital repertoire. For example, one 1875 letter from Wilhelm Taubert stipulates the repertoire for a court concert that week.[10] Soon, however, she was able to program her own recitals, as indicated by another letter from Hahn who, despite his evident frustration at a lack of decision on

Table 10.1. Chronological table of all the composers whose Lieder Lehmann added to her repertoire.

1872	Robert Franz, Franz Schubert
1874	Wilhelm Taubert, Frédéric Chopin, Robert Schumann
1875	Ignaz Brüll
1876	Ferdinand von Hiller, Franz Poenitz, Franz Liszt, Anton Rubinstein, Johannes Brahms, Franz Abt
1878	Johann Naret-Koning
1879	Max Bruch, Richard Wagner
1880	Ludwig van Beethoven
1881	Gabriel Fauré, Gustav Mahler
1886	Eduard Lassen, Alban Förster
1887	Carl Loewe
1890	August Bungert
1894	Peter Cornelius, Reinhold Herman, Friedrich August Naubert, Alexander von Fielitz
1896	Johannes Lechner, Hans Hermann, Fritz Steinbach
1901	Edvard Grieg
1903	Hugo Wolf
1904	Fritz Koegel
1906	Oskar Kolbe
1907	Richard Strauss
1911	Jakobus Kenyen

Source: Repertoire book, box 3, Lilli Lehmann Collection, US Library of Congress, Washington, DC.

Lehmann's part about a concert program, deferred to her final decision.[11] In a letter to the conductor Franz Wüllner (1832–1902), Lehmann makes repertoire suggestions, explaining the character of some unfamiliar Lieder by Bungert, to help Wüllner choose from the selection she offered.[12] When she began singing at the Berlin Court Opera in 1870, she came into contact with several contemporary composers, and her Repertoire book shows that she was particularly interested in performing their works (see table 10.1). The contacts allowed her to sing songs prior to their publication, for example Taubert's "Kuss und Lied" that she sang in 1874 before it was published in 1875.[13]

Lehmann sang the role of Christine in the world premiere of Ignaz Brüll's (1846–1907) opera *Das goldene Kreuz* on December 26, 1875, at the Berlin Hoftheater. This performance was soon followed by a brief recital accompanied by Brüll on January 5, 1876, which was the first record of a Lehmann recital dedicated to Lieder without any arias. It included a group of three of his songs and Liszt's "Mignons Lied." Thereafter, she remained friends with Brüll, living near to him in the Salzkammergut in Austria. She enjoyed performing settings of Goethe's work and she asked Brüll in 1902 to set the "Goeth'sche Maxim: Edel sei der Mensch," for which he charged sixty florins.[14]

Lehmann remained on contract in Berlin for fifteen years. During that time, she generally gave about twenty-five guest concerts per year, of which only two or three usually included Lieder. She described such events as "Conzerte." On November 4 and 18, 1882, it appears she gave dedicated Lieder concerts in Magdeburg and Erfurt, describing the program for the first time as "Lieder." The first time she used the term *Liederabend* was at the Steinway Hall in London on October 22, 1885, but, in fact, her program for it consisted of a mixture of arias and Lieder, suggesting that the boundary between the terms was still porous.[15]

In 1883, Lehmann's mother died, enabling her to take control of her life and realize her vocal ambitions. She performed several dramatic roles that she had been preparing for some years. It is perhaps significant that, also within eighteen months of her mother's death, she met and fell in love with tenor Paul Kalisch, whom she would marry in New York in 1888. She also managed to arrange permission to take up a temporary guest contract at the Metropolitan Opera in 1885. Thus, on November 4, 1885, she boarded the SS *Eider* to travel to the New World. Lehmann's move to the United States was marked by her own compositions appearing in public. One of her songs, "Fahr' wohl," she claimed had been stolen from her and published without her consent in 1889 by the New York publisher Schirmer and the Berlin publisher Friedrich Luckhardt as her opus 1 (fig. 10.1).[16] Lehmann confirmed in her autobiography that it was a private work and that she was mortified at its publication because she did not regard herself as a composer.[17] The text of this highly romantic song, expressing regret at leaving a loved one, is by Lehmann herself. The triumphant concluding chords, however, imply that the sorrow is not entirely sincere. One might interpret the song biographically; the move to the United States was an escape from what she viewed as poorly paid near-drudgery in the Berlin court opera. Furthermore, she was leaving behind memories of her earlier failed relationship with Fritz Brandt (the former stage engineer of the Bayreuth Festival) and embarking on a new life with Kalisch.[18]

For her debut in the United States, Lehmann chose to present herself as Carmen, a role with which she had had great success in Germany, and it was positively received at the Metropolitan Opera.[19] Having demonstrated her histrionic and vocal skills in *Carmen*, with careful strategy Lehmann built up her reputation at the Metropolitan Opera in the dramatic *Fach*, soon becoming renowned for her performances of all Wagner's Brünnhildes, Amelia in *Der Maskenball*, Valentin in *Die Huguenotten* by Meyerbeer, and Aïda, among other roles. The account ledgers from this era show that Lehmann was the highest paid singer

Fig. 10.1. Lilli Lehmann, "Fahr' wohl" (New York: Schirmer; Berlin: Friedrich Luckhardt, 1889).

on the Metropolitan Opera books, earning even more than her male contemporaries, such as Albert Niemann.[20] When the opera season finished on March 6, 1886, with a final performance of Karl Goldmark's *Die Königin von Saba*, Lehmann began a concert tour in which she gave seventy performances in two and a half months (March 8, 1886–June 24, 1886). The programs usually consisted of a mixture of arias and Lieder. At first, they were repeated over two days in one place and then altered for the next two concerts. After the fifteenth concert, the pattern was changed and each night of the tour she gave a different program using the same repertoire of songs.

Perhaps unexpectedly, Lehmann's recital fee was the same, and sometimes even higher, than her earnings for an opera performance. A slip of paper in her Repertoire book lists her performance fees from January to April 1896, according to which she was paid $1,250 to sing Isolde in New York on March 17, but for a recital on February 4 she received $1,495. She observed in her autobiography that the fee Steinway and Sons offered her for a thirty-day concert tour was the equivalent of three years' pay at the Berlin Opera.[21] She therefore decided to break her contract in Berlin and remain in the United States. Her action resulted in not only a fine of 13,500 Marks but also a ban on her performing in German-speaking theaters after 1886. (The ban was lifted in 1890 by Kaiser Wilhelm II.) During this period, Lehmann worked frenetically in the United States, Denmark, and Budapest (under Mahler), eventually collapsing from exhaustion, breaking off her 1892 US tour, and going home to Berlin to rest.

Lehmann described this period of convalescence in her autobiography: "Lonely and alone I bethought me of [Bungert's] songs. Should I really never sing again? The impulse to inner deliverance was strong once more, and triumphed over all the warnings of my physicians. So, I began to study again, practiced very softly at first, then steadily louder, until I had become assured that my heart would never offer resistance to such work, though the nerves of my head might often still be of another opinion."[22] The admission that her "nerves" might also be a contributing factor in her illness, encourages speculation about her suffering some kind of depression during this period. After leaving the whirl of performance life in the United States, she was now lonely, and evidently her life with Kalisch was not affording her the company and intellectual stimulation she desired.[23]

She sought consolation in her work, studying in particular the songs of August Bungert. This successful composer was able to offer her intellectual stimulation and companionship. The only times she mentioned having worked with Bungert previously was in 1890 when they gave a concert together in Berlin consisting of excerpts from some of her famous roles, such as Brünnhilde (*Götterdämmerung*) and Rezia's aria "Ozean du Ungeheuer" from Weber's *Oberon*, followed by a group of Bungert Lieder; and, on November 3, 1891, in Trier, when she sang an aria from *Fidelio* followed by some unidentified Bungert Lieder. She repeated this program the next day in Cologne and then two days later in Wiesbaden.[24] In her autobiography, Lehmann perhaps reveals the dual appeal of performing these songs in the pleasure of exchanging ideas about music, art, and philosophy with Bungert in combination with her strong identification with the texts he set:

AUGUST BUNGERT! This name awakes rich memories of the eminent man, the fortunate tone poet, the true friend, and of the happy, intellectual hours in which he, full of the Homeric spirit, transported us to other worlds, intoxicating us with classical idealism. . . . His songs had already aroused my lively interest, and the words of Odysseus at the close of the Nausicaa: "Passing hence, I perceive / That the will of man is one / With the divine will. By renouncing, / I fulfil life's inmost meaning!" took strong hold on my heart as he sang them to me once. Who does not know the word Renunciation, that, in my life, also, has played so harsh a part?

Bungert had described to her the creative idyll he often inhabited at Schloss Mon Repos, Neuwied, in which Queen Elisabeth of Romania, who wrote under the pseudonym Carmen Sylva, produced poetry that he immediately set to music for it to be performed by the princess's family. The appeal of working with him and the potential influence of royalty must therefore have made joining his circle at this time an attractive option for Lehmann. After nine months of recuperation, Lehmann reentered the performing world with her new recital program of no less than twenty Lieder by Bungert. It was still unusual to dedicate a recital entirely to Lieder by one composer at the time. The first person to do so had been Gustav Walter in 1876, with his recitals of Schubert songs in Vienna every March.[25] Walter's agent, Albert Gutmann, had intended to develop the idea into a series of similar Liederabende by other singers, including Lilli Lehmann, and, according to Edward Kravitt, Gutmann claimed he had undertaken the project, though no such venture is recorded in Lehmann's Repertoire book. The singer Amalie Joachim, five years before Lehmann, had given three Lieder recitals in 1888, each dedicated to a different composer: Schubert, Schumann, and Brahms, on three separate evenings.[26] It is revealing that Lehmann kept a review of Amalie Joachim's Lieder recitals in her album of press clippings, perhaps indicating a sense of competition with Joachim. In the review, Joachim's Lieder recital was criticized because it evidently bored the audience, and the reviewer contrasted this with Lehmann's performance the previous Friday: "Something of what I felt may well have also been felt by the audience. I saw many bored faces and heard nothing of the explosive applause of the previous Friday, where in the same place a crowd of giddily joyful people had been enraptured."[27]

Between December 2, 1892, and January 25, 1893, Lehmann gave six Bungert recitals in Dresden, Berlin (two recitals), Neuwied, Leipzig, and Cologne. The attraction for Lehmann may have been in part the creative process of working with Bungert and Carmen Sylva, who valued her creative contributions on equal terms to their own.[28] At a time that she repeatedly depicts in her autobiography as being a lonely period, she discovered in Bungert and Carmen Sylva attentive friendship and support.[29] Another attraction for Lehmann was Bungert's instinct for the dramatic in his settings, a skill that Max Chop compared to that of Franz

Schubert.³⁰ Furthermore Bungert chose to set to music not only the poetry of Sylva, whose work Lehmann deeply admired, but also many of her other favorite German poets, in particular Goethe. Not only did the nationalist focus of much of his work appeal to her, but she may also have judged it as likely to be widely popular, as it chimed with current burgeoning German patriotism.³¹

Her choice of Bungert was something of a mystery to several of the reviewers of the recitals. Paul Gerhardt, after attending the recital in Leipzig on January 11, 1893, wrote that in the course of the recital, the listener increasingly longed for her to sing composers who were worthy of her brilliant interpretation.³² Other reviewers agreed with Gerhardt that despite composing some good songs, Bungert was not worthy of being included in the canon of great German composers.³³ In Lehmann's diaries, however, she reports repeated success with the Bungert Lieder.³⁴ A few years later, her unbroken loyalty to Bungert despite criticism from some quarters is explained by comments in her diaries in 1901 and 1903, when she reveals that she was concerned for Bungert's financial well-being and was keen on helping him, perhaps therefore also continuing to regularly perform his works until two years after his death in 1917.³⁵

In contrast, Robert Franz's music, which Lehmann chose to sing in her recitals the following year, was highly praised.³⁶ Some critics, however, complained about Lehmann's general inclination to perform music by contemporary composers whose compositions they judged to be of inferior quality. One critic complained with levity that while Bungert was indeed an artist, if not a particularly great one, the same could not be said of Lechner nor of Hans Hermann, who, according to one reviewer, was so privileged by Lehmann's attention that he now had more commissions than he could cope with.³⁷ Another reviewer commented that Lehmann had now set the composer Alexander von Fielitz "on the map" by performing his work, reflecting the power Lehmann's programming choices might have on the lives of composers.³⁸

Lehmann's performances from memory also attracted comment from several reviewers.³⁹ Furthermore, she encouraged the audience to reserve applause for the end of the entire concert, creating a concentrated, reverent atmosphere during her performance. One reviewer commented that "the audience was completely hushed until the hurricane-like applause."⁴⁰ Lehmann apparently presided over this pious atmosphere like a priestess, and this kind of religious imagery was frequently used in descriptions of her later performances.⁴¹ Her elegant stature also lent her a regal air, which was repeatedly commented on; she was called the "Queen of the art of singing" by one reviewer.⁴² In 1913, the president of the Mozarteum, Dr. Franz Stibral, wrote of her performance, "How Lilli Lehmann's regal bearing filled the room, every inch a queen and then how she sang again the queen: the queen of dramatic singing there was a stirring in the room and then the storm of admiration broke out."⁴³ At an exclusive soirée held at Mme. Lemaire's Parisian painting academy, she was described as more regal than all the aristocratic audience members "who appear to be like so many pitiful dolls."[44]

A contrasting image that also pervades reports of Lehmann's appearance and behavior in concerts, however, is her aura of humanity or *Menschlichkeit*. For the composer Uso Seifert, an important part of her charisma arose from the sense of equality she created with the audience.[45] Leopold Schmidt also recalled a Schubert recital Lehmann gave much later in Berlin, on December 28, 1900; reflecting on the humanity of great performers in general, he commented that it was *Menschlichkeit* as well as pure technical ability that "causes her audience's eyes to light up and make young hearts beat faster and . . . creates the atmosphere of intimate reverence that surrounds her."[46] Her attractive facial expression was noted in a description of a recital in Berlin: "It was a special sight to see the erect personage with her chiseled features, leaning gently against the piano and to watch her intelligent face come alive during her singing and then again return to still marble."[47] The fact that Lehmann became so still afterward captures an element of the very controlled nature of her performances, which were so carefully "worked out," as described by her student Geraldine Farrar.[48] Photographs of the singer from various stages of her career illustrate her ability to endow the statuesque with a glimpse of humanity. A publicity still from 1914 shows her more glamorous side (see fig. 10.2).[49] A series of professional photographs were made of Lehmann and her husband (see fig. 10.3), some of which were published in contemporary newspapers, perhaps to reassert publicly the solidity of their marriage. (Fig. 10.4 and other photos prove that her villa in Scharfling has remained largely unchanged since 1903 with all the original furniture and fittings.)

Lehmann's recordings of 1906 confirm that vocally she embodied the ideal balance Edward Kravitt describes between the clarity of German articulation and the fluidity of a beautiful Italianate line.[50] Lehmann was fortunate in her combined experience of Italianate vocal technique, learned from her mother, and a knowledge of Germanic declamation, learned from working with Wagner.[51] Her expression of the drama of the text was of prime importance, though, as she explained in her letters to her close friend the baritone Victor Maurel, one had to restrain volume for the sake of the beauty of the vocal line.[52]

Lehmann's Lieder singing was also much admired by Hugo Wolf, who attempted to seek her out in January 1894 in Berlin to interpret his songs.[53] Ernst Décsey cited Richard Sternfield's claim that Lehmann failed to recognize and support Wolf's great talent, but the claim is not quite accurate according to Lehmann's Repertoire book. She first performed Lieder by Wolf on November 20, 1903, in Berlin, including "Gesang Weylas" and "Anakreons Grab." She continued to perform his songs regularly as part of her recital programs. Some of

Fig. 10.2. Lilli Lehmann, publicity photograph (undated). Lilli Lehmann in concert dress (ca. 1912). Lehmann's own copy of the photograph found in her house in Scharfling, now preserved at the *Internationale Stiftung Mozarteum: Mozart-Archiv*. Lilli Lehmann Nachlass. Standort: Depot 1, Inventarnr.: 009 054.

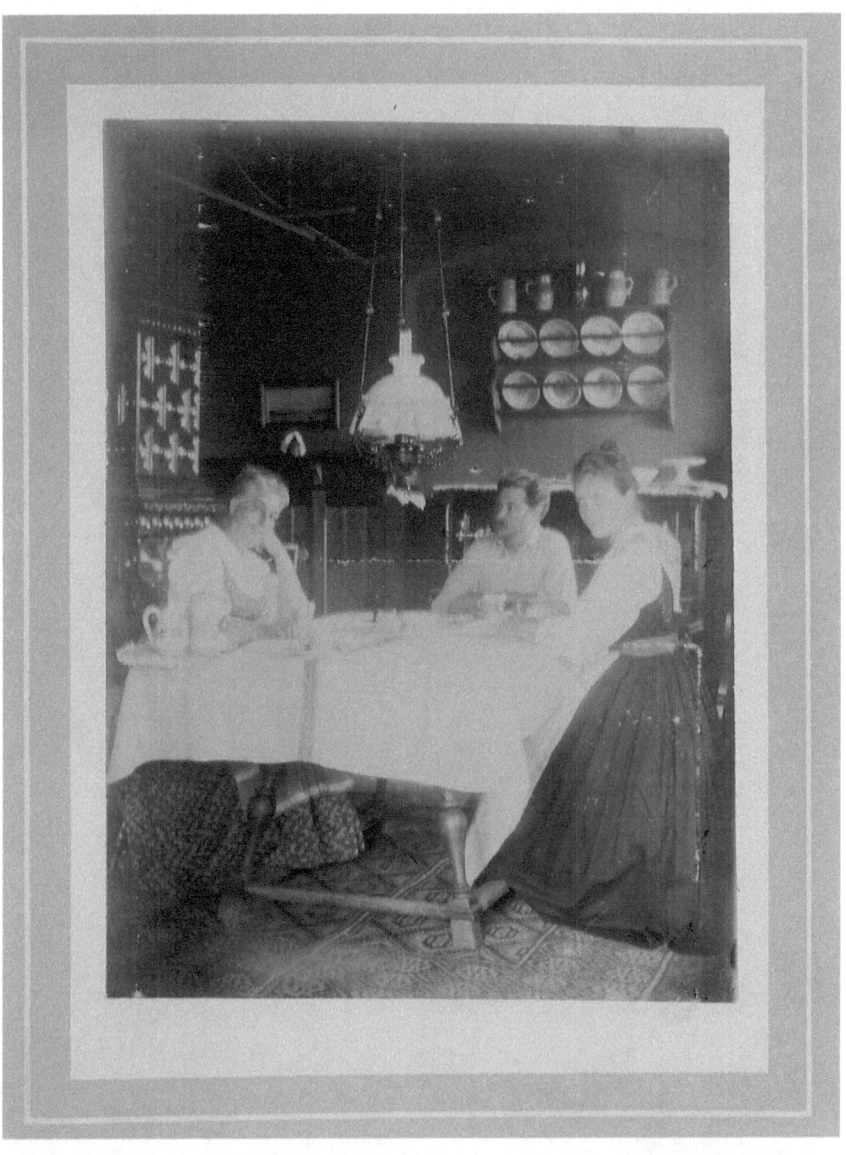

Fig. 10.3. Photograph of Lilli Lehmann with Paul Kalisch and Hedwig Helbig (ca. 1903). It and the other photos in this album prove that the Villa has remained largely unchanged since 1903 with all the original furniture and fittings. *Source: Internationale Stiftung Mozarteum: Mozart-Archiv.* Lilli Lehmann Nachlass. Fotoalbum von Scharfling 5. ca. 1900–1903. 105 professionelle Bilder. Standort: Depot 1, Inventarnr.: 009 089. Seitenr:16.

Fig. 10.4. Photograph from Lilli Lehmann's own collection in her villa in Scharfling am Mondsee. It was taken in 1920, the year in which she gave her final public recitals at the age of seventy-two. *Source: Internationale Stiftung Mozarteum: Mozart-Archiv.* Lilli Lehmann Nachlass. Standort: Depot 1. Inventarnr.: 009 095.

the songs became regular encore pieces, such as "Gesang Weylas," which between 1903 and 1917 she sang forty-eight times.

Lehmann was celebrated for her tasteful rendition of the texts of the songs she performed.[54] In particular, her use of vocal color and dynamics to communicate text was consistently remarked on by reviewers.[55] Her stage experience was thought to be evident in her song performances, and many reviews mention her ability to capture the essence of each contrasting song for the audience. In a 1917 Lieder recital of eighteen songs by Brahms, Bungert, and Wolf, the reviewer in the *Preussische Zeitung* commented on the way she vividly depicted the coquettish character when singing the line "Ich lieb deine Küsse" in the Bungert song "Bei der Trösterin." He asked, "which of the younger artists of today could act like this?"[56] Nevertheless, he noted that despite bringing the songs alive "visually," she did not grab at effects. Indeed, a characteristic feature of Lehmann's performances of Lieder seems to have been her restraint in expression and her ability to remain within the appropriate bounds of decorum suitable for the concert podium; likewise, she did not indulge in the extreme facial expressions fashionable among of some of her contemporaries, such as Ludwig Wüllner.[57] On May 13, 1904, Lehmann wrote in her diary about her increasing desire to reduce her movement in performance.[58] Similarly, when she presented humorous songs, she communicated the humor with restrained taste, according to Leopold Schmidt.[59]

Lehmann's Bungert and Franz recitals were both accompanied by Professor Reinhold Herman, who had regularly accompanied her during their recital tours in the United States. He was also a good friend outside the concert hall: Lehmann's diaries mention him coming to her house to play card games with her in the evenings. He is constantly commended in reviews for the quality of his playing. One review for a Franz recital, however, strongly reminiscent of accounts of Strauss in recital with Pauline de Ahna, criticized his improvised interludes between Lieder, despite their quality, as detracting from the simple perfection of Franz's compositions because of their complexity.[60]

Lehmann's programs of Lieder devoted to one composer and developed in the early 1890s were gradually broken up and used in other concert programs, initially often in combination with opera arias. Nevertheless, she did give several other pure Lieder performances dedicated to individual composers: Franz, in the Berlin Philharmonie on December 23, 1899; Schubert at the Berlin Philharmonie on December 28, 1900; Franz, in Munich on November 15, 1910; Brahms at the Berlin Philharmonie on January 19, 1911; Wolf in Dresden on January 24, 1912; and Franz at the Berlin Philharmonie on January 7, 1916. Lim Lai noted that she also performed *Die schöne Müllerin* in 1912, but the cycle is not included in the Repertoire book for that year: she had performed the whole cycle on November 22, 1907, in the Berlin Philharmonie. *Die schöne Müllerin* had previously been performed on various occasions by Amalie Joachim, Julius Stockhausen, and

Gustav Walter, but Beatrix Borchard and Natasha Loges point out that these performances may not have adhered strictly to our modern concept of the work.[61] In contrast, Lilli Lehmann appears indeed to have performed all twenty of the Müller Lieder in her concert in 1907.

Lehmann retired from the stage in 1910, but, as mentioned, she continued to give regular recitals until 1920. They occasionally contained operatic arias but mostly consisted only of Lieder, usually organized in groups of three or four Lieder by three different composers. As Lehmann grew older, there were occasional comments about her age and the slight deterioration of her voice, but mostly the response to her performances continued to be rapturous. The reviewer of a Berlin recital on January 16, 1917 debated whether she ought to stop singing but concluded that "she is just as present [and youthful] as ever before."[62] Another reviewer of her final concert dedicated to Franz Lieder in 1916 stressed that her voice, while not quite so full at the top, was still a pure pleasure to experience.[63]

According to Lai, in her later years, Lehmann also sang Hans Pfitzner and regularly sang Mahler, but in fact there is no record of Pfitzner in her Repertoire book, and she seldom performed Mahler Lieder.[64] Instead, her programming during the last decade of her career focused increasingly on the songs of an earlier age, including those of Schubert, Schumann, and Beethoven. Nevertheless, the songs of Bungert and Franz remained in her repertoire until the end.

Through this exploration of the development of Lehmann's programming of Lieder recitals, it becomes clear that Lehmann with characteristic originality and resourcefulness was able, when emerging from a personal crisis, to define a new form of artistic expression, namely a new Lieder recital form, focusing solely on presenting the work of one composer. Later in her career, we see that she then went on to develop programs that were to take a form that became familiar later in the century, concentrating on performing groups of Lieder that were to become established as the core German repertoire, with singers also tending to include some choices that reflected their personal connections and tastes.

The creation of dedicated Lieder programs in 1892–93 permitted her to successfully negotiate a period of vocal difficulty and to rebuild her stage career, also prolonging her professional career by an additional decade as a recitalist. In later life, she advocated this balance of Lieder and opera in a singer's repertoire for her students. In one postcard that she sent her student Geraldine Farrar, she wrote,

> Dearest Geraldine,
>
> I was very much pleased with your dear letter and I am glad to know you feel well and strong again. Good for you to have only concerts. You will be fresh again when you come back to the opera.[65]

A year before she died, when she was still teaching at the Mozarteum in Salzburg, she wrote one of the last of her regular letters to Farrar, concluding with the recommendation that she start to incorporate more Lieder into her programming:

> I would very much like you to put together some groups of the lovely Schubert songs of which there are so many; they are of course not easy, but they keep their promises and one can perform them for the public one's whole life. I have several hundred in my repertoire and they were always a success for the artists' art and brought happiness and honor. Likewise, there are such delightful ones from Carl Loewe that never grow old. Take me as your example, as an artist you can only profit from.[66]

Notes

1. "Den Besuchern ... dürfte ausnahmslos klar geworden sein, daß die große Künstlerin mit vollstem Recht als eine der vollkommensten, außerlesensten Gesangsmeisterinnen der Gegenwart bezeichnet wird." Paul Gerhardt, *Erste Beilage zur Leipziger Zeitung*, January 12, 1893. 127–30. She was also described as the "best Lieder interpreter of our time" ("die hervorragendste Lieder-Interpretin der Gegenwart") in the *Dresden Neueste Nachrichten*, November 12, 1903. Many of the reviews cited come from Lehmann's own album of newspaper reviews in an uncatalogued private collection soon to be acquired by the Mozarteum, Salzburg, currently held in Scharfling am Mondsee [hereafter, SaM].

2. The tour was from November 27, 1891, through February 15, 1892. In total, twenty-one performances were given in Chicago, New York, and Brooklyn.

3. The book, labeled "Repertoire," was sold to the Library of Congress in 1996 as part of a collection of Lilli Lehmann's papers. It is kept in box 3 of the unprocessed Lilli Lehmann Collection [hereafter, Lehmann Collection] in the Music Division there. See also Lim Lai, "Lilli Lehmann," *Record Collector* 26, nos. 7 and 8 (February 1981): 150–90. Lai's article provides an overview of Lehmann's entire career, including her broad repertoire of opera and oratorio, apparently based on her published autobiography, collected programs, and newspaper articles.

4. Edward Kravitt, *The Lied: Mirror of Late Romanticism* (New Haven, CT: Yale University Press, 1996), 22. Lehmann mainly portrays her childhood in the autobiography as a disciplined preparation for a career as a professional singer, the only way out of poverty that their mother, Marie Loew, was able to offer Lilli and her sister.

5. "Ohne irgendein Wort erhob sie sich nach dem Kaffeee und ging zum Flügel. Wir hätten sie niemals um ein Lied zu bitten gewagt, sie schenkte uns diesen Genuß freundlicherweiße aus eigenem Willen." On another occasion: "Nach dem Abendessen ging sie zum Klavier: ... Und dann sang sie ... Lieder, von denen sie wußte, daß ich sie liebte.... Es war schon spät—da schloß sie mit dem süßen Abendlied von Brahms: 'Guten Abend—gute Nacht—Mit Rosen bedacht'" (Käthe Damm, "Jugenderinnerungen an Lilli Lehmann," unidentified newspaper, Staatsbibliothek zur Berlin: Mus.Nachl. L. Lehmann. Kasten 7: Zeitungskritiken, unbearbeitete Briefe und Karten an L. L. Kritiken, New York 1897, 1 Band). This collection is henceforth referred to as D-B Lehmann.

6. The Repertoire book was obviously kept by Lehmann for practical purposes, with the titles of the Lieder given in note form, often idiosyncratically spelled. The resultant ambiguity can usually be clarified through cross-referencing. Lehmann's very first program included "Haideröslein," which, despite the unusual spelling, is probably the Schubert setting of Goethe's 1771 poem "Heidenröslein." She regularly included this song in her programs until the end of her career, for example, in her penultimate performance in Vienna on January 8, 1920, where it is recorded in the Repertoire book, this time spelled with an *e* and no *n* but clearly marked as being by Schubert.

7. Lai, "Lilli Lehmann," 182. Lai notes that the last concert Lehmann gave was in Berlin on February 13, 1921, consisting of Mozart, Beethoven, Brahms, and Loewe. This concert is not indicated in written references and presumably a record of it is contained in Lai's private collection of concert programs and newspaper articles. Lehmann does not mention it in her Repertoire book, perhaps implying it was a less formal event.

8. D-B Lehmann Mus. Nachl. Lehmann L.2, 19. Undated letter from Reynaldo Hahn to Lilli Lehmann (approx. 1903).

9. Entry of February 13, 1896, diary 1894–97, box 2, Lehmann Collection.

10. D-B Lehmann Mus. Nachl. Lehmann L.3, 201. Letter from Wilhelm Taubert to Lilli Lehmann, Montag Abend der March 15, 1875.

11. D-B Lehmann Mus. Nachl. Lehmann L.2, 4. Undated letter from Reynaldo Hahn to Lilli Lehmann.

12. Staatsbibliothek zur Berlin.Signatur: Mus.ep. Lehmann, L. 3. Letter from Lilli Lehmann to Franz Wüllner, Berlin, August 1, 1891.

13. With Tauber conducting, she sang the role of Maria in the premiere of his opera *Cesario* on November 13, 1874 (Repertoire book).

14. D-B Lehmann, Staatsbibliothek zu Berlin, Musikabteilung; Signatur: Mus.Nachl. Lehmann, L. 1,61. Letter from Ignaz Brüll to Lilli Lehmann, September 17, 1902. This charge he accompanied with the wry comment: "I am myself but a poor musician" (Schumann).

15. The program was the aria *Martern aller Arten* (Mozart), followed by the Lieder "Träume" (Wagner), "Mignon's Lied" (Liszt), "Fragen soll feierlich," and "Lied" (Swedish folk songs) (*The Times* [London] October 22, 1885).

16. Lehmann, Lilli, Fahr' wohl: Lied für eine Singstimme mit Begleitung des Pianoforte, op. 1 (Berlin: Luckhardt, 1889) Bildarchiv und Grafiksammlung, Österreichische Nationalbibliothek.

17. "I perpetrated a song once only for a very special reason, which was taken away from me as sometimes happens with my writings against my wish, and was printed without my consent being asked. I can say, however, that I condemned myself to be hanged for it, even if it found but one reader, and I consigned to the infernal regions 'the robber and printer against my will'" (Lilli Lehmann and Alice Benedict Seligman, *My Path through Life* [New York: Arno, 1977], 242).

18. Her decision not risk contact with her former fiancé by taking up the work at Bayreuth in 1882 despite months of preparation and the happy prospect of working with Wagner again suggest that this was still a painful memory. (Lehmann and Seligman, *My Path through Life*, 304.)

19. Although one German critic commented on her US debut that "A better Carmen the sadly prematurely deceased composer could not have wished for. . . . Only thus can this wild, hot blooded gypsy have behaved and loved" (unsigned and undated New York newspaper

review ca. November 26, 1885, from Internationale Stiftung Mozarteum, Bibliotheca Mozartiana. Zeitungsausschnitte Sammlung von Lilli Lehmann, ca 130 Bl, NL L-K Doc 353.). Henry Krehbiel, however, remembered her apparently rather serious performance as being a "puzzling phenomenon to some experienced observers"; Henry Edward Krehbiel, *Chapters of Opera: Being Historical and Critical Observations and Records Concerning the Lyric Drama in New York From 1908 to 1918* (New York: Henry Holt, 1909), 319. Nevertheless, W. J. Henderson noted that "the audience was quick to recognize Fräulein Lehmann's excellences" (W. J. Henderson, *New York Times*, November 25, 1881).

20. Unpublished paybooks, 1886, p. 89, Metropolitan Opera Archives, New York. This shows Lehmann was paid $16,800 ($5,000 more than all the other performers listed in this document).

21. Lehmann and Seligman, *My Path*, 346.

22. Lehmann and Seligman, *My Path*, 402.

23. Much later, in 1902, she expressed her disillusionment with her marriage to her friend and ally Victor Maurel. In her close correspondence with Maurel in 1898–1903, she sought friendship and intellectual stimulation until his remarriage and move to the United States. It seems that this pattern of seeking intellectual exchange and friendship outside her marriage continued to recur, as explored in Rosamund Cole, "A Critical Study of the Performance Style, Writing and Directing of Lilli Lehmann (1848–1929)" (Unpublished doctoral thesis, Royal Northern College of Music, Manchester, 2018).

24. The *Fidelio* aria was replaced with the second Constanze aria (Repertoire book).

25. Kravitt, *The Lied*, 18.

26. Beatrix Borchard, "Amalie Joachim und die gesungene Geschichte des deutschen Liedes," *Archiv für Musikwissenschaft* 4, no. 58 (2001): 265–99.

27. "Etwas von dem, was in mir vorging, mag wohl auch das Publikum empfunden haben. Ich sah viele gelangweilte Gesichter und hörte Nichts von jenem exploßiven Beifall, zu dem am Freitag vorher an derselben Stelle ein haufen freudetaumliger Menschen hingerissen wurde" (newspaper clipping album, p. 9, *Berlin Fremdenblatt* [undated, author unidentified], D-B Lehmann, L.10/1).

28. This attitude is revealed in the dedication Carmen Sylva wrote in a copy of her essays: "'In remembrance of the threefold interpretation of the sorceress' by which she meant her song, *The Lorelei*, composed as a poem by her, set to music by Bungert, and sung by me" (Lehmann and Seligman, *My Path*, 411).

29. Lehmann and Seligman, *My Path*, 403. This friendship is also confirmed in a dedication on the front of Bungert's Neue Volkslieder, op. 49, vol. 2, in Lehmann's extant sheet music collection: "Die Meisterin Frau Lilli Lehmann dem lieben, tapferen Kamaraden. 1899."

30. Max Chop and August Bungert, *August Bungert . . . mit 46 Bildern* (Berlin: Stahl, 1917), 326.

31. For similar reasons, despite her personal declarations of her love of France in her letters to Maurel, she eschewed almost all French *mélodies* in her Lieder programming, possibly to avoid the disapprobation of her German audiences. See the letter from Lehmann to unidentified addressee (author assumes Victor Maurel). Internationale Stiftung Mozarteum, Bibliotheca Mozartiana NL L-K Doc 39 Lilli Lehmann, ohne Empfänger, New York, s. a. [ca. 1899], 3 Bl. mit 5 beschriebenen S.

This (possibly unsent) letter appears to be part of the group of letters between Victor Maurel and Lilli Lehmann, collated by the author in previous research. See also

Rosamund Cole, "A Critical Study of the Performance Style, Writing and Directing of Lilli Lehmann (1848–1929)" (Unpublished doctoral thesis, Royal Northern College of Music, Manchester, 2018, 169–220).

32. "Angesichts der künstlerischen Heldenthaten der herrlichen Meisterin erschien uns die Wahl ihrer Lieder mit ausschließlicher Berücksichtigung des Componisten August Bungert um so bedauerlicher, als dadurch die im Verlaufe des Abends immer dringlicher empfundenen Wünsche, sie Lieder von Componisten singen zu hören, die einer solchen Interpretation völlig würdig wären, leider gänzlich unerfüllt bleiben müßten!" (Paul Gerhardt, "Erste Beilage," *Leipziger Zeitung*, January 12, 1893, SaM).

33. "Jedenfalls aber waren wir nicht im Stande, unter diesen Liedern auch nur eines ausfindig zu machen, das in Bezug auf Werth und Bedeutung, auf Selbständigkeit, Reife Individualität etc mit den hervorragenderen Werken unserer große deutschen Liedmeister in eine Linie gestellt werden konnte" (Paul Gerhardt, *Leipziger Zeitung*, January 12, 1893, SaM).

34. "'Die Rosenlaube' gefällt immer Kolossal. Es freut mich für Bungert" ["'Die Rosenlaube' is always a huge success. I am so pleased for Bungert"] (diary 1901–5, 48, January 17, 1902, box 4, Lehmann Collection).

35. "Paul e ich wollen für Bungert eine Kleinigkeit geben e ihm helfen obwohl ich nicht einmal weiß ob er es will. . . . Ich glaube aber, daß er nichts hat e daß ihm sehr willkommen sein dürfte" ["Paul and I want to give Bungert a little something and help him although I am not even sure if he wants it. . . . I believe, however, that he doesn't have anything and that it might be very welcome"] (diary 1901–5, 103, February 7, 1904, box 4, Lehmann Collection).

36. "Hat er so Bedeutendes, so Vollendetes geschaffen, daß wo von deutschen Liedmeistern geredet wird, sein Name neben den ersten, neben Schubert und Schumann genannt werden muß" (*Preussischer Zeitung*, November 8, 1893, SaM; located in Internationale Stiftung Mozarteum, Bibliotheca Mozartiana. Zeitungsausschnitte Sammlung von Lilli Lehmann, ca 130 Bl, NL L-K Doc 353).

37. "Vielleicht hat sie ihn sogar, mit dem besten Willen Gutes zu thun, in seiner gesunden Entwicklung geschädigt, denn Hans Hermann ist seither in eine Massenproduktion hineingerathen, die ihn, dem man ein gewisses Patent gar nicht absprechen kann, verflachen muß" (*Vossische Zeitung* [Berlin], November 5, 1896; located in Internationale Stiftung Mozarteum, Bibliotheca Mozartiana. Zeitungsausschnitte Sammlung von Lilli Lehmann, ca 130 Bl, NL L-K Doc 353).

38. "Neu war ein Lied von Fielitz, eines Komponisten, den Lilli Lehmann erfolgreich auf die musikalische Landkarte gesezt hatte" (newspaper clipping album, p. 1, D-B Lehmann, L.10/1).

39. "Mit feinem Geschmack hatte sie sich drei größere Gruppen Lieder zusammengestellt, die sie sich geistig so zu eigen gemacht hatte, daß sie die zwanzig Lieder ohne daß störende Notenblatt in der Hand außwendig singen konnte und es gewahrte einen eigenen Reiz" (newspaper clipping album, p. 6, D-B Lehmann, L.10/1).

40. "Die viertausend Zuhörer folgten mit wahrer Andacht, mit einer hier selten erreichten lautlosen Ruhe, sie hingen förmlich an den Lippen der Sängerin. Mit solch athemloser Stille ist hier noch nie eine Künstlerin gehört worden . . . ein Beifallsorkan" (newspaper clipping album, p. 3, D-B Lehmann, L.10/1).

41. "Da steht sie vor uns Königin und Priesterin zugleich," Adolf Weißmann (newspaper article), January 22, 1917 (untitled), SaM. Now located in Internationale Stiftung Mozarteum; "La grande-prêtresse de Mozart" (Reynaldo Hahn, "Notes sur des Notes," *Femina*, May 15, 1910, 265);

Bösenwein [no first name identified], "Keiner von den Anwesenden wird ohne Herzklopfen und andachtsvolle Begeisterung dieser wunderbaren Frau jetzt sein Aufmerksamkeit schenken" (*Preußische Zeitung*, March 25, 1910, Mappe 3, D-B Lehmann, L.10/1).

42. "Diese Königin der Gesangskunst ist Lilly [sic] Lehmann." D-B LehmannL.10/1 Mappe 3, newspaper article, April 15 (ca. 1905).

43. August 6, 1913, was the date of her last performance to raise money for the Mozart fund in Salzburg. "Wie Frau Lilli Lehmanns königliche Erscheinung herabkam über die Oberstufen des Podiums—jeder Zoll die Königin—und wie sie dann sang—wieder die Königin: die Königin des dramatischen Gesanges—da ging tiefe Bewegung durch den Saal und dann brach der Sturm der Bewunderung los" (*Feuilleton*, September 9, 1913, newspaper clipping album, D-B Lehmann, L.10/1, Mappe 3).

44. Bösenwein [no first name identified], "Und die Pariserinnen in den wunderbaren Toiletten mit Diademen oder Gold und Silbergaze um den Kopf gewunden, sahen wie erbärmliche Puppen neben der königlichen Gestalt im himmelblauen Samt aus" (March 25, 1910, D-B Lehmann, L.10/1, Mappe 3).

45. "Der Gesang ist so überaus menschlich ... und weil er uns zu sagen scheint: was ich kann, könnt ihr alle" (Uso Seifert, "Konzert" *Dresdner Anzeiger*, December 3, 1892, SaM. Now located in Internationale Stiftung Mozarteum, Bibliotheca Mozartiana. Zeitungsausschnitte Sammlung von Lilli Lehmann, ca 130 Bl, NL L-K Doc 353).

46. "Nur ist dieser Zusammenhang nicht immer um einzelnen nachweisbar.... Ich mag nicht immer von der Stimme und der Technik dieser Frau reden. Sie sang Schubert, und was alle Augen leuchten, junge Herzen höher schlagen machte, das was ganz gewiß nicht die Meisterschaft allein.... So ist denn auch die Atmosphäre innigster Verehrung, die sich wie von selbst um sie verbreitet" (Leopold Schmidt, "Aus den Konzerten," newspaper and date unknown, SaM).

47. "Die hochaufgerichtete Gestalt mit dem feingeschittenen Köpfe, statuarisch ruhig gegen den Bechsteinschen Flügel gelehnt, zu betrachten wie sich die geistvollen Züge während des Singens belebten und dann wieder zu marmorner Unbeweglichkeit erstarren" (*Die Post*, Berlin, author unknown, undated, SaM).

48. Frederick H. Martens, *The Art of the Prima Donna and Concert Singer* (New York: D. Appleton, 1923), 90.

49. A-Sm, Mozarteum, Bibliotheca Mozartiana, NL Lehmann, Lilli. This photo was published in the 1914 English edition of Lehmann's autobiography *My Path through Life*.

50. Lilli Lehmann, *Lilli Lehmann: The Complete Recordings* (East Barnet, UK: Symposium Records, 1997).

51. Kravitt, *The Lied*, 53.

52. Lehmann advised Maurel, "Votre voix et douce, résonante et noble, ... mais, vous forcé sur la scène.... Ce que nous donnons au public doit être agréable, et beau" (Letter from Lilli Lehmann to Victor Maurel. Gresac Papers, Yale University. GEN MSS 1363 – Beinecke, pp. 23 and 20, January 28, 1899).

53. Ernest Newman, *Hugo Wolf* (Mineola, NY: Dover, 2012), 98; Kravitt, *The Lied*, 70; Ernst Décsey, *Hugo Wolf* (Leipzig: Schuster and Loeffler, 1904), 3: 118.

54. "Und nun der Vortrag! Für jede Stimmung findet Frau Lehmann den passendsten Ausdruck, jeder noch so feine Unterschied im Texte wird durch eine entsprechend feine Nüance im Gesange gekennzeichnet" (newspaper clipping album, D-B Lehmann, L.10/1).

55. "Freilich auch eine Künstlerin, die den Geißt der Lehman [sic] hatte, könnte so nicht wirken, wenn ihr nicht zugleich auch in so reichem Maße die Gabe verliehen wäre, den Klang des Organs verschieden zu färben" (*Die Zeit*, December 6, 1916, newspaper clipping album, D-B Lehmann, L.10/1).

56. *Preussische Zeitung am Mittag*, January 22, 1917, newspaper clipping album, D-B Lehmann, L.10/1.

57. For a detailed account of Wüllner's performance style, see Kravitt, *The Lied*, 90.

58. "Ich bin sehr ruhig auf dem ganze e versuche immer weniger bewegungen zu machen e [sic], mehr ausdruck zu geben." 1901–1905 diary, box 4, Lilli Lehmann Collection, Library of Congress, Washington, DC. In the same vein, during the singing lessons she gave Geraldine Farrar she insisted on stopping her gesturing with her hands by tying them behind her back. "One day she took them and tied them behind my back and then I had to use my face. She thought over-gesturing was as weak as continually underscoring a letter whose contents were not important enough to carry without that means" (D-B Lehmann L.10/1, Mappe 4. "Unjust! Miss Farrar Cries. Criticism from the Prima Donna's Point of View," *The Baltimore Sun*, March 1, 1908).

59. "Kein Gebiet des Liedergesangs ist ihr verschlossen, und zum Schluß belohnt sie ihre Bewunderer gern mit einem kleinen Scherz. Wenn er zum Pikanten neigt, da weiß sie zum Lächeln, so verschmizt, so vielsagend,—aber vornehm auf alle Fälle" (no author or title, April 15, ca. 1905, SaM).

60. "In Herrn Professor Reinhold Herman aus New York hatte die Künstlerin einen durchaus feinfühligen Begleiter am Klavier gefunden. Nur seine allzuweit ausgreifenden, im übrigen jedoch sehr geschmackvollen Überleitungen und Interludien wollten sich in den zumeist einfachklassischen Rahmen der Franzischen Gesänge nicht recht paßend einfugen" (Untitled, Berlin *Dresdner Anzeiger*, December 3, 1892, SaM).

61. Beatrix Borchard, *Stimme und Geige: Amalie und Joseph Joachim; Biographie und Interpretationsgeschichte* (Vienna: Böhlau, 2007), 436; and Natasha Loges, "Julius Stockhausen's Early Performances of Franz Schubert's *Die schöne Müllerin*," *19th-Century Music* 41, no. 3 (2018): 206–24.

62. "Soll sie wirklich aufhören? Sie kann es nicht. Sie glaubt es nicht zu dürfen.... Auch sie, das hofft sie, wird trotz solchen kämpfen al seine einzige in der Erinnerung fortleben. Erinnnerung? Nein sie ist da, gegenwärtiger denn ja" (*Preussische Zeitung*, January 22, 1917, SaM).

63. "Aber wie hat Lilli Lehmann die alten lieben Sachen gesungen!... Daß das Organ in der höchsten Lage nicht mehr den bezaubernden satten Klang und daß der Ton in der Tiefe nicht mehr ganz so fest 'steht' wie einst.... Trotzdem war fast alles ein reiner Genuß!" (*Preussische Zeitung*, January 7, 1916, SaM).

64. Lai, "Lilli Lehmann," 183.

65. Postcard from Lilli Lehmann to Geraldine Farrar dated April 15, 1928, folder 9, Geraldine Farrar Collection, Library of Congress, Washington, DC.

66. "Ich wünschte wohl sie legten sich einige Gruppen der köstlichen Schubertlieder von denen es so viele giebt; leicht sind sie natürlich nicht, aber sie halten was sie versprechen u [sic] man kann sie sein ganzes Leben lang dem Publicum wieder vorsingen. Ich habe einige hundert auf m. Programme, u immer waren sie Erfolge die der Kunst dem Künstler glücke Ehrungen brachten. Auch von Carl Loewe gibt so Entzückende die niemals veralten. Nehmen Sie ein Beispiel an mir, man kann als Künstler nur dabei gewinnen" (Letter from Lilli

Lehmann to Geraldine Farrar dated July 22, 1928, Salzburg Mozarteum, Geraldine Farrar Collection, 1895–1943, box-folder 10/8, Library of Congress, Washington, DC).

Bibliography

Borchard, Beatrix. "Amalie Joachim und die gesungene Geschichte des deutschen Liedes." *Archiv für Musikwissenschaft* 4, no. 58 (2001): 265–99.

———. *Stimme und Geige: Amalie und Joseph Joachim; Biographie und Interpretationsgeschichte.* Vienna: Böhlau, 2007.

Chop, Max, and August Bungert. *August Bungert . . . mit 46 Bildern.* Berlin: Stahl, 1917.

Décsey, Ernst. *Hugo Wolf.* Vol. 3. Leipzig: Schuster and Loeffler, 1904.

Hahn, Reynaldo. "Notes sur des Notes." *Femina* (May 15, 1910): 265–66.

Kravitt, Edward. *The Lied: Mirror of Late Romanticism.* New Haven, CT: Yale University Press, 1996.

Krehbiel, Henry Edward. *Chapters of Opera: Being Historical and Critical Observations and Records Concerning the Lyric Drama in New York from 1908 to 1918.* New York: Henry Holt, 1909.

Lai, Lim. "Lilli Lehmann." *Record Collector* 26, nos. 7 and 8 (February 1981): 150–90.

Lehmann, Lilli, and Alice Benedict Seligman. *My Path through Life.* New York: Arno, 1977.

Loges, Natasha. "Julius Stockhausen's Early Performances of Franz Schubert's *Die schöne Müllerin.*" *19th-Century Music* 41, no. 3 (Spring 2018): 206–24.

Martens, Frederick H. *The Art of the Prima Donna and Concert Singer.* New York: D. Appleton, 1923.

Newman, Ernest. *Hugo Wolf.* Mineola, NY: Dover, 2012.

ROSAMUND COLE is a researcher at the Universität Salzburg.

11 "Eine Reihe bunter Zauberbilder"
Thomas Mann, Hans Pfitzner, and the Politics of Song Accompaniment

Nicholas Attfield

We begin by opening the diary of Thomas Mann at the entry for Sunday, October 26, 1919. On that evening, at the Munich Four Seasons Hotel, Mann attended a recital given by two singers, the soprano Maria Ivogün and the tenor Karl Erb. They perform numerous Lieder, but the "pièce de résistance"—to borrow Mann's phrase directly—is a rendition of Schumann's Eichendorff *Liederkreis*, op. 39. Awestruck, Mann records the following: "The most remarkable impression from Eichendorff! That poem with the line 'Hast du einen Freund gefunden [sic], Trau ihm nicht zu dieser Stunde'—[this is] art of romantic demonic confusion of feeling ('romantisch-dämonischen Gefühlsverworrenheit')."[1] The reference here is to the tenth song of opus 39, "Zwielicht" ("Twilight"), in which the poet speaks of the treacherous hour when "dusk spreads its wings": the hour of approaching horror, of hunters roaming dark forests, and of the seeming friend whom you must not trust.[2] As Mann's (mis)quotation suggests, it is this latter image of romantic doubleness—he who "seeks war in a deceitful peace"—that especially enchants him at this moment, and the artistic effect of which he attempts to grasp through the peculiar term *Gefühlsverworrenheit*, "confusion" or "obscurity" of feeling. Indeed, these were aesthetics in which his own work had long been steeped. In his *Reflections of a Nonpolitical Man*, published in German the year before the concert, Mann had praised art's ability to "present, cultivate, and celebrate passion and unreason" and of its propensity to "hold primordial thoughts and instincts in honor." More vehemently still, he had written that it was art alone that could keep those innermost stirrings of humanity "*awake*" or "reawaken them with great force—the thought and instinct of war, for example."[3]

Strikingly, it was not only Eichendorff's poetic text, however, that so moved Mann on that evening. In the same diary entry, he draws our attention to the fact that the pianist for this recital had done something rather unusual: he had not only played Schumann's written piano accompaniments for the Eichendorff songs but had provided what Mann calls "connecting music" (*verbindende Musik*) between them.⁴ This, we infer, had certainly contributed to the overall "romantic-demonic" impression, and perhaps even made it possible in the first place; so too it had generated the confused state of feeling in which Mann revels and to which he so closely relates.

The pianist in question was the composer Hans Pfitzner. In one of his own essays from a few years later, Pfitzner refers to the same pianistic accompanimental technique, which he says he had practiced for many years and in many different ways, both privately at home and publicly in concert, with singers present and without. Indeed, he cites it especially with regard to Schumann's song cycles, not least *Dichterliebe*, op. 48, and the *Liederkreis*, op. 39, about which latter he makes the following remarks:

> Because of the unusual intensity of atmosphere in these songs [*Gebilde*] and their drastic brevity, I have always felt the drop back into sober reality after the last chord particularly keenly—even when I heard all twelve sung together. But if one refuses to let the sounding element [*Tonelement*] break off, a something [*ein Etwas*] comes into existence, something that appears to present itself as a whole, and yet obviously isn't and could easily be berated as styleless. For what do the individual texts have to do with one another? Even so, in this specific case (and not in every case, for heaven's sake!), I sensed that romantic atmosphere [*Stimmung*] was the main point and that the conceptual content of the words simply paled beside it; a series of colorful magic images [*eine Reihe bunter Zauberbilder*], drawn together by a common bond.⁵

Pfitzner would have us believe, then, that his romantic intuition had led him to sense a hidden connection spanning these songs, quite in spite of the apparent stylistic discontinuity of Schumann's arrangement of Eichendorff's texts. As a musician, he had been able to bring this connection to the perceptible forefront as what he calls atmosphere [*Stimmung*], a process that had turned each song into something visual before the mind's eye—his use of the noun *Gebilde* is rather telling here—and the whole into a "Something" defined as a "series of colorful magic images." Thomas Mann, as we have seen, was one listener enthralled by the result.

If it is Pfitzner's "magic images" that give my chapter its title, then it is the subject of their "drawing together by a common bond" that will form its content. This is, in one sense, a music-technical and aesthetic matter: through consideration of a related practice and a related work, we can first speculate on what Pfitzner's "verbindende Musik" might have sounded like and how it might have been prepared and delivered. Yet, no less important, we can also inquire after the broader resonances of the "something" that its composer—and some of his listeners—believed it created. The concert in Mann's diary, we ought not forget, took place in Munich in 1919: a place and a time in which, I shall suggest, a "romantic-demonic" musical practice on the concert platform could be easily galvanized into far more threatening and repellent form, an armor for the purposes of both defense and assault. In this sense, even as it seems to retreat behind the abstruse fog of romantic atmosphere and ascend to the safe haven of Mann's "nonpolitical" man, Pfitzner's "verbindende Musik" takes on a finely honed political edge and issues a rallying cry to the very "primordial thoughts and instincts" that Mann's view of art had posited. The magical something that Pfitzner claims to feel, and which Mann so enjoys, has a presence that extends into the early 1920s and the composer's expressly romantic cantata, *Von deutscher Seele*: "Of the German Soul."

Pfitzner's Schumann Celebration

Beyond giving the term itself, Mann's diary entry is brief indeed: it does not indicate of what Pfitzner's "verbindende Musik" for the *Liederkreis*, op. 39, consisted. Pfitzner himself, in his essay "Von deutscher Seele," is only slightly more revealing in technical musical terms. He writes laconically of "improvised interludes" ("improvisierte Zwischenspiele") performed "at the right moment, within a small circle of listeners, with the lights dimmed, and without a score," and thus seems to wish to emphasize the creation of a Romantic-intimate atmosphere above all else. He adds that these interludes would be "inspired with the breath of the *Kapellmeister*"—an obscure phrase presumably intended to imply, once again, the apparent spontaneity of the practice in the right setting and its source in the well-versed and authoritative musician.[6]

In search of a richer explanatory context, we might instead choose to historicize the practice in terms of the German Romantic legacy to which Pfitzner and Mann self-consciously laid claim. As Valerie Woodring Goertzen has shown, Clara Schumann (to cite only one example) had publicly improvised preludes and transitions between small forms throughout much of her career as a concert pianist in the first half of the nineteenth century; thus she created characterful "mosaics" of short keyboard works by Bach, Beethoven, and her own Romantic contemporaries, and in turn fostered the finding of connections—musical and spiritual—within the burgeoning piano repertoire.[7] Moreover, these were improvisatory practices that extended long into the twentieth century, encompassing the likes of Pfitzner's concert contemporary (and public adversary) Ferruccio Busoni.[8] Although he remains tight-lipped on any such legacy—as part of a larger claim of inspired spontaneity, as we shall later see—it would not be unreasonable to place Pfitzner as directly observant of it, an inheritor of the "preluding" tradition within the specialized realm of Lieder accompaniment.

At his own suggestion, we might also turn to a published work of Pfitzner's to which, albeit momentarily, he does allude, suggesting that it "captures the same principle in notation."[9] The work in question may, by present standards,

Table 11.1. Pfitzner's selection from Schumann's choruses, opp. 69 and 91.

Title	Author of text	Schumann's Opus Number	Key
1. "Klosterfräulein" [The novice]	Kerner	Op. 69 no. 3	D minor
2. "Waldmädchen" [The forest girl]	Eichendorff	Op. 69 no. 2	A major
3. "Die Kapelle" [The chapel]	Uhland	Op. 69 no. 6	F major
4. "Soldatenbraut" [The soldier's bride]	Mörike	Op. 69 no. 4	A minor
5. "Jäger Wohlgemut" [The hunter's good spirits]	Des Knaben Wunderhorn	Op. 91 no. 2	Bb major
6. "Der Wassermann" [The waterman]	Kerner	Op. 91 no. 3	G minor
7. "Meerfey" [The mermaid]	Eichendorff	Op. 69 no. 5	A minor

not actually be a work at all: currently unrecorded and typically absent from lists of Pfitzner's œuvre, it is his addition in 1910 of an orchestral accompaniment to a selection of Schumann's Unaccompanied Choruses for Women's Voices, opp. 69 and 91.[10] The original twelve choruses, otherwise known as "Romanzen," had been composed by Schumann for the Dresden Verein für Chorgesang in 1849, and bring together settings of texts from the anthology *Des Knaben Wunderhorn* with those by Eichendorff, Mörike, Justinus Kerner, and other Romantic poets.[11] But beyond a folksy or folkloric tone, a (young) woman protagonist in most cases, and a certain tendency toward the tragic, the texts in each opus collection have little in the way of a common thread, and the resulting impression of colorful variety is only exacerbated by Pfitzner's choice of seven of Schumann's settings for his orchestral accompaniment (see table 11.1). Nonetheless, the lavish Universal Edition title page of Pfitzner's score (see fig. 11.1) proudly proclaims that Schumann's choruses had not only been "furnished with an instrumental accompaniment" ("mit Instrumentalbegleitung versehen") but also, as a consequence, "bound together into a whole by Hans Pfitzner" ("zu einem Ganzen verbunden von Hans Pfitzner"). Thus, against the poetic texts, a strong claim is made for the role of the music within.

Perhaps the most immediately striking point about this score is not one of recompositional license—as one might imagine promised by such a title page—but instead that Pfitzner shows an unbending commitment to Schumann's settings. Rather as if handling rigid, mosaic-like pieces, each beautiful in its own right, he takes the original vocal parts of these choruses almost entirely verbatim, observing not only notes, but also their assigned keys, dynamics, phrasing, and other expressive markings. Before and between these settings, his orchestra—

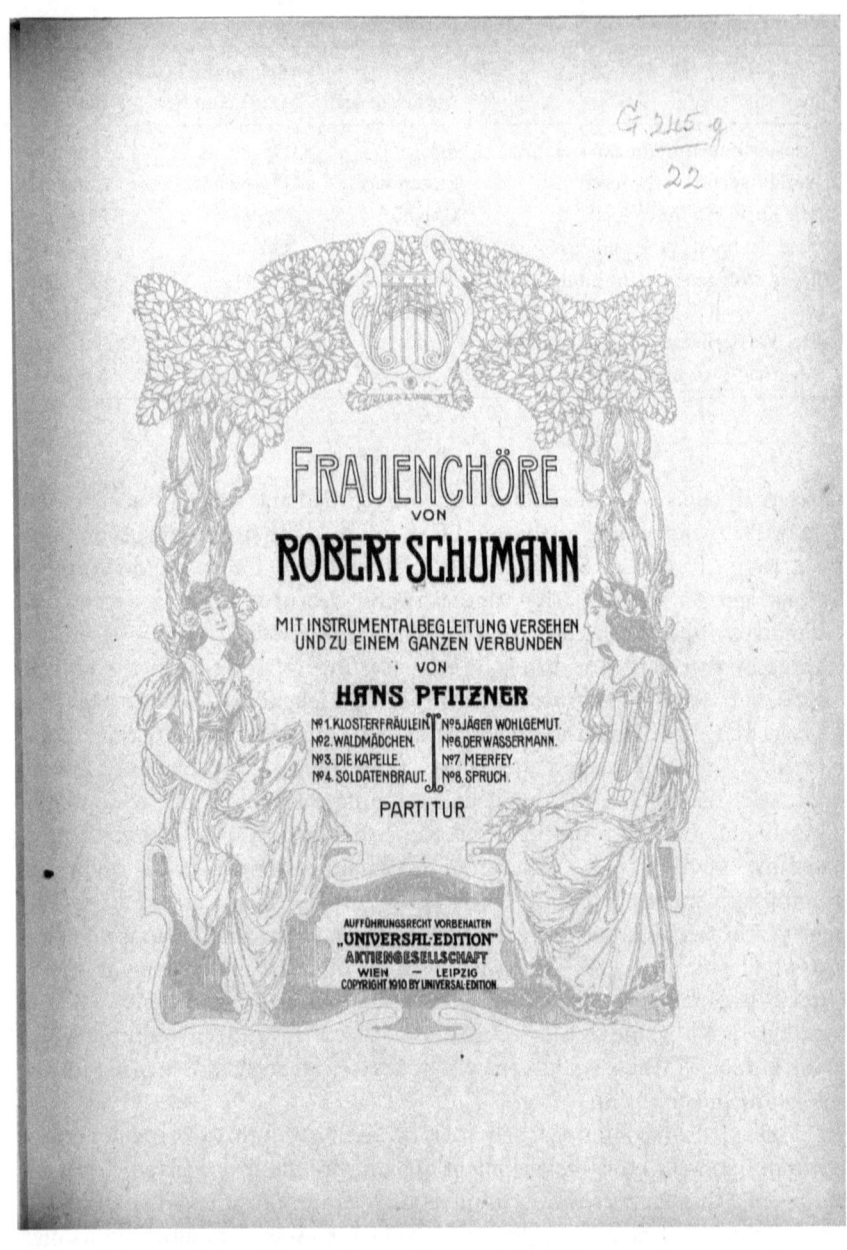

Fig. 11.1. Title page of Hans Pfitzner, *Frauenchöre von Robert Schumann*. Source: UE 2679 (Vienna: Universal Edition, 1910).

a large and colorful ensemble that includes cor anglais, bass clarinet, contrabassoon, harp, and organ—delivers short modulatory passages that typically presage the principal thematic material and effect of the number to follow. The somber dotted tread of the *Klosterfräulein* into her confinement, for example, is preceded by a few bars of mournful woodwind counterpoint founded on the same rhythm; the offbeat semiquavers at the end of the number provide a bridge into those of the rather livelier "Waldmädchen."

Pfitzner's preludes and transitions are, of course, merged into continuous accompaniments for each vocal setting, contrapuntal weaves of orchestral sound that fill Schumann's *a cappella* silence with motivic material and thus juxtapose the "stylized naïveté" of his original with a rather more modern complexity.[12] But Pfitzner also uses his orchestral body to propose narrative links between the choruses: the semiquavers at the end of "Klosterfräulein" are actually introduced in the flutes as part of the third stanza's text, in which the novice glimpses birds flying high outside her barred window; as they lead into the second number, the semiquavers also prepare us for the arrival of what she so longs to be, the unfettered forest girl whose whirlwind dance is first presented by an elaborate viola solo. In the sixth chorus, meanwhile, Pfitzner takes the inherent death-and-the-maiden drama of Kerner's text as another cue for this kind of pictorial writing: as the ghostly suitor approaches the dancing maiden with whom he will descend to the depths, the muted *tremolando* violas describe a semitone alternation (D–Eb) that soon rises through two octaves and dissolves into eerie trills across the upper strings; as this number transitions into the next, the same semitone acquires an upward leap of a sixth as tailpiece and becomes a central melodic part of "Meerfey"—another image of watery peril, though here with roles reversed so that it is the doomed sailor who founders on the mermaid's rock.

In the case of his Schumann choruses, then, Pfitzner's "verbindende Musik" certainly imparts an overall sense of shape and trajectory and manages changes in tempo, key, and predominant emotional tone. (Here silence can be as effective as sound: the lack of transition at the end of "Die Kapelle" serves to sharpen the effect of the opening military rhythms of "Soldatenbraut.") Thus it might be said that Pfitzner creates the impression of a whole out of texts by five different authors with little direct connection to one another—and indeed, a "work" out of a group of choruses that were not necessarily intended to be sung together. Yet, for all this apparent unity, we must also comment on the presence of disjunction in these orchestral settings, and in particular the tendency of some of Pfitzner's unruly instruments to solo, rather as if they were improvising within and against the larger ensemble, and as if they were not so much preparing as *producing* the next stanza or next number. Music speaks, text follows. The rumbustious solo viola of "Waldmädchen"—its influence soon spreading through the other strings and eventually reaching the flutter-tongued flutes—is a case in point, but perhaps the best example comes from the end of the seventh setting, "Meerfey," when the organ adopts the desolate A minor chord in order to break through, *fortissimo* and *volles Werk*, on a transitional path toward a teetering dominant seventh. Thus, it is as if it interjects in order to produce the climax, culmination, and coda of Pfitzner's orchestration: an eighth Schumann setting, not of anything from the opus 69 or opus 91 choruses, but of the last of his three Lieder for three accompanied women's voices, opus 114.[13] That this is a *Spruch* (proverb, in this case by Friedrich Rückert) is highly significant. Led by the solemn tones of the organ, the voices reflect inward and upward, exhorting the listener to gaze toward the "stars that never err from their paths" and seem to reveal the preceding folkloric scenes as colorful and characteristic appearances only—all the bewilderments of the world, these, now set in their rightful place against the eternal firmament and solemnized by the presence of the organ and the full weight of Pfitzner's orchestra.[14]

Coming back down to earth again momentarily, and to the evening concert of October 1919, it is worthwhile to speculate how these orchestrations might help us to understand Pfitzner's accompaniment for the op. 39 *Liederkreis*. Bearing in mind his *werktreuerisch* attitude toward the original vocal parts for Schumann's choruses, it is surely unlikely that he meddled with the given piano parts of opus 39, whatever the dramatic or pictorial temptations of, for example, "Waldesgespräch" or "Auf einer Burg" might have been. On the other hand, it seems probable that he interjected into the silences between the songs motivic transformations, as well as harmonic and dynamic transitions. And again, though he hints that it was a practice developed across many such performance occasions, it may too have been designed to give the impression of an improvisation, as though with each transition the pianist were guiding the cycle's course toward its next station and final conclusion. Indeed, it can readily be imagined how, at the end of the penultimate song, Pfitzner might have returned to the huntsman's 6/8 that characterizes much of its rhythmic surface and transformed it into the rapid semiquaver triplets of the finale, thereby turning the heartfelt shudder amid nature of the former song's close into the ecstatic affirmation that concludes the latter one—and, of course, brings the entire cycle to an end.

The potential of this affirmative moment leads us onward, moreover, to our other focus in this chapter: if "something"—*ein Etwas*, to borrow Pfitzner's word—was here created by this accompanimental technique, what were its boundaries, and how far did it resound? Beyond the borders of an impressive *aesthetic* whole, how did the circumstances in which it was created, performed, and received condition the shape and identity of this "something"? In terms of the 1919 *Liederkreis*, it will be the task of the remainder of this chapter to address these questions. But, as a preliminary to doing so, we can briefly turn back one final time to Pfitzner's 1910 Schumann choruses, for which a survey of the composer's contemporary letters reveals that the score was in fact an occasional one, created for the festivities in Strasbourg (then German Strassburg) for the centenary of Schumann's birth; accordingly, the choruses formed part of Pfitzner's duties as director of the city's conservatory and as chief conductor of its symphony orchestra.[15]

We might be led to wonder, then, whether the whole created by Pfitzner's orchestration was understood to stand in some sense for the municipal whole, and it is striking to find a regional report that hints at just this. The Strasbourg correspondent for the *Musikalisches Wochenblatt* proposes that Pfitzner should be congratulated for inspiring and directing the majority of the festival's musical events, not least because in so doing he had managed to turn away from "regressive local patriotism" and to unite the city's people in a Schumann celebration to rival those of other German centers, most of all Munich. Moreover, the same commentator, Emil Rupp, identifies Pfitzner's newly accompanied choruses as essential to this effect, situating them (and particularly their closing Rückert *Spruch*) as a fitting climax to the festivities: here the audience encountered something "simply overpowering" and responded with a "storm of applause."[16]

It should be added that, in spite of Strasbourg's history as part of a disputed territory, there is no obvious anti-French sentiment in this response. On the contrary, Rupp stresses how welcome in its subtlety the Parisian Alfred Cortot's rendition of Schumann's Piano Concerto had been, in spite of the expected accusations of "superficial *Romanentum*"; likewise praised is the "overtone-rich" construction of the Pleyel instrument on which he performed.[17] Such statements only reinforce the impression that Rupp considered the Schumann festival as a presentation of (his view of) Strasbourg's unique cultural identity—at the heart of which, in 1910, stood Pfitzner as director. In his conducting of the Concerto, his rendition of the "Rhenish" Symphony ("here a unique musical personality became one with that of the assembled listeners!"), and his orchestration of the choruses and their grand peroration with Rückert's turn to the infinite stars, Pfitzner's Schumann festival delivers something around which the people of Strasbourg might rally: communal consciousness, in Rupp's words, of an "experience of greatness."[18]

Violation and Vainglory

Bridging from this Strasbourg "experience of greatness" back to the Munich Lieder recital with which we began, we might usefully consider another document of reception, in this case Alfred Einstein's review in his capacity as music critic for the *Münchener Post*. At first glance, it seems that there are some rather petty differences of aesthetic viewpoint expressed in it. Einstein complains, for example, that the singers, Maria Ivogün and Karl Erb, had not only divided the songs of the *Liederkreis* between them, and had sung the finale together, but—to its considerable detriment—had dramatized *Waldesgespräch* by playing the poem's implied roles of rider and witch. The device is simply "horrible [*schauderhaft*]" in effect, Einstein concludes, and a dire misappropriation of the balladic tradition; it beckons, in fact, toward a state of affairs in which four singers will be needed to give a rendition of Schubert's *Erlkönig*—"Goethe, who begins the discourse and, shuddering, brings it to a close; father, son, and the *Erlkönig* himself."[19]

But far more profound is Einstein's direct response to Pfitzner, by whom he is clearly angered and unsettled, in spite of his "indescribable subtlety" as a Lieder accompanist.[20] Specifically with his interludes between the songs of opus 39, Pfitzner is judged to have created "something frightful [*etwas . . . Furchtbares gemacht*]":

> [Pfitzner] seems to think that his inner relationship with his kindred-by-choice [*Wahlverwandten*] Robert Schumann gives him the right to violate him. For that is what this is, a violation [*Vergewaltigung*], to attempt to weave the op. 39 *Liederkreis* "into a whole" by means of interludes, however discrete they may be. It robs Schumann's intended song-beginnings and endings of their aesthetic effect; also, I simply don't believe that Schumann meant anything by the ordering of his songs—one only has to think of the succession of "Andenken" [i.e., "Intermezzo"] and "Lorelei" [i.e., "Waldesgespräch"]![21]

The reference to the idea of Schumann as *Wahlverwandten* points, of course, in the direction of Goethe and his 1809 novel *Die Wahlverwandtschaften* (usually translated as "Elective Affinities"). Einstein thus deliberately distances himself from Pfitzner's particular appropriation of the German Romantic tradition in favor of his own—one that seems to value the clarity of the fragment, of distinct beginnings and endings, of the non sequitur, and even of Eichendorff's original poem titles over Schumann's song titles (hence the "wrong" titles in the last line). His apparent quotation of "into a whole" (in the original German: "zu einem Ganzen zu verweben") suggests, too, that the phrase was present before him in one of the paratexts for the recital, just as it had stood on the published cover of the Schumann choruses in 1910; it thus forms part of the overall "violation" of the tradition to which Einstein objects.

Moreover, in striking this distanced pose, Einstein adds a telling piece of information that Thomas Mann's diary entry omits: that the lights in the Four Seasons' recital room were extinguished during the rendition of Schumann's opus 39. We might speculate variously on reasons for this—Einstein himself quips that he "thought those days were over," perhaps a reference to the dimming of lights because of fuel shortages during the war[22]—but one inevitably wonders whether it was an attempt to recreate the treacherous twilight of the tenth song and diffuse it throughout the experience of the work, thereby fostering the "romantic-demonic" state of emotional confusion that Mann's diary celebrates.

Certainly, the lighting had been similarly treated in the Lieder recital that formed part of Pfitzner's Schumann festival in Strasbourg in 1910, and there had inspired one reviewer to write of a *Stimmungsmache* ("cheap atmospheric effect" or even "propaganda") that threatened to overwhelm the effect of Schumann's "immortal songs."[23] In any case, the darkness clearly contributes to Einstein's similar reaction against the Ivogün-Erb rendition of opus 39. Far from "profound," he finds it "alienating and embarrassing [*befremdend und peinlich*]."[24] We might say that his review persona assumes, overall, a Settembrini-like role for the reader, eager to cast an exposing light on the whole charade, to flick the lights on just at the moment that Pfitzner revels in the effect of turning them off.[25]

If so, we might also draw from Einstein's review that what this Lieder recital actually staged was something like a boundary perimeter: a line that divided those within the Munich Pfitzner circle from those beyond—a dark inner circle of initiates surrounded by apostates in the garish light of its periphery. Ivogün and Erb were very much ensconced within this Pfitzner group—they had, indeed, taken two of the principal roles in his opera *Palestrina*, premiered to huge acclaim in Munich only two years before, and still prominent in the repertory there and elsewhere.[26] Thomas Mann was also, of course, at this time still a devotee of the composer, having established a close friendship with him around the time of *Palestrina*'s first performances and having delivered a glowing homage to that opera in 1918's *Reflections of a Nonpolitical Man*.[27] In fact, in June 1918, Mann had been leading light at the founding in Munich of the *Hans Pfitzner-Verein für deutsche Tonkunst* ("Hans Pfitzner Association for German Composition"), a pressure group intended to consolidate Pfitzner's post-*Palestrina* reputation among his public and foster his aesthetics as national style.[28] In a celebratory after-dinner speech to this association of a year later, indeed, Mann had made remarks that gently recalled the Schopenhauerian terms of Pfitzner's organic "something" and continued to expand its compass to embrace and embody the national collective in explicitly political terms:

> But art, gentlemen, is an irrational sphere, just like life itself, and its graspability through concepts like romanticism and reaction, or modernity and progress, is extraordinarily limited. We know of gigantic cases of artistry—think of Wagner and Dostoyevsky—in which elements that we are accustomed to calling romantic and reactionary (the national element, for example) combine organically with those we name revolutionary. . . . Gentlemen, I believe that in Germany's present historical situation . . . this musical-romantic art holds more future-building power and significance than many apparently more contemporary.[29]

Pfitzner, of course, is for Mann just such a giant of artistry—as much a musical revolutionary as an archromantic[30]—and this identification permits the collision of contradictions in the toast at the very end of the speech, in which our previous dark-light dichotomy is inverted and the composer becomes the torchbearer and light bringer for his "people": "Long live Hans Pfitzner! May he live the noble, strict, and heartfelt life that, dreaming deeply and enthusiastically of the past, drives the German future. May he live in high renown, immortally, a beacon [*Fanal*] for his people [*Volk*]. Long may he live!"³¹ Mann's heavily inflated rhetoric of contradiction here and his emphasis on the potential of art as irrational sphere also point directly toward numerous passages in the *Reflections of a Nonpolitical Man*. Just a few pages before the famous homage to Pfitzner's *Palestrina*, for example, he had suddenly released the brakes on an astonishing tirade that frames art as a violent reactionary, perhaps national-political, force to be reckoned with:

> Let every utopia of progress, let the sanctification of the earth by reason—every dream of social eudemonism be fulfilled, the pacified, Esperanto world become reality: air buses breeze over a "human race" that is clothed in white, pious with reason, statelessly unified, monolingual, in the ultimate mastery of technology, with electric television: art will still live, and it will form an element of uncertainty and preserve the possibility, the conceivability, of relapse. It will speak of passion and unreason; it will present, cultivate, and celebrate passion and unreason, hold primordial thoughts and instincts in honor, keep them *awake* or reawaken them with great force, the thought and instinct of war, for example.³²

We saw the final sentence at the beginning of the present chapter, in our opening consideration of Mann's "romantic-demonic"; the reason he emphasizes the word *awake* seems to be because, only a page before, he had prepared this tirade with the citation of an Eichendorff poem called *Klage* ("Lament," 1809). It begins with the romantic poet lying down in the deepest woods to dream away the "foolish" and "God-forsaken" world around him and concludes with the breaking of a new dawn and a call to arms similarly emphasized by Mann: "Da wacht, ihr Getreuen, *auf*" ("Then you, o loyal ones, *awake*").³³ Thus Mann follows Eichendorff in making the deep dream a necessity for the new day; and no sooner has he cited this brazen ending than he points out that Pfitzner had set the whole poem to "magnificent" orchestral music in 1915. This could hardly be any more provocative, particularly in the context of a call to the loyal: as Mann was certainly also aware, Pfitzner had dedicated the resulting work to Admiral von Tirpitz, commander of Germany's Imperial Navy and shortly to be the chair of its populist and war-committed Fatherland Party.³⁴

Largely through Mann's agency and prestige, then, Pfitzner's romantic-steeped aesthetics—not least those of "verbindende Musik" and its resulting organic "something"—had been drawn into a much larger ideological nexus by the war's end. If in 1910 these had been placed at the heart of a Schumann festival in an embattled territory, they now strained under a greater national burden. With a distinctly contrary logic, the provincial *Kapellmeister* of Strasbourg is here proclaimed as a restorative national genius and his creations made the domain of a dangerously productive irrational art. Precisely on account of something that appears as the very antithesis of the political, namely their "dreamful gaze backward" [*träumerische Rückwärtsgewandtheit*], art and artist are identified as the driving force of the German future—the fire signal for the corralling of its people, and perhaps even, with von Tirpitz in mind, for the launch of its battleships.[35] Aided and abetted by Pfitzner, the "nonpolitical" German of Mann's *Reflections* here becomes primed to stride onto the central public stage.

"Mund und Sprecher"

With Mann's overtly contradictory logic still in view, we might turn at length to our final written source, Pfitzner's own commentary on his "verbindende Musik" practice—actually part of a prefatory essay to his newly composed "romantic cantata" *Von deutscher Seele* ("Of the German Soul"), completed in 1921. We have already made reference to this essay and its general tendency toward disingenuity, but now we are in a position to propose that its obfuscation is actually far more thoroughgoing: it can be identified as a considered study in denial and contrariness that draws directly on Mann's 1918 framing of the apolitical man. At the core of its style and substance, in short, stands Mann's romantic notion that the deepest dreams and darkest woods might conceal the most eruptive, the most productive, the most revolutionary in the German character.

Pfitzner's epigraph for his essay is taken from Gurnemanz's entreaty to Parsifal ("Tell me what you do know, for you surely must know something"), and this image of the "pure fool" informs his attitude throughout. Ever the good Schopenhauerian, Pfitzner claims that he had "willed" and "striven" for nothing in creating the new cantata; nor had he sought to give expression to any "worldview," preferring instead to allow a "drive for form [*Gestaltungetrieb*]," a "higher instinct for creation [*höherer Spieltrieb*]" to take its course and deliver his cantata as a "thing in itself [*Ding für sich*]." Accordingly, it had grown from a few small sketches for settings of Eichendorff's aphorisms into a "drama of songs [*Liederspiel*]" intended for voice and piano alone and linked into a whole by Pfitzner's accompanimental practice. From there it had become a large-scale orchestral work showcasing interludes of considerable length—small tone-poems in themselves, indeed, often dwarfing the vocal settings of Eichendorff's words. At all times, Pfitzner-as-Parsifal concludes, music had been the "leading power" in this formation process, marshaling the texts according to its "secret instructions." Thus, for him, the cantata deserved the title "Of the German Soul," since it was music's special prerogative to speak this out in all its complexity and splendor.[36]

The resulting work might readily invite an "autumnal" reading, that is, a nostalgic revisiting of a Romantic aesthetic all too painfully gone by in the early 1920s. Yet, against the context developed in this chapter, it seems that we must trace a far more polemical edge to the work. Worthy of note, for example, is the transformational nature of its numerous orchestral interludes, which, as if responding directly to Mann's description of art as an "irrational sphere," facilitate the cantata's rapid shuttling from one mood or state to another. This structure, of course, demonstrates the central conceit of music as a "common bond" holding Eichendorff's "magic images" together, delivering a whole that is in turn a cipher for the "German soul" of the work's title. Just as at the end of the 1910 Schumann choruses, moreover, it leads to a demonstrative *Schlussgesang* comprising chorus, full orchestra, and organ.

Taking the cue of Mann's knowingly contrary "apolitics," however, we might also home in keenly on the cantata's apparently most innocuous moments and expect them to be the most polemically charged of all. Indeed, it is in this very regard that a sequence in the work's third part—the so-called *Liederteil*—has become notorious. The setting here is of Eichendorff's *Der Friedensbote* ("The Envoy of Peace") and it would be hard to imagine a moment more intimate than its beginning, in which a father sings a cradle song to his slumbering child— "*Schlaf ein, mein Liebchen, schlaf ein*"—while the sounds of nature rustle comfortingly outside the window. As the setting proceeds, however, Pfitzner draws on the mention of war in Eichendorff's text in order to turn the song into a militarized zone, first through thundered timpani and then, on the poem's last word, a scarcely credible *tutti* surge from *piano* to triple *fff*, emblazoning a chord of C major across the orchestra. This has often been suspected simply as a case of bad composition: even a strong advocate of Pfitzner's music like John Williamson writes that the song here slips out of focus and exceeds all its own terms.[37] The closing line, "Das Land ist ja frei" ("The land is indeed free"), it might be said on this view, occasioned such patriotic excitement in Pfitzner that he momentarily lost the otherwise exceedingly subtle control of his compositional means.

But, after all, that could very well be the point. We might say instead that Pfitzner—bunkered behind the guise of "the music itself" and its "secret instructions"—unleashes with this paragraph a highly calculated presentational act, not unlike, in its own way, the vainglorious toast at the end of Mann's after-dinner speech for the Pfitzner Association. For these early postwar romantics, just as a lament might be dedicated to the commander of battleships, so a cradle song can be a political statement, and so the deepest dreams of Eichendorff's forested past might drive the future. From his Parsifalian stance of knowing ignorance, Pfitzner chooses exactly this unlikeliest of moments: his intimate song to a child turns outward suddenly into a form of public address. Through the cantata created by the practice of "verbindende Musik," Pfitzner here outfits himself as the national composer that he and his circle had foreseen in the earliest days of the war's aftermath.

This goal was not lost on contemporary commentators. Responding to the cantata's first performances in 1922, the reviewer for *Musikblätter des Anbruch* begins from what he calls a "Freudian slip," labeling Pfitzner as political when his intention (or so he feigns) was to write "polemical."[38] The specific arrangement of Eichendorff's poetry in *Von deutscher Seele* was most certainly beholden to an intention, the reviewer continues, and the intention was something quite different from the harmlessness indicated by the work's section titles. The "frailty" of the overall construction out of small parts, moreover, and the mode of delivery of the work's finales could hardly be named a great success. Even so, the reviewer confesses his susceptibility to the effects of the "extortionist sentimentality," the emotional blackmail practiced by Pfitzner's Romantic style and substance, not least in the extensive instrumental sections that joined the cantata together. Even the young German of the 1920s should never be ashamed, he ultimately proposes, of feeling his inner sympathetic strings resonate with Pfitzner's. Indeed, in this composer's cantata-led "optimism," he finds (sounding rather like Thomas Mann in 1918) the "hope for our future": namely, the "rebirth of the German spirit out of the German soul."[39]

Rather less enthusiastic, finally, was Alfred Einstein. Already a veteran, as he points out, of the experience of Pfitzner's "verbindende Musik," Einstein complains that what Pfitzner's chosen title "Of the German Soul" actually betrayed was a lack of corrective "inner shame" in the blunt proclamation of nationalistic feeling. None in the exalted tradition from Bach to Brahms would ever have trumpeted such a thing, he insists, which had the effect of reducing Pfitzner to the level of Edward Elgar and his supposed "Spirit of England." Symptomatic of this problem was the issue at the center of the piece: whether Pfitzner in his fervor to capture the German soul had, in fact, simply emphasized a catastrophic incongruity between Eichendorff's "intimate, intensive lyricism" and the "extensive [orchestral] apparatus" of the late Romantic cantata.[40]

But in pointing to this paradox at the heart of the work, Einstein also draws attention to its spark of productivity. With the creation of *Von deutscher Seele* and the claims he had made about that work, Pfitzner was attempting, thought Einstein, to redefine his individual relationship with the "totality"—specifically the "totality of the people [*Volksgesamtheit*]." The extreme "esoteric and egocentric" aspects of *Palestrina* were becoming revalued, inverted, turned outward, and its originator made "Mund und Sprecher"—both "mouthpiece and spokesperson"—of a far larger German collective.[41] Perhaps with events like the op. 39 *Liederkreis* concert in mind, Einstein had once written that Pfitzner was the kind of figure who could only ever have a "community" (*Gemeinde*, a word with strong connotations of "congregation") at his disposal, and never a "public."[42] In 1922, listening to the cantata *Von deutscher Seele* and the "orchestral songs without words" that sought to bind it together, Einstein seems to wonder whether these two bodies might merge into one and the same entity.[43] Pfitzner's nationalistic commitment—proclaimed by the cantata's end and expressed with a new fervency and virulence in exclusionary writings like the *New Aesthetics of Musical Impotence* (1920)—might yet propel him, his ideas, and his growing entourage to a position of public prominence.[44]

Notes

1. Thomas Mann, *Tagebücher 1918–1921*, ed. Peter de Mendelssohn (Frankfurt: S. Fischer, 1979), 310. All translations are my own unless otherwise stated.

2. I translate here the German text found in the Breitkopf and Härtel edition of opus 39 (Leipzig, 1883), edited by Clara Schumann.

3. Thomas Mann, *Reflections of a Nonpolitical Man*, tr. Walter D. Morris (New York: Ungar, 1983), 291; I have used the translation in conjunction with the original German found in *Betrachtungen eines Unpolitischen*, reproduced in *Politische Schriften und Reden*, ed. Hans Bürgin (Frankfurt: S. Fischer, 1968), 1: 297. The emphasis on "awake" [*wach*halten] is Mann's own; I shall return to the significance of this later in the chapter.

4. Mann, *Tagebücher 1918–1921*, 310.

5. Hans Pfitzner, "Von deutscher Seele: Eine romantische Kantate," *Neue Musik-Zeitung* 43, no. 11 (1922): 161.

6. Pfitzner, "Von deutscher Seele," 161.

7. See Valerie Woodring Goertzen, "Clara Wieck Schumann's Improvisations and Her 'Mosaics' of Small Forms," in *Beyond Notes: Improvisation in Western Music of the Eighteenth and Nineteenth Centuries*, ed. Rudolf Rasch (Turnhout, Belgium: Brepols, 2011), 153–62.

8. On the specific case of Busoni, see Kenneth Hamilton, *After the Golden Age: Romantic Pianism and Modern Performance* (Oxford: Oxford University Press, 2008), 101–3. Instances of similar practices performed by eighteenth-, nineteenth-, and twentieth-century pianists are treated in Valerie Woodring Goertzen, "By Way of Introduction: Preluding by 18th- and Early 19th-Century Pianists," *Journal of Musicology* 14, no. 3 (1996): 299–337.

9. Pfitzner, "Von deutscher Seele," 161.

10. These choral orchestrations are without opus number and are therefore not found, for example, in the list of works given in Peter Franklin's "Pfitzner, Hans" (January 20, 2001), in *Grove Music Online*, www.oxfordmusiconline.com. My source for the score is Pfitzner, *Frauenchöre von Robert Schumann*, UE 2679 (Vienna: Universal-Edition, 1910).

11. On the genesis of opp. 69 and 91, see John Daverio, *Robert Schumann: Herald of a "New Poetic Age"* (Oxford: Oxford University Press, 1997), 398–99. My sources for the scores are the Breitkopf and Härtel editions (Leipzig, 1887) edited by Clara Schumann; both collections there carry the title *Romanzen für Frauenstimmen*.

12. It might be noted here that Schumann later added piano accompaniments to these choruses as basic harmonic and melodic guides for the singers; I leave them to one side, because they appear to have left no trace on Pfitzner's orchestrations. On Schumann's

accompaniments, see Daverio, *Robert Schumann*, 424; the phrase "stylized naïveté" also comes from Daverio, *Robert Schumann*, 399.

13. These three Lieder are another work of 1849 (Daverio, *Robert Schumann*, 424).

14. The full text—which I draw from the Breitkopf and Härtel edition (Leipzig, 1887) edited by Clara Schumann—is as follows: "O blicke, wenn den Sinn dir will die Welt verwirren, zum ew'gen Himmel auf, wo nie die Sterne irren!" ("O look up, when the world would confound you, to the eternal heavens, where the stars never err from their paths!").

15. See, for example, the letter of 1908 to the publisher Henri Hinrichsen in Bernhard Adamy, *Hans Pfitzner Briefe* (Tutzing, Ger.: Schneider, 1991), 145–46.

16. Emil Rupp, "III. Elsaß-lothringisches Musikfest," *Musikalisches Wochenblatt* 41, no. 10 (1910), 203–4.

17. Rupp, "Elsaß-lothringisches Musikfest," 204.

18. Rupp, "Elsaß-lothringisches Musikfest," 204.

19. Alfred Einstein, *Münchener Post*, November 5, 1919, as reproduced in Kurt Dorfmüller, "Alfred Einstein als Musikberichterstatter," in *Festschrift Rudolf Elvers zum 60. Geburtstag*, ed. Ernst Herttrich and Hans Schneider (Tutzing, Ger.: Schneider, 1985), 134.

20. Dorfmüller, "Alfred Einstein," 134.

21. Dorfmüller, "Alfred Einstein," 134.

22. Dorfmüller, "Alfred Einstein," 134.

23. See Arthur Neißer, "Das III. Elsässische Musikfest," *Der Merker* 1, no. 4 (1910), 909. Gustav Altmann's review of the Strasbourg festival in *Die Musik* makes it clear that Pfitzner was the piano accompanist for these Lieder performances, which included *Dichterliebe* and *Frauenliebe und -leben*; the singer was Marie Gutheil-Schoder ("Strassburg: III. Elsaß-Lothringisches Musikfest (11.-13. Juni)," *Die Musik* 9, no. 20 [1910]: 123–24).

24. Dorfmüller, "Alfred Einstein," 134.

25. The reference here is to the enlightened humanist Ludovico Settembrini in Thomas Mann's novel *Der Zauberberg* ("The Magic Mountain," 1924); to cite only one example, in the chapter "Ewigkeitssuppe und plötzliche Klarheit," Settembrini appears in the protagonist Hans Castorp's darkened room in a "blinding blaze of light," having flicked on the light switch immediately upon entering (Thomas Mann, *Der Zauberberg* [Berlin: Fischer, 1958], 177).

26. Ivogün and Erb were also the dedicatees of Pfitzner's *Alte Weisen* (op. 33, 1923), a collection of songs after Gottfried Keller, the published score of which includes a note insisting that its eight songs "belong entirely together, and are only to be performed together and in this order" (Pfitzner, *Alte Weisen* [Berlin: Fürstner, 1923]).

27. See the end of the "On Virtue" chapter of Mann's *Reflections*, 297–314.

28. As discussed in my *Challenging the Modern: Conservative Revolution in German Music, 1918-1933* (Oxford: Oxford University Press), 46–51.

29. Mann, "Tischrede," reproduced in the collection *Rede und Antwort: Gesammelte Abhandlungen und kleine Aufsätze* (Berlin: Fischer, 1922), 286–87.

30. Mann, *Rede und Antwort*, 287.

31. Mann, *Rede und Antwort*, 288.

32. Mann, *Reflections*, 291.

33. Mann, *Reflections*, 290–91.

34. On Tirpitz and his relationship with the Fatherland Party, see Patrick J. Kelly, *Tirpitz and the Imperial Germany Navy* (Bloomington: Indiana University Press, 2011), particularly 419–21.

35. The term "Rückwärtsgewandtheit" is found in Mann, *Rede und Antwort*, 287.
36. Pfitzner, "Von deutscher Seele," 161–62.
37. See John Williamson, *The Music of Hans Pfitzner* (Oxford, UK: Clarendon, 1992), 269.
38. R. S. Hoffmann, "Von deutscher Seele," *Musikblätter des Anbruch* 4, nos. 5–6 (1922): 88.
39. Hoffmann, "Von deutscher Seele," 88.
40. Alfred Einstein, *Münchener Post*, August 31, 1922, as reproduced in Dorfmüller, "Alfred Einstein," 136–37.
41. Dorfmüller, "Alfred Einstein," 136.
42. Quoted in Dorfmüller, "Alfred Einstein," 136.
43. Dorfmüller, "Alfred Einstein," 137.
44. That Einstein had read an advance copy of Pfitzner's *Impotence* essay is evident from a review of December 1919, reproduced in Dorfmüller, "Alfred Einstein," 135.

Bibliography

Adamy, Bernhard, ed. *Hans Pfitzner Briefe*. Tutzing, Ger.: Schneider, 1991.
Altmann, Gustav. "Strassburg: III. Elsaß-Lothringisches Musikfest (11.-13. Juni)." *Die Musik* 9, no. 20 (1910): 123–24.
Attfield, Nicholas. *Challenging the Modern: Conservative Revolution in German Music, 1918–1933*. Oxford: Oxford University Press, 2017.
Daverio, John. *Robert Schumann: Herald of a "New Poetic Age."* Oxford: Oxford University Press, 1997.
Dorfmüller, Kurt. "Alfred Einstein als Musikberichterstatter." In *Festschrift Rudolf Elvers zum 60. Geburtstag*, edited by Ernst Herttrich and Hans Schneider, 117–55. Tutzing, Ger.: Hans Schneider, 1985.
Goertzen, Valerie Woodring. "By Way of Introduction: Preluding by 18th- and Early 19th-Century Pianists." *Journal of Musicology* 14, no. 3 (1996): 299–337.
———. "Clara Wieck Schumann's Improvisations and Her 'Mosaics' of Small Forms." In *Beyond Notes: Improvisation in Western Music of the Eighteenth and Nineteenth Centuries*, edited by Rudolf Rasch, 153–62. Turnhout, Belgium: Brepols, 2011.
Hamilton, Kenneth. *After the Golden Age: Romantic Pianism and Modern Performance*. Oxford: Oxford University Press, 2008.
Hoffmann, R. S. "Von deutscher Seele." *Musikblätter des Anbruch* 4, nos. 5–6 (1922): 88.
Kelly, Patrick J. *Tirpitz and the Imperial Germany Navy*. Bloomington: Indiana University Press, 2011.
Mann, Thomas. *Betrachtungen eines Unpolitischen*, reproduced in *Politische Schriften und Reden*, vol. 1, edited by Hans Bürgin. Frankfurt: S. Fischer, 1968.
———. *Rede und Antwort: Gesammelte Abhandlungen und kleine Aufsätze*. Berlin: Fischer, 1922.
———. *Reflections of a Nonpolitical Man*. Translated by Walter D. Morris. New York: Ungar, 1983.
———. *Tagebücher 1918–1921*. Edited by Peter de Mendelssohn. Frankfurt: S. Fischer, 1979.
———. *Der Zauberberg*. Berlin: Fischer, 1958.
Neißer, Arthur. "Das III. Elsässische Musikfest." *Der Merker* 1, no. 4 (1910): 909.
Pfitzner, Hans. *Frauenchöre von Robert Schumann, UE 2679*. Vienna: Universal-Edition, 1910.

———. "Von deutscher Seele: Eine romantische Kantate." *Neue Musik-Zeitung* 43, no. 11 (1922): 161–64.
Rupp, Emil. "III. Elsaß-lothringisches Musikfest." *Musikalisches Wochenblatt* 41, no. 10 (1910): 203–4.
Williamson, John. *The Music of Hans Pfitzner*. Oxford, UK: Clarendon, 1992.

NICHOLAS ATTFIELD is Lecturer in Music at the University of Birmingham. He is author of *Challenging the Modern: Conservative Revolution in German Music, 1918–1933* and coeditor of *Music, Modern Culture, and the Critical Ear: A Festschrift for Peter Franklin.*

12 Performers' Reflections

Natasha Loges and Laura Tunbridge

How do Lieder performers approach the process of assembling a song recital program today? And how does this relate (if at all) to the histories of song performance discussed in this collection? This closing chapter draws together, under several themes, responses to semistructured interviews the authors conducted with leading performers of German song in 2017. The responses have not been analyzed systematically but have rather been woven into a salon-style conversation. They are not intended to be a record of authoritative stances or definitive statements; instead, our aim is to provide a sense of commonalities and divergences in current attitudes toward performing German Lieder onstage. We approached many artists, trying to incorporate as broad a range as possible of nationalities and ages, as well as the voices of both singers and pianists. The singers we spoke to were Benjamin Appl (BA), Ian Bostridge (IB), James Gilchrist (JG), Thomas Hampson (TH), Sophie Karthäuser (SK), Mark Padmore (MP), Sarah Walker (SW), and Kitty Whately (KW); the pianists were Eugene Asti (EA), Julius Drake (JD), Martin Katz (MK), Sholto Kynoch (ShK), and Simon Lepper (SL). Most responses offer an Anglo-American perspective on Lieder programming, with London's Wigmore Hall signifying a very clear set of expectations from all sides. The role of conservatoire education has not been developed further here, but conversations inevitably touched on these artists' formative experiences and training. Although the business end of concert life is raised in various contexts, such as when deciding which programs will "sell," for understandable reasons artists were reluctant to offer details about their financial situations as recitalists in comparison with other performance work. (It seems highly unlikely that they earn more for recitals than opera performances, as Lilli Lehmann and Frieda Hempel did.) Beyond these pragmatic concerns, it becomes apparent on comparing responses to aesthetic questions about how to approach a concert that some of the ideas expressed chart deep-seated ideologies about what constitutes good and faithful performance; that these values might be open to question in light of the historical findings of previous chapters is something we have tried to tease out in our commentary.

Practical Considerations

When asked for their thoughts on programming a recital, most respondents mentioned practicalities first, principally the size and location of the venue. "It starts really from the hall itself, how you stage it is important," according to BA. The venue shapes technical and expressive choices; as IB explained, one has to accommodate oneself "to the acoustic, the size of the hall and the audience," adding that "big halls can work [for Lieder] but require something different." More important, however, each concert venue brought a raft of aesthetic expectations and limitations. Cross-currents like national origin, class considerations and urban-rural identity certainly shape these; for example, big urban centers are possibly more in dialogue with one another (London–New York–Berlin–Amsterdam–Vienna–Paris) than with smaller towns in their own countries. The contradictions also are intriguing: such as in national perceptions of audiences.

> The marvelous song cycles op. 35 and op. 39 can be a bit long for general publics, especially in America. Now, England has a very wonderful tradition; if you're singing a recital at the Wigmore Hall you have more freedom to be more specific. (TH)

> One of the difficulties is working out the audience's relationship with this repertoire and I think it does get harder, because if you're singing in this country, in England, normally an audience has very few who are German-speaking, and then you've got a different relationship between music and text. (MP)

Artists also had clear views about what was acceptable in different places:

> In Vienna you'll be surprised how little Hugo Wolf is sung. It always depends on the place and the mandate: for example, if I'm in Vienna and in the hinterlands that kind of program would be completely inappropriate. (TH)

> In Germany you have the problem that people are unfamiliar with the repertoire, ... in some ways that can be good, unfamiliarity doesn't lead to overfamiliarity, but I think people are reluctant often [to hear something new]. (MP)

There is a perception that the rules of engagement are different in the provinces: budgets, audience demographic, and promoter priorities determine both who is hired and what they perform:

> If I was just going to Manchester (just to pick a random city) I would probably think more along the "bouquet" line of things and in the English language as well as the German language. (TH)

[Pianist] Anna [Tilbrook] had put together some programs which were beautifully thought through, designed to appeal to [the English city of] Hull. And in some respects, the actual themes were neither here nor there. One was about Hull as a port, so we tried to find music which was connected to the sea, to seafaring, to commerce.... We found things to do with the slave trade, and it was fascinating doing songs by Samuel Coleridge Taylor and Chevalier Saint-George. To some extent, I don't think it matters whether the audience knows what we're finding, but I felt that Anna was able to put together a group of works of music that shared something. (JG)

Some respondents implied that assumptions about venues and audiences were worth challenging:

I think that there are times when you can lose an audience with pitching things a bit too high, a bit too difficult for them; although I've also sung Schubert songs to GCSE classes in comprehensive schools [freshman year, public high school], who are not necessarily going to be quickly impressed by anything, and they've been knocked out by "Der Doppelgänger." (MP)

Others, however, expressed concerns about how much a performer could demand from an audience:

In times of technology and smartphones, are people able to listen to classical music at such length? (BA)

There is, of course, also the practical issue of timing:

For full-length programs generally thirty-five to forty-five minutes (maximum) is a good, manageable length for the first half, followed by a twenty-minute interval, and a thirty- to thirty-five-minute (maximum) length for the second half, perhaps having an additional two to five minutes for an encore (or encores). For lunchtime (or "hour-long") programs with no intervals, around fifty minutes maximum of music is probably ideal. (TH)

I also pay attention to the length of the program, usually not more than thirty-five minutes of music in the first part and more or less the same in the second part. (I prefer an audience asking for more encores at the end than an audience falling asleep being bored.) (SK)

And, considering the audience's ability to concentrate, it is important to bear in mind demands on the performers:

I'm well aware that to do a full-length recital is difficult for me as a performer. But it's also quite difficult for the audience. I think to listen to any one voice for any great length of time [means] you can tire of it.... So that's another thing—to engage the audience and maintain some freshness of the voice by not actually singing at them for an hour and a half.... I tend to overprogram, I make my programs too long. And I think it's a big mistake.

It slightly goes back to stamina, both for the performers and of the audience, but most of all of the audience.... When I go to a concert, if I hear twenty songs beautifully sung, I'll be much happier than if I've heard forty songs and I've got bored by the thirtieth. (JG)

A further issue is the amount of time it takes to rehearse and memorize programs, since most recitals involve just one singer, for financial and other pragmatic reasons:

I really try to do the majority of what I do by heart because I think it engages the audience more effectively. Therefore, on a very practical level, I simply cannot provide an hour and half's new music every time. To some extent that gets easier as you have more experience because there's more in the bag for you to draw upon. But it does mean that my evolution of programs is slow. My gold standard, which I have never yet achieved, would be to have a kind of program each year that I try to produce as one work. (JG)

Having a variety of different voices is a way of adding further variety in programs for both audience and performers—but it is usually a luxury, as it usually winds up being more expensive for the venue/promoter—and it can also create practical problems in terms of finding adequate rehearsal time where the multiple artists are available at the same time. (EA)

I often find you agree [on] a program with someone, but you need to start rehearsing it before you know what the order will be, for example. If you've selected certain songs and you know they work together and you think they've got a good balance of things, then you start to rehearse it and then you think we have to sort this and this, take this out, so that sometimes needs the rehearsal process to sort it. I don't usually program whole programs that I'm not involved in playing. With the [Oxford Lieder] Festival I request certain things, I very rarely if ever have said, "Will you perform this program, these songs from beginning to end?" I've sometimes said, "Can you include these ten songs and then make the rest of it around that and build it from there?" So I've made requests, but I've never suggested an order really because they have to find what works for them. (ShK)

Alongside these considerations, the type of repertoire chosen can affect the length of programs, especially if cycles are included:

Given that there is such an extraordinary repertoire and that you have to spend quite a lot of time on a program, you have to be quite selective, and if you want to sing the great cycles, or the great songs, again you can't pack in too much into a program. (MP)

What Makes a Good Recital Program?

Performers are clear that the interest required for all-Lieder recitals today is specialized, and that such experiences are downright demanding. "For recitals, I think it's a very niche audience, a very special audience," explains BA. This musical world seems to privilege connoisseurship, raising the question of what makes an audience member want to be "inside" this world, and what forges a connection with this repertoire in the first place. An opposition is being created between the idealized "truth" of the world of art song and the pragmatic environment of concert making, as if the two were incompatible without compromises:

> I do think that those of us ... who are deeply devoted to this kind of repertoire and experience, live a kind of schizophrenic existence, for there are immediately two or three pressures on us; firstly from the side of what we know to be the truth of the Lieder repertoire in whatever language; and secondly the reality of the publics that we're singing to and to some extent, if you'll excuse me, the fragility of the presenters [promoters] themselves who invite you because they think they'll sell some name and that you're going to show up.... I'm not a pessimist about it but I am a realist about it. (TH)

> It's also in the hands of a good performer to try to keep this tradition of the Liederabend (not quite as Schubert's) to continue to find a way to keep the intensity and delivery of the music, to keep the format running, and to discover new possibilities of length, text. (BA)

The sense of the need to sustain a particular tradition in the modern age was a recurrent refrain in responses. Are, though, the aesthetic concerns of today's musicians when programming recitals the same as they were for musicians in the nineteenth century? There have been some significant shifts in attitudes toward the recital program since the middle of the twentieth century:

> Lucia Popp, [Gundula] Janowitz would come to the Wigmore, would do six songs by Schubert, then go off, then come back, do another group.... They were rigid programs, groups of songs which complemented each other, but you could have sat at home and put the record player on, or a Spotify playlist. (SW)

Many musicians cited pianist and programmer Graham Johnson as having had a profound effect on the way in which Lieder recitals have been put together in Britain, particularly through the foundation of the Songmakers' Almanac in 1976 and the series of recordings of Lieder made for Hyperion. Johnson has explored unfamiliar swathes of the repertoire for voice and piano and made numerous complete recordings of songs by individual composers and presented dedicated recitals as well.

For the majority of the musicians interviewed, three tensions repeatedly emerged in the desire to achieve interest: theme, sequence, and contrast; that is, the need to create a coherent program, to construct a meaningful narrative, and to incorporate variety and interest:

> To make something that's not boring, that has some sort of continuity. (JD)
>
> I think a nice Lieder program involves a good balance of different elements to keep the audience "awake"! Variety might be a key word here in moods, tempi, languages. (SK)
>
> I want to keep the audience interested, minute to minute. (JG)
>
> It's about a balance of moods and finding something that has a kind of logical progression from one song to the next without thinking anything beyond "that works," rather than necessarily that it has to be so intellectually connected. (ShK)
>
> [A program is] most compelling when in essence it has a kind of dramaturgy, some kind of flow and experience that draws someone into ninety minutes' or two hours' reflection. It can be musical language driven or, "more Thomas Hampson," with various composers assigned by a common literary poet or subject matter. (TH)

Within this, contrast was a recurring priority, although it was generally clear that contrast operated within quite strict limits of genre and style:

> Beauty is only a matter of contrast, not an absolute quality. (IB)
>
> I think the most important factor in a recital program, be it Lieder, or mélodie, or songs in any language, is contrast. By this, I mean contrast within a set of songs (excluding cycles, of course) and then also between sets of songs. (MK)

Some also had notional models that helped them allocate time and material to three stakeholders in the concert experience—the audience, the critics, and finally the musicians themselves.

> A famous singer (I think Christa Ludwig?) once said she always tried to build a program in three different parts: one third to make the audience happy, another third to make the press happy, and the last third to make herself happy! (SK)

Against the idea of contrast was the overwhelming, unquestioned investment in coherence, both as a means of holding the program together in the musicians' heads and as a way of helping the audience to make sense of an experience that is constructed of many fragments (although it was not clear how successfully the musicians' notions of coherence were perceived by audiences):

> I always like to see at least some thought or through-line running through the program in the choice of composers, poets, thematic idea, et cetera. I think this helps the performers as well as the audience to keep focus and maintain direction through the recital. (BA)

> I try and find some logical thread that ties the two other than just random amusement. . . . It's pretty obvious, one wants to have some kind of dramaturgy, some kind of experience for the evening, that can be either musical language-based, poetry-based, or period-based. (TH)
>
> In general, it's a program which has a musical narrative (not necessarily an explicit poetic narrative) which can carry the audience through from beginning to end of each half without emotional interruption. In other words, something absorbing and compelling which drives through and doesn't allow for lapsed concentration. . . . Of course, there are different sorts of recital (with a few groups in each half, or a couple of smaller cycles) but the most satisfying I do as an artist is building and singing this sort of program. (IB)
>
> When you're not singing cycles, it's really difficult to have the same program with the same intensity as a cycle. (BA)

Perhaps the most elusive of these is the idea of constructing a narrative of a program, since this need not (indeed almost certainly will not) be a narrative in a traditional sense of events happening to a protagonist. It is perhaps most simply conceived as an emotional arc or journey. For some, the solution lies in comparing a program with a meal, or interior design, or other metaphors:

> The idea of having a starter might mean something that might introduce, or get the listener into the mood for, a potential "idea" or "theme" for the program, followed by the main course (serious repertoire—often Lieder), then the interval, followed by perhaps French (or other "lighter" language) repertoire and finishing with songs in English (if you are performing to an English-speaking audience). (EA)
>
> I would struggle to do a Finzi-Schubert program. It is like organizing a meal; it's not just if each dish is good, it's what you're putting before and after it, and whether it is then a nice surprise. (MP)

Mezzo-soprano Sarah Walker was considering her experience of coaching vocal students at the Guildhall School of Music and Drama, helping them to compile programs that make sense and flow smoothly:

> You wouldn't have your ice cream to start with, followed by three courses of steak, followed by prawn cocktail. . . . [A program] should balance in the same way that a painting, a play, a beautiful menu balances. But that doesn't say you have to move through chronologically. You can go from Purcell to Gershwin if you know how to do it. (SW)

Collaborative pianist Simon Lepper also draws on metaphor to explain his approach:

It's like interior design, or any kind of design (which I guess is what programming is), because we don't make the furniture, but we can place it in a way that people will enjoy. Some people have a knack for that. (SL)

The idea of programming themed recitals that explore a single topical image is a relatively recent trend that evoked mixed responses. For some, it was a powerful programming strategy that automatically lent coherence to an experience and also simplified the process of short-listing songs for a program when the available repertoire is so vast (that is, themed programming is a strategy for both musicians and audience):

Personally, I like programs that have a theme; it's probably not essential, but I find it interesting myself. It's a good starting point and a good way of unearthing some unusual songs rather than the best-known song cycles that get done to death. (KW)

I quite often try to find some sort of thematic link towards programming and I do find this enormously helpful; it's a bit like trying to write an essay when you've got no idea what you want to say, and actually just have a thought, and it doesn't even have to be articulated that there's any sort of theme behind it—it doesn't have to have a subtitle—it just helps me feel about how things work together. (JG)

Often I start thinking about Lieder programs with poets as much as composers. So, I like doing concerts which have a poetic connection as much as a musical one. (MP)

For others, such strategies can seem like a modern rather than a nineteenth-century tool: "I can get a theme like freedom and take us from Schubert to contemporary poetry" (TH).

Without a doubt, the most obvious programming strategy beyond the performance of complete cycles or opus groups was the construction of programs based on poets:

If I'm just thinking of a straight Liederabend of German Lieder I'm more likely to be looking for different reflections on the same poet or of the same poetic epic or essence, for instance Heine and his school seen through the eyes of various composers. (TH)

Various musicians, however, felt that their experience of programming a single poet, poetic character, or even a single composer, had not worked:

I'm not particularly excited by songs being grouped as one composer from this date to that. (KW)

> One thing I have experimented with and which I feel doesn't work very well is having a poet-led program.... One ended up—rather than having several facets of the same jewel—with similar Xerox copies. And I could feel the audience sagging, and I sagged a bit as well. So, I've avoided doing that since. Not entirely, I think sometimes it can work beautifully but there's a danger with it. (JG)

> If we're talking about Lieder to an English-speaking audience, I'm not sure they really feel the subtleties, the differences in language between Heine and Goethe enough for it to be worth basing a program around it. It's a nice way to collect things. Brahms collected those bouquets in a sort of "boho chic" way, I suppose, it's kind of mix and match. Now we're more into cataloguing and "I'm going to do the whole of opus 100." That's enough for programming because it looks good on the page—and I'm not sure what looks good on the page translates to what actually is a visceral experience. (SL)

The pianist Julius Drake has given many tightly themed programs but recognizes their pitfalls too:

> It's difficult not to become a bit recherché; I want to resist becoming an expert, I want it to appeal to everybody. I'm in favor of Bryn Terfel-type programs, much more a mish-mash, because I want people to respond to songs/texts with piano accompaniment, the richness of the repertoire. The old-fashioned programs that my mum used to love, i.e. [those of the singer] Victoria de Angeles—the first half was never worth hearing but by the second half she'd warmed up, was singing in her own language, and she was wonderful. (JD)

JD went on to say that he likes IB's approach, with "one composer in each half, and you might highlight a particular poet, and then the fun is putting the songs together so in a way you make a cycle out of them—so there would be contrast or similarity of mood, you might have a long song followed by a short, brief narrative song leading into something more emotional, just like *Dichterliebe* does." The creative aspect of programming—of "composing cycles" out of preexisting songs indicates how compelling narrative coherence is.

EA espouses "balance, contrast, tonality." Although balance and contrast are a common preoccupation of the interviewees, it is striking that pianists give tonality a special status. (By contrast, IB explains "we sing words and not notes, which has a huge impact on how to articulate a line.") The question is whether one believes that one should either keep to the original keys or, if one has to transpose, to aspire somehow to retain the composer's original harmonic scheme. A related question is whether the progression of keys between songs is actually important in the creation of some kind of logic or coherence:

> I did two of the Wigmore Hall's Schubert series where everything, down to the order, the keys, who was singing what, was organized by Graham

Johnson. That was really illuminating, because Graham is such a famous programmer and creates these amazing running orders, and to live through it, experience it from the inside rather than just to hear it. At first glance on paper I didn't see the internal logic of it, but actually when you came to play it, it was absolutely brilliant. (ShK)

ShK's concern for the importance of keys is reduced within his own programs:

> The only time I care is when the keys stay the same. There are some things that I know well enough where it disturbs me for an eighth of a second where it starts in a different key, but I'd always rather hear a song sung comfortably—though some songs are designed not to be comfortable. I would much rather hear singers do things in keys that work well for them, particularly if you're transposing anyway. [There is] something to be said for [using] composers' original keys, but then the pitch was different, and the instruments were different anyway, so what are we hoping to achieve by saying it has to be in this key? And even if it were exactly the same, and you thought the composer heard C major in a particular way, 99.9 percent of the audience don't have any response like that, don't have perfect pitch or any attachment, they just hear what's comfortable. Very occasionally there are lovely connections to be made but that's a nice added bonus, I certainly wouldn't alter anything to find that. If you have a sequence of songs in the same key, particularly if it's the same key but a very different mood, it can be jarring. Semitone shifts can be jarring, but it depends how the song starts. And so long as you think about how to pace things, you don't have to make an effort to connect the two.

The interviewees also had strong feelings, based on their experiences, of what had not worked in terms of composer pairing or mood. For some the judgment depended on their perception of what an audience would enjoy:

> I remember when I had too many Lieder with a sad, intense emotion and a slow tempo following each other (some cycles are sometimes built like that) and having those finishing the first or second part of the recital, it was hard for the audience to clap with enthusiasm (either they were bored, sleepy, or too much involved in the "dark side" of the texts they just heard for at least twenty minutes). I do remember singing the three Schubert Mignon Lieder followed by the four intense Wolf Mignon songs, and it was definitely quite a tense emotion for too long. . . . If you can feel this onstage, you usually can be sure the audience can feel it too! (SK)

In contrast with that empathy with an audience, other performers trust that if their own conception of the program has integrity, it will be effective:

> I am pretty sensitive to composers who need to be in completely separate halves of the program or not together at all. I personally find it very difficult

to program anyone else with Hugo Wolf.... I would never put Brahms and Wolf in the same program, Wolf and Schumann perhaps, that works okay; to some extent Schubert, but I would certainly never have them in the same half. Another thought process: my natural instinct with recital programs is to think in halves, not quarters, even though I may have four groups. I tend to like a half where I spent a whole forty-five minutes without leaving the stage, as it's more engrossing. (TH).

Along similar lines, MP explained that Schubert and Schumann on the same program do not seem "as compatible as certain other composers."

Use of Languages

Although in the nineteenth century it was fairly common practice to sing Lieder in translation, according to the country in which they were being performed, it is no longer the norm. Singing in the local language can help engage the audience, who do not have their heads buried in their programs. In the original language, however, the timbral and rhythmic qualities of the poetry can shine (consider the awkwardness of hearing Dvořák in translation into English or, even worse, German).

> When you're putting across poetry, syntax makes a huge difference, and one of the pleasures of singing German is it's flexible, the way that the verb falls.... The most important word in the sentence is the verb and you find in German that sometimes it's actually at the beginning for poetic reasons. (MP)

Singers are expected to sing songs in the original language, hence the quality of diction and responsiveness to poetry plays a huge part in the way in which they are received. This is built into professional training at conservatories and into competition structures, in which one expects to hear competitors sing in a range of languages. The languages chosen are also determined by the geographical location of audiences.

> To build a program, I personally pay attention to hav[ing] at least two different languages (usually German and French as I'm more familiar with those two, and also because I have recitals mainly in Belgium, France, Germany, Austria). (SK)

As in implicit in SK's bilingual programming, singers' ability to perform "in well over a dozen languages" (SW) becomes another way of bringing variety to programs.

Introducing Unfamiliar Repertoire

There are tensions and overlaps between what might be considered, in the academy, canonic repertoire, accorded historical and aesthetic significance in scholarship, and what might be called performing canons—those songs that are heard most often on concert programs. Many canons are self-propagating, in that scholarship on a certain cycle or song encourages more scholarship on it, and likewise, songs one regularly hears are likely to be sung again. Although a work such as *Winterreise* might have a firm hold in both scholarly and performing canons, there is little to suggest that the two necessarily interact: academia's obsessions over lesser-known works might not be matched by performers, and the most frequently performed songs are not necessarily those most written about. Performers, however, have strategies for bringing new repertoire into their programs: they are concerned about how music is learned, the requirements of promoters, and how unfamiliar music can be sold to audiences. Are events showcasing an artist or a repertoire? Under what circumstances can one introduce lesser-known repertoire? One of the special situations is the music festival, in which people have bought into a particular project and so are more open-minded or receptive. On the other hand, they might have subscribed to the festival because they expect it to be a glut of all their favorite things.

> If you're performing in a little festival somewhere, they may not have that acquaintance and you've got to convince them that it's worth going back and hearing another Lieder recital. I now speak much more to the audience than I used to. I do think allowing the audience into the room, as it were, is a very good idea. You've got to understand that the audience is part of it, you've got to want them to be a partner in the whole experience. (MP)

Sometimes music both performers and academics would think uncontentious or popular prove not to be for certain audiences, at least as far as perceived by the promoters, fearful of box-office losses:

> I tend to work with presenters, to know what their publics want, what they're used to, what they're like. It'll probably surprise you, but some presenters say, well, you know, our public really doesn't like Schubert; I feel like hanging up, but you go, what about Schumann, or Brahms, or Mahler? And they say, Schumann and Brahms they like; Mahler, don't think they know much of Mahler. Why don't we give them a dose of what they want and then maybe some Schubert songs that make sense with the rest. (TH)

Some performers are invested in introducing new repertoire:

> I have always been interested in trying to present songs that are neglected in programs whenever possible—but this can prove problematic if the chosen singers don't have enough time in their busy schedules to commit to learning such repertoire. And it can also alienate an audience if they see too much unfamiliar repertoire on a program. So, I guess a healthy balance of less well known and some more well-known repertoire in a program is also a good

idea for practical reasons—both for artists and audience (and concert venues and promoters if they hope to draw in a decent public). (EA)

Choosing repertoire was based first of all on availability of singers, and then depending on what kind of musician that person was, whether they had their own discrete set of repertoire they sang—to base thing around their core repertoire, rather than learning a whole load of new songs. That's a lot of learning for one concert. My skill set as an accompanist is one who should be able to get involved in lots of different musical styles, lots of different kinds of singers. But a singer ought to be honing a repertoire which is based on their personality. So, I am personally reluctant to program "for" a singer when they have to stand there and sing these texts, whereas asking me to play lots of different notes is no problem; you have to enjoy lots of different notes, shapes, and sounds. (SL)

There is some concern for the way new works fit into more familiar programs. One singer recommended

a chronological order of the different composers involved—or at least not too big contrasts in style or big jumps in different periods (and actually not too many different composers if possible), always making either a nice group of songs for each composer or a cycle, a few unknown or less known pieces. (SK)

One factor that certainly adds pressure on the performer is the expectation that programs be memorized:

It is very liberating to do programs from memory. It's hard work and you've got to understand that it takes time I think for anybody to learn—there are of course people who seem to learn things with no effort at all—certainly I have to sing things a lot. And you have to practice them a lot, and you have to practice with a pianist a lot. (MP)

One pianist gave an example of an all-Mendelssohn day, including two recitals, which raised the issue of which performers can be expected to learn new repertoire:

Because this program involved young artists, I was able to ask them to learn unusual repertoire knowing that they would be more than happy to do so and that they would enjoy the challenge.... This is not always so easy to do when working with more established artists who generally have far less time to prepare too much new and unusual repertoire with their busy lives and (often operatic) careers. (EA)

The challenge for the festival programmer is to balance keeping the performer happy while persuading him or her to learn unfamiliar repertoire because of thematic considerations:

> My own experience in terms of programming the [Oxford] Lieder Festival is obviously that we're trying to program to an overarching theme. So, then, you're looking for connections to be made that go beyond that evening's performance and feed into everything else, as well as thinking about balance and coherence and ticking off some boxes for the completist element of what we're trying to do. . . . I think there's a lot to be said for the importance of the performer as well and for them feeling very comfortable with their program. There's a danger that it becomes an intellectual exercise when trying to program things in a festival within a theme. (ShK)

Festivals seem to have their own logic because they are immersive and demand commitment (often involving travel to a special location or hearing works in less typical venues), but on the other hand, audience expectations are more flexible. Often audience members and performers can feel a strong sense of loyalty to a festival, though on other occasions it may be that a festival discourages specialization:

> For making programs, . . . you want to think a little bit about how an audience will react to different repertoire. I think doing a whole program of obscure Schubert songs for a little festival would be a real trial and might put people off. . . . The word I always use as a performer is *generosity*, you need to *want* the audience to experience something that's really worthwhile. (MP)

What the Singer Does on Stage

The basic set-up of singer and piano on stage might seem straightforward, but the mode of performance in a Lieder recital is considered to be unusually focused:

> Classical "singing" can be very alienating—the communication should be so direct that the audience doesn't know that you are singing. (IB)

What does direct communication mean?

> How you concentrate is a very big issue for musicians. Because you can perform and think about shopping! I think two words that feel very important to me are *attention*, really noticing what's going on. And then there's *intention*, because you've got to mean something when you sing. (MP)

> My gift is involvement with the text, I just know instinctively how to deliver it, I like to explore the fact that I can do that, with the tiniest—if any—gesture. (SW)

> When performing Lieder, I think you must first keep in mind the main emotion you want to express when you start a Lied. Sometimes your mind needs to jump from a joyful piece to a very intense dark one, so you must establish the precise atmosphere before producing the first sound or the first chord of the piano introduction, using your face and body language (but

avoiding pushing this too far, I mean: trying to do this as naturally as possible by really deeply feeling that emotion—that sometimes involves thinking about personal situations in your own life, in my case!—I think an audience is clever enough to see and feel when it's fake, artificial; that's my bigger first challenge once I step on stage). I guess I'm always trying to share my emotions with the audience, to try to make the story I'm (singing) talking about real. Text and subtext are as important as the music, they help, support each other. (SK)

It's interesting, when I go to vocal recitals, I find myself wary of wanting to catch the eye of the performer. I often find my physical attention focused somewhere else. I want to be able to see them out of the corner of my eye. But I don't want to actually eyeball them because I find that almost too . . . (*long pause*) too upsetting isn't quite the right word, but too, too intimate. And in fact, when I'm performing, I increasingly try not to look. . . . I try to find a place to focus my attention which is somewhere else. I think a lot of my colleagues do the same; they feel that actually to eyeball the audience is too much, really. . . . Of course, I'm just me, standing in a suit on a platform—but I try to put myself in the place of the poet. And addressing whoever he or she wants, so, an imaginary figure. But it's very concrete in my mind. Very concrete. I think I deliberately try to "de-realize" myself and put myself in a physically different place. (JG)

The decision about what is alienating or overdone is generally culturally conditioned. What is considered good song singing in the United States is perhaps unrecognizable in Germany, as can be discovered when singers receive mixed responses on tour.

Directness is sometimes conflated with a notion of drama, despite the fact that the Lied is predominantly a lyric form. IB sums it up succinctly:

The Lied is a dramatic art form. Every performance is different and live performance can afford to be extreme. [IB]

Difference and extremity can be accentuated in theatrical interpretations (or, as IB puts it, "Lieder as theater"), which are growing in popularity but also have a long heritage. (One can think of four singers performing Schubert's "Erlkönig" in the nineteenth century, or the staged versions of Schumann's "Die beiden Grenadiere" captured on early sound film.) The musicians interviewed had mixed feelings about overtly theatrical approaches:

It's not that I want to make a new drama; I'm just trying to help the songs feel "in a setting," rather than that they stand totally alone. I'm quite a dramatic artist anyway, I'm not very good at standing still. I like to become physically involved. I like to try and imagine, even in a very small way, staging, not that I want the theater to get in the way of the songs. I just wanted to place it there. Now, I know this is a bit radical. And it's increasingly where I am going as a programmer. (JG)

In the last twenty or thirty years there has been an advance in what a singer is expected to be at home doing. They're expected to have a dramatic conception onstage; they don't just stand and sing on stage in terms of opera and the same applies to Lieder. . . . But I really don't approve of theatrical versions. They are usually overplayed. . . . it would have to be done in television or film style. (SW)

It is essentially storytelling. My thing about Lieder singing is that it's not about beautiful voices, and actually people with fairly indifferent voices could make fantastic Lieder singers if they have the right kind of poetic imagination. (MP)

There seems to be a resistance to the notion that a theatrical or dramatic element is something imposed from outside a Lied's text and poetry and, in its place, an investment in the drama coming from within. That internalization of expression and representation resonates with some of the themes discussed in earlier chapters in this book, about "intimacy," for example, but that does not necessarily imply a historically informed perspective on how nineteenth-century Lieder were interpreted at the time of their composition.

Responses to a Program by Clara Schumann

The musicians were shown a recital program from 1872, devised by Clara Schumann, which ran as follows:

1. Schumann *Fantasie*, op. 17
2. Schubert Lieder "Willkommen und Abschied" and "An die Leier"
3. Beethoven Variations in C minor, WoO 80
4. Schumann *Dichterliebe* nos. 1–8
5. Schumann "Nachtstück" in F major, op. 23 (no. 2 or no. 4), and "Scherzino" from *Faschingsschwank aus Wien*, op. 26 no. 3
6. Mendelssohn Scherzo from *Sommernachtstraum*, op. 21
7. Schumann *Dichterliebe* nos. 9–16

They were then asked to give their first impressions:

I think it's really bizarre. Nobody would program like that anymore. (JG)

There would be complete outrage at the Wigmore to break up [a cycle]. . . . I did a *Frauenliebe* [*und -leben*] where, after each song, there was a poem that reflected the same theme. And I thought that was really interesting, and we included the poem, Chamisso's extra poem, in English. I really liked it, but some people were outraged at breaking up the cycle with something else. (KW)

Everything was long in those days [the nineteenth century]: formal meals were long, operas were, and I imagine recitals also had people talking through them.... Lotte Lehmann's *Winterreise* was broken up left, right, and center. We're much more purist now, and we know a lot more about it. All the performers are immensely knowledgeable. (SW)

I think the attention-span thing, which we all think of as a modern phenomenon—it obviously vexed [Clara Schumann] hugely. And she was very anxious about putting long works in a program; she much preferred putting in short dribs and drabs of highly varied programming.... I think modern audiences—I may be wrong—would not be happy with that sort of programming. I feel they would feel—I won't quite say short-changed, but they would [*hesitantly*] want to see the bigger timescale. I mean, *Dichterliebe*, I cannot conceive of performing it today split up. Even *Winterreise*, which until quite recently was very often performed with a little interval in the middle of it, I would be loath to do that.... And I know it's a big ask of audiences. But my own feeling is that—when it works—it's what audiences are wanting at the moment.... Perhaps it's when people make the effort to come to a concert, they actually want something that is different from their day-to-day life, which is, you know, pinging with emails and everything. And they want to be able to think over the longer timescale. That's what I feel. (JG)

Other musicians found Clara Schumann's approach to programming appealing or at least intriguing:

It's something I'm working towards. It means working with a pianist who is as comfortable in solo repertoire as in Lieder or chamber music. Unfortunately, we live in a world where artificial divisions are set up. (IB)

I have been talking about doing programs like that. I do occasionally do solo things and there are some pieces that I think I can play that would work well in a song program. It's there in the back of my mind. [Imogen Cooper's and Stephan Loges's at Wigmore][1] programming seemed very organic (organic is a horrible word, isn't it?) and there was something about it; she chose movements [from *Kreisleriana*] that sounded like they'd sprung brilliantly from out of what they'd just sung, so it actually felt it could be part of the cycle, it didn't interrupt, it was more a pause to elaborate on the thought we'd just been through. I could tell there was great artistry behind that, what kind of music—aria that followed a récit or something, you got the action out of the way and then had chance to think about it and reflect a bit purely musically. It helps when it's a great performance as well. I am quite happy with the role of accompanist, but I also think it's a good thing that people remember there is a pianist in the room as well. I like the idea that we can get a bit of the limelight as well—I know others would probably kill me for suggesting that, but I think it's not a bad thing and I think it makes people listen to things a bit differently. It's not just the limelight making people think those piano parts are really interesting, if Imogen Cooper is playing *Dichterliebe*, the piano parts must be extraordinary. (Many in the audience don't realize that's where 90 percent of the musical interest lies.) (ShK)

We just have to be imaginative about programming. I'm not sure we'd want to recreate a Liszt recital now and those stories of him leaping on stage from the audience and tearing off his white gloves sound rather more Lang-Lang than perhaps one would imagine. There would be lots of things about a nineteenth-century piano recital that I think one would find fairly intolerable, the improvisation, stuff going on between movements, all sorts of things, or listening to an *Elijah* where there's encores demanded of arias. So, I think there's a limit to how much one wants to go for historical reconstruction, but I think conversations within a program of different things [are good], and I love singing at chamber music festivals partly because of that. So I love Lieder being in the midst of the other repertoire which it would have been known with. And the other thing to remember about Lieder is that it isn't concert-hall music on the whole. *Dichterliebe* wasn't performed in its entirety until twenty years after Schumann died, the song recital didn't exist in their imaginations, so they were essentially writing something that would have been performed at home. (MP)

The musicians on occasion justified their opinions by invoking the composer's intentions over concerns for performance situations:

I try to be sensitive to what the composer is searching for. . . . [In the nineteenth century], "the industry of recital repertoire" didn't exist in that context, the strictures of today probably weren't that important. (TH)

Some, though, felt that it was important for attitudes toward programming to change according to the times:

We do not owe a responsibility to the dead composer but to the living audience. (IB)

It is apparent that there is no single approach to Lieder programming in the minds of the musicians interviewed; there seems to be a strong sense, though, of what works and what does not that is informed by practical and commercial concerns as much as by creative ones. A history of Lieder performance in the twenty-first century may well be as varied as the history of nineteenth-century practices revealed in this volume—certainly the geographical reach of this music is far greater than had previously been the case, not least because of the dissemination of performances via audiovisual media (a topic that is beyond the scope of this book). At the same time, however, localities remain important, as does the individuality of interpretation.

How different, then, are the attitudes of today's professional performers from those of the nineteenth century, and to what extent can they be considered to perpetuate a particular lineage? For the most part, it seems that today's practices have a much more recent history, one shaped by the specialization of performance pedagogy and recording technology, rather than by the hybrid programs that occupied earlier concert stages. The emphasis on coherence and balance, and a conception of "inner" drama, put forward by many of the musicians interviewed is at odds with the previous generations illustrated in other chapters. It does, though, tally with some of the aspirations of figures like Clara Schumann, determined to cultivate a more serious approach to concertizing (despite her splitting up of song cycles). Cultural gatekeepers such as critics, professional virtuosi, concert managers and promoters, editors, and academics determine the way in which music is presented today no less than they did in the nineteenth century. If the musicological essays in this volume suggest, through historical studies, a much freer approach to Lieder programming than performers seem to feel at liberty to pursue today, that is simply evidence of those gatekeepers' influence. Yet having set out to unsettle some assumptions about German song onstage, it feels appropriate to suggest that the time may have come to divert energies to, if not necessarily changing, then at least questioning what is meant by a Lieder recital. A conscious effort to preserve a recently-constructed past, an "invented tradition," might then be displaced by borrowing from an older history of performance practices that inform and invigorate, to ensure the survival of this form of live music making for decades to come.

Note

1. ShK is referring to a concert at Wigmore Hall in February 2016 given by baritone Stephan Loges and pianist Imogen Cooper in which Schumann's *Dichterliebe* was broken up with a selection from *Kreisleriana*.

NATASHA LOGES is Head of Postgraduate Programmes at the Royal College of Music. She is author of *Brahms and His Poets: A Handbook* and coeditor of *Brahms in the Home and the Concert Hall: Between Private and Public Performance*; *Brahms in Context*; and *Musical Salon Culture in the Long Nineteenth Century*.

LAURA TUNBRIDGE is Professor of Music at the University of Oxford. She is author of *Schumann's Late Style*; *The Song Cycle*; and *Singing in the Age of Anxiety: Lieder Performances in New York and London between the World Wars* and coeditor of *Rethinking Schumann*.

Timeline

1732	Birth of Joseph Haydn
1749	Birth of Johann Wolfgang von Goethe
1750	Death of Johann Sebastian Bach
1756	Birth of Wolfgang Amadeus Mozart
1758	Birth of Carl Friedrich Zelter
1770	Birth of Ludwig van Beethoven
1774	Publication of Goethe's *Sorrows of Young Werther*
1783	End of the American Revolution
1784	Birth of Marianne von Willemer
1785	Birth of Anna Milder-Hauptmann
1788	Birth of Joseph Freiherr von Eichendorff
	Birth of Friedrich Rückert
1789	French Revolution
1791	Death of Wolfgang Amadeus Mozart
1794	Birth of Wilhelm Müller
1795	Publication of Goethe's *Wilhelm Meister*
1797	Birth of Franz Schubert
	Birth of Heinrich Heine
1804	Birth of Wilhelmine Schröder-Devrient
	Birth of Eduard Mörike
1805	Premiere of Beethoven's opera *Leonore*
	Birth of Fanny Mendelssohn
1808	Publication of Goethe's *Faust*, Part 1
1809	Death of Joseph Haydn
	Birth of Felix Mendelssohn
1810	Birth of Robert Schumann
	Birth of Frédéric Chopin
1811	Birth of Franz Liszt
1812	Publication of Lord Byron's *Childe Harold*

1813	Birth of Richard Wagner
1814	Schubert composes "Gretchen am Spinnrade" (published as his opus 2 in 1821)
	Premiere of Beethoven's revised *Fidelio*
1815	Battle of Waterloo, defeat of Napoleon Bonaparte
	Congress of Vienna
1815	Schubert composes "Erlkönig" (published as his opus 1 in 1821)
	Beethoven, *An die ferne Geliebte*, op. 98
1818	Conradin Kreutzer, *Neun Wanderlieder von Ludwig Uhland*
1819	Publication of Goethe's *West-östlicher Divan*
	Birth of Clara Wieck
	Peterloo Massacre
1820	Birth of Jenny Lind
1821	Premiere of Carl Maria von Weber's *Der Freischütz*
	Publication of Wilhelm Müller's *Gedichte aus den hinterlassenen Papieren eines reisenden Waldhornisten*
1822	Premiere of Schubert's opera *Alfonso und Estrella*
1824	Publication of Schubert, *Die schöne Müllerin*, op. 25
1825	Schubert, "Suleika"
1826	Birth of Julius Stockhausen
	Publication of Joseph von Eichendorff's *Aus dem Leben eines Taugenichts*
1827	Death of Ludwig van Beethoven
	Death of Wilhelm Müller
	Publication of Heine's *Buch der Lieder*
1828	Death of Franz Schubert
	Publication of Schubert, *Winterreise*, op. 89
1831	Birth of Joseph Joachim
1832	Death of Johann Wolfgang von Goethe
	Death of Carl Friedrich Zelter
	Publication of Goethe's *Faust*, Part 2
1833	Birth of Johannes Brahms
	Abolition of Slavery Act, British Empire
1837	Coronation of Queen Victoria

1838	Death of Anna Milder-Hauptmann
1839	Birth of Amalie Schneeweiss
1840	Marriage of Robert Schumann and Clara Wieck
1845	Birth of August Bungert
1847	Death of Fanny and Felix Mendelssohn
1848	Marx and Engels, *Communist Manifesto*
	German uprisings
	Birth of Lilli Lehmann
1849	Death of Frédéric Chopin
1850	Death of Nikolaus Lenau
1852	Publication of Emanuel Geibel and Paul Heyse's *Spanisches Liederbuch*
1856	Death of Robert Schumann
	Death of Heinrich Heine
	Birth of Christian Sinding
1857	Death of Joseph Freiherr von Eichendorff
1860	Death of Marianne von Willemer
	Death of Schröder-Devrient
	Birth of Alexander von Fielitz
	Birth of Gustav Mahler
	Birth of Hugo Wolf
1863	Marriage of Joseph Joachim and Amalie Schneeweiss
1864	Birth of Richard Strauss
1865	Premiere of Wagner's *Tristan und Isolde*
	13th Amendment to the US Constitution (abolition of slavery)
1866	Death of Friedrich Rückert
	Death of Franz Liszt
1869	Birth of Hans Pfitzner
1870	Franco-Prussian War
1875	Death of Eduard Mörike
1877	Thomas Edison invents the phonograph
1880	Birth of Nikolai Medtner
1883	Death of Richard Wagner
1887	Death of Jenny Lind

1891	Publication of Wolf's *Spanisches Liederbuch*
1892	Publication of Wolf's *Italienisches Liederbuch*
1896	Death of Clara Schumann
1897	Death of Johannes Brahms
1899	Death of Amalie Joachim
1901	Bechstein Hall opens, London
1903	Death of Hugo Wolf
1905	Premiere of Richard Strauss's *Salome*
1907	Death of Joseph Joachim
1911	Death of Gustav Mahler
1914	World War I begins
1915	Death of August Bungert
1918–19	End of World War I
1929	Death of Lilli Lehmann
1930	Death of Alexander von Fielitz
1941	Death of Christian Sinding
1949	Death of Hans Pfitzner
	Death of Richard Strauss
1951	Death of Nikolai Medtner

Index

Page numbers in *italics* refer to figures. A suffix t indicates a table. Page numbers with n refer to notes. For example, 108n40 means note number 40 on page 108.

Abraham, Gerald, 157
accompanists, 77–78, 146–47, 184, 235, 244–58, 262, 270, 274, 278–79
amateur music-making, 87, 94, 129n43, 210–14. *See also* domestic music-making
Andersen, Hans Christian, 146
Andrae, Natalia. *See* Macfarren, Natalia, Lady
Annenkov, Pavel, 156
anti-German feeling, 195–96
Appl, Benjamin (BA), 262, 263, 264, 266, 267, 268
archaic language, 103
Arne, Thomas, 194
arrangements of songs, 212, 213
Asti, Eugene (EA), 262, 265, 268, 270, 274
atmosphere of concerts, 108n40, 179, 187–89, 230–31, 252–53. *See also* performance style
Auber, Daniel, 89
audiences: behavior of, 108n40, 187–89, 215; education of, 72, 143, 162–63, 164, 165, 204–10; expectations of, 72, 73, 74–77, 78, 275; twenty-first century, 263–65, 266, 271, 273, 275; working class, 203–17
Auslander, Philip, 52
authenticity of performance, 52–63, 72–73, 79, 90

Bache, Constance, 88
Bailey, Lillian (Mrs. Henschel), 117, 184, 185t, 187–88
Barbi, Alice, 138, *147*
Barker, George, 100, 101, 102
Beethoven, Ludwig van, 77, 162; *An die ferne Geliebte*, op. 98, 111, 113, 115, 117, 119, 120, 121, 122, 123, 146, 163

Beliy, Andrei, 159, 161, 163, 165
Bellini, Vincenzo, 62
Benson, Robert Henry, 88
Berlin, 203–17; Arbeiterbildungsschule concerts, 215–16; educational concerts for working classes, 204–10, 206t, 208t, 209t; the Joachims in, 138, 144; Lilli Lehmann in, 225–26, 228; Anna Milder and Friederike Liman in, 19; miscellany program example, 12–13; nonmusical societies' concerts, 214–17; Sing-Akademie, 137, 139–40, *141*, 143–44; working-class choirs, 210–14, *211*
Biden, Stephen, 123
Bispham, David, 116, 117, 119, 121–24, 187, 188, 190, 192, 193t
Blum, Carl: "Gruss an die Schweiz," 21, 22–23; "Der Troubadour," 10, 42n5
Boosey & Company, 182
Borwick, Leonard, 190
Boston, 113, 114, 115t, 118, 119, 122–23
Bostridge, Ian (IB), 262, 263, 267, 268, 270, 275, 276, 278, 279
Brahms, Johannes: and Amalie Joachim, 138–40; in London programs, 181, 191; onstage persona, 53; song cycle performances in his lifetime, 122; translations of his songs, 94–95
Brahms, Johannes (works): folk songs, 143–44; *Gesang der Parzen*, op. 89, 95; *Gesänge für Frauenchor*, op. 17, 95; "Ein kleiner, hübscher Vogel," op. 52 no. 6, 96–99, 98t, *99*, 102t; *Liebesliederwalzer*, op. 52, 94–102, 139; *Magelone* Romances, op. 33, 119, 120, 121, 122, 123, 124, 125, 146; *Mir lächelt kein Frühling*, WoO25, 95; "Muss es eine Trennung geben," op. 33 no.

Brahms, Johannes (*Cont.*)
12, 121; *Neue Liebeslieder*, op. 65, 95, 139; "Rede, Mädchen," op. 52 no. 1, 95–96, *97*, 98t, 100, 101t; *Schicksalslied*, op. 54, 94; *Sieben Lieder für Chor*, op. 62, 95; "Treue Liebe dauert lange," op. 33 no. 15, 122; *Vier ernste Gesänge*, op. 121, 118, 122–23, 124, 191; "War es dir, den diese Lippen bebten," op. 33 no. 7, 121; "Wiegenlied," op. 49, No. 4, 142; *Zigeunerlieder*, op. 103, 139, 190, 192; *Zwei Motetten*, op. 74, 95
Brandt, Fritz, 226
Bratenskaya, Anna (wife of Nikolai Medtner), 159, 173, 177n64
Breitkopf and Härtel, 94
Brema, Maria, 121
Brüll, Ignaz, 225–26
Bungert, August, 223, 228–30, 235
Bürde, Jeannette: "Der Berghirt," op. 4 no. 1, 19, *20*
Burgmüller, Norbert, 54
Butt, Clara, 186

canonic repertoire, 180–82, 181t, 190–92, 230, 272–73
Chadwick, George, 117
Chappell & Co., 182
Chicago, 113–14, 115, 119, 124
choirs, working class, 210–14, *211*
Clark, Charles W., 124
Clément, Edmond, 188
coherence in programming, 10–13, 77–79, 80–81, 84n55, 190, 266–72
Cologne, 73, 114
composers: canon of, 180–82, 181t, 190–92, 230; paired in programs, 271–72; performers' fidelity to, 53, 72–73, 279; single-composer programs, 229, 235, 236, 269–70
contemporary music programs, 194–96, 225, 230
Cooper, Imogen, 278–79
Cornelius, Peter, 181–82; *Six Christmas Songs*, 120, 121
Cox, Garnet Wolseley, 195
Culp, Julia, 186, 192

d'Alheim, Pierre (Piotr), 163
Damm, Käthe, 223
Damrosch, Leopold, 113
Damrosch, Walter, 123
Dannreuther, Edward, 183
d'Aubigné, Lloyd, 122
Daumer, Georg Friedrich, 96, 98
Davies, Walford, 95
Debussy, Claude, 195
Décsey, Ernst, 231
Delius, Frederick, 195
Dent, Edward, 100, 105n13
Deutscher Arbeiter-Sängerbund (DAS), 212–14
Devrient, Eduard, 89
Ditters von Dittersdorf, Karl, 41
domestic music-making, 78, 87, 140, 143, 182, 185. *See also* amateur music-making
Drake, Julius (JD), 262, 267, 270
Dresel, Otto, 113
Dürr, Walther, 13
Durylin, Sergei, 160, 172
Dustmann, Louise, 138
Dvořák, Anton: *Zigeunerlieder*, op. 55, 118

education of audiences, 72, 143, 162–63, 164, 165, 204–10
Eichendorff, Joseph von, 244–45, 254, 256, 257
Einstein, Alfred, 251–53, 257–58
Elgar, Edward, 189
Elisabeth of Romania, Queen (Carmen Sylva), 229–30
Elwes, Gervase, 186, 188
emotion, 56–57, 61, 268, 271, 275–76. *See also Innigkeit* (sincerity of feeling); theatricality
Engel', Yuliy, 171
Engelhard, Henriette, 189
England, 122, 263–64, 266. *See also* London
Engle, Marie, 122
English-language performances, 113–14, 116, 118, 123
English translations. *See* translation and translators
Erb, Karl, 244, 251–52, 253
Eweyk, Arthur von, 144

Farrar, Geraldine, 231, 236–37
Fielitz, Alexander von, 182, 230; *Eliland: Ein Sang vom Chiemsee*, 120, 182
Fillunger, Marie, 191
financial considerations, 73, 224, 226–27, 228, 262, 265
Fleming, Renée, 52
folk and folk-style songs, 142–45, 156, 157, 204, 208–10, 213
Foster, Muriel, 186
Fox-Strangways, Arthur, 100
Franz, Robert, 182, 230
Frege, Livia (née Gerhard), 146
Freiligrath, Ferdinand, 216
French, Florence, 114
Fuchs, Albert, 192
Fuller-Maitland, John Alexander, 191

gender: the concert hall as gender-neutral, 132–47; men singing female roles and vice versa, 114, 139, 145–46
Gerhardt, Elena, 186, 189–90, 191, 191t
Gerhardt, Paul, 230
German culture, resistance to, 195–96
Gilchrist, James (JG), 262, 264–65, 269, 270, 276, 277, 278
Glinka, Mikhail, 156
Goethe, Johann Wolfgang von: *Erlkönig*, 90–93; Lilli Lehmann's admiration for, 230; Nikolai and Emilii Medtner and, 155, 159, 160, 161, 165–71; on Anna Milder, 20–21; Schiller-Theater company "Goethe-Abend," 205, 206t; *Der west-östliche Divan*, 21–22, 27–30, 47n57
Goodrich, William O., 123
Grahl, Heinrich, 144
Greene, Harry Plunket, 124, 126n8
Grieg, Edvard, 89, 189, 195
Griesinger, Georg August, 19
Grimm, Herman, 27
Gutmann, Albert, 229

Hafiz, 24–27, 28–29
Hahn, Reynaldo, 224–25
Hale, Philip, 118–19
Hall, Marguerite, 121, 122, 123
Hamburg, 62, 73, 75t, 76t, 137–38

Hammer-Purgstall, Joseph von, 27
Hampson, Thomas (TH), 262, 263, 264, 266, 267, 268, 269, 272, 273, 279
Hanslick, Eduard, 72
Harty, Hamilton, 194
Haydn, Joseph, 15
Heine, Heinrich, 157
Heinrich, Max, 117–18, 119, 124, 125
Heinrich, Wilhelm, 116, 118–19
Heinz, Hugo, 179
Henschel, George, 117, 119, 138, 180, 184–86, 185t, 187–88; *Serbisches Liederspiel*, op. 32, 117, 184
Henschel, Lillian (née Bailey), 117, 184, 185t, 187–88
Henson, Medora, 118
Herman, Reinhold, 235
Hermann, Hans, 230
Hiller, Friedrich, 73
Hiltz, Grace, 114
Hostater, Julia, 192

idealism of Lieder and their performance, 52–63, 72–73, 191–92, 204
Ilyin, Ivan, 154
Innigkeit (sincerity of feeling), 54, 55–56, 62
Isaac, Heinrich, 142
Italian language, 89
Ivogün, Maria, 244, 251–52, 253

Janowitz, Gundula, 266
Jensen, Adolf, 182, 191
Joachim, Amalie, 132–47, 136, 142; career overview, 133–38; Lilli Lehmann's sense of competition with, 229; as Lieder specialist, 138–45, 191, 229, 235–36; performance style, 144–46; and Heinrich Reimann, 120, 133, 134, 135, 141–42, 143; sources for, 132–33, 138–40; Villa Witney White studies with, 119, 121
Joachim, Joseph, 53, 71, 72, 78, 132, 138, 140, 182
Johnson, Graham, 23–24, 33, 46n47, 266, 270–71
Jordan, Julius (Jules), 116
Joseffy, Rafael, 118

Kalbeck, Max, 138
Kalisch, Paul, 224, 226, 233
Karatygin, Vyacheslav, 173
Karthäuser, Sophie (SK), 262, 264, 267, 271, 274, 276
Katz, Martin (MK), 262, 267
keys, 77, 79, 80–81, 84n55, 270–71
Kirchner, Theodor, 78
Kirkby Lunn, Louise, 186, 192
Kirpal, Margaretha, 118
Klein, Bernhard, 41
Koenen, Tilly, 186
Kreissmann, August, 112–13
Kreutzer, Conradin: *Neun Wanderlieder von Ludwig Uhland*, 20–21
Kynoch, Sholto (ShK), 262, 265, 267, 271, 275, 279

languages, 108n40, 188, 263, 268, 270, 272. *See also* English-language performances; translation and translators
Lechner, Johannes, 230
Lehmann, Lilli, 223–37, *227*, *232*, *233*, *234*
Lehmann, Liza, 95; *In a Persian Garden* (1896), 124
Leighton, Frederic, 183
Leipzig, 54–55, 75t
Lemmens-Sherrington, Helen, 185
Leonhard, Hugo, 113
Lepper, Simon (SL), 262, 268–69, 270, 274
Liebling, Leonard, 123
Lieder, idealism of, 52–63, 72–73, 191–92, 204
Lierhammer, Theodor, 186
Liman, Friederike, 19–21, 45n39
Lind, Jenny, 61–62, 63, 114
Lissmann, Eva Katharina, 194
Lissmann, Hans, 194
List, Elise, 56–57, 61
List, Emilie, 60
Liszt, Franz, 53, 157
Little, Lena, 118
Liverpool, 189
Lockwood, Elisabeth M., 100, 101, 102
Loewe, Carl, 181–82, 214
Loges, Stephan, 278

London, 179–96; Bechstein Hall (now Wigmore Hall), 80, 179, 189–96, 191t, 193t, 195, 195t, 263, 277–79; David Bispham in, 122; canon of composers, 180–82; early development of vocal recitals, 182–89; George Henschel in, 184–86; miscellany concerts, 179–80, 182–84; Prince's Hall, 184–85, 185t; programming in 1910, 189–96; Steinway Hall, 226; St. James's Hall, 182, 183t, 184; Wigmore Hall (*See* Bechstein Hall *above*)
Lonsdale, Gertrude, 194–95, 195t
Löw, Martina, 132
Löwenfeld, Raphael, 205, 207

MacDowell, Edward, 195
Macfarren, Natalia, Lady (née Andrae), 88–93, 94–103
Macfarren, Sir George Alexander, 88
MacKenzie, Alexander Campbell, 117
Magnus, Helen, 79
Mahler, Gustav, 236
Mann, Thomas, 244–46, 253–55
Marx, Adolf Bernhard, 89
Maurel, Victor, 231
Mayer, Andreas, 23
Mayrhofer, Johann, 13
Medtner, Emilii, 159, 160, 161, 172, 174
Medtner, Nikolai Karlovich, 154–55, 158–74, *161*; *Goethe Lieder*, op. 6, 155, 161, 166, 171; *Goethe Lieder*, op. 15, 155, 164, 165–66, *167*, 167–71, *169*, *170*, *171*; *Goethe Lieder*, op. 18, 155, 164, 165, *165*, 166, *166*; *Sonata-Vocalise* and *Suite Vocalise*, op. 41, 162; *Three Romances*, op. 3, 160
Meerti, Elisa, 54–56
memory, performing from, 184, 230, 265, 274
Mendelssohn, Felix, 41, 78, 181, 189; "Auf Flügeln des Gesanges," op. 34 no. 2, 55; "Frühlingslied," op. 34 no. 3, 54, 73; "Volkslied," op. 47 no. 4, 58–60, *59*, 66n33
Mengelberg, Wilhelm, 161
Meyerbeer, Giacomo: *Margherita d'Anjou*, 10
Meyn, Heinrich, 119, 122
Mikhaylov, Mikhail, 157

Milder-Hauptmann, Anna Pauline, 10–21, 14, 23, 24, 37, 41
miscellany concerts, 10–13, 11t, 41–42n1, 72–81, 112–15, 179–80, 182–84, 192–94
Morozova, Margarita, 159, 172
Moscow, 155, 158–60, 162–65, 171–72, 174
Moser, Andreas, 138
Möser, Carl, 10–11
Mozart, Wolfgang Amadeus: "Dove sono" (*Le Nozze di Figaro*), 37, 41; "Wiegenlied," 145; "Wiehe des Gesangs" (*Die Zauberflöte*), 213
Müller, Wilhelm, 19, 100
multiple singer performances, 122, 251–52
Munich, 244–46, 251–52, 253
music festivals, 273, 274–75

Napoleon Bonaparte, 19
nationalism, 257–58
Neukomm, Sigismund von, 15
Newman, Ernest, 180–81
New York, 113, 114, 115, 118, 119, 122–24
Nicholls, Agnes, 192, 193t, 194
Nikisch, Arthur, 186
Novello and Company, 88, 89, 91, 100

Odoyevsky, Prince Vladimir, 155
Olenina-d'Alheim, Maria, 155, 162–65, 172–73
opera, comparisons with, 52, 53, 56, 60–62, 63, 84n46, 186, 188, 192–94
orchestral accompaniment, 247–51
Osgood, George L., 111, 114, 115t

Padmore, Mark (MP), 262, 263, 264, 265, 268, 269, 272, 273, 274, 275, 277, 279
Parthey, Gustav, 41
Parthey, Lili, 41
Paur, Emil, 118
Perabo, Ernst, 113
performance style, 179, 187–89, 275–77; Amalie Joachim, 144–46; Lilli Lehmann, 230–31, 235; person, persona and character, 52–63, 73; theatricality, 53, 61, 63, 72, 145, 193–94, 251–53, 276–77; *Werktreue* performance, 53, 60, 72, 79, 90

performing spaces, 132–47, 213–14, 263–64. *See also* Berlin, Sing-Akademie; *and individual venues under* London
Peters (publishers), 94
Peyser, Herbert, 100
Pfitzner, Hans, 236, 244–51, 252–58
pianists, 77–78, 146–47, 184, 235, 244–46, 252, 262, 270, 274, 278–79. *See also individual pianists*
Plunket Greene, Harry, 186, 190
political use of songs, 215–17
Popov, Boris, 158
Popp, Lucia, 266
popular entertainment, 213–14
private salons, 183. *See also* domestic music-making
professionalization of Lieder-singing, 179
programming: composer pairing, 271–72; in London, 179–87, 189–96; metaphors for good, 268–69; miscellany concerts, 10–13, 11t, 41–42n1, 72–81, 112–15, 179–80, 182–84, 192–94; poet-based, 269–70; practical considerations, 262–65; single-composer, 229, 235, 236, 269–70; of song cycles (*See* song cycle programming); song recitals (*See* song recital programming); theme, sequence and contrast, 73, 74, 165, 265–72, 274–75; unfamiliar repertoire, 223, 225, 263, 272–75; in the United States, 111–25; working-class choir concerts, 211, 213; working-class educational concerts, 205–10, 206t, 208t, 209t; working-class nonmusical societies' concerts, 214
publishing of songs as cycles, 80

Rachmaninoff, Sergey, 154
recordings, 81, 231, 266
Reger, Max, 182
Reimann, Heinrich, 120, 133, 134, 135, 141–42, 143
religious nature of art. *See* spirituality
Rellstab, Johann Carl Friedrich, 15–18
repertoire: canonic, 180–82, 181t, 190–92, 230, 272–73; programming unfamiliar, 223, 225, 263, 272–75

reviews: criticizing improvised interludes, 235, 252; of Amalie Joachim, 119, 139–40, 144–45, 229; of Lilli Lehmann, 223, 236; of London recitals, 179, 185, 187–88, 191–94; of Anna Milder, 21; of a miscellany concert, 12–13; of Hans Pfitzner, 251–53, 257; of Clara Schumann and Julius Stockhausen, 77–78; of US recitals, 11, 114, 118–19, 122–24
Rieter-Biedermann (publishers), 94
Rollwagen, Louise, 118
Rooy, Anton van, 124, 186
Rothery, W. G., 100
Rubinstein, Anton, 88
Rückert, Friedrich, 250
Rumford, Kennerley, 186
Rupp, Emil, 251
Russia, 154–74

Saint Petersburg, 45n39, 156, 161
Sams, Jeremy, 103
Schiller-Theater company, Berlin, 204–7
Schmidt, Leopold, 231, 235
Schröder-Devrient, Wilhelmine, 57–60, 61, 90, 146
Schubert, Franz, 13, 19, 21, 23, 24, 37, 41; "Am Meer," D957 no. 12, 57; "Ave Maria," D839, 55, 213; "Du bist die Ruh," D776, 52; "Erlkönig," D328, 21, 89–93, 252; "Die Forelle," D550, 12, 42n2; "Frühlingsglaube," D686, 67n42, 73; "Geheimnis," D491, 13; "Gretchen am Spinnrade," D118, 61; "Heidenröslein," D257, 145; "Der Hirt auf dem Felsen," D965, 19, 21, 23; *Die schöne Müllerin*, D795, 71, 72, 79, 103, 114, 116, 118, 119, 120, 121, 122–23, 124, 129n43, 146, 163, 235–36; *Schwanengesang*, D957, 103, 116, 124, 146; "Ständchen," D957 no. 4, 113; "Suleika" songs, D717 & D720, 13, 21–41, 25–26, 32, 34–35, 36, 38, 39–40; *Winterreise*, D911, 79, 103, 116, 118, 119, 123, 124, 146, 163, 278
Schulz-Curtius, Alfred, 186–87
Schumann, Clara: assessment of singers, 53–63; *Dichterliebe* performances with Stockhausen, 71–73, 74–78, 80, 81;
improvisatory practices, 246; present-day responses to a program by, 277–79; recitals in London, 182, 183t
Schumann, Robert: assessment of singers, 53–63; on Clara Schumann's performance of his works, 78; influence in Russia, 157; Liederalbum for Wilhelmine Schröder-Devrient, 57–58
Schumann, Robert (works): *Dichterliebe*, op. 48, 57, 71–81, 75t, 76t, 113–14, 116, 118, 123, 124, 125, 126n8, 163, 179, 270, 278, 279; *Drei Romanzen*, op. 28 no. 2, 77; *Fantasie*, op. 17, 77; *Frauenliebe und -leben*, op. 42, 58, 78, 80, 111, 114, 117–18, 120, 121, 123, 129n41, 146, 163, 277–78; "Frühlingsnacht," op. 39 no. 12, 73, 214; *Fünf Lieder*, op. 40, 146; "Ich grolle nicht," op. 48 no. 7, 57; *Kreisleriana*, op. 16, 78; "Liebhabers Ständchen," op. 34 no. 2, 194; *Liederalbum für die Jugend*, op. 79, 62, 120–21; *Liederkreis*, op. 24, 60, 61, 73, 146; *Liederkreis*, op. 39, 58, 116, 163, 214, 244–45, 250, 251–52; *Myrthen*, op. 25, 58, 120, 146; *Novelette* in D major, op. 21 no. 2, 77; "Der Nussbaum," op. 25 no. 3, 120; Piano Quintet, op. 44, 78–79; *Requiem für Mignon*, op. 98b, 74; *Romanze* in D minor, op. 32 no. 3, 77; Romanzen (Unaccompanied Choruses for Women's Voices), opp. 69 and 91, 247–51, 247t; *Sechs Gedichte und Requiem* op. 90, 114; Three Lieder for women's voices, op. 114, 250; "Waldesgespräch," op. 39 no. 3, 58; "Widmung," op. 25 no. 1, 120
Schumann-Heink, Ernestine, 121
Scott, Sir Walter, 90, 91–93
Scriabin, Aleksandr, 154
Seidler-Wranitzky, Karoline, 11–12
Seifert, Uso, 231
Senfft, Klara von, 144
Senfl, Ludwig, 142
Shaginian, Marietta, 173
Sharpe, Ernest, 194
Shaw, George Bernard, 188
Sieber, Ferdinand, 12
Simrock, Fritz (publisher), 94–95, 100, 140

Sinding, Christian, 182
song cycle programming: *Dichterliebe* performances by Julius Stockhausen and Clara Schumann, 70–81, 277–78; by Lilli Lehmann, 235–36; present-day perspectives, 263, 265, 277–78; in Russia, 163; in the United States, 111–12, 119–25, 263. *See also individual cycles under their composers*
song recital programming: by Amalie Joachim, 139–40, 141–45; by Lilli Lehmann, 224–26, 227–28, 229, 235–36; in London, 179–80, 184–86, 189–96; present-day perspectives, 265–75; in Russia, 163, 165; in the United States, 111–12, 115–19
Spies, Hermine, 138, 146, 191
spirituality, 159–60, 162–72
Stacey, Clara D., 113–14
Stanford, Charles, 95
Sterling, Antoinette, 186
Sternfield, Richard, 231
Stibral, Franz, 230
Stieler, Kaspar, 120
Stockhausen, Julius, 71–79, 74, 80, 81, 114, 116, 128n38, 137–38, 146, 182, 183t, 188, 235–36
Strasbourg, 251, 253
Strauss, Richard, 124, 181, 191
Stravinsky, Igor, 174
Stümmer, Heinrich, 12
Stuttgart, 75t
Süßmayr, Franz: "Juno wird dich stets umschweben," 15, *16*, *17–18*
Swinton, "Elsie" (Elizabeth) (née Ebsworth), 186
Sylva, Carmen (Queen Elisabeth of Romania), 229–30

Taneyev, Sergei, 157
Tappert, Wilhelm, 142
Taubert, Wilhelm, 225
Tchaikovsky, Pyotr Ilyich, 195, 214
theatricality, 53, 61, 63, 72, 145, 193–94, 251–53, 276–77
Thomas, Theodore, 113, 114
Tomaschek, Johann Wenzel (Václav Jan Tomášek), 15

tonality, 77, 270–71
Townsend, Stephen S., 118
translation and translators, 87–103; Heinrich's English-language editions, 118; Natalia Macfarren's career, 87–88, 100, 103; Natalia Macfarren's "Erlkönig" translation, 89–93; Natalia Macfarren's *Liebeslieder* translation, 94–102; need for and use of, 87–88, 94, 100, 103–4, 119, 182, 188; Russian translation of Heinrich Heine, 157. *See also* English-language performances; languages
transposition, 77, 80–81, 84n55, 270, 271
Troutbeck, John, 88
Trubetskoy, Evgeny, 158–59
Turgenev, Ivan, 156

United States, 111–25; Lilli Lehmann in, 226–28; miscellany concerts, 112–15; song cycle programming, 119–25, 263; song recitals, 115–19; sources for studying Lieder performance, 111–12
Uthmann, Gustav Adolph, 213

Van Rooy, Anton, 124, 186
Varnhagen von Ense, Karl August, 19
Varnhagen von Ense, Rahel, 19
Vaughan Williams, Ralph, 195
Velden, Johannes, 207–10, 208t, 209t
venues, 132–47, 213–14, 263–64. *See also* Berlin, Sing-Akademie; *and under* London
Viardot-Garcia, Pauline, 60–61, 146
Vienna, 10–13, 15, 73–74, 79, 116, 144–45, 263

Wagner, Richard, 194, 216; *Parsifal*, 172
Wahrheit (truth), 54, 60, 61, 62
Walker, Ernest, 95
Walker, Sarah (SW), 262, 266, 268, 275, 277, 278
Wallenreiter, Karl, 116
Walter, Gustav, 115, 138, 229, 236
Waterston, Jean, 192
Werktreue performance, 53, 60, 72, 79, 90
Werrenrath, George, 115–16
Whately, Kitty (KW), 262, 269, 278

White, Maude Valérie, 189
White, Villa Whitney, 119–21, 124, 144
Whiting, Arthur, 116
Willemer, Marianne von, 21–22, 27–30, 37–41, 47n57
Williamson, John, 256
Wolf, Hugo, 27, 37, 124, 180–81, 191, 231–35, 263, 272
Wolff, Hermann, 141
Wolfsohn, Carl, 113–14, 115
Wolgast, Heinrich, 204
Woolfe, Zachary, 52, 53, 63

working-class engagement, 203–17; choirs, 210–14, *211*; educational concerts, 204–10, 206t, 208t, 209t; political and social dimensions, 214–17
World War I, 100, 173–74, 195–96
Wüllner, Franz, 225
Wüllner, Ludwig, 118, 124, 186, 235
Wurm, Mary, 146, *147*

Zelter, Carl Friedrich, 20–21
Zingarelli, Nicola: *Giulietta e Romeo*, 12
Zurich, 75t
Zur Mühlen, Raimund von, 184, 189

www.ingramcontent.com/pod-product-compliance
Lightning Source LLC
Chambersburg PA
CBHW031759220426
43662CB00007B/465